BBC and Television Genres in Jeopardy

BBC and Television Genres in Jeopardy

JEREMY TUNSTALL

PETER LANG
Oxford • Bern • Berlin • Bruxelles • Frankfurt am Main • New York • Wien

Bibliographic information published by Die Deutsche Nationalbibliothek
Die Deutsche Nationalbibliothek lists this publication in the Deutsche Nationalbibliografie; detailed bibliographic data is available on the Internet at http://dnb.d-nb.de.

A catalogue record for this book is available from the British Library.

Library of Congress Control Number: 2014955808

ISBN 978-3-0343-1846-4 (print)
ISBN 978-3-0353-0687-3 (eBook)

Hochfeldstrasse 32, CH-3012 Bern, Switzerland
info@peterlang.com, www.peterlang.com, www.peterlang.net

This publication has been peer reviewed.

Printed in Germany

Contents

Acknowledgements

My thanks to these people who gave me taped face-to-face interviews, in almost all cases at their place of work: Dan Adamson, Pablo Aguirre, Dawn Airey, Kenton Allen, Tess Alps, Geoff Atkinson, David Attenborough, Matt Baker, Glenn Barden, Emily Bell, Roger Bolton, Jeremy Bowen, Kate Bulkley, Ed Braman, Dorothy Byrne, Doug Carnegie, John Clarke, Andrew Cohen, Danny Cohen, Tony Cohen, Charles Constable, Michael Crick, Mark Damazer, Martin Davidson, Jeremy Dear, Conor Dignam, Jonathan Dimbleby, Greg Dyke, Clive Edwards, David Elstein, Ben Fenton, Peter Fincham, Alastair Fothergill, Ben Gale, Mike Gardner, Steven Garrett, Tony Grant, Eleanor Greene, Toby Hartwell, Kate Harwood, Edward Havard, Lorraine Heggessey, Steve Hewlett, Tim Hincks, Alison Hindell, Patricia Hodgson, Susan Hogg, Richard Holloway, Claire Horton, Jay Hunt, Sue Inglish, Faisal Islam, Andrew Jackson, Paul Jackson, Dylan Jane, Clive Jones, Martha Kearney, Richard Klein, Nichola Koratjitis, Jonathan Lewis, David Liddiment, Mark Linsey, Patricia Llewelyn, Kevin Lygo, Laura Mackie, Angus Macqueen, Graham McWilliams, David Mannion, Andrew Marr, Eamonn Matthews, Paul Mitchell, Stephen Mitchell, Patrick Morris, Thomas Morris, Gerry Morrissey, Neil Mortensen, Roger Mosey, Graham Mytton, Bill Neely, Neil Nightingale, Craig Oliver, Peter Pagnamenta, Tony Pastor, Charlie Pattinson, John Perkins, Robert Peston, Jon Ploman, Stephen Price, Keiran Roberts, Nick Robinson, Peter Salmon, Diederick Santer, Samir Shah, John Silver, John Simpson, Jon Snow, Martin Spence, Nigel Stafford-Clark, Ben Stephenson, Kevin Sutcliffe, Ceri Thomas, Deborah Turness, Adrian Van Klaveren, Jeremy Vine, Bella Vuillermoz, David Walker, Sarah Walmsley, Richard Wilson, David Wood, Mark Wood, Michael Wood, Colin Wratten, Steven Wright, John Yorke, Jenny Abramsky.

Thanks also to John Pilger who gave me an e-mail interview.

Special thanks to the following people, each of whom gave me two (or more) separate interviews: Tom Bradby, Phil Craig, Gary Gibbon, Daisy Goodwin, Alex Graham, Peter Horrocks, Roly Keating, Stephen Lambert, Anne Lapping, Norma Percy, Phillip Whitehead.

Special thanks also to the following people who gave me a recent interview as well as an interview back in 1989–91: Peter Bazalgette, Jana Bennett, Roger Bolton, Nigel Chapman, Paul Hamann, John Willis, Alan Yentob.

Extra special thanks to Brian Lapping, who spoke into my tape recorder for a total of about fifteen hours.

Many thanks to Rebecca, Helena and Paul for tolerating my television obsession; and to Sylvia for allowing me to do the average Brit's four hours of TV viewing per day.

Thanks also to Richard Barron, John Cowley and Bruce Hanlin, who laboured through this book in draft and made sage suggestions.

Finally, thanks to Frances Bruce for excellent secretarial and research assistance.

Introduction

The 'Death of Television' has been greatly exaggerated. The average Brit (over the age of two) watches TV for about twenty-six hours per week, or nearly four hours per day. Americans view more. People today also spend huge amounts of time looking at other screens, but this other screen viewing has been added to – not subtracted from – television viewing.

The British television industry's largely freelance labour market is presided over by a few hundred executive producers, who work either inside an independent production company, or within a broadcaster, such as the BBC, ITV, or Channel Four. These executive producers employ, and then manage, the presenters, writers, directors, comedians, actors, researchers and technical people who make the programming. These executive producers have to get their work financed and accepted by senior channel executives and genre commissioners; most of those senior people are themselves former executive producers.

This book focuses on executive producers and on British television's twenty-one genres. Not only does British television offer an extremely wide range of genres, but it specialises in many series runs as short as six or eight half hours per year. Although there are also some big, long-running, series, British TV's output is highly fragmented; which is why it is hard to summarise or comprehend.

Since the economic crisis of 2008, less money has been available for new television productions. Some of the twenty-one genres discussed in this book are not in the best of health. Seven genres have been declining and are now in jeopardy. These declining genres are Education, Natural History, Science, Arts, Children's, Religion and Current Affairs. These seven are predominantly factual genres, with public service broadcasting traditions. All seven of these declining genres were, in the past, especially strong within the BBC.

In much better health are another six genres, which are especially strong in commercial television, rather than the BBC. These broadly healthy genres are Soap Drama, Big Entertainment, Talk, Homes/Housing, Quiz/Game and Reality.

A further seven genres are still in goodish health – primarily on the BBC, but also on other channels. If these seven genres decline in the future, then not only will the BBC, but the entire British television enterprise will be in danger. These genres are Drama, News, Documentary, History, Travel, Comedy and Cooking. Especially significant here are Drama and News – British television's biggest and most prestigious two genres.

The twenty-first genre is Sports, where the BBC's limited output remains popular. But Sports TV is financially dominated by American-controlled BSkyB, whose main sports competitor is British Telecom.

The biggest change in British television since 1989–90 has, of course, been the increase from four channels to several hundred channels – with the great majority of these numerous small channels being American.

In 1990, when Rupert Murdoch received a nod and a waive from Margaret Thatcher, Britain was still a world television leader. Today many of Britain's TV and media players are American owned-and-operated from New York and Los Angeles – including BSkyB, Virgin Media, Channel Five, Reuters news agency and most of the larger 'independent' TV production companies. Google's dominance of internet advertising is draining much of the life from both UK newspapers and commercial television. London is no longer a world media and TV hub, but is rapidly becoming a colonial media outpost of the United States.

David Abraham, chief executive of Channel Four, chose a slightly different metaphor when he said:

> Our free-to-air channels have become the must-have accessories, the tiny dogs of 2014, amongst US companies eager to stay ahead of each other by internationalising their revenues, priming their distribution pipes and shielding their tax exposure.[1]

1 David Abraham, MacTaggart lecture at the Edinburgh TV Festival, 21 August 2014.

CHAPTER 1

The BBC and Public Service Genres in Jeopardy

In 2012 the British Broadcasting Corporation seemed to have one of its best years since the birth of the BBC ninety years earlier. But in the twelve months from late 2012 to late 2013 the BBC quickly went from triumph to disaster.

The BBC, in 2012, still commanded almost one third of the UK's TV viewing. BBC Radio had over half of all UK Radio listening. The BBC in 2012 still had about two-fifths of all UK TV viewing and radio listening hours. However, summer 2012 was probably the very last great highpoint in recent BBC history. The BBC's summer coverage of the London Olympics achieved huge domestic UK audiences. The BBC provided in summer 2012 the main television and radio coverage of the celebrations which marked Elizabeth's sixty years as Queen.

The BBC's unprecentedly disastrous 2012–13 year had several overlapping components:

- It became apparent that Jimmy Savile – a top BBC entertainer during 1964–94 – had sexually molested literally hundreds of girls and boys; many of these events had occurred inside BBC buildings.
- *Newsnight*, a flagship BBC news output, badly mishandled this story. *Newsnight* then accused a completely innocent retired Conservative politician (Lord McAlpine) of sexual molestation.
- A major BBC computer project – intended to make big amounts of old programming available online – collapsed with losses of £100 million.
- The BBC was accused of making hugely excessive payouts to retiring senior managers.

- Several top BBC executives were unimpressive performers when interrogated by two Parliamentary committees. In September 2013 the BBC Chairman and the recently departed Director General engaged in a remarkably belligerent public feud in front of the House of Commons Public Accounts Committee, and in front of TV cameras.
- In late 2012 George Entwistle served as BBC Director General and CEO for less than two months. His was much the worst DG performance in BBC history.

These BBC events generated large quantities of negative coverage across the Press and across TV and Radio (including the BBC's own news outputs). Less coverage was awarded to some BBC responses. In fact Jimmy Savile's record of sexual molestation in several hospitals had been even more shocking than his BBC behaviour. Although *Newsnight*'s initial performance was poor, BBC journalists and BBC News gave massive coverage to the BBC's multiple disasters. The BBC's Digital Media Initiative collapse was not its first major computer project disaster; but its DMI failure was less horrible than some other big computer disasters in several UK government departments. The BBC did make several pay-offs of £500,000 or more, but these one-off payments significantly reduced the BBC's spend on executive salaries. The conflict between the Chairman (Lord Patten) and the recently ex-Director General (Mark Thompson) was nothing new; there had been numerous BBC Chairman v Director General conflicts in the past. When George Entwistle 'resigned' as DG he was only the most recent of several BBC Director Generals who left in a hurry.

So what was genuinely unusual about the 2012–13 sequence of triumph and disaster? In 2012 the BBC was experiencing the early impact of a huge 16 per cent real value cut in its revenue. The BBC was bleeding; the BBC's old rivals in the press, and its new competitors (commercial TV, cable, satellite and online), were alerted. British journalists, as well as politicians, have always been attracted by the smell of blood.

BBC 'public service': Outdated by digital?

Since the 'Digital Revolution' of the 1990s, it has increasingly been argued that BBC 'Public Service' is outdated and redundant. A key justification for the original monopoly of the BBC (from 1922 as a 'Company', and from 1927 as a 'Corporation') was the then scarcity of radio frequencies. The sole British radio broadcaster could only have one or two national outputs because the scarce frequency spectrum had to be shared with neighbouring European countries and other services. But the 'frequency scarcity' argument – used also in early television – was indeed largely removed by the Digital Revolution, with its multi-channel and multi-platform opportunities.

The BBC grew up under the wing of the British state in general and of the Post Office in particular. For its first sixty years (1922–82) most of the BBC's Director Generals had served in the military during one of the two world wars. John Reith (the founding BBC DG, 1922–38) was badly wounded in the 1914–18 war. All of the BBC's DGs during 1952–72 had served as military officers in 1939–45.[1]

A longish list of its public service goals and stances has posed dilemmas for the BBC in both the distant past and the recent past:

- Political Neutrality has been a key assumption of public service broadcasting in recent decades. Typically new governments receive much friendly news coverage; but news tends to be negative and most incumbent governments eventually come to regard BBC public service as political hostility.

1 Sir Ian Jacob (DG 1952–9) was an Army General who turned the BBC from a mainly radio, into a mainly television, operation. Hugh Carleton Greene (DG 1960–9) held senior positions both during the war and subsequently at the BBC European and World Services, which were directly funded by the British government. Charles Curran (DG 1969–77) was an Indian Army Officer and held senior positions at BBC World Service. Ian Trethowan (DG 1977–82) served as a Fleet Air Arm Officer during 1939–45.

- Regional Balance. The BBC has always been London dominated. But the BBC has always retained operations in the 'Nations' (Scotland, Wales, Ulster) and in the English regions. There were also network production centres in places like Birmingham and Manchester. Since the early 1990s and especially since 2000 the BBC beefed up its presence in the three 'Nations' and in Salford-Manchester.
- Social Class. 'Too middle class' is a traditional criticism of the BBC. The BBC trinity of Inform, Educate and Entertain does have a ring of condescension. The BBC offers some programming with a strongly working class flavour – but the *EastEnders* soap opera is London based and even much BBC comedy is quite middle class.
- Ethnic Minorities. The BBC aims and claims to present Britain's full multi-ethnic character on screen; but it is criticised for not employing enough Afro-Asian talent in drama, comedy and other genres.
- The Age Problem. Public Service television needs to reach all age groups. Both BBC TV and BBC Radio have difficulty in reaching the 10 to 34 age group. Most BBC TV audiences are skewed towards the over 50 age group.
- The Gender Problem. Women are still struggling to occupy even one third of the most prominent BBC on-screen roles. Less visible to the viewer is that more than one third of the most important and powerful BBC executive roles are now occupied by women.

The Licence fee continues to be the BBC's most vulnerable feature. The Licence fee at about £3 (or 5 US dollars) per household per week is cheap compared with the prices of newspapers, satellite and cable. But the Licence Fee, as a compulsory charge on households is a regressive tax, from which only those over age 75 are exempt. A lowly paid single householder with one TV set pays the same as a large wealthy household with several TV sets.

Public service broadcasting

Advertisement for new BBC Director General in 2012

The BBC is the world's leading public service broadcaster. Its mission – to inform, educate and entertain – is unchanging, but the way it fulfils that mission must evolve over time.

Public Service Broadcasting, 1986, according to Michael Tracey:

- Geographical universality.
- Catering for all interests and tastes.
- Catering for minorities.
- Concern for national identity and community.
- Detachment from vested interests and government.
- One broadcasting system directly funded by the corpus of users.
- Competition in good programming rather than for audience numbers.
- Guidelines to liberate programme makers and not to restrict them.

Mark Thompson, BBC Director General, 2004–12:

I've tried to do four things:

1. Focus the BBC on a rather traditional, even classical, view of its mission ... The best journalism in the world; outstanding children's content; outstanding British drama and comedy ... Knowledge and culture.
2. The BBC ... Has to undergo a revolution, thus my total commitment to digital.
3. The BBC should be ... For the whole of the UK and, in some of what it does, for the whole world.
4. To open up the BBC and its privileges and advantages to others. Every week we've literally hundreds of partnerships across broadcasting, technology, the arts, sport and other fields.

An Independent Producer:

PSB seems to include cheap quiz shows and ancient crime movies or any other old rubbish the BBC wants to screen.

Several other complexities surround the Licence Fee issue. The BBC is heavily, but not entirely, dependent on the Licence Fee. The BBC in practice has additional sources of income. Its foreign arm, BBC Worldwide, however, spends nine tenths of its £1.5 billion additional revenue on the additional expenditure of running its BBC Worldwide marketing operation; Worldwide also remakes BBC series into local American and other versions.

The BBC, during its long life, has emphasised a variety of different strengths or virtues. Most basic of all, it has emphasised its Britishness. But there was always some American content and in the 1970s this was semi-officially fixed at a quota of American content which occupied not more than fourteen per cent of BBC (and ITV) transmission time. However American programming (Hollywood's most popular films and TV series) tended to get more than fourteen per cent of the BBC's total TV audience. Of course Hollywood movies had dominated British cinema screens since 1914–18; and the USA/Hollywood component within BBC output has been through several phases:

- During 1943–55 American pop music played a leading role on BBC Radio.[2]
- During 1955–65 first the new ITV, and then the old BBC imported large numbers of American TV series.[3]
- During 1965–90, and not least in the 1980s, American series were amongst the most popular output on BBC TV. The full 356 episodes of *Dallas* ran on BBC1 during 1978–91. Other high profile Hollywood shows which ran on BBC television were *Dynasty* (1981–9) *Knots Landing* (1980–3, 1986–94), and *Cagney and Lacey* (1982–8).
- Since the 1990–1 arrival of Sky (with its massive quantity of Hollywood offerings), the BBC has tried to downplay its own Hollywood imports. But much American material still appears in small audience areas of BBC output – especially across daytime. In high audience time slots

2 Christina L. Baade, *Victory Through Harmony? The BBC and popular music in World War II* (New York: Oxford University Press, 2012).

3 Asa Briggs, *Competition, 1955–74* (Oxford University Press, 1995), 143.

the BBC's involvement with American TV often includes some kind of co-production, which is less visible to most audience members.

Whether or not Hollywood TV is part of the BBC's DNA, certainly much language used by past and present BBC producers has American origins. For example: 'Stripped', 'Common Carrier', 'Has Legs', 'Must Carry', 'Network', 'SciFi', 'Sitcom', 'Smartphone', 'SmartTV', 'Soap'. In recent years Google, Apple, Facebook and Twitter have also invaded BBC vocabulary.

Many Britons have complex (positive and negative) attitudes towards the BBC and the Licence Fee. Survey research – depending on the wording of the questions – reveals very contradictory responses. Most people want to keep the BBC, but many don't like paying the Licence Fee.

A common weakness of both the BBC Licence Fee and the Public Service project is that governments can subject both to frequent small cuts. Since 2010 the BBC has had less money, but more obligations. For example, the BBC must now fund its radio world service, plus several other fresh small items.

Since the 1990s the BBC's leaders have worked hard to combine new technologies with old licence fee. Digital Terrestrial TV (DTT) allowed the BBC to develop several new channels and services. But in 2005 the BBC faced strong opposition, when it announced that an additional £220 million of Licence Fee money would be devoted each year to 'new media' projects.[4] Commercial competitors – newspapers, commercial TV and 'new technology' companies – objected to three key BBC developments. Firstly, BBC JAM (a digital curriculum project for school age children) was launched with a budget of £150 million in 2006, but was closed down in 2007, following a legal challenge from competitors. Secondly the BBC iPlayer has been quite successful in providing a large replay service; but the iPlayer has faced difficult financial problems. Thirdly, the BBC website is huge by European standards – especially in news; but it also has been restricted by regulatory decisions. A fundamental problem is how to

4 Maria Esposito and Geoff White, 'Extra £220m for BBC new media ...', *Broadcast*, 3 June 2005.

combine pay-per-view with the one-price-fits-all BBC License Fee, while still calling the result a 'Public Service' broadcasting system.

David Elstein has long made cogent arguments against the BBC Licence Fee. He refers to the Licence Fee's 'dark side' – poor householders who fail to pay the Licence Fee have been vulnerable to severe legal penalties.[5] Some basic BBC services, Elstein argues, should be free to all households. Meanwhile most services would move over to subscription funding. If Elstein's argument prevails, 'Public Service' will consist of News and a few other Genres offered free to all households. But most of the twenty-one Genres discussed in this book will go onto subscription.

Without any Licence Fee, another 'dark side' would be revealed. The least affluent households might get some News and some Entertainment without charge; but many of the least affluent people would overall receive less Education, less Information and also less Entertainment than under the Licence Fee system.

The BBC and national newspaper hostility

Many executive producers, and other senior people inside and outside the BBC, believe that the British national newspapers are broadly hostile to the BBC. In particular, it is widely believed that the billionaire families behind the *Mail*, *Telegraph*, *Times* and *Sun* newspapers are hostile to the BBC. This kind of hostility is also seen as having been in place during most decades since the 1920s.

In the 1920s and 1930s the newspapers succeeded in preventing the BBC from employing its own team of news journalists. But this changed drastically during 1939–45, when the BBC cemented its relationship with

5 David Elstein, 'The licence fee and the question of BBC funding', in John Mair, Richard Tait and Richard Lance Keeble, eds, *Is The BBC In Crisis?* (Bury St Edmunds: Abramis/Arima Publishing, 2014), 274–84.

the British state, the Monarchy, the Church of England and the war effort. Subsequently the BBC actively promoted democracy and western values by its transmissions in Russian and other east European languages.

During 1955–90 the newspapers were especially worried by ITV, because of its strength as a rival for advertising. But since 1990 national newspaper hostility towards the BBC has increased. The BBC has, since 1990, been seen as a threat to both newspaper news and newspaper finances. While the newspapers have since 1990 lost around half their daily sales, the BBC news effort, on both TV and Radio, has expanded (see Chapter Five). Another big change is that the BBC has become a major online player; the newspapers see the BBC as unfairly using general Licence Fee funding to expand its large online news output.

Meanwhile the BBC feels obliged to devote many late night and early morning (radio and TV) minutes to summarising the newspapers' lead stories. Moreover when, as in 2012–13, the newspapers give massive coverage to BBC shock-horror-crisis-disaster, the BBC feels obliged to give its own massive news coverage to the same disaster stories.

The newspapers do not want the BBC to carry advertising – this would take revenue from the newspapers. But a steadily declining BBC Licence Fee, and a reduction in BBC output, would please most of the newspapers.

BBC: Twenty-one TV genres and twenty TV/radio channels

The BBC's senior people see their public service mission as an obligation to carry a very broad range of genres, especially on the two large audience channels, BBC1 and BBC2. The BBC frequently rearranges its departmental titles. But most BBC executives would probably agree with most of this chapter's list of twenty-one genres. In addition the BBC shows theatrical movies. Pornography is the main example of a TV genre which the BBC avoids.

The national audience is well aware of the difference between Cooking and Current Affairs or between Natural History and History. Most people recognise the BBC1 sequence through the evening of news, family entertainment, soaps, more adult and high profile programming at 9pm, and news again at 10pm. Regular viewers of a series already know what to expect. To assist non-regular viewers, producers signal which genre their series belongs to; these signals include the opening titles, the music and the first few spoken words. Each genre has its distinctive history. TV Drama and Comedy derive from live performance, movies and radio. News derives from newspapers and radio. Arts programming derives from the art gallery and other art venues.

The BBC has always defined its public service mission as being to Inform, Educate and Entertain. But the BBC has been deliberately vague as to what precisely these three words mean; vagueness is necessary in order to accommodate change. Information (News) has strengthened since the early days of radio. Formal Education has weakened. Entertainment has grown hugely.

Today's broadcasters in general, and BBC producers in particular, often seek a mix of information, education and entertainment. Many factual entertainment shows offer a few newsy facts, provide a brief background educational summary, and then deliver an entertaining presentation. Often a popular entertainer, a comedian, or a journalist, is employed to present something serious in an entertaining way. This is not merely Info-tainment; the BBC favours Info-Educ-Tainment wrapped together in one series.

BBC television genres

	Book Chapter	Genre Origins	Mainly Information, Education or Entertainment	Cost per Audience Hour
DRAMA	4	Book, Stage, Radio, Movie	Ed/Ent	High
SOAP DRAMA	4	Radio	Ent	Low
NEWS	5	Press, Radio, Agency News	Ed/Inf	Low
CURRENT AFFAIRS	6	Press, Radio	Ed/Inf	Medium
EDUCATION	7	School	Ed	High
NATURAL HISTORY	7	Film	Ed/Inf/Ent	High
SCIENCE	9	School, Radio	Ed/Inf/Ent	High
ARTS	7	Live Performance, School, Radio	Ed/Inf/Ent	Medium
CHILDREN'S	7	Radio, School	Ed/Inf/Ent	High
RELIGION	7	Church, Radio	Ed	Medium
DOCUMENTARY	8	Sponsored Film	Ed/Inf/Ent	Medium
HISTORY	8	School, Radio	Ed/Inf/Ent	Medium
TRAVEL	8	Book, Film	Ed/Inf/Ent	Medium
COMEDY	9	Live performance, movie, radio	Ent	High
BIG ENTERTAINMENT	9	Stage, Movie	Ent	High
TALK	9	Radio	Ed/Inf/Ent	Low
COOKING	10	Radio, Press, Stage	Ed/Inf/Ent	Medium
HOMES	10	Radio, Press	Ed/Inf/Ent	Medium
QUIZ/GAME	10	Radio	Ed/Ent	Low
REALITY	10	Radio	Ed/Inf/Ent	Medium
SPORT	11	Live Performance, Radio	Ent	High

Meanwhile the BBC maintains its traditional moral hierarchy. Information and Education are seen as being superior to Entertainment. Yes, Entertainment has increasingly been regarded by the BBC as important in its own right; millions of Licence Fee payers must be entertained. But entertainment is also seen as luring audiences into, and subsidising, more informative and educational programming.

Different genres are scheduled in very different ways. Some genres – notably News and Soap Drama – are 'stripped' and appear frequently each week, every week, and at the same times. Some prestigious programming, such as short Drama series of a total four hours, is scheduled in the top time slot of 9pm on BBC1. Scheduling plays a key role in the BBC's public service project. For example, *Panorama* has for decades been seen as the BBC's number one, flagship factual show. For most of its long life, *Panorama* has received helpful BBC1 scheduling on Monday evening. *Panorama* at 8.30pm has been scheduled between the *EastEnders* super-popular soap at 8pm and other high profile series at 9pm. This is called 'hammocking' (and it does mean that *Panorama* is normally scheduled against ITV's super-popular *Coronation Street*).

On-air publicity provides another way of boosting the ratings of prestige public service programming. High profile, and high budget, drama series are boosted by publicity blasts at TV and Radio programming junctions; these blasts are the nearest the BBC gets to expensive 30-second commercials. Factual or Current Affairs series are often boosted in advance on BBC news outputs – both TV and Radio. Today's multiple platforms and catch-up services are also deployed in pursuit of public service goals. The News incorporates its own catch-up service through its extremely frequent outputs and through its 24 hour TV and Radio all-news channels. The BBC supports its most popular entertainment with repeats, online catch-up services, and additional programming. The BBC online Archive output also gives primacy to 'classic' drama, comedy and other factual genre outputs of the past.

Genres include sub-genres, which are often seen as located within hierarchies of cost and prestige. 'Serious' or 'Classical' BBC drama is seen as more prestigious and is better funded than soapy drama. Scripted comedy is better funded and more prestigious than panel comedy. Premier League

Football is more expensive and more prestigious than lower league Football. But the most prestigious and best funded drama is typically not as popular as soap drama. Thus on a cost-per-viewer basis the prestige sub-genre can be very much more expensive than the higher rating sub-genre. In practice the executive who commissions a particular genre spreads the available finance. Some prestigious-but-expensive programming is commissioned; the majority of hours are allocated to less prestigious programming which is also much cheaper-per-viewer. Genres rise and fall over time. Three falling BBC genres are Education, Religion and Children's (see Chapter Seven).

The genres are living things, driven by their own teams of TV workers. Genres compete with each other, critique each other, and seek to invade each other's territory. Comedy makes fun of most of the other genres. BBC History programming can select from, and manipulate old BBC output from several different genres.

The remixing of genres is a common phenomenon. Producers in most genres, including the News, like a joke or two, some judicious sprinkling of comedy. In factually formatted entertainment, there are restless attempts to 'tweak' the format with an added ingredient. Cooking series may incorporate humour, travel, history or science. Travel series may incorporate almost any of the other twenty genres.

Each genre looks out towards the world it covers. TV Drama looks to the live theatre and the acting profession; the News looks toward Politics and public figures; cooking series focus on restaurants; football producers look towards both UK and European football; talk shows must monitor and invite entertainment stars. But each genre has its more private life both within the BBC and within the BBC's competitors. A specific genre is typically located on a particular open-plan floor. Within each genre there are career ladders. Everywhere there is a key producer hierarchy from assistant producer via series producer to executive producer. Genres have very distinctive timetables. News works on daily timetables, and sport on weekly timetables. But some genres – such as drama and comedy – may be given six or nine months in which to generate three or four hours of programming. In some genres, people routinely work across the weekend; in other genres people are routinely out of the UK for months on end.

Members of two diverse genres, despite having nearby offices, may see very little of each other precisely because their work timetables differ so much. Moreover, when producers and other TV people travel home, and when they reach home, they tend still to be locked into their own genre. They read and write genre documents and proposals; they view the output of their own genre competitors. They continue to inhabit a private genre world.

BBC DOMESTIC TELEVISION AND RADIO CHANNELS	
TELEVISION CHANNELS	MAIN PROGRAMMING
BBC1	News, Drama, Entertainment
BBC2	Factual, Factual Entertainment
BBC3 (until 2015)	Youth (16–34)
BBC4	Arts, Documentary, History
BBC News	24-Hour News
CBeebies	Pre School Children
CBBC	School Children
Parliament	Parliamentary Debates, Committees, Discussion
BBC HD	Selection of High Definition output
S4C	Welsh
RADIO CHANNELS	
Radio One	Pop Music (16–34)
Radio Two	Pop Music (35+)
Radio Three	Classical Music
Radio Four	News, Talk, Comedy, Drama
Radio Five Live	News, Sport, Talk
1Xtra	Pop Music
BBC 6 Music	Music
Radio 4 Extra	Talk
Asian Network	Music
BBC World Service	News and Talk

The BBC's output is segmented not only by twenty-one genres, but this output goes out on about ten domestic TV channels (according to definition) and about ten UK radio channels. So if we think in terms of both genres and channels, we are looking at hundreds of specific channel genre offerings.

Nor is this all. The BBC also has big external, or world, services in both television and radio. If we then think of genre outputs across many outside-the-UK language channels, we are looking at hundreds more specific country-genre offerings.

The most important of these external offerings, not least in terms of finance, is BBC Worldwide, the BBC's foreign marketing effort. Why does the BBC put so much effort into external operations which (if external radio is included) cost at least £1.5 billion annually and still make an overall loss? The BBC has done all of this, because it has been asked by successive governments to win prestige for the UK as not only the best, but the most active, Public Service Broadcaster in the world. This is why the BBC has a big marketing network across the USA and across the world, and why the BBC is such an active TV producer, especially in the United States. BBC Worldwide is a large and energetic dog which pulls Auntie BBC in directions which she might prefer to avoid. Worldwide's most financially successful BBC export efforts have been Quality-Popular entertainment series such as the car comedy series, *Top Gear*.

Quality/popular BBC1 and 2 and specialist BBC3 and 4

During the 2003–13 decade the BBC offered four mainstream television channels – the big audience BBC1, middling audience BBC2, and small audience BBC3 and BBC4. Less than 10 per cent of BBC funding and less than 10 per cent of BBC audience went to BBC3 and BBC4 combined.

BBC3 was designed as a Youth channel and BBC4 as primarily an Arts and Culture channel.

BBC1 and BBC2 carried some high prestige programming (especially most high prestige drama) and BBC1 carried the News. But most BBC1 and BBC2 output has aimed to be quality/popular – superior entertainment, or popular programming, delivered by top-of-the-range talent.

Like most other TV channels, BBC1 and BBC2 have always relied heavily on a smallish number of established series, each of which may eventually run to hundreds or thousands of episodes. *The News* on BBC1 does four shows each day; *EastEnders* is the BBC's main daily soap. There are many established annual outputs; the BBC has done two TV weeks of Wimbledon tennis since 1946 and big batches of Promenade Concerts since 1927 (on radio, and from 1946 continuously on TV).

But an equally prominent part in BBC television has been played by a group of long-running television shows, mostly offering some kind of factual entertainment, some mix of information/education/entertainment.

- *Songs of Praise* began in 1960. Each Sunday's show came from a different church, chapel, or other place of worship. The focus was on amateur choirs singing hymns – backed up by personality presenters.
- *Film* ... was another cheap concept – it began as *Film '71*. This was a film review show which used clips provided by the movie companies, and often interviewed a star, promoting his or her new movie.
- *Top Gear* began as another cheapish show in 1978 by doing serious consumer reviews of new cars. The show was briefly stopped, but then restarted in 2002 as a factual comedy show. Three middle-aged men, led by Jeremy Clarkson (born 1960), engaged in colourful pranks such as driving expensive cars up mountains.
- *Antiques Roadshow* began in 1977. Each show visited a different locality (often a grand country house) where locals brought along their family antiques to be assessed and valued by professional experts. The *Roadshow's* multiple appeals included the mildly eccentric experts and the splendid settings. The *Roadshow* also provided history lessons on

nineteenth- and twentieth-century furniture, china, painting, jewellery, toys and much else.

- *Crimewatch* began in 1984 as yet another cheapish series: the Police who provided most of the personnel and the Crime information were the good guys. The extraordinary prevalence of CCTV in the UK allowed for the action replay of many street crimes.
- *Watchdog* began in 1985 as a Consumer series which reported on defective products and shoddy service. The bizarre tricks of the crooked businesses provided outlandish humour.
- *Countryfile*, launched in 1988, went through several facelifts but continued to inform a mainly urban audience about rural Britain. One common approach was to provide a loose narrative which focussed on a single issue in a single place, such as sheep farming in Yorkshire.
- *Who Do You Think You Are?* launched in 2004, was a history series dressed up as a celebrity interview show. The selected celebrity's family history was investigated; the focus then switched to an ancestor or ancestors who had done colourful things perhaps one hundred years ago. The invited celebrity was deployed as the week's professional presenter.
- *The One Show*, launched in 2007, was unusual as an early evening factual show doing 250 episodes a year. The *One Show* did four short films for each weekday; these films were mostly commissioned from producers far away from London. The show featured happenings, bizarre news stories, the weird detail. *The One Show* followed in the footsteps of *Nationwide* (BBC1 1969–83).[6]

Most of these BBC shows use a magazine pattern; each episode includes several items, whose popularity can easily be researched. These shows mostly combine small helpings of information and education with a large helping of entertainment. Comedy is salient, as are history and nostalgia. These shows

6 Charlotte Brunsden and David Morley, *Everyday Television: Nationwide* (London: British Film Institute, 1978).

are not radical, edgy or avant-garde. Big popular shows like these enhance big popular presenter personalities, who then help to 'carry' the show.

Such shows often come from outside London; we mostly meet warm-hearted provincial Britain, not the capital city. Successful shows generate follower series – both linked BBC series and competitor series on ITV and Channel Four. These popular BBC shows are also provided with outlets on additional platforms. This may make a successful series more expensive over time – there are more lights, more cameras, more researchers; the presenters become more expensive. But the audience tends to remain loyal.

Although they aim at family viewing, these are not shows for the 16–34 age bracket. In most cases the majority of the audience is aged over 50. Most of the people who produce these shows are younger than 50. One of the ways in which senior executives can 'freshen up' BBC1 and BBC2 – as well as their long-running shows – is by sacking or 'moving on' long-established presenters. The sacking of 'much loved presenter' on much loved BBC series is a much loved newspaper story.

The Controllers in charge of BBC1 and BBC2 pursue linked, but somewhat different, strategies. The BBC1 Controller has £3 million to spend each day of the year, while the BBC2 Controller has one third as much. Broadly, BBC1 goes for 'majority' programming – trying to reach everyone some of the time – while BBC2 does a range of 'minority' programming. Some shows which achieve strong ratings on BBC2 are moved across to seek still higher ratings on BBC1.

Jay Hunt, when controller of BBC1, told this author that her focus was primarily on drama and entertainment. BBC1's median viewer is aged over 50, and the Controller tries hard to seek out fresh big ratings comedy and factual entertainment. BBC1 is the leading UK exponent of Public Service Broadcasting, as Hunt said:

> I have fixed commitments around news, the hours of current affairs, around original drama, original arts programmes, sport, regional production and the amount of stuff made outside London.

Danny Cohen became BBC1 Controller in 2010 at age 36. He came from running BBC3, the BBC youth channel. Cohen quickly decided to weed out some older programming; there were, he said, too many middle aged white males conducting murder investigations across BBC1's evening hours.

BBC2's output (since its 1964 birth) has been broadly quality-popular, like BBC1. BBC2's audience is as old as BBC1's. Critics say that BBC2 is the channel for middle class pensioners. BBC2 focuses on more demanding Arts, Comedy and History; it also covers several high profile Sports. BBC2 carries some programming which might seem too edgy or controversial for BBC1. Another genre strongly favoured by BBC2 has been the Quiz. On some weekday afternoons and evenings BBC2 has scheduled as many as four separate Quiz shows; these were mostly the more demanding quiz shows, which emphasise information and education as well as entertainment. But in 2013 BBC2 was told to stop commissioning fresh daytime programming. BBC2's daytime programming now consists entirely of repeats.

Both BBC3 and BBC4 became established as lesser TV channels which only started transmission at 7pm. This disadvantage of a late and slow start also generates a low 24 hour share of perhaps one per cent of total UK viewing; however, a BBC3 rating of about 1.4 per cent concealed a rating-while-on-air of a more respectable 2 per cent. Both BBC3 and 4 prided themselves on using about 90 per cent UK and EU programming. Both, however, relied on a small amount of very popular US programming. Both BBC3 and 4 commission a very large number of short running series.

While BBC3 aimed at the 16–34 demographic, about half of its audience was aged 35 and over. However this was youthful for any British TV channel. BBC3 has always prided itself on its more daring, and more edgy, material. BBC3 liked startling series titles such as *Young, Dumb and Living off Mum*, *My Weapon is my Dog*, *Is it Cos I is Black?*, and *Alice and Her Six Dads*.

But after a decade of somewhat controversial existence, BBC3 was told in 2013–14 that it was to be closed down as a TV channel; it would continue online, with a much smaller budget. With BBC2 reverting to a daytime entirely made up of repeats, and with BBC3 exiled to a low budget online existence, the BBC's mainstream Public Service offering was being squeezed.

Conflict: BBC chairman versus BBC director general

During 2012–13 no less than three separate individuals occupied the BBC's chief executive role of Director General. Mark Thompson reached the end of his 2004–12 eight year term as DG; George Entwistle in late 2012 occupied the DG role for a mere two months; and a third Director General – Lord Tony Hall – took over as DG in April 2013.

While conflicts between the 'professional' Director General and the 'amateur' Chairman had occurred previously,[7] it was only in the three decades after 1982 that these conflicts became increasingly common and increasingly public. Across the twenty years of 1992–2014 the BBC had a succession of forceful Director-Generals, namely John Birt (1992–2000), Greg Dyke (2000–4) and Mark Thompson (2004–12). All three of these BBC DGs were television and broadcast professionals; they had an average age of 49, when taking up the DG post.

These three DGs shared a pattern of hyperactive macho management, and workaholic obsessiveness. All three BBC Director Generals had had experience outside the BBC in advertising-funded television. All three were eager to embrace new technology, and to slash or abolish BBC sections and departments, while also launching big new initiatives.

Most BBC Chairmen were broadcasting amateurs who had had extensive experience in public affairs, politics or finance. BBC Chairmen, both during 1992–2012 and across the BBC's whole history, entered office at an average age of 61 and served until age 65 or 66. Typically the Chairman arrived at the BBC to work with an incumbent DG; two and a half years later the typical BBC Chairman, now aged 63 or 64, took the lead in appointing a new Director General aged about 49.

Most newly arriving Chairmen went through a honeymoon phase of less than one year. The BBC Chairmanship was supposedly not a full-time job; it was advertised in 2010 as requiring 'a time commitment of 3–4 days

7 Asa Briggs, *Governing The BBC* (London: BBC, 1979). Charles Curran, *A Seamless Robe: Broadcasting – Philosophy and Practice* (London: Collins, 1979), 313–32.

per week or 12–16 days a month'. The new BBC Chairman was allowed to continue as an outside director of big companies, and Chris Patten also continued as Chancellor of Oxford University. For most of his first year, the new Chairman probably only did BBC work for half as many hours as his hyperactive Director General. On arrival at the BBC, most new BBC Chairmen admit that they don't view much television; but they do like BBC Radio Four. The new Chairman typically announced special interest in about two (of the twenty-one) genres – most often News and one other genre.

However, the chairman tends in effect to terminate the honeymoon phase, after having written the Chairman's Foreword to one *BBC Annual Report and Accounts*. In June 2013 Chris Patten listed his favourite 'high points' for 2012–13 – These were the BBC Olympic coverage, the *Hollow Crown* Shakespeare series, and one big Documentary.[8] The remaining eighteen genres apparently had no high points.

After a brief honeymoon period, most BBC Chairmen then want to take the lead in what they regard as the current big issues. This 'take charge' approach is not very surprising, in view of the British political tradition that a Minister can do a number of big government jobs in quite quick succession. Chris Patten, had during an 18 year period, held five major public positions – as a Thatcher appointed Minister in two different London Departments, as Chairman of the Conservative Party, as the last Governor of Hong Kong (before its handover to China) and finally Chris Patten was Brussels European Commissioner for External Relations. Chris Patten could perhaps be excused for thinking that being in charge of the BBC should be comparatively easy. He subsequently admitted that the BBC job was very much more demanding and complex than he had anticipated.

But when Chris Patten took office as BBC Chairman in May 2011 he found himself working with the hyperactive Mark Thompson, who had been an effective Director General for seven years. Their honeymoon

8 Lord Patten, 'Chairman's Foreword', *BBC Annual Report and Accounts, 2012/13* (June 2013).

period was rather brief; indeed the conflict, which went public after Thompson became chief executive of the *New York Times* company, was extremely acrimonious and damaging. It was distinctly lacking in traditional BBC gravitas.

Because BBC Chairmen were in charge of appointing new Director Generals, occupancy of the two posts was staggered. Each DG typically worked for more than one Chairman, and each Chairman worked alongside two different DGs. In a thirty-year period (1982–2012) there were twelve such pairings, with each pairing typically lasting only two or three years. Most of the pairings involved a brief honeymoon period, followed by steadily increasing conflict.

Both BBC Chairmen and Director Generals tended to leave abruptly. During 1982–2012 three of five Director Generals – Alasdair Milne (1982–7), Greg Dyke (2000–4) and George Entwistle (2012) were sacked by the Chairman and his team. Of eight men who acted as BBC Chairman during 1980–2014, no less than seven departed suddenly and unexpectedly. George Howard (1980–3) and Stuart Young (1983–6) both grew ill and died. Christopher Bland (1996–2001) departed suddenly to British Telecom; Gavyn Davies (2001–4) resigned over the Hutton report on the BBC and the Iraq war. Michael Grade (2004–6) departed suddenly to ITV, and Sir Michael Lyons (2007–11) 'resigned', or was terminated by the Cameron Conservative government. Chris Patten (2011–14) departed due to ill health.

Any BBC Chairman or DG faces difficult challenges. The Director General needs to understand News, to have experience across other genres, to have a grasp of finance and audience data, as well as an ability both to cut and to build. The DG needs to be a good speaker and public performer in front of internal BBC audiences, Parliament, the OFCOM regulator, the press, radio and TV. Finally, the DG needs political and diplomatic skills. George Entwistle clearly lacked the public speaker skills and performed horribly badly on his own BBC Radio and TV.

Greg Dyke (2000–4) was in several respects an effective Director General; but he lacked gravitas, political skill, and any element of diplomacy. Greg Dyke told me that he was appointed as DG and protected by Christopher Bland (as BBC Chairman); Dyke and Bland were friends and colleagues from London Weekend (ITV). Dyke, who liked confrontations, mishandled BBC relations with the British Government of Tony Blair over BBC reporting of the Iraq War. Greg Dyke also antagonised key Governors. He told me:

> The truth about the governors was you took people who knew fuck all about broadcasting and they just sat there.

Easily the most inadequate BBC Chairman of recent years was Marmaduke Hussey (1986–96). Hussey was a former senior executive of the Murdoch controlled Times Newspapers; Hussey was sacked by Murdoch but retained as a consultant. Hussey admired Murdoch and his standard tactic, when arriving at a new property, of sacking the top man. To sack the BBC CEO was an even more enticing prospect for Hussey because Alasdair Milne was already highly unpopular with several leading BBC Governors and several leading Tory politicians, including Mrs Thatcher. Within two months of Duke Hussey's arrival at the BBC, Alasdair Milne was sacked. Milne's book, which focuses heavily on his dismissal, is one of the best written and most revealing books on the BBC.[9] Marmaduke Hussey's book is also a revealing read. Duke Hussey provides an interesting account of how he fell out not only with Alasdair Milne but also with the next two Director Generals, Michael Checkland and John Birt.[10]

Chris Patten was another shortish stay BBC Chairman (2011–14) who nevertheless worked with three Director Generals – Mark Thompson, George Entwistle and Tony Hall. Chris Patten and Tony Hall (BBC Director General from April 2013) worked together for only 13 months; Chris Patten retired in May 2014 due to ill health. The two men seem to have worked together fairly amicably. Tony Hall had had plenty of senior

9 For a revealing account of Alasdair Milne's state of mind about a year before he was sacked, see this interview: Martin Jackson and Peter Montieth, 'Riding the Bumpy Years'. *Broadcast*, 6 December 1985: 22–7.

10 Alasdair Milne, *DG: The Memoirs of a British Broadcaster* (London: Hodder and Stoughton, 1988). Marmaduke Hussey, *Chance Governs All: A Memoir* (London: Macmillan, 2001).

experience at BBC News and, like Patten, he was an accomplished book author. But for twelve years (2001–13) he had been chief executive at the Royal Opera House, Covent Garden.

During their 2013–14 cohabitation chairman Chris Patten had his sixty-ninth birthday and DG Tony Hall had his sixty-second. Many in the BBC's aging audience will probably have felt sympathy when they saw Chris Patten and Tony Hall together on BBC television. Both Patten and Hall were members of the unelected House of Lords; both had white hair, and both appeared to be worried men. Millions of younger people may have wondered why Public Service Broadcasting was being run at the BBC by this Lordly couple with a combined age of 131 years.

But Chris Patten resigned in 2014 and his successor broke with tradition. Rona Fairhead was the first woman to chair the BBC; and, at age fifty-three, she was ten years younger than her Director-General, Lord Tony Hall. However, Fairhead followed tradition in other respects – she was a newspaper manager (*Financial Times*) with no previous experience in broadcasting.

In retrospect it seems likely that BBC governance changes, introduced by 2006 legislation, exacerbated the tendency to Chairman versus Director General conflicts. In January 2007 the BBC 'Governors' were replaced by BBC 'Trustees'. The Chairman was now Chairman of the BBC Trust and Trustees. The Trust was given a strengthened staff of 70 people. The BBC Executive Board, still led by the Director General and including six other top BBC executives, was 'strengthened' with four non-executive Directors and eight other Directors. Politicians, who had often accused the BBC of having too many senior positions, had now surrounded the BBC with several newly powerful groups – the Trustees were added to the new communications regulator (OFCOM) and to several newly active Parliamentary Committees. This meant that more and more external and internal committees had an increasingly assertive role in trying to decide what 'BBC Public Service Broadcasting' really meant. An unintended consequence was to make two stressful roles – Chairman and Director General – increasingly difficult to perform.

BBC technology and survival strategies

The BBC has long been known as a 'Great Survivor', but survival has become more difficult. The BBC faces conflicting demands from its audiences, as well as from politicians, the press, and its TV and online competitors. The BBC must appeal both to the mass public and to the national elite. The BBC is urged to be more efficient and commercially competitive, while also delivering high quality across twenty or twenty-one genres.

'New Technology' has, at least since the 1980s, posed big dilemmas for the BBC. Until the 1980s the BBC had been seen by successive governments as the chosen national technology innovator in radio and then in television. The BBC pioneered both black and white, and colour, television as well as FM Radio. But in the 1980s the BBC failed to pioneer in either satellite or cable. Since 1990 the BBC has been involved in several other important technology innovations. Its strong support for Digital Terrestrial TV (DTT) enabled the BBC to become a leader in Freeview's multi-channel offer. The BBC has also established a strong online presence. The BBC iPlayer (which allowed viewers to catch up on BBC output of – initially – the last week) responded to five million catch up requests per day in 2011 and eight million per day in 2014. But the BBC (like ITV) has fallen behind both Sky and Virgin new technology.

As technology change has speeded up, some established BBC assets have developed awkward new characteristics. There is now a marked tendency for very senior BBC star performers to criticise the BBC's politics and performance. Some of these talkative star performers are now 'too famous to sack'; some are near retirement or have recently departed to other prestigious roles (such as head of an Oxford college). A number of these senior ex-BBC stars are now appearing on Sky.

The BBC makes both strategic and tactical responses to its critics. Tactical responses include the following:

- The BBC employs at least 150 public relations people. Some big entertainment shows have their own PR team.

- The BBC does some direct paid advertising, typically featuring a 'major new TV series'.
- The BBC does much on air promotion mainly of certain selected new series. Big BBC1 in particular does promotions for series on smaller BBC TV channels.
- The BBC commissions numerous specialised reports from public figures and academic experts. These report writers are carefully chosen and typically produce a broadly positive account, with some additional 'must try harder' points.[11]

The BBC also engages in a number of more strategic activities, such as:

- Many elected politicians, national and local, come into regular contact with BBC journalists and producers. The BBC's local radio stations are in regular contact with local Members of Parliament. This news gathering operation enables BBC managers to be well informed in their political lobbying efforts.
- The BBC has spent at least £10 million a year on management consultants in most recent years. The BBC first employed McKinsey in 1969[12] and it was still using McKinsey in the 2010s.
- One of John Birt's innovations was to establish a BBC Policy and Planning operation; which was directed by Patricia Hodgson (1987–2000). Several researchers from BBC Policy and Planning went on to senior positions in broadcasting, in politics, and at the OFCOM regulator. Hodgson herself became Chairman of OFCOM in 2014.
- The BBC has continued to be a major player on the British arts and cultural scene. In addition to maintaining its orchestras, the BBC co-operates in many projects and much programming with the British

11 By 1972 there were already 720 publications – mostly books and book length reports – about the BBC. See: BBC, *British Broadcasting: a Select Bibliography* (London: BBC, 1972). Since 1972 this literature has greatly expanded.

12 Tom Burns, *The BBC: public institution and private world* (London: Macmillan, 1977), 229–38.

Museum, the British Library, the National Trust, the National Gallery and many other cultural organisations.

Over its long life the BBC has developed numerous survival tactics and strategies. But these cannot entirely defend the BBC from an increasing number of threats and challenges. In particular the BBC has lost its once commanding position as a developer of 'new technology'. Moreover despite – or perhaps because of – its huge complexity and its 21 genres, the BBC is more vulnerable than ever to short sharp headlines such as 'BBC Sex Scandal' or 'BBC Cash Scandal'.

Finance will continue to be the BBC's greatest single problem. BBC Licence Fee income will probably continue to fall further and further behind the revenue available to its commercial television competitors.

CHAPTER 2

UK Commercial Television Trembles

Commercial television (of various kinds) attracts about seventy per cent of all UK TV viewing. The two main ways of funding this commercial television are advertising and subscription. The licence fee is reserved for the BBC (and its thirty per cent of viewing).

Despite the huge growth of the internet and of handheld devices, the typical Briton still views television programming for about twenty-six hours a week compared with twenty-one hours in 1982. This includes about eighteen hours a week of viewing commercial TV (against eight hours watching BBC). Viewing on mobile phones and other mobile devices has largely been added to time spent viewing conventional television. This parallels the continuing strong UK performance of Hollywood TV, to which has been added the strong UK performance of Silicon Valley.

ITV (Independent Television) had a monopoly of UK commercial television for twenty-seven years (1955–82). The legislative intention was to combine the best of the BBC with the best elements of early 1950s American television. In the early 1950s the US television industry was still located in New York and the programming was produced by advertising professionals. Madison Avenue advertising was deeply implanted into the programming with, for example, the comedy star smoking the sponsor's cigarettes and stressing the health benefits. The London 1953–4 legislative process focused heavily on reducing such advertising abuses, but largely ignored programming issues. However, after the Pilkington Committee report (1962), ITV was more severely regulated. During the remainder of the 1960s and 1970s, ITV was a heavily regulated advertising monopolist – another BBC1, but with advertising.

In the 1970s the UK audience was about equally divided between the two BBC channels with fifty per cent and the sole ITV channel with its fifty per cent. Since the 1970s the BBC's audience share has fallen from about half to about thirty per cent of today's TV viewing. But the commercial television audience is now spread into three parcels, each having about twenty to twenty-five per cent of the total audience:

- ITV is now no longer a cartel of regional companies, but is dominated by a single ITV company.
- Channels Four and Five, plus the UKTV group of eleven channels.
- The satellite and cable channels – some owned and operated by BSkyB. Most of the remainder of the programming is supplied by American channel groups such as Discovery and the Hollywood majors.

British policy has continued to follow, and often to misunderstand, the latest changes in United States commercial television. In particular UK policy followed but misunderstood American satellite-and-cable as well as Silicon Valley's new technologies in the 1980s and 1990s. British policy lacked commercial and technological realism and relied too much on 'punching above our weight' and similar nostalgic-fantasy catchphrases.

British policy consistently failed to grasp the sheer size and the extreme scale economies of American commercial media. Whereas the UK now has two significant commercial TV outfits (ITV and Channel Four) Hollywood has about twenty traditional TV networks and significant cable TV channels. Together with these Hollywood entities and the top Silicon Valley players, British commercial TV is confronting California and other US conglomerate companies whose dollar revenue is at least thirty times larger than the combined ITV and Channel Four revenue.

Meanwhile both Hollywood and Silicon Valley have chosen London as a, or the key, hub location in their global strategies. The big population countries where more than half of the world's population reside (China, India, Bangladesh, Pakistan, Indonesia, Japan, Russia, Nigeria, Brazil) are largely media self-sufficient.[1] Consequently the Hollywood export focus

1 Jeremy Tunstall, *The Media Were American* (New York: Oxford University Press, 2008).

is on the numerous, smaller population, wealthier nations of the Middle East, Latin America and especially western and eastern Europe. London neatly fits this strategy:

- London is the favourite location for EMEA (Europe, Mid East, Africa) marketing by American media companies.
- London is the lead city for a group of English speaking countries (Australia, Canada, Ireland, New Zealand, UK) with a combined population of 120 million.
- London is a, or the, leading European location for advertising, international law, and political media lobbying.

ITV and advertising-funded television leadership

In 2015 ITV had its sixtieth anniversary and ITV spokespersons strongly asserted that the years 2010–15 had been some of the best in its 1955–2015 history. True, ITV now has only one third of ITV's 1970s audience share. But an expanding family of new ITV channels has significantly improved this picture. ITV2 (targeted at younger women), ITV3 (older women) and ITV4 (macho male) have each averaged a UK audience share of about two per cent.

ITV in the 2010s was re-establishing its reputation for making quality-popular drama. ITV productions (mainly the *Coronation Street* and *Emmerdale* soaps) had more than half of the top twenty UK ratings each week. This enabled ITV to claim that it had the answer to 'audience fragmentation', because each weekday it routinely delivered to advertisers audiences of between five and eight million. ITV News was still doing quite well, especially at 6.30pm. ITV was making much of its own programming at ITV Studios; and ITV was busily buying up successful Independent Production companies in both the UK and US.

Throughout the 1970s and 1980s ITV had changed very little. ITV then had a monopoly of television advertising; this continued even when

Channel Four arrived in 1982, because ITV initially sold the new channel's advertising and also produced a large fraction of its programming. The proceeds of the TV advertising monopoly were spent on three main things – generously budgeted production of programming, very generously paid unionised personnel, and strong profit performance by the initially fifteen (later sixteen) ITV regional companies. The ITV network was dominated by initially four (later five) 'networking' companies, which made most of the programming. But each of these networking companies only produced fifteen per cent, or less, of this one channel's programming. Each of the ITV networking companies only made about twenty hours of programming per week, including its local news.

In the 1970s and 1980s, ITV was a system of cross-subsidy – the smaller and more remote regions were subsidised by the bigger companies based in London, Birmingham, Manchester and Leeds. The IBA regulator was flexible on programming detail, but conservative – indeed rigid – on everything else. The IBA regulator saw itself as refereeing the petty squabbles between the bigger and smaller ITV companies. This refereeing in practice meant keeping everything rigid and unchanging.

1988–91 was a period of ITV panic and chaos. A Thatcher government White Paper in 1988 made it clear that ITV's comfortable cartel was coming to an end. Not only did Rupert Murdoch's BSkyB bulldozer itself onto the commercial TV scene. But following the 1990 Broadcasting Act, the renewal of ITV Licences would depend upon an auction; this auction occurred in 1991 and Thames Television – previously ITV's most dynamic and successful company – lost its licence. By the end of 1993, ITV had sacked one third of its workforce; by 1995 nearly half of the workforce had gone. The previously strong trade unions were defeated and ITV was being casualised in employment terms.

1992–2003 were eleven years of merging the ITV cartel into a single company. In a period during which BSkyB, Google and other American companies grew so rapidly, it took ITV eleven years simply to shake down into a single company. This failure was due, partly, to inept UK policy and regulation. But ITV management failures included the following:

- ITV misused its allocation of new DTT television channels. It launched a new 'On Digital' offering (1998–2002) which, as a pay TV service, was a disastrous failure.
- ITV launched a hopelessly under-resourced twenty-four hour news channel (2000–5). ITV also closed down its highly regarded current affairs shows, *This Week* and *World in Action*, which together occupied only about thirty hours of screen time per year.
- ITV had online failures, in particular 'Friends Re-united' which ITV acquired in 2005 and sold in 2009 with a loss of £145 million.
- ITV cut back on one of its main advantages – namely its strong regional identities in the English Midlands and North.
- ITV was involved in several 'phone-in scandals' which involved cheating its own audience members.

ITV's first fifty years (1955–2005) were marked by ludicrous levels of internal in-fighting and antagonism. When the separate ITV companies were merging, during 1992–2003, the regional owners and managers continued to direct their belligerence at their ITV colleagues rather than at BSkyB. The leading executives, towards the end of the ITV merger process, were resented as ignorant and incompetent outsiders, by many producers. At Granada (the ultimate ITV winner) the two key executives, Gerry Robinson and Charles Allen, were known as the 'caterers' because they came from the chain catering, and not the television division, of Granada. The caterers were seen (by, for instance, sacked current affairs producers) as overly obsessed with delivering daily ratings to advertisers.

For two full decades (1990–2010) ITV suffered from badly flawed government policy and regulation, plus its own weak management, plus plenty of bad luck. Only in 2010 did a more talented management team begin to assemble at ITV. Soon ITV achieved improved audience ratings; its profits, and its share price rose steeply. The ITV of the 2010s was a much more commercial version of commercial TV than the ITV of the 1960s or 1970s. Sponsorship of an entire series, once forbidden, was now commonplace. Advertiser funded programming (AFP) is now allowed as is product placement within programming. The ITV programming hour is now only forty-six minutes, compared with fifty-three minutes in the early days. One reason why ITV1's audience share remains stubbornly below twenty per cent, is that not everyone wants to be a typical ITV audience member who views forty TV commercials each day and three hundred TV commercials each week.

Moreover each of the successful lesser ITV channels tends to depend on very heavy repetition. ITV2, for example, depends on repeating ITV soaps and big entertainment; it also carries American series and made-in-America versions of British programming formats. ITV may be in danger of losing some of its UK identity by doing so much importing of made-in-USA productions, by owning Hollywood independent production companies and by participating in high profile ITV-US co-productions.

ITV has said that it is successfully boosting its TV series production output. But much of this series production is being made for transmission on the ITV channels. ITV is still very heavily dependent on advertising. UK advertising on the internet surpassed advertising on ITV for the first time in 2008. By 2015 about half of all UK advertising expenditure was on the internet, with Google the largest single location. Only thirteen per cent of UK advertising expenditure now goes to the ITV channels.

Also advertising funded: Four, Five, UKTV

In addition to ITV, the UK has three other advertising financed channel families. These are Channel Four (launched 1982), Channel Five (launched 1997) and UKTV (which began on a small scale in 1992). These three 'families' together offer more than twenty-five channels. Together Four, Five and UKTV have a twenty per cent share of the British TV audience. The three channel families have these characteristics in common:

- All three channel families are financed by advertising.
- All three have much lower programming budgets than either BBC1 or ITV1.

- All three of these commercial channel families also include a 'public service' element. Four and Five have public service obligations (to carry news and some other non-entertainment programming). UKTV, which is not formally subject to public service obligations, is half-owned by the BBC.
- None of these channels makes any of its own programming. They depend on 'commissioning' programming – mainly from independent producers – and on 'acquiring' existing programming.
- All three-channel groups depend on acquisitions from Hollywood. Channels Four and Five import hundreds of Hollywood series each year; UKTV is half owned by the BBC and half by the American Scripps Networks Interactive company.

After six years (1982–8) of gradual growth, Channel Four had achieved a ten per cent share of the UK TV audience. Now as a family of eleven small channels, Four still has a ten per cent audience share. But the main Channel Four achieves only half of the Four total. E4, Film4, More4 and 4Seven – plus another six mini-channels – deliver the other half of the Four audience.

Channel Four initially claimed to be 'different-but-not-too-different.' C4 has always tried to be young, affluent and attractive to advertisers. In fact C4's profile is not hugely different from the UK population; but C4 does appeal to advertisers because the C4 audience is somewhat younger and more middle class than the ITV audience. Channel Four has always managed to win prizes and newspaper praise by producing some top of the line short series and one-offs. C4 has always presented itself as 'edgy', youthful, risk-taking, and a little left of centre politically. In fact audience research showed – even in its earlier more risky years – that C4 was not seen by the great British public as being hugely different from either the BBC or ITV.[2] Today Channel Four's main four channels together schedule at least thirty hours of American programming per 24 hours. This is

2 David Docherty, David E. Morrison and Michael Tracey, *Keeping Faith? Channel 4 and its audience* (London: John Libbey, 1988); Barrie Gunter and Paul Winstone, *Television: The Public's View, 1992* (London: John Libbey, 1993).

about 11,000 hours of Hollywood movies and TV/Cable series in one full year. Of course, much of this is scheduled into the lowest audience times of these low audience channels.

Paradoxically for a Public Service broadcaster, Channel Four has not been very successful at several traditional public service genres – such a children's TV, religion and science. Channel Four's big successes have mostly been in factual programming. This includes News, Current Affairs and Documentary. C4 has been especially strong in Lifestyle (Cooking and Homes) programming as well as in Quiz, Games and Reality. C4 has done quite well in Music/Culture/Arts, in History and in Natural History. C4 has even been moderately successful in the expensive genre of Sport – including Horseracing. 'Documentary' on C4 has meant many things. C4 has scheduled numerous traditional documentaries; it has specialised in 'rig shows' which use many fixed cameras within a single location. C4 has done many 'Shock Docs' (also known as Schlock Docs or soft pornography).

Channel Four has been successful in establishing significant additional channels. E4, which is young and female, specialises in entertainment, much of it American. More4 is also female-skewed but older and it specialises in re-runs from the main Channel Four. Film 4, which is older and male-skewed, focuses on movies, predominantly American, but also British and European.

Channel Four has consistently supported the low budget British film industry. These 'films' in practice differed very little from single TV dramas; they had similarly low budgets. In the early years these 'films' appeared on the sole C4 channel and in some UK cinemas.[3] 136 films were co-funded in Channel Four's first nine years – fifteen films per year. There were several early successes. But the great majority of these films had very small audiences both in cinemas and on Channel Four. In more recent years C4 has continued to fund and co-fund a small number of films.

Channel Four has always reflected the ideas of its current top management. Jeremy Isaacs was C4's first CEO – 1982–8, plus two years pre-preparation. Isaacs was a very accomplished producer of current affairs

3 John Pym, *Film on Four* (London: British Film Institute, 1992).

and history. He had been a senior executive at Thames (the ITV London weekday company); Isaacs liked opera, literature and art. He surrounded himself with a strange assortment of senior colleagues, several of whom had no TV experience.[4] Channel Four showed full length operas once a month; and it commissioned much untried factual entertainment as well as philosophy and Berliner Ensemble.[5] Despite the publicity emphasis on 'independent production', the majority of C4's broadcasting output came from the old ITV companies and Hollywood.

Few journalists or politicians in 1981–2 had realised that C4 would have to rely heavily on Hollywood.[6] As Jeremy Isaacs recalled:

> Much of what we broadcast, I knew, but was not yet saying, would be acquired material, foraged from the bazaars of the world.

Most of these bazaars were located in Los Angeles. In the Isaacs years, C4 acquired UK rights to super successful US TV series such as *Cheers*, *The Golden Girls*, *The Cosby Show*, *St Elsewhere*, and *Hill Street Blues*. On Hollywood movies, Isaacs writes:

> Throughout 1981 and 1982 Derek Hill and Leslie Halliwell recommended to me movies for purchase. We bought several thousand. Halliwell bought in Hollywood.[7]

In the early 1980s bulk buying of Hollywood series and movies was extremely cheap, because there was only modest competition within the UK market.

When Jeremy Isaacs departed in 1988,[8] Channel Four already had a UK audience share of 8.9 per cent. So the next C4 CEO, Michael Grade

4 Dorothy Hobson, *Channel 4: the early years and the Jeremy Isaacs legacy* (London: I.B. Tauris, 2008).

5 Michael Kustow, *One in Four: a year in the life of a Channel Four commissioning editor* (London: Chatto and Windus, 1987).

6 Stephen Lambert, *Channel Four: television with a difference?* (London: British Film Institute, 1982).

7 Jeremy Isaacs, *Storm Over 4: a personal account* (London: Weidenfeld and Nicolson, 1989), 31–2, 115.

8 Jeremy Isaacs, *Look Me In The Eye: A Life in Television* (London: Little, Brown, 2006), 324–71.

(1988–97) found it comparatively easy to reach the ten per cent target. During the 1990s C4 became increasingly successful in generating advertising revenue. From 1994 onwards C4 was importing *ER*, *Friends*, *Frasier* and many other Hollywood series.

The next C4 CEO was Michael Jackson (1997–2001) and during his years some key changes occurred. Michael Jackson launched *Big Brother* on Channel Four in summer 2000. This format, from the Dutch Endemol company, allowed viewers to observe the sealed off inmates of the Big Brother house on a live or 'near live' basis. In fact the whole proceedings were recorded and quickly edited. In the UK, as in several other countries, *Big Brother* was a spectacular ratings success. When the ratings grew, *BB* was scheduled into longer and earlier runs, over a greater number of weeks and into earlier weeks each summer. Moreover *Big Brother* was streamed live online and generated additional linked TV programming – such as *Big Brother's Little Brother* and *Celebrity Big Brother*. The third year, 2002, attracted the largest audience.[9]

The new C4 CEO, Mark Thompson (2001–4) stuck with *Big Brother*, perhaps against his better judgement. But *BB* was extremely cheap, while it still remained under a fixed price contract. In 2006–7 Endemol, the production company, demanded a massive increase in the fee, which C4 paid, but only for one year. Again it was Michael Jackson, followed by Mark Thompson, who established and maintained C4's new channels. Film Four (1998) and E4 (2001) were both launched by Jackson and sustained through initial losses under Mark Thompson. This new multi-channel strategy, and the huge ratings success of *Big Brother*, effectively transformed Channel Four from a single channel public service into a multi-channel public business.

In its first three decades (1982–2012) Channel Four achieved much. But it is still very dependent on massive Hollywood imports as well as on factual genres and formats. *Big Brother* in the 2000s had supplied elements of drama, soap drama, comedy, and big entertainment. But, arguably, C4

9 Maggie Brown, *A Licence To Be Different: the story of Channel 4* (London: British Film Institute, 2007), 304–19.

needed to develop long running series in each of these genres – if it was to protect its 10 per cent multi-channel share. In 2010 a formidable new senior management team – led by David Abraham and Jay Hunt – took charge of C4's early middle age.

Channel Five launched in 1997 as the UK's fifth 'Public Service' mainstream analogue TV channel. Ever since 1997, Channel Five (with its channel group) has been known as the six per cent (UK audience share) channel, which carries a huge amount of Hollywood crime. For a decade, beginning in 2001, Channel Five was heavily dependent on *CSI: Crime Scene Investigation* (and its spin-off New York and Miami series). Almost equally successful were *Law and Order* and its two additional series. Other American successes on Five were *NCIS*, *The Shield*, *Prison Break*, *The Mentalist* and *Person of Interest*. Non-crime US successes included *House*, *Grey's Anatomy* and *Ice Road Truckers*.

In its very earliest days (1997–2000) Channel Five scheduled Hollywood made-for-TV movies almost every day in the key 9pm slot. Subsequently, Channel Five began to buy American television series each of which, typically, made about twenty-three episodes per year. When the schedule today says '10/23, Series eleven', you are looking at something like the 240th episode of that series. From year 2000 onwards Channel Five filled its hours between 2pm and midnight predominantly with Hollywood TV series and movies, plus Australian daily soaps. The main evidence that Channel Five retained some public service element was the two half hours of News per weekday; but even this News was supplied by American controlled BSkyB.

'Films, Fucking and Football' was a phrase which haunted Channel Five for at least a decade after it was made by Dawn Airey (then Chief Executive at Five) in 2001. Airey was not advocating an FFF scheduling strategy; she was asserting that Channel Five was no longer an FFF channel. In fact its quantity of football and late night soft pornography had always been quite small. But this sleazy image stuck. Channel Five's audience was older and smaller than Channel Four's audience which made Five much less appealing to advertisers.

TV channels – like most people and organisations – are strongly marked by their early years. Channel Five was launched in 1997 with little finance and very unrealistic public service goals. It was also hugely handicapped in terms of technology. Its early coverage initially excluded about one third of UK homes. Channel Five was further handicapped by initially being owned by a group of four incompatible companies. These included one American bank, the German RTL (Bertelsmann) television giant, and two British losers in the struggle to control the UK's slowly merging ITV.[10] Meanwhile David Elstein, as chief executive of Channel Five, was required to avoid the looming disaster. Elstein saved Channel Five with a virtuoso display of management skill. Possessing an unrivalled combination of creative and management experience, plus persuasive skills, Elstein turned looming disaster into early success. He was supported by other talented senior people such as Dawn Airey and Tim Gardam. Having held a senior position at BSkyB, David Elstein did not hesitate to introduce several American commercial TV practices. Elstein decided to 'strip' popular shows across the week – keeping the schedule largely the same on all five weekdays. Elstein admitted that he did not himself view much of this stuff, but he did know the numbers (money and ratings) and he impressed the advertising agencies. Meanwhile the warring and incompetent owners failed to appreciate Elstein. After just twelve months (in 1997–8) Channel Five's audience share reached 6.3 per cent, but the owners then starved it of money and the channel group never subsequently reached seven per cent.[11]

After David Elstein departed in late 2000, Dawn Airey took over as chief executive for two years. The German RTL was now the majority owner and RTL became the 100 per cent owner in September 2005. In 2006 Five launched two infant channels; but the combined audience share of the three channels remained stuck at about 6 per cent. At Channel Five's tenth

10 Chris Horrie and Steve Clarke, *Citizen Greg* (London: Simon and Schuster, 2000), 213–36.

11 'What C5 needs is for its bickering shareholders, RTL and United News and Media, to grant that much heralded £60m rise in its programming budget to £180m'. Katy Elliott, 'Homegrown hits still eluding C5', *Broadcast* (9 March 2001). Meg Carter, 'More dash than cash', *Broadcast*: 'Special Supplement. The Story So Far, C5 – 1997–2002', 10–11.

birthday in 2007 a celebratory trade press supplement concluded that the Channel's greatest success had been in 'the buying game'.[12] For a decade Five had acquired several of the best popular-quality Hollywood series. But next year, in late 2008, the Euro-American financial crisis exploded. Channel Five – as the six per cent ratings channel – quickly lost much more of its advertising revenue than did ITV or Four. The RTL management duly panicked and rehired Dawn Airey (now with senior experience at both BSkyB and ITV) for her second stint as chief executive at Five. Airey arrived back at Five in October 2008.[13] A few months later, Dawn Airey told me:

> It was almost a perfect storm. On my very first day back at Five, I announced a thirty per cent cut in our programming budget. In seven months we've reduced our staff from 330 to 250. Our key assets here are speed, simplicity and self-confidence. Eighty per cent of our programme suppliers have agreed to have their money reduced. Sacking and cutting is not nice, but if you're direct with them, people understand. We're in commercial survival time here.[14]

After Airey had saved Channel Five for them, the German owners decided to sell.

The new owner of Channel Five from August 2010 was Richard Desmond, best known for his history as the UK's leading owner of pornographic print magazines and pornographic satellite TV channels. Desmond quickly introduced a new strategy which aimed to modify Five's rather isolated business position. Desmond already owned two seven-day national newspaper franchises – the *Express* and *Star* papers. He also had long owned *OK!* Magazine, both the UK and international editions. Desmond, as a successful purveyor of 'celebrity' journalism in print, was determined to cross-promote new young celebrities between

12 Jessica Rogers, 'The buying game', *Broadcast*, Five is 10: celebrating Five's first decade (30 March 2007) 14–15.

13 Jon Rogers and Katherine Rushton, 'Five get to axe one third of staff', *Broadcast* (27 February 2009). Amanda Andrews, 'Five's advert revenue falls 27pc on audience figure fears', *Daily Telegraph* (21 January 2009).

14 Author interview with Dawn Airey at Channel Five (13 May 2009).

his print media and Five's TV channels. 'Celebrities' discovered on Five were ruthlessly promoted in print; celebrities from his newspapers were put onto television. Desmond also heavily cross-promoted his advertisers and their products.

One big Desmond advantage was simply that he was an aggressive individual mogul with no debt and with a strategy to rescue Channel Five. In 2010 he had about £1 billion of his own money and was happy to invest some of it in the channel. Desmond's father had been a senior advertising man, but Desmond had done some of his growing up in poverty with his mother. He was a street fighter, a raucous and obscene, self-made media mogul. Perhaps Desmond was right in thinking that too many senior Channel Five people had had first class Oxford degrees. Desmond also faced the fierce hostility of some other national newspapers, which continued to describe him as a pornographer.

Channel Five remained hugely dependent on imports of American series and movies. In some cases Five may have paid too much to Hollywood, but it was legally locked into long-term deals. Channel Five was still an All American Crime Scene, when in 2014 Desmond sold Five to Viacom, the Hollywood major.

'UKTV' is a collection of eleven television channels which together have about a five per cent share of the British audience. Each of these is a small channel with a typical audience share of 0.4 per cent. UKTV relies primarily on re-running old programming from BBC1, 2, 3, 4; but it also shows old ITV programming and some (mainly newish) Hollywood product. UKTV is jointly US/UK. The American fifty per cent has been sold between several different American companies. UKTV offers these channels: Alibi (crime drama), Blighty (British nostalgia), Dave (male and comedy), Drama (British drama), Eden (natural history), Gold (old comedy), Good Food (food), Home (home and garden), Really (female reality, lifestyle), Watch (entertainment), Yesterday (history). Most of these names were adopted during 2007–9; previously each of the titles had been prefixed by 'UK', which involved names such as UK Food, UK History and UKG2 (later Dave). UKTV's eleven channels have undergone a total of at least sixteen name changes between them.

All eleven of these 'new' channels were genre specific – in line with the trend towards genre specific channels since 1990. But UKTV managers know that even genre specific channels sometimes need to wander sideways (onto other genre territory) in line with audiences and ratings. Overall the eleven UKTV channels made quiet moves towards more entertainment; for example the Yesterday channel now used less straight History, but more films and personal accounts of past events. Around 2012 UKTV started to acquire more Channel Four programming.

Programming from Hollywood also increased. The new policy was not to buy big expensive Hollywood runs in the Channel Five style. But UKTV managers were spending more money on buying short bursts of fresh American programming, which could buttress the channel brand and could be cross-promoted on other UKTV channels. For example *Storage Hunters*, a very cheaply filmed US reality show about domestic junk auctions, achieved ratings success on the Dave channel in 2013–14. After 2010 UKTV made a big effort to become more of a multi-platform operation. Additional re-run, catch-up, mobile and streaming activity was especially difficult for UKTV because of the complex rights details involved in reusing so much old BBC and other programming.

UKTV had emerged from the 1990 wreckage of BSB – the 'official' UK satellite operator which was defeated, and absorbed, by Murdoch's Sky. UKTV's first channel was Gold which launched in 1992 to replay BBC and Thames programming. Cox (the US Cable company) owned an initial 65 per cent at the launch of UK Gold. As UKTV slowly grew from a 1.5 per cent bundle of channels in 2000 to a five per cent audience bundle after 2010, the value and price of UKTV inevitably increased. Meanwhile the BBC – with many new developments – was always short of enough cash to take full ownership.

The biggest UKTV dependence is on American controlled BSkyB and Virgin Cable. Seven of the eleven UKTV channels cannot be viewed on Freeview – but only via BSkyB or Cable. There is a strong correlation between a UKTV channel's audience and its position on the Sky Electronic Programme Guide (EPG). The more successful UKTV channels have EPG positions like 109, 110 and 111. The less successful UKTV channels tend to have much worse positions such as 532 and 537.

BSkyB and Virgin cable: UK subscription, US ownership

In addition to licence fee and advertising, the third main source of TV funding in the UK is subscription. The two dominant subscription TV suppliers are BSkyB and Virgin Media. These two companies are in a combined total of fifty per cent of households; and that percentage is only increasing very slowly. The typical BSkyB or Virgin household pays a total subscription which is about four times the BBC licence fee.

Both of these two dominant subscription TV suppliers are American controlled. BSkyB has been controlled since 1989 by the Rupert Murdoch family. Another American media mogul, John Malone, through his Liberty Global company achieved control of Virgin Cable in 2012. But British cable had been dominated by other American companies for the two previous decades. So how did it happen that the UK – with it long tradition of strong national broadcast policymaking – allowed these major new technologies to develop into an American owned satellite monopoly and a cable monopoly? And why was each of the two new monopoly companies controlled by an American billionaire? This long-term outcome clearly derives from the Margaret Thatcher decade of the 1980s.

Today the typical Sky or Virgin subscriber household can receive several hundred channels. A Sky subscriber will receive all of the public service (BBC/ITV/Four/Five) channel bundles, plus all of UKTV. Sky itself offers its own Sky One, Sky Two and other Sky-labelled channels. A basic subscription also includes a large number of American entertainment, children's, and factual channels. For additional payments, the customer can receive a large group of Sport channels and a large group of Movie channels. Other specialised channel bundles are available for yet more subscription payments.

This huge armada of Sky or Virgin channels is very different from the initial Sky offer of 1988–92. Then the offer was of a mere handful of fresh channels, in particular two or three (Hollywood) movie channels. But especially in 1992, when Sky began to offer big quantities of live sport, it was becoming obvious that Sky was delivering programming for which some householders were willing to pay sizeable subscriptions.

National UK policy weakness played a large part in this outcome. During the 1980s, British broadcasting policy went through a chaotic sequence of false starts and false hopes. Both Thatcher's Conservatives and the Labour opposition failed to grasp some very basic dimensions of the 'new' Satellite and Cable media. British policymakers (like policymaker across Europe and the world) looked at the American experience, but still failed to grasp some of its most basic essentials. In particular Satellite and Cable need significant subscription revenue to pay for many thousands of fresh programming hours; most of these new hours would need to be entertainment.

British policymakers in general, and 1980s Conservative policymakers in particular, failed to grasp the basic raw economics of satellite and cable. They were misled by two apparent Thatcher-Conservative successes. Firstly, Channel Four (launched 1982) seemed to show that Mrs Thatcher's preferred combination – more competition, with high programming standards – could be achieved. But in retrospect Channel Four now looks more like BBC2-with-commercials; Channel Four did fairly little to satisfy the popular demand for more Entertainment with less Education and Information.

British policymakers were also misled by the apparently successful privatisation of the UK telephone system. The selling off of the UK telephone system (two Acts in 1981 and 1984) was very strongly influenced by the break-up of the American AT&T into eight separate companies. The Thatcher policy intention was that the UK should become the European leader in competitive and lightly regulated telephone and satellite TV. New commercial satellite TV channels in Scandinavian, and other, languages were encouraged to base themselves for both legal and up-linking purposes in the UK.[15]

Both the Channel Four and British Telecom innovations had occurred without any significant government expenditure. This encouraged the

15 Michael Palmer and Jeremy Tunstall, *Liberating Communications: policymaking in France and Britain* (Oxford: Blackwell, 1990), 219–312.

Thatcher Conservatives to think – right through the 1980s decade – that they would be able to introduce both satellite and cable services, with some kind of public-commercial formula, but without government finance.

1990 was a key year for Murdoch, for Thatcher, and for BSkyB. In 1990 Murdoch's News Corporation was on the verge of collapse; its spectacular Fox acquisition in Hollywood and its launch of the Fox TV network had left News Corp with $7 billion of bank debt. 1990 was the year in which Margaret Thatcher's lengthy premiership came to an end. 1990 was also the year in which BSkyB took shape.

Most people in Britain knew of Murdoch only as a newspaper owner. But Murdoch had been in fact focused on television, as well as press, since 1957 – when (aged twenty-six) he toured the western United States, with his wife, visiting TV stations. In 1958 he repeated the US television tour;[16] and in 1959 he launched his, and Adelaide's, first TV station. Twelve years later in 1971 Murdoch briefly acquired control of London Weekend Television (LWT) in London.[17]

Before his 1985–6 Fox Studio acquisition, and the Fox TV network launch,[18] Murdoch had become involved in American satellite-to-home television. This 1983 venture was Skyband, which closed the same year with a loss of $20 million. Murdoch recognised two weaknesses. His home dishes were too large and too expensive; secondly, Skyband lacked attractive programming.[19]

Murdoch's second satellite-to-home television enterprise was called Sky and was successful by 1989 in reaching fifteen million European cable homes, mainly in Germany, Netherlands, Belgium and Switzerland. This

16 William Shawcross, *Rupert Murdoch: ringmaster of the information circus* (London: Chatto and Windus, 1992), 91–8.

17 David Docherty, *Running The Show: 21 years of London Weekend Television* (London: Boxtree, 1990), 69–75.

18 Michael Wolff, *The Man Who Owns The News* (London: Bodley Head, 2008), 296–308.

19 Jerome Tuccille, *Rupert Murdoch*. (New York: Donald I. Fine, 1989), 103–5. Michael Leapman, *Barefaced Cheek: Rupert Murdoch* (London: Coronet, 1983), 308–10.

European Sky was acquired by Murdoch[20] from a London TV producer, Brian Haynes, who had called it 'Satellite TV'.

When Murdoch launched his third Sky effort, he targeted it at the United Kingdom. The European Sky had generated almost no revenue; the British Sky was subscription financed. Murdoch used his previous experience to launch in 1989, more than a year ahead of the officially regulated British satellite enterprise, namely British Satellite Broadcasting (BSB). The official and well funded BSB was beaten by Murdoch's cheap-but-quick Sky. Both companies had spent lavishly on Hollywood movies. But Sky won the contest because, strongly assisted by the Murdoch newspapers, it sold a lot more of its home dish antennas. Sky's cheap technology worked efficiently, whereas BSB's high tech technology worked badly. Murdoch had a much better understanding, than BSB, of the complexities of satellite-to-home, both in the USA and in Europe.

The Murdoch-Thatcher meeting at 10 Downing Street on October 29 1990 came at a key moment for both. Rupert Murdoch's News Corporation was very close indeed to financial collapse.[21] Margaret Thatcher was in her last week as British Prime Minister. Murdoch briefly informed Thatcher of the impending merger. She listened passively. Murdoch went off to save News Corporation and to merge the two satellite companies into a single BSkyB; News Corporation initially owned fifty per cent and also operated the new company.

By 1990 Murdoch had lived in the US for seventeen years, against only four years as a media owner in the UK (1969–73). He had been a US citizen since 1985. His instincts and attitudes were now primarily American, secondly Australian, and only thirdly British.

There have been at least three turbulent periods in BSkyB's history. During 1991–4 the merged BSkyB was fighting for its life;[22] but the expensive Hollywood movie contracts were renegotiated downwards. In May 1992

20 Jean K. Chalaby, *Transnational Television in Europe* (London, I.B. Tauris, 2009), 12–13, 34–7.

21 Richard Belfield, Christopher Hird and Sharon Kelly, *Murdoch: The Decline of an Empire* (London: Macdonald, 1991), 228–77.

22 Mathew Horsman, *Sky High: the inside story of BSkyB* (London: Orion 1997).

BSkyB signed its first exclusive deal to carry live Premier League Football. During 1991–4 Sky subscriptions trebled to 3.4 million households and loss turned to profit. A second turbulent period was 1999–2002. BSkyB was going digital, which required big fresh investment and produced losses in each of the four years. However, the new digital system now allowed Sky to offer hundreds rather than mere dozens of channels. Most, but not all, subsequent years produced big profits.

A further period of BSkyB turbulence commenced in 2010. The Murdoch News management made an offer to buy up the 61 per cent of shares not owned by News. But there were objections. The bigger non-Murdoch shareholders (the ten largest owned twenty-six per cent of the shares) wanted more money. Other commercial players said that News Corp dominance of both TV and press in the UK would be excessive. Then the UK phone hacking scandal erupted. Numerous *News of the World* journalists were hacking into private phone messages – criminal behaviour by News/Murdoch employees.[23] The sixty-one per cent share purchase attempt was vetoed and the Murdoch family were humiliated, while giving evidence on live (BBC) television. (More on this in Chapter Twelve).

By 2013 the Murdoch UK interests were recovering from the scandals. The (unprofitable) UK newspapers were split off, while cable and movies continued as a separate, highly profitable and highly acquisitive, Hollywood major company.

Also in 2013, John Malone's Liberty Global company acquired the entire British Cable business – in the then form of Virgin Cable. John Malone had since the 1980s been the outstanding executive in the United States cable industry.[24]

23 Tom Watson and Marti Hickman, *Dial M for Murdoch: News Corporation and the Corruption of Britain* (London: Allen Lane, 2012).

24 'John Malone, chief executive of TCI … and his small group of managers, housed in a very modest office building in an outer Denver suburb, are the most admired and feared management in cable … TCI specializes in rescue missions after cable companies get into trouble. Malone aides are despatched to inspect the ruins, and return with plans for surgery economy, efficiency and more profits for the TCI bottom line.' Jeremy Tunstall, *Communications Deregulation* (Oxford: Blackwell, 1986), 135–7.

In the 1980s TCI (Telecommunications Inc) became, under John Malone's management, the largest American cable company. John Malone understood more quickly than almost anyone else that successful delivery of cable TV required a combination of effective technology, attractive programming, big finance and aggressive marketing.

- Technology was a Malone strength – he had a Yale Electrical Engineering degree and a Johns Hopkins PhD.[25] He was good at deciding on new technologies and then purchasing in bulk. He was the first major cable leader to announce that cable would soon provide 400 or 500 channels.
- Attractive programming meant providing new channels such as CNN, ESPN, MTV, USA and Nickelodeon, all of which became available in 1979–81.[26] Malone also acquired minority shareholdings in many channels.
- Big Finance meant bank borrowing for building new cable systems and taking wires down streets. Malone's management consultancy experience at McKinsey focused him on growing capital value and carrying enough debt to avoid paying tax.
- Marketing was vital in the American suburbs and smaller cities where cable was initially most successful. Malone pioneered numerous marketing devices subsequently used by BSkyB and many others.

But British cable in the 1980s and 1990s failed to grasp most of John Malone's lessons. A key fact about British cable is that there was never much of it. From the 1980s onwards, the most active players on the UK Cable scene were American managers and companies.

After winning the UK's May 1979 Election, the Thatcher Government was interested in the then fashionable topics of cable and satellite. In just fourteen months of 1982–3 the Thatcher Government generated three

25 'The Cowboy: John Malone's Cable Kingdom, *The New Yorker* (7 February, 1994). Reprinted in Ken Auletta, *The Highwaymen: Warriors of the Information Superhighway* (New York: Random House, 1997), 25–55.

26 Tunstall, *Communications Deregulation*, 121–41.

separate reports on cable policy; these led to a Cable Act (1984) and a new Cable Authority (January 1985).[27] The policy involved encouraging the rapid growth of very high technology versions of cable and satellite. Cable and satellite would supposedly enthuse British industry, encourage new technology, and boost the economy.[28] Even at the time, the Cable Act (1984) was critiqued as shallow and naïve.

Despite some quick glances at Europe and North America, British cable policy failed really to comprehend how United States cable operated. Also ignored was the fact that Britain lacked the Belgian/Swiss/Canadian situation of a large same-language neighbour. Britain's closest same language large neighbour was the United States, and Britain was in obvious danger of following Canada into cable dependence on the USA. British cable policy and the British cable industry failed on all four of the Malone points:

- Technology. The chosen UK focus on very high technology plus the UK requirement to dig-up-streets (rather than string wires cheaply between telephone poles), lacked commercial viability.
- Attractive programming. UK policymakers had failed to grasp that multi-channel cable would require thousands of hours per week of fresh programming. The BBC and ITV might provide some old programming, but the bulk of programming would inevitably be Hollywood movies and TV series.
- Big Finance. The UK banks were willing to supply funds for pilot schemes – wiring a few streets to test demand. When the pilots were largely unsuccessful, UK bank finance dried up (although American bank finance continued).
- Marketing. Often this was poor. UK cable companies acquired a reputation for over-promising and under-performing.

But while British companies struggled and failed, a number of American companies in the 1980s were interested in acquiring UK cable franchises.

27 Discussed at greater length in concluding chapter.

28 Palmer and Tunstall. *Liberating Communications*, 262–81.

In December 1983 the US Supreme Court agreed to the break-up of AT&T, the dominant American phone company. AT&T's local Bell operating companies were split into seven 'Baby Bells' – each covering about seven states. Some of these Baby Bells quickly looked at Europe in general and at the UK in particular. Meanwhile UK telecommunications was deregulated in two distinct steps, the Acts of 1981 and 1984.

Both Baby Bells and US cable companies, from 1984 onwards, were especially focused on one aspect of the UK market. In the UK a single company could now supply both cable television and telephone service. This was a commercially attractive combination, not yet permissible under US law. By entering the UK market, an American phone company could go international; secondly it could gain experience of the cable/phone double play; thirdly it could make losses to set against its high profits in the US home market. During the entire 1985–94 decade UK cable was driven by American money. By 1994 the largest investments had been made by Telewest (TCI and US West), Nynex (another Baby Bell) and Bell Cable Media (of Canada). Of the then ten largest UK cable companies, six were US and two were Canadian. By 1994 four million UK homes were passed by cable, but only one million were subscribing.[29] The contest really consisted of US phone companies versus Murdoch's BSkyB; and Sky was winning.

During 1998–2000 BSkyB was still far ahead, but Sky was undertaking a huge digital investment which put it into loss. NTL, another American company, decided to outsmart Sky by buying up all, or most, of UK cable. By May 2001 NTL had spent $34 billion on UK cable acquisitions and fresh investment. NTL acquired the UK cable interests of twenty-seven companies.[30] But within another twelve months, NTL was close to bankruptcy; it only survived by allowing its banks to take control.[31]

Only two other companies wanted to stay outside NTL. These were Telewest and Flextech. Telewest (TCI and US West) was the larger of the

29 Peter Goodwin, 'The First Million', *Broadcast* (2 June 1995) 18–19.

30 Nuala Moran, 'Powerful position in the race to roll out broadband services' *Financial Times* (May 16 2001).

31 Carlos Grande, 'Bondholders will emerge with core NTL', *Financial Times* (April 17 2002).

two and in 2000 it bought out Flextech, which specialised in content and channels, not in wires-down-streets and households. Flextech could rely – in addition to significant US programming – on several kinds of UK channels. These were old BBC and old ITV series; Sky's own-branded channels; and Flextech also developed some channels of its own such as Challenge, Trouble and Bravo. But these latter three channels only accounted for 1.6 per cent of all viewing in UK cable and satellite homes in April 1999.[32]

The combination of Discovery/TCI/BBC/Flextech was quite complex. Discovery (part owned by TCI) established a major alliance with the BBC; Discovery now distributed much BBC programming in the US. Meanwhile Flextech (also part owned by TCI) established a joint Flextech/BBC enterprise, UKTV, which in 1999 was offering five UK channels – Gold, Arena, Horizons, Style and Play.[33]

The years around 2000 were the era of the 'Triple Play'; a single cable company, like NTL or Telewest, supplied three services – cable TV, fixed line phone, and broadband. But the American-owned NTL, now the UK's largest cable company, by late 2001 had huge debts and only about one million triple play customers. Flextech was also having difficulties with its focus on content; in 2000 Flextech merged into Telewest. By year 2005 Quadruple Play was the new multiple offer – cable TV, fixed line phone, broadband, and mobile phone. This brought cable companies more directly into competition with phone companies; in 2007 British Telecom launched a TV service, BT Vision, with big expenditure on original programming.

Meanwhile, in a 2006 three way merger, NTL acquired Telewest and Virgin. The three entities were renamed Virgin Media, because the Virgin name was thought more acceptable to younger UK adults. But the new Virgin Media had the familiar problem of competing with the much larger BSkyB. In 2010 Virgin Media gave up its attempt to market its own Virgin channels. BSkyB paid only a semi-token £160 million for Living,

32 European Networks Guide '99, *Multichannel News International* (October 1999).

33 John Birt, *The Harder Path* (London: Time Warner, 2002), 465. Jeremy Tunstall and David Machin, *The Anglo-American Media Connection* (Oxford University Press, 1999), 152–61.

Challenge, Bravo and Virgin I. In 1999 John Malone sold TCI to AT&T for $48 billion. AT&T then merged into Comcast. John Malone switched his full attention to his Liberty company and its international wing, Liberty Global. Malone began to build an international version of the old TCI. This involved merging numerous European and Latin American cable systems, as well as the one and only UK cable system, namely Virgin.

Hollywood, Silicon Valley and British commercial television

> In the end Britain lost interest in the struggle, and it is doubtful if British officials ever achieved a realistic appreciation of the situation ... For the entire thirty years [1920–50] ... British officials and businessmen clung to the fond hope that some strategy or other would create a second Hollywood on the Thames ... They discounted the burgeoning economic strength of the American industry; and they had only a glimmer of the effective strategy that was producing the American success.
>
> — IAN JARVIE, *Hollywood's Overseas Campaign* (1992)[34]

Ever since 1916, Hollywood has had extraordinary success in getting its products onto British screens. Also since 1916 successive British governments have failed adequately to comprehend the Hollywood presence in London. Since Ian Jarvie's chosen period of 1920–50, the California-to-UK pipelines have been expanded to carry television and cable, as well as Silicon Valley, products.

ITV, the leading British commercial TV enterprise, spent the eleven years of 1992–2003 painfully merging into a single company. British TV executives and political policymakers were aware of some dramatic developments in both Hollywood and Silicon Valley; but few were fully aware of the scale and speed of the current changes.

34 Ian Jarvie, *Hollywood's Overseas Campaign: the north Atlantic movie trade, 1920–1950* (Cambridge: Cambridge University Press, 1992), 247–72.

In the 1990s and the 2000s Hollywood became a cable-led industry. Cable is now first in Hollywood importance; the old television networks are second, and movies are third. The big Hollywood companies now are multi-media conglomerates. For example, Comcast is the biggest US owner of local (monopoly) cable systems, but it also owns NBC-Universal. The Murdoch family control Twenty-First Century Fox which is a major producer of television series and movies; Fox also owns the Fox TV network (and a group of local stations) as well as controlling Sky in the UK, Italy and Germany. Disney, a major TV and movie producer, owns the ABC TV network and the Disney theme parks; it also specialises in brand merchandising. These three companies, plus three other Hollywood conglomerates have annual revenues which, taken together, are more than thirty times those of Britain's ITV.

Silicon Valley (between San Francisco and San Jose) also has a few large and fast-changing companies – such as Apple, Google, Facebook and Twitter – which have had a huge impact in the UK and across Europe. Other internationally significant locations in the western US are Seattle (Amazon and Microsoft) and Denver (cable). Also relevant to the UK and Europe are satellite providers (such as DirecTV) and the big Telecoms companies.

British television policy and British television executives, in the past, largely failed to note that Hollywood and Silicon Valley shared a number of common characteristics:

- New technology, which is so central to Silicon Valley, has also been vital to Hollywood.
- Both Hollywood and Silicon Valley companies have been led by high-profile macho entrepreneurs.
- Bank finance and venture capital have been crucial to the explosive early growth of many California companies.
- Both Hollywood and Silicon Valley companies have been involved in numerous anti-trust legal cases.
- Support from Washington has often been important for Hollywood. Military funding for Lockheed, and for space/aviation micro-electronics, was vital to the birth of Silicon Valley. Military funding also created the internet.

- Both Silicon Valley and Hollywood[35] had a strong occupational community – in which work life and non-work life tended to overlap or merge.
- Both locations were dependent on huge sales of selected new products and updated models. Hollywood TV series and movie franchises paralleled Silicon Valley's annual updates of gadgets and handheld devices.

Perhaps the key similarity between Hollywood and Silicon Valley is that economies of scale take an extreme form. The focus is on funding blockbuster hits.[36] Reaching ten million customers is not enough; the target is to reach a billion customers. With the development and production tasks already completed, subsequent millions of consumers should hugely increase profitability. This means that, for both Hollywood and Silicon Valley, the 'natural' (or at least target) market is the whole world.

Some of the most successful Hollywood and Silicon Valley products find more than half of their customers outside the United States. Often the UK accounts for five or ten per cent of global revenue. In the UK, partly because of cultural proximity and language, the import tends to be especially strong. For example, in the early Facebook-and-Twitter years (since Facebook's 2004 launch), UK policymakers and TV producers could notice American social media having an impact on many things British. These included UK audience research, books, celebrity, conversation, dating, education, family, followers, friendship, games, gossip and so on.

After year 2000, several British TV producers had successes in Hollywood big entertainment TV and in reality format TV. Any British producer, with a UK-successful TV reality format to sell, has an advantage over most European or American format pitchers. The UK show is

35 Everett M. Rogers and Judith K. Larsen, *Silicon Valley Fever: growth of high technology culture* (New York: Basic Books, 1984). 'Beverly Hills: occupational community', in Jeremy Tunstall and David Walker, *Media Made in California* (New York: Oxford University Press, 1981), 29–49.

36 Anita Elberse, *Blockbuster* (London: Faber and Faber, 2014). Arthur De Vany, *Hollywood Economics: how extreme uncertainty shapes the film industry* (London: Routledge, 2004).

in English; secondly the UK producer typically has an up-and-running show and thus video material, not just a paper proposal, to show to the American commissioning executive. Numerous UK formats have been sold; but the fee is typically only a few per cent of the production cost of the new American version.

The BBC, ITV, Channel Four and some UK independent producers have since the 1980s all had some modest success in selling series to the United States. But this overall effort has always been,[37] and still is, a niche effort. Most UK series sales are into slots well away from prime time on the larger US channels; and most UK series sales have been of short runs of less than twenty episodes. The leading British exporter has been the BBC, and, as a public service broadcaster in a relentlessly commercial American market, the BBC is a niche player. Across six decades (1928–90) British actors won twenty-four per cent of all 'Best Actor' and thirty per cent of the 'Best Actress' Oscars. In nearly all of these cases, however, the British winners were performing in American produced and financed movies.[38] This tradition continued with, for example, Daniel Day Lewis as *Lincoln* (2013). The most successful 'British' movie franchises – the James Bond and Harry Potter series – involved British writers and leading actors, but Hollywood finance and distribution. Hollywood producers tend to like British drama in period costume and almost anything about the royal family.

Both Hollywood and Silicon Valley have well established marketing pipelines which run from California, via New York, to Europe and the UK. There have been some tendencies towards a merging of these two industries and two sets of export pipelines. An early example was provided by Steve Jobs, who, between his two famous spells at Apple, was instrumental in creating Pixar and merging it into Disney. Video games depended on Silicon Valley technology, but relied on Hollywood-style creativity. Netflix was an internet-based service which began as a DVD-by-mail operation,

37 Jeanette Steemers, *Selling Television: British television in the global marketplace* (London: British Film Institute, 2004), 120.

38 Emmanuel Levy, *And The Winner Is: the history and politics of the Oscar awards* (New York: Continuum, 1990), 75–85.

but subsequently moved towards the Hollywood mainstream. YouTube takes internet channel multiplication to extreme numbers, but also relies on movie-TV style creativity.

Major new high technology products originating from Silicon Valley, but also from Amazon, Samsung and others, are said to be merging TV and the internet. SmartTV sets allow consumers to view TV and internet on a single screen. Tablets allow consumers to access a big range of video product and to consume them through the day, or in bed at night. Such trends as these mean that Silicon Valley companies can diversify into (somewhat) less risky areas; and Hollywood can benefit from some of Silicon Valley's surging wealth.

From 1916 onwards, Hollywood worked with Washington, and especially with the Commerce and State Departments.[39] Hollywood (both movies and TV) has always focused on a few genres – such as action adventure and crime dramas, comedy, and children's/family entertainment. Since the early use of cheap movie serials, Hollywood has relied on series and frequent reruns.[40] Hollywood has for a century been dominated by a group of five or six major companies.[41]

For a hundred years Hollywood has cast London and the UK in the role of best supporting actor. The UK has continued to play this helpful (to Hollywood) role through five distinct historical periods.[42]

The era of Hollywood Silent Movie (1916–26), world dominance involved new (camera) technology, the star system and big foreign marketing, mainly to Europe.[43] Hollywood controlled over 80 per cent of the UK cinema market during these years.

39 Garth Jowett, *Film: The Democratic Art* (Boston: Little, Brown, 1976), 164–84.

40 Derek Cumpare, *Re-Run Nation: how repeats invented American television* (New York: Routledge, 2005).

41 Douglas Gomery, *The Hollywood Studio System* (London: British Film Institute/Macmillan, 1986).

42 Bill Baillieu and John Goodchild, *The British Film Business* (Chichester: John Wiley, 2002).

43 Benjamin B. Hampton, History *of the American Film Industry from its beginning to 1931* (New York: Dover, 1970).

The Talkie Movie era (1926–50) involved big investments in sound technology.[44] Hollywood movies continued to dominate and not least in the UK. Two British policy decisions (in 1927 and 1947) were especially inept. A 1927 Act required minimum quotas of films shown in the UK to be made in the UK; this resulted in the 'Quota Quickies' disaster. A 1947 attempt to impose heavy taxation on imports-from-Hollywood led to a total boycott and a UK government surrender.

The Television and Movie era (1950–85) saw American television migrate from New York to Hollywood, while conquering the (non-Communist) world. In 1954 the US had 32.5 million TV sets, the UK had 4.2 million and no other European country had more than one million. Hollywood continued to dominate UK movie screens, but the TV 'Gentleman's Agreement' (BBC + ITV + Trade Unions) controlled the quantity of Hollywood movies and TV series.

The Cable, Network TV and Movie era (1985–2000) allowed the average US household to advance from about ten channels in 1985 to more than one hundred in 2000.[45] A much weaker version of this growth occurred in the UK; it was dominated by one monopoly pay-TV supplier (BSkyB) and by Hollywood product.

The Hollywood and Internet era dates from about 2000. In the case of the UK, nearly all of the major innovations were delivered by American companies in general. BSkyB and Google have offered more and more American-style content and services.

Google and other American internet companies have had a huge impact on the British media and TV scene. Today the internet attracts about half of all UK advertising expenditure. Back in 1980 a sole advertising-funded channel (namely ITV) attracted 27.1 per cent of advertising spend while national and regional newspapers had 41.7 per cent.[46] But since 1980 the newspapers have lost over two-thirds of their former advertising share.

44 Tino Balio, ed., *The American Film Industry* (Madison: University of Wisconsin Press, 1976).

45 Tunstall, *Communications Deregulation*, 64–79, 121–41.

46 Jeremy Tunstall, *The Media in Britain* (London: Constable, 1983), 72–3.

Most of that old newspaper share has gone to Google and the rest of the internet. The internet companies have developed a more efficient way to market houses, cars, jobs and much else.

Television still has a quarter of all UK advertising spend but ITV is no longer a sole TV advertising channel. ITV now has to share this advertising spend with Sky, Virgin, Channels Four and Five and with UKTV. All of these latter companies have been outplayed – in terms of advertising revenue – by the internet's extraordinary surge from nothing in the 1980s to about half of all UK advertising in the 2010s.

Google, of course, does many things beyond search and advertising – such as Gmail, Google Chrome, maps, smartphones and Android. Also active in the UK is YouTube which *Time* magazine has described as needing to consume attention and to excrete cash.[47] Google has faced criticism and legal action across Europe. In the UK there has been criticism especially of Google for locating itself for (non) tax purposes in Ireland. Google has a new London HQ building and a commitment to Washington-style lobbying. Like the Murdoch family, Google hosts a grand annual party for top politicians (UK and US), UK royals and upmarket celebrities.[48]

HBO is another example of a Californian entity which has done especially well in the UK. HBO initially offered premium sport and new movies (hence 'Home Box Office') to US households willing to pay extra. While it continued to show movies, HBO – through the 2000s decade – also developed a new type of TV drama with series such as *Sex and the City*, *The Sopranos*, *The Wire*, *Boardwalk Empire* and *Game of Thrones*. These TV drama series differed from traditional 23-hours-a-year Hollywood TV fiction. The HBO dramas typically did only about ten hours per year, had much higher budgets-per-hour, and used better and higher paid writers, actors, directors and executive producers (or 'show-runners'). These were

47 Lev Grossman, 'The beast with a billion eyes', *Time* (April 2 2012), 38–43.

48 Adam Sherwin, 'The great Google gathering', *The Independent* (22 May 2012).

TV dramas for the top third or half of the US population in terms of willingness-to-pay extra for some higher quality and fewer commercials.[49]

Top-of-the-line TV dramas from HBO (and others such as Showtime) did well in the UK, especially on Channel Four – which could promote itself as offering something new and better. Channel Four used the HBO dramas to help in branding the channel. The BBC was involved in the $100 million, eleven hour, HBO/BBC co-production of *Rome* (2005–6) which delivered sex, violence and strong British acting performances in some quantity. A number of British actors played prominent roles in several other HBO series, including *The Wire*. English speaking audiences were probably a little more adept at comprehending New Jersey or Baltimore crimetalk and ghetto-speak than were audiences elsewhere in Europe. Executives at BSkyB observed the appeal of these HBO sagas to some affluent UK viewers and to most upmarket newspaper critics. BSkyB duly signed an exclusive deal for future HBO series to appear on its Sky Atlantic channel.

How American is British commercial television?

To what degree has British TV in general, and British commercial TV in particular, been Americanised or come under American ownership and control?

- Commercial TV has about seventy per cent of total UK TV audience time. USA owned companies (Sky, Virgin, Channel Five and half of

49 '*HBO at 25*', *Variety* (November 3–9 1997), 82 pages. Marc Leverette, Brian L. Ott and Cara Louise Buckley, *It's Not TV: watching HBO in the post-television era*. (New York: Routledge, 2008). Brett Martin, *Difficult Men: Behind the Scenes of a Creative Revolution* (London, Faber and Faber, 2013).

UKTV) have about forty per cent of that seventy per cent – or about twenty-eight per cent of all UK viewing.

- Made-in-USA programming across all of UK television (including the BBC) has about forty per cent of all UK audience viewing time.
- Much programming, which appears on UK channel groups, is commissioned from UK-based 'Independent Production' companies. But the majority of the larger independents are now American owned.
- If we add made-in-USA programming to programming made by UK based-but-US owned-producers, then over half of all audience time spent with UK commercial channels is being spent with American owned and controlled programming.
- The BBC uses much smaller proportions of made-in-USA programming. But the BBC does rely quite heavily on drama and other programming made by US-owned, UK-based, independent producers.
- Another important trend of recent years has been the very rapid advance of Google and other American internet companies in the UK. Any future merging of television and internet is likely to involve further Americanisation of UK media.
- Much of this is equally true of most other European countries. However, the UK is unique in the extent to which one Hollywood major – the-Fox-Murdoch interests – is in a commanding position in UK domestic television and is also in a commanding position in the UK national newspaper market.

There are a few contrary trends, such as British Telecom's now strong position in providing premium live sports programming. But overall the trend is towards more, not less, owned and operated American product on UK screens. Channel Five and Virgin Media can both be expected to grow their UK audience share.

After two chapters which have attempted to outline key elements of both BBC and UK commercial TV, attention now switches to British TV producers and to twenty one separate TV genres. Because BSkyB and Virgin depend overwhelmingly on American product, this book now focuses mainly on the channel groups of the BBC, ITV, Channels Four and Five, and UKTV.

CHAPTER 3

Executive Producers, Independent Production and Celebrity

Executive Producers are senior creative managers within British television. A typical hands-on executive producer is likely to be in charge of several million pounds per year of TV production spending. He or she is currently the immediate boss of perhaps fifty or 100 people across the peak weeks of a year. This might be a total of ten or twenty hours of TV per year on one of the bigger channels. British television has several hundred of these hands-on executive producers.

There are two main categories of hands-on executive producer. Firstly many producers work inside the BBC or ITV. But secondly many other executive producers work for Independent Production companies, which make much of the programming shown on Channels Four and Five and other smaller channels. Executive producers in independent companies also make a substantial quantity of all programming shown on the BBC and ITV channels.

This book mostly focuses on these two types of hands-on executive producer. But there is a third type of executive producer, who typically is not a hands-on producer. This senior executive producer is normally the working boss of several hands-on executive producers. In-house producers are senior people in the TV production hierarchy and very senior people within their own particular genre.

The hands-on executive producer is in charge of the broad creative approach of the particular TV series. The executive producer is the financial manager of the operation, usually supported by a production manager who keeps track of the numerous costs and payments involved in any TV series. The executive producer is also in charge of technology, including the camera system and the main editing and post-production approach.

Most importantly, the executive producer hires and manages the teams which make the production.

But if these executive producers are the hands-on managers 'and employer', why do we hear writers, directors, actors and presenters talking about 'my next series'? Everyone knows that television, like football, is a team game. A football striker or goalkeeper may talk about 'my team'; but everyone knows there are ten other players on the field, and a manager and staff just off the field. In this freelance TV system, writers, directors, actors, film editors, and many others, need employment and need to sustain their careers. Talk about 'my next series' is convenient also for the print journalist. It's easier to construct a readable narrative if you, as a journalist, can write about the character and career of a television author, or actor, or director, whose new show starts next week.

Television people usually refer to just three phases – Development, Production/Filming, and Post Production. But they are well aware of two other phases – at the beginning and the very end of the sequence – where the executive producer is largely in lone charge. These two additional and vital phases are 'Commissioning' (which includes getting the project financed) and a final fifth phrase after postproduction, but before transmission. The following five-stage summary applies especially to such genres as Drama, Comedy, Documentary, Natural History, History, Science, Lifestyle and Factual Formats. These parts refer to a new short series of perhaps six hours or twelve half hours; the entire five-stage sequence for such a series might see the executive producer involved for between ten and thirty months:

1. *Commissioning* typically lasts between three and twelve months. The executive producer is in charge of the bid to a potential commissioner. This bid presents the broad strategy, the filming approach, likely setting (Studio, outdoor location, or abroad), the intended scheduling (daytime, early evening etc) and the requested level of finance.
2. *Development* involves active preparation of scripts and/or research. Key appointments must be made, the filming locations chosen, and the post production house selected. Important in this phase are the series producer, the director and casting specialist, the designer, and

the chief camera person. But it is the executive producer who has assembled this team over a period of perhaps two to six months.

3. *Production/Filming* obviously focuses on the lead performers, or presenters, the director or directors and the series producer, who is in a day-to-day charge but is working under the executive producer.
4. *Post Production/Editing* involves a small team. Editing is crucial and a rough edit is followed, after discussions, by a more precise and detailed edit. Sound-dubbing and music are also salient. In drama a senior person is the colourist who can manipulate the overall look of the production. All executive producers monitor the post-production process and some executive producers are very active and hands-on during this phrase.
5. *After Delivery*, and *before Transmission*, important things can still be done by the executive producer. During a period of perhaps one to three months, legal points, which caused earlier difficulty, may be finally decided. Scheduling issues could involve the executive producer trying to improve on the time slot and transmission days initially allocated. Quite often the sequence of factual episodes is altered in order to put the 'strongest' episode into the opening slot. Here and more generally, the executive producer is seeking publicity – especially, for bigger budget productions, some advance promotions on the channel and some kind of paid advertising. Executive producers try to secure press interviews for the more glamorous of their creative team.

The executive producer does not usually pursue personal publicity. He or she will be judged by the production on its ratings, its press coverage, its on-line buzz and what the top channel executives have in mind. The executive producer is well aware of how much power he or she exercises over the whole production.

Writers are often salient, especially in scripted drama and comedy. All executive producers agree that, in these genres, the script is vital. Nevertheless it is very often the executive producer who made the strategic decisions such as to televise a particular novel in a particular period style. A factual series may be conceived by the executive producer as similar to some other show, but with one big difference. In factual shows the research team can be as vital as the writers in drama and comedy.

Performers are in a strong position once the series is in production. The same is true of directors – both the on location TV version of the movie director and the inside director of cameras in the electronic studio. There certainly are frequent conflicts between the assembled creative egos. But most writers, performers and directors will not want to antagonise an executive producer who is making the series for one of the few relevant big commissioners.

Each genre has its own production sequence. Soap has a production sequence which lasts about ten weeks, and Current Affairs similarly often takes perhaps three months from conception to transmission. Many series are long established and thus not requiring much fresh commissioning. Nevertheless the executive producer tends to be in an exceptionally strong strategic position in both Soap Drama and Current Affairs.

Two genres – News and Sport – involve much live output with some, often earlier-in-the-day, recording. Here again executive producers (or 'Editors' in news) are salient. However, the live talkers are crucial, because they not only talk but generate most of their own material. The 'Talk' genre itself is another live – or near live – genre in which the chief talker is crucial. But equally salient are the guests and this means that the producer (or executive producer) chooses 'guest' names and arranges interviews through their agents.

An individual executive producer may in one year control two or three short series, with combined budgets of several million pounds. Executive producers, as a category, together spend much of the TV industry's money and effectively employ most of the active work force. Executive producers now employ much less unionised, and much less secure, working teams than in the 1980s. Back in the 1980s each television employee carried a precise rank and a precise job description. The BBC had eighty-two job titles within its Film Group and ninety-one job titles for its electronic studio operations. Work areas responsible for the visual side of TV production – TV costume, graphic design, make up, scenic operations, scenic construction, TV design and TV visual effects – recognised 150 separate job titles. The make-up career ladder alone had fifteen job titles (from Head of Make Up

Design, Television, down to Trainee Make Up Assistant).[1] Most of the people on these career steps had staff, or semi-permanent, status.

Compared with the 1980s, today's work force is largely casual and freelance. There are many more women in formerly male gendered jobs,[2] such as camera operator. A much higher proportion of today's executive producers are women. Today's executive producers are virtually unanimous in saying that since the 1990s, and especially since 2008, they have to do more things with less money. Before 1990 most producers did not know the true cost of their own productions. Today's executive producers are much more numerate and financially aware. They talk and think about the cost of everything. Unlike their 1990 predecessors, they are very serious about audience research numbers. Today's executive producers routinely quote such numbers as cost-per-audience-member.

In contrast with the 1980s, today's executive producers are extremely aware of rapid technology change.[3] The BBC, in particular, provides many short courses designed to educate its producers in new technology and its costs. Most producers focused on High Definition, when it was being introduced after year 2000. Executive producers routinely organise websites, enthuse about catch-up technologies and try to acquire more finance for more multi-platforming. Most executive producers want even better cameras and lighting in order to make their output look better.

But the biggest single impact on the role of executive producers has come from the emergence of Independent Production companies – outside the big broadcasters – which produce much of today's television programming.

1 BBC and BETA, *Pay Relativities: Banding Charts, Principal Posts and Categories Throughout The Corporation* (Effective, June 1985).

2 Institute of Manpower Studies report (1989).

3 The monthly publication *Televisual* is an excellent source of information on new television production, and post-production, technology.

The hierarchy: Producers, channel controllers, commissioners

British television production is dominated by a producer hierarchy. This producer hierarchy resembles the engineers in an engineering company or the officers in an army. An executive producer can see himself, or herself, as located towards the top of a career ladder with at least twelve levels:

Channel Controller
Genre Commissioner
(In house) Senior Executive Producer
(Hands on) Executive Producer
Series Producer
Director
Line Producer
Production Manager
Producer-Director
Assistant Producer
Researcher
Runner

Within this hierarchy the hands on executive producer will be paid about twice as much as the producer or production manager, and about four times as much as the researcher.

There are two other important smaller hierarchies within TV production. One is the Director of Photography/Camera Operator hierarchy; the other is Post Production which involves job titles like Dubbing Mixer and Editor (offline and online).

Each big broadcaster (such as BBC, ITV, Channel Four) has its group of channels and its own teams of controllers and commissioners. The detailed technology and responsibilities tend to change quite frequently. But basically this is a Two Tick system. No new series or continuing series is approved and funded until it has been accepted by both a genre commissioner and a channel controller. Typically each commissioner handles everything within one or two genres – such as all of Drama or Natural History plus Science. Genre commissioners and channel controllers (and their schedulers) plan ahead many months into the future. Bigger budgets normally indicate that a production is destined for BBC1, BBC2, ITV1, or the main Channel Four. Smaller budgets are allocated for daytime programming and for lesser channels such as BBC4 or ITV2, 3 or 4, or the small UKTV channels.

From the viewpoint of an assistant producer, much power and patronage is located at the Executive Producer levels. As seen from the executive producer level, much power and patronage is located at the Channel controller and genre commissioner levels.

If we take BBC1 as an example, we can see that the Controller of BBC1 has normally come up through the producer ranks. Across two decades (1993–2013) seven separate individuals were Controller of BBC1 (with a budget today of over £1 billion). All seven have been kind enough to talk with me at some point in their fast moving careers. The first six of these individuals (who were BBC1 controller between 1993 and 2010) had an average age on appointment of forty-three years. Danny Cohen, the seventh, was aged thirty-six on appointment in 2010. All seven of these BBC1 controllers were university graduates (three out of seven from Cambridge and Oxford). This was in sharp contrast to earlier BBC1 controllers, such as Bryan Cowgill (1974–7) and Bill Cotton (1977–81) who were not graduates. Bryan Cowgill was a former newspaper journalist with a special interest in sport, and Bill Cotton came from a showbiz dynasty.[4]

Two 1990s BBC1 Controllers were Alan Yentob (1993–6) and Michael Jackson (1996–7); both came from Documentary and Arts, both had been Controller of BBC2 previously, and both went on to higher things (at the BBC and Channel Four). Alan Yentob spoke with me when he was still running BBC2, and Michael Jackson was still producing *The Late Show* which did late evening Arts on BBC2 four nights a week. Both Alan Yentob and Michael Jackson were charming and talkative; both had a distinctly artistic, mildly eccentric, personal style. These controllers of both BBC1

4 Bryan Cowgill, *Mr Action Replay* (Swadlincote: Sports Masters International, 2006).

and BBC2 in the 1990s reported to Will Wyatt, the 'Managing Director, Network Television'. Will Wyatt explained to me that he, Jackson and Yentob, worked in adjoining offices and spoke together several times a day. One of the few difficulties, said Wyatt, was a tendency for the BBC1 controller to try to seize any successful new BBC2 series. In his autobiography, Will Wyatt is positive about both Yentob and Jackson, but does criticise their lack of punctuality and Michael Jackson's odd habit of 'taking his shoes off and walking over the office furniture.' A big shock at this time was the speeding up of research findings by a new regime of 'overnights', research data on last night's programming.[5]

Peter Salmon was the next BBC1 Controller. He had spent the 1980s in several junior producer roles and was head of TV features, at BBC Bristol – in charge of a handful of factual series. He then held senior programming jobs at Channel Four and Granada/ITV, before becoming BBC1 controller (1997–2000).

Lorraine Heggessey was the first woman to be BBC1 Controller (2000–5). She had had two decades of experience on major current affairs series and was the producer of such factual series as *Q.E.D.*, *The Human Body* and *Animal Hospital*. She headed BBC children's television for two years. Lorraine Heggessey told me:

> Running BBC1, you're on call seven days a week. So, early in my skiing holiday in Canada, I'm told on the mobile phone: 'In two minutes BBC1 will be announcing the Queen Mother's death'. I went into a mountainside restaurant and rescheduled BBC1 for the next few days – on a conference call with my scheduler and the BBC head of news back in London. I was also running BBC1 when 9/11 happened. We pulled some other programming which we thought might be unfortunate at such a time.

The next BBC1 Controller was Peter Fincham (2005–7). His career has been unusual in other respects, but he was a successful executive producer (at Talkback) of numerous comedy and drama series.[6]

5 Will Wyatt, *The Fun Factory: A Life in the BBC* (London: Aurum Press, 2003), 238–40.

6 Including various *Alan Partridge* series, *They Think It's All Over*, *Never Mind The Buzzcocks*, *Smack The Pony*, *Shooting the Past*, *Bo' Selector* and *Look Around You*.

Jay Hunt was the second woman controller of BBC1 (2008–10). She had a classic fast track career in BBC news and current affairs; she was Editor (executive producer) of two key outputs – *Panorama* and the *Six O'Clock News*. In a sideways career move, Jay Hunt stepped off the prestige news ladder and went to Birmingham as 'Executive Producer, BBC Daytime'; she then became 'Controller of BBC Daytime and Early Peak' – the entire BBC1 and BBC2 network output between 9am and 7pm. After another move to Channel Five, Jay Hunt became the BBC1 Controller when aged forty-one. She told me, after she had been there one year:

> Obviously I'm familiar with the BBC1 daytime output, which is mostly stripped across five days a week. The News, Sport and Children's on BBC1 have fixed slots and largely look after themselves. For its Controller, BBC1 is mainly a Drama and Entertainment/Comedy channel. I spend most of my time with these two and with factual, although factual is not our main genre.
>
> It's vital to refresh the schedule, not least with new factual series. It's especially hard to do Comedy on BBC1. There are a few old comedy jewels which have had continued potency with the audience for many years. People are hugely nostalgic about them. They give an important flavour to the channel.
>
> I'm constantly looking at costs and cutting costs. Research is vital. At 9.45 am the Overnights are part of the rough-and-tumble of the day. I also see focus group research, and sometimes follow a focus group – looking through the one way glass. I also see the log of people who call and email in.
>
> I have a weekly meeting with my promotion team and the marketing team, as to which pieces we're going to promote on air. We promote the whole BBC portfolio, not just BBC1.
>
> I'm much more regulated and constrained than my predecessors. I have fixed commitments on news, on current affairs in peak time, on original drama, on regional – and outside the M25 – production. Quite an elaborate jigsaw. I'm very proud that BBC1 has an almost entirely British generated schedule with only a very few American imports.

In 2010 Jay Hunt made another sideways move to become Chief Creative Officer at Channel Four, in charge of C4's entire bundle of channels. Then in October 2010 the BBC announced the appointment of 36-year-old Danny Cohen as BBC1 Controller; he would be paid £260,000 a year and would have an annual BBC1 budget of £1.1 billion. By career background he was a commissioner rather than the traditional executive producer. He had held a series of appointments at Channel Four, and its E4 partner, during 2000–7. For the next three years (2007–10) he had been controller of BBC3, targeting the 16–34 age bracket. In most other respects he was within the recent BBC1 tradition. He did an Oxford English Literature degree and spent an American year with a music group which performed in bars without much success. 'We went to forty states.' His first London TV job was at Diverse Productions (small independent producer) where he became Head of Development.

Danny Cohen, before going to BBC1 talked to me about the very different task he faced as controller of the BBC's 'youth' Channel, BBC3:

> Audiences don't always know what they want, until they're shown it. BBC3 now has more serious programming than previously and an increased audience share. During the hours we're on air – from 7pm onwards – we get a bigger audience than our main competitor, ITV2.
>
> We have the very brief news, and the BBC3 website also has brief news. We take 15 hours a year from the Current Affairs commissioners and we do other Current Affairish stuff. We've done whole hours on other countries, including Afghanistan. We like to use young pop celebrities as presenters of serious factual programmes of interest to young adults.
>
> Our best audience hours are 10pm to 1am. Yes we do follow several big BBC1 series with repeats and add-on programming. We focus on *EastEnders*, *Top Gear*, and *Total Wipeout*. We do a lot of *Dr Who* – there's huge interest in its plot detail and craft – how it's made. New technology is easier for us in the BBC with its resources. We want to maintain a sense of BBC3 community with the website and Facebook. In this EPG age you're missing a trick if you don't have grabby titles. You need clarity and grabbiness of title, but must avoid offending people.
>
> Yes, *EastEnders* repeats, and the American *Family Guy* series, are our most popular, late evening, output. But our primary purpose is to commission British producers to make things in Britain for the British public. Seventy per cent of our programme time has to be BBC commissioned; unusually for a small channel, only thirty per cent of BBC3 is acquisitions and films.
>
> Part of our remit is to innovate. It's part of our service licence. One of the challenges of the job is to decide what you stop doing, so that you can do new things.

The careers of Jay Hunt and Danny Cohen encapsulate some key dilemmas and paradoxes of British TV in general and of BBC TV in particular:

- Jay Hunt was the second woman to head BBC1. When Danny Cohen left BBC1 (to head all of BBC TV programming) in 2013, he was succeeded as BBC1 controller by Charlotte Moore. By now, three of the last five BBC1 controllers had been women. But the proportion of women at the executive producer is much smaller.
- Danny Cohen, who had been such an enthusiast for BBC3 as a youth channel, subsequently played a leading role in demoting BBC3 from TV channel to an internet only service (with a much smaller budget).
- All five BBC1 controllers since year 2000 have been youngish executives with a broad range of previous experience.

There are now numerous fast moving youngish, but seniorish, executives who have worked as an Independent Producer and at either the BBC, ITV, C4, or C5 and at either Sky or one of the all-American outfits such as Discovery, Disney or National Geographic. During their sideways-and-upwards quick career moves, these youngish executives have typically been involved in several different genres. Quick career movers open up spaces for yet more additional quick career movers. One big move, such as a new CCO (Chief Creative Officer) at Channel Four, triggers a chain of other career moves. Some disappointed applicants for the job move out; other ambitious career movers arrive and their previous job role now needs to be reoccupied.

All of this is very different from the situation before 1990, when many British TV producers and executives either stayed in the BBC or ITV for their whole careers or made one career move, typically from the BBC to ITV. Today's rapid circulation of the programming elite contributes to the overall sense of impermanence, quick change, and insecurity. This also makes human connections, and relationships with key executive producers, even more salient. Junior producers follow their previous patrons in search of additional work.

Today's channel commissioners are not secretive about their programming requirements. Commissioners announce what programming they want – on websites and in trade press interviews. Commissioners also speak frequently at gatherings of independent producers, both inside London and outside. There is a widespread belief in British television that commissioners prefer to stick to producers with whom they've worked successfully in the past. Peter Fincham, while in charge of all programming on the ITV channels, told me:

> There's a TV saying that people don't commission ideas, they commission people. An executive producer of good repute and track record who comes to you with a barmy idea may well be worth commissioning. A person who comes to see you with a perfectly sensible idea – but they themselves don't know how to make decent programmes – I'd say generally avoid them ... That may sound too cliquey. But people who've made good programmes often go on and make more good programmes.

Independent producers: Going corporate and US/European owned

Until 1982 there were only two UK television operators – the BBC and ITV – and they produced almost all of their own programming. To do this, both BBC and ITV employed large numbers of people. In 1982 Channel Four became the third British broadcaster, but it did not make any of its own programming. In its first (1982–3) twelve months, Channel Four commissioned 900 hours of programming from new 'independent production' companies. All of these new producers were small and most specialised in a single genre. Almost all of these 1982 independents were owned-and-operated by British people, most of whom had been producers at the BBC or ITV.

Three decades later, UK independent producers were making not 900 hours, but 16,000 hours of new TV programming per year. In addition to this eighteen fold increase in TV hours produced, there are other important changes. In 1982–3 there were about thirty significant small independents; now there are about a dozen very much larger dominant independents. In 1982–3 the typical larger independent was owned and controlled by one executive producer who was concentrating on a single genre. Each of today's dozen large independents includes about six smaller indies which it has acquired. Today's multi-indie independent typically now spreads itself across a much wider range of genres.

Another big change since the 1980s is that today most of the UK's largest 'independent producers' are in fact owned by American or European companies. Until 2014 All3Media was still the largest independent TV producer in the UK. All3Media had itself acquired ten smaller indie companies. But in early 2014 All3Media was acquired by American interests (Discovery, John Malone and Liberty Global). After this ownership change the fifteen largest UK-based independents (combined revenue of £1.7 billion or $2.8 billion) fell into these three categories:

- Five American companies accounted for over half the combined revenue of the top-fifteen-revenue group. These five companies were firstly the Discovery, Liberty, All3Media group; William Morris Endeavor (the big Hollywood agency group); Shine (the Fox/Murdoch owned group).
- Nearly one third of the top-fifteen-revenues belonged to four European and one Japanese group – Endemol, Fremantle, Zodiak, Studio Canal and Sony.
- Only about one sixth belonged to the five largest UK-owned independents.[7]

7 Indie Survey, 2014 (*Broadcast*, 21 March 2014).

British deregulatory policy – aimed at generating a new production sector of small British enterprise and creativity – led to a very American-style deregulatory result. The Broadcasting Act of 1980, which set up Channel Four and largely created the independent production sector, is to blame – along with the subsequent Broadcasting Acts of 1990, 1996 and 2003. Once again British media policy was sentimentally patriotic, naïve, and poorly informed as to what an American concept (in this case 'Deregulation') really meant.

Despite the great strength of non-UK-owned indies, there are several significant all-UK indies. In addition, at least a further fifty lone 'genuine' independents each do at least £1 million of production per year. Most of these smaller UK indies stick to the older single-genre model. Several are 'talent indies', built upon the careers of successful comedians, cooks, or actors. But because these talent indies are so dependent on individual talents, and only do one or two genres, their revenues tend to be uncertain. Some of the small indies are run by very well known, long established, producers. An established producer may be able to use his or her industry contacts and reputation to obtain a steadyish stream of two or three million pounds of commissions per year within a particular sub-genre.

This last category of small indie producers represents a survival from the early days of indie production between 1980 and 1990. By 1990 both the BBC and ITV were buying some programming from independents. But despite this BBC-ITV-Channel 4 patronage, only about twenty-five independents had annual revenues of £3 million by 1990. At least two hundred new indies had annual revenue of under £1 million. Most of these pioneering indie producers had established a reputation within their own genre and within either the BBC or ITV. By television standards, they were not especially young; many were in their forties.

Several indie producers did say, in 1990 interviews, that they had seen independent production in terms of personal professional freedom. They had taken the redundancy money offered by their BBC or ITV employers. They then had perhaps one full year in which to establish a viable independent production business. Most, even moderately successful, independents said in 1990 that they were making little profit. It was a culture shock for a newly minted independent producer in 1990 to recognise the many issues and decisions which he or she now had to face without the daily support of auntie BBC or uncle ITV. Now the new independent producer had to focus on agent negotiations (over talent), archive film and where to buy it, small business problems of many kinds, copyright issues, camera technology and cost, contracting out of post-production, car parking for employees, debt and finance, editing personnel and plans, film crews, the greenlighting of projects, international sales, junior staff employed short term, kitchen-in-the-office provision, London office rentals, make up, music, and many others.

The new indie producer also needed to view a lot of television to keep up with the competition and the talent. In pursuit of publicity, newspaper journalists and critics needed to be talked to and lunched. But for the new independent producer the biggest task was likely to be trying to get new programmes commissioned by the BBC, ITV or Channel Four. Two successful new independents said this to me in 1990:

> Most of my time is spent writing proposals and trying to sell programmes. Making programmes can become a distraction. (Brian Lapping)

> The amount of energy required to sell a programme is excessive. (Peter Bazalgette)

Most independent producers in 1991 were confined to a single genre. Sixty-four per cent of all 1991 independents said they specialised in Documentary and/or Current Affairs; much of this 'documentary' was what later became known as 'factual' or factual entertainment.[8] The drama specialists were the financially most successful of the 1990 independent producers. They made relatively few hours, but drama hours were much the most highly priced. Independents making dramas for ITV were paid an average of £671,000 per hour in 1989–91. One such drama indie was Zenith which

8 Key Note Report, *Independent TV and Film Production* (London, 1991). Richard Paterson, ed., *Organising for Change* (London: British Film Institute, 1990). Jeremy Tunstall, *Television Producers* (London: Routledge, 1993), 157–72.

began making *Inspector Morse* in 1987. Other drama independents were Carnival, Chatsworth, September Films and Cinema Verity.[9]

Successful comedy specialist independents in 1990 were led by Humphrey Barclay (a producer-writer of numerous comedies), Talkback, Hat Trick and SelecTV. Sports specialist independents in 1990 included Sunset and Vine, Grand Slam, Cheerleader, and Transworld International (TWI); this latter company, TWI, was unusual at the time in being American owned and already being quite large. Of these twenty-four independent producers in 1990 only one – TWI – survived the next twenty years as a separate entity. The other twenty-three companies merged into much bigger companies. One problem was the age of the successful insurgents – most were in their forties in 1990 and thus in their sixties by 2010.

Prevailing business conditions made life difficult for the single genre indies. But Channel Four, the BBC, and ITV were all wary of allowing any independents to become too powerful. Channel Four around 1990 was still sticking to its early policy of spreading its commissions around literally hundreds of small independents. The BBC and ITV (like Channel Four) were also insistent that they retain the foreign rights, meaning that few early independents sold any series – or series formats – to America or Europe. Brian Lapping, who insisted on holding onto the foreign rights, then had to make numerous trips to European market events and to Boston, New York and Washington DC.

Many independents were established by two partners, both of them television producers. There was a subsequent tendency for one partner to focus on the creative side of production and one on the business side; in some cases more business-oriented producers, or even accountants, joined the indie top leadership/ownership. Some ambitious indies took on significant debt. Typically this eventually led to the indie being acquired by a bigger indie company which was spreading itself across several genres.

The 1990s were a decade of quotas, growth and factual formats for the UK's independent producers. The Broadcasting Act of 1990 required both the BBC and ITV to commission significant amounts of programming

9 'State of Independents', *Broadcast* (16 April 1993), 24–8.

from independent producers. These quotas were set at twenty-five per cent, but did not apply to news and some other programming. By the mid-1990s the independent production sector had grown significantly with the largest commissioner in 1995 being the BBC, followed by ITV, with Channel Four in third place.[10]

Factual format genres saw the biggest growth in the 1990s, and this growth was best exemplified by Peter Bazalgette and his Bazal independent production company. From 1982 Bazalgette produced a successful BBC2 series, *Food and Drink*; when the BBC needed to fulfil its independent production quota, he was allowed to make *Food and Drink* the basis of his new indie company. From 1996 onwards Peter Bazalgette generated a succession of new cooking and other factual formats. *Changing Rooms* (BBC2 and 1, 1996–2004) was the first UK do-it-yourself and housing series; *Ground Force* (BBC2 and 1, 1997–2005) was a successful gardening format. In year 2000 Peter Bazalgette launched the British version of *Big Brother* for the (then) Dutch company Endemol to which he had sold his Bazal company. The year 2000 also marked the arrival of a fresh era of international super-independents like Endemol which bought up smaller indies; *Big Brother* required a huge production team and complex, high priced, commissioning.

A perhaps even more significant indie production development in the new millennium was the UK's Broadcasting Act 2003, which enabled independent producers to hold onto the additional rights. Previous to 2003 a UK indie producer typically was required to sell the entire production rights to the commissioning broadcaster (usually BBC, ITV or C4). Now in 2003, the independent producer could retain the additional rights; this would enable an indie with a new format show to sell the format rights inside the US and other national markets. These 2003 changes altered the entire commercial prospects of UK independent production. UK indies

10 James Hogan, *Let A Thousand Flowers Bloom – Independent Producers and Democratic Representation* (London: Department of Sociology, London School of Economics. Working Paper 13. 1997). Ian Potter, *The Rise and Rise of the Independents: a television history* (London: Guerrilla Books, 2008).

became much more interested in the US market. A largely unanticipated consequence was that American companies became much more interested in acquiring, not just British formats, but the entire British production company with all of its formats, programming and personnel.

A subsequent change was what the BBC called its Window of Creative Competition (WOCC). The BBC would produce internally fifty per cent of its television output. Independents would be commissioned to make at least 25 per cent of BBC output; and the remaining 'window' of twenty-five per cent would be available for competition between BBC departments and independent producers. Across four major genres – Drama, Comedy, Entertainment and Children's – the independents provided a substantial 36 per cent of BBC programming hours in 2006. From 2010 onwards, both the BBC and ITV commissioned the great majority of their high-priced Drama and Comedy from independent producers. It was these drama and comedy specialist indies that the American and European acquisitors especially targeted. BSkyB began to commission expensive UK scripted productions – especially in comedy but also in drama. Other American players, such as Discovery, began to source more programming from UK independents. American (and British) venture capital companies became interested in acquiring UK indies.

Single-genre independents proved vulnerable to the whims of broadcaster commissioning. Larger merged groups of independents tend to be more commercially successful. Larger groups usually get better access to key commissioners. Larger groups provide group benefits such as better legal advice and financial support. Larger groups are better informed as to the workings of the freelance labour market; small independents, who have acquired a commission, are often uncertain as to suitable people for actually making the production.

Many small independent producers, who had become workaholic obsessives in their early indie years, did not relish having to continue overworking themselves on a permanent basis. Especially hard was having to employ producers, writers, researchers and others for short periods of only a few weeks or months. Many independents in their forties or fifties decided to sell out to a bigger company. The majority of surviving small independents were working mainly in factual genres; but these factual genres were now more competitive than in the 1990s.

Producer power: Defining celebrity

Several common factors have influenced British national celebrity over the last 200 years. Celebrity has always been media driven – initially by print and now by television, print, radio, online and film. Television is the leading conferrer of UK celebrity. Moreover since TV is a producer-driven medium, TV producers play a permanent role in deciding who becomes celebrated, famous or notorious.

Celebrity and fame are very time sensitive. If you are a UK royal prince, you can be a celebrity for your entire life. If you are a successful contestant on a TV talent or quiz show, you might be famous for a few weeks. Short term TV celebrity can follow some publicity in a small circulation magazine, or on a radio show, or as a pop music choice. Such celebrity is usually confined to one genre and, at most, two media outputs. In recent years online and social media have greatly increased the quantity of short term and narrow celebrity.

A second category is celebrity which lasts for several years or perhaps a decade. Here television producers play a key role, because decade-long celebrity often involves numerous television appearances – perhaps in several popular TV series. This level of celebrity, while TV dominated, also depends on radio, newspapers and the largest UK online celebrity sites, such as Mail Online. Actors and presenters from successful TV series may also achieve longer on-screen life through online replay.

Celebrity mechanisms vary significantly between countries, as do the media. In the UK London dominates both the mass media and national celebrity mechanisms. Terms such as 'Expert', 'Great and Good', 'Public Intellectuals' and 'House of Lords' encompass a very mixed bag of assorted individuals who appear on British factual television. This classification differs radically from United States attempts to define and measure, for example, 'Public Intellectuals' or 'Media Intellectuals'. In the US there is no equivalent of the BBC or Channel Four. Richard Posner has tried to quantify 'Public Intellectuals' by counting the contents of low circulation print publications.[11] Ronald Jacobs and Eleanor Townsley have tried to quantity 'Media Intellectuals' by counting appearances on very low audience television talk shows.[12]

In the UK 'Experts' are typically professionals (such as historians, scientists, economists, lawyers) who do brief interviews and are often used by producers to provide neutralising balance. In the UK some experts 'get their own TV series' about their own specialist field. Subsequently an expert, such as a historian of the eighteenth century, can be found commenting amateurishly on twenty-first-century politics; this was a phenomenon which Richard Posner disapproved of in the US.

'Great and Good' is a very British category, which often refers to unpaid committee membership; membership of one such public committee tends to be followed by others. This then leads on to television appearances, as an expert from that committee of a few years ago. Another adjacent, or overlapping, category is the *House of Lords* with its nearly 800 members; there is a huge supply of Lord and Lady expertise on almost any topic. Lords and Ladies are, for producers, easy to locate; their television readiness is easy to inspect; and – like some other experts – most Lords and Ladies are cheap.

A third celebrity category are the elite talents or TV stars, often with their own-name series. Top TV celebrity or stardom typically stretches across more than one decade and can span several genres. The BBC revealed that in the year 2008 about forty individual talents each received over £1 million for BBC TV and radio appearances. (After 2008, BBC pay levels declined).

11 Richard A. Posner, *Public Intellectuals: A Study of Decline* (Harvard University Press, 2001). Amitai Etzioni and Alyssa Bowditch, eds, *Public Intellectuals: An Endangered Species?* (Lanham, Maryland, 2006).

12 Ronald N. Jacobs and Eleanor Townsley, *The Space of Opinion: media intellectuals and the public sphere* (New York: Oxford University Press, 2011).

The agents who represent elite talent are likely to negotiate above the executive producer level – with channel controllers and top genre commissioners. Elite talent is seen as part of the reputation, or brand, of an entire channel. Sometimes two or even three channel controllers are involved – if, for instance, a top talent is being signed up to do separate series on two BBC TV channels and one BBC radio channel.

The BBC and ITV have employed most of British TV's recent top talent. Channel controllers try to employ the top one or two talents within each of the twenty-one genres. But elite talents tend to have unique television qualities; one individual may appear in contrasting genre and roles. Ant and Dec, for example, became ITV1's favourite Saturday night nice-boys-next-door hosts, while also being cruel to 'celebrities'. Clare Balding went from being a virtuoso of horse-racing commentary to outperform most, if not all, male commentators across a big sporting range. Simon Cowell exhibited a big talent for inventing, controlling, and appearing in big entertainment formats. Stephen Fry excelled as comedian, as actor, as quiz host and television polymath. Martin Clunes and Miranda Hart exemplified the comedian/comedy actor with other, wider, interests. Jonathan Ross provided edgy talk, as well as film and disk jockey expertise. These people (and other elite talents) were following the lead of David Frost, who combined comedy and satire with political interviewing of British Prime Ministers and American Presidents.[13] Yet other varied talents belonged to Clive James who fronted extreme low brow as well as extreme high brow TV series, while also writing many volumes of poetry, journalism and autobiography.

Top talents tend to operate as co-executive producers of their shows. The top talent often has his or her own small independent production company. Alongside an agent, the top talent often talks direct to the channel controller. Top talents tend to pursue their own distinctive business plan; this can mean retaining the foreign rights to the show. Simon Cowell has been uniquely successful among British talents in building a lucrative web of contracts with both TV production outfits and music companies. The

13 David Frost, *Frost/Nixon* (London: Macmillan, 2007).

top talent's personal team tends to include agent, managerial, business and legal expertise.

But top talents do not focus solely on financial success. They also like winning awards[14] and honours. The top talent typically does some public form of good works – often through his or her very own charity. Elite talent is partly defined by a long, as well as successful, career. Whereas most performer careers peak before age fifty, the elite talent career tends to march onwards into the sunlit uplands beyond age sixty. David Attenborough and David Frost, like Mick Jagger, were still famously active beyond age seventy.

Jimmy Savile was a highly idiosyncratic elite talent on BBC television. He died in 2011, and in 2012 an ITV television show revealed that Savile had been a career paedophile, who sexually molested literally hundreds of teenage, and even younger, girls over several decades. Jimmy Savile (born 1926) left school at fourteen and worked as a coal miner. He had a long struggle as a radio disk jockey, but eventually achieved television fame. He presented the very first *Top of the Pops* on 1 January 1964. The first show of this super-successful BBC series featured The Rolling Stones, the Dave Clark Five and The Hollies; there were film inserts, in this first programme, of The Beatles playing 'I want to hold your hand' and of Cliff Richard and The Shadows. A decade later, Jimmy Savile got his own-name show, *Jim'll Fix It*, which achieved huge audiences for the next two decades; in this show, Jim fixed extraordinary requests from children. Because *Jim'll Fix It* involved such bizarre children's wishes – flying in Concorde, driving a racing car, and so on – the show in fact required a lot of producer effort.[15]

Jimmy Savile projected a unique middle aged/teenager/clown persona with assorted props – cigar, Rolls Royce, lengthy dyed blonde hair, and tracksuit. Savile certainly had executive producer insight – he had managed a chain of dance halls in his youth. Jimmy Savile won many awards, was courted by politicians and knighted by the Queen. He ran many marathons

14 James F. English, *The Economy of Prestige: Prizes, awards and the circulation of cultural value* (Cambridge, MA: Harvard University Press, 2005).

15 Steve Blacknell, *The Story of Top of the Pops*. Foreword by Jimmy Savile, OBE, KCSG (London: Patrick Stephens, 1985).

in support of his own and other charities. Savile also had a very long career. He was a top TV talent for three decades (1964–94) and only retired from *Jim'll Fix It* when aged 68.

That Savile could sexually molest, and rape, a long succession of teenage girls, across several decades, tells us something about the power both of the elite individual talent and the TV producer hierarchy. Several producers, it seems, either suspected or knew what Savile was doing. But no producer, or top executive, was willing to challenge Savile in public.[16] Producers will have realised that under British legal conditions, including the libel law, teenage girls would have been reluctant or weak witnesses against this famous man and his lawyers. No producer, it seems, wanted to be held responsible for challenging the top talent of a long-running top BBC series. Few senior BBC executives have had pop music backgrounds or are familiar with big entertainment.

According to Fred Inglis, Lord Byron was one of the first people to be recognised by the British public as both famous and notorious.[17] Lords and Royals became famous beyond London and Brighton in the years around 1800, mainly due to print publications. In *Don Juan* Byron frequently refers both to daily newspaper titles and to periodical 'reviews'. The years 1838–63 saw the expanding newspaper press greatly increase the scope of fame and notoriety. In September 1838 Grace Darling (1815–42) became the heroine of a shipwreck saga off the Northumberland coast; her story in local Northumberland newspapers was picked up by *The Times* in London. Within the next fifteen months Grace Darling became the subject of books, plays, panoramas, songs, pottery figurines, paintings and sculptures. The Darling story was also used by the novelist Walter Scott and by the poets, Wordsworth and Swinburne.[18]

16 Dan Davies, *In Plain Sight: the life and lies of Jimmy Savile* (London: Quercus, 2014), 109–13, 196–200, 266–73, 310–15.

17 Fred Inglis, *A Short History of Celebrity* (Princeton, NJ: Princeton University Press, 2010), 37–73.

18 Hugh Cunningham, *Grace Darling: Victorian Heroine* (London: Hambledon Continuum, 2007).

The Times was not reluctant to carry murder stories in great detail – such as one particularly gruesome murder of 1849; Charles Dickens paid to observe the resulting execution from a nearby roof; Madame Tussaud immortalised this murder in her new waxwork enterprise.[19] The 1850s greatly boosted the boundaries of fame and notoriety. The Crimean War was photographed and war news was sent by the new electric telegraph.[20] *The Illustrated London News* pictured the news each week and helped to establish Florence Nightingale as the heroic inventor of modern nursing. The *ILN* also pictured Queen Victoria, the funeral of the Prince Consort (1861), the marriage of the Prince of Wales (1863), and the American Civil War (1861–5).[21]

The 1890s saw another much larger surge in the diffusion of fame and notoriety. The London mass press arrived with Northcliffe's *Daily Mail* (1896) and then *The Daily Express* (1900). The new popular press and the new entertainment industry were inter-dependent. Three linked professions – the theatre, journalism, literature – expanded hugely.[22] Some individuals were engaged in all three. One such was Oscar Wilde who, while writing plays, also wrote many reviews for an evening paper, the *Pall Mall Gazette*. Wilde was destroyed by the famous court case of 1895 and by the coverage of the case in the newspapers.

In the twentieth century new types of media generated new types of fame and notoriety. The new media of the twentieth century tended to be supported by big publicity in the older media, especially the printed press. Movies and movie stars were boosted by press, by personality gossip, by news stories, and by reviews and advertising. Radio and TV stars similarly were supported by print coverage; and online today draws heavily on television coverage. Since the 1850s, news agencies have massively boosted the stars of print, movies, radio, TV and, today, online.

19 Judith Flanders, *The Invention of Murder* (London: Harper, 2011).

20 Paul Kerr, *The Crimean War* (London: Boxtree, 1997).

21 Leonard De Vries, *History as Hot News the World of the early Victorians through the eyes of the Illustrated London News, 1842–1865* (London: John Murray, 1967).

22 Michael Baker, *The Rise of the Victorian Actor* (London: Croom Helm, 1978), 160–74.

Executive producers and genres

The next eight chapters focus on twenty-one UK television genres and on the role of executive producers within these genres.

Drama and Soap (Chapter Four) are the most popular genres, and (non soap) drama is the most expensive. The bigger soaps are produced by ITV and the BBC. But much Drama is made by independent production companies which tend to be American owned. Not least because of the big scale, executive producers are salient in both Drama and Soap.

News (Chapter Five) has unique status, especially at the BBC, but also at ITV, Channel Four and Sky. News is the most British of British genres, although there are some American-controlled elements. News executive producers (or 'Editors') are salient especially in the BBC output and BBC hierarchy.

Current Affairs (Chapter Six) is a very British, and very BBC, genre which is now in decline. The few executive producers are prominent and powerful within the declining genre. Here again, executive producers are prominent, not least in choosing topics, approaches and presenters. But these genres have largely retreated from commercial TV and are now mostly based at the BBC. Executive producers, even at the BBC, are facing declining audiences and declining finance.

Flourishing Public Service Genres (Chapter Eight) include Documentary, History and Travel. Documentary has shown itself to be a flexible, popular and cheapish genre. History and Travel also have cost-per-audience benefits; successful series often depend on a partnership of prominent presenter and powerful executive producer.

Comedy, Big Entertainment and Talk (Chapter Nine) are key genres across British television and especially for BBC1 and ITV which badly need very popular output. These genres generate many failures, but some hugely successful hits; this again casts the executive producer as a (or the) key player.

Factual Entertainment and Formats Prosper (Chapter Ten). These four genres – Cooking, Homes, Quiz/Game and Reality – have become more prominent in recent decades. Independent producers focus on these format genres, because a successful format can become a lucrative hit – both at home and abroad. Executive producers (and development executives) are key to inventing the format, selling it to a channel, and 'tweaking' it into long life.

TV Sports: Live, Formatted, Monetised (Chapter Eleven). Since 1990 live sport has played a key role in UK television and especially in television's finances. The work of series producers is salient, but the key sports executive role involves liaison and negotiation over contracts and finance.

British television is more than ever a hit driven business. This makes it more than ever an executive producer driven business. At the top end of each genre, the executive producer's main role is to develop and sustain series which are popular hits with favourable cost-per-audience.

At more modest levels of each genre, the executive producer is key to the development of smaller series which offer a reasonable cost-per-audience and which attract some prestige and/or some advertisers.

Increasingly British producers are expected to seek additional US or European finance.

Back around 1990 executive producers had the option of leaving the BBC or ITV, to set up a new independent production company. Many of these people subsequently sold their independent company and (after a work out phase) were rewarded with a few million pounds.

Today the latter route has largely ceased to exist. But today's ambitious executive producer has other, newer, career prospects. A successful forty-year-old producer can now work for an American (or European) owned large 'independent' or for one of the UK versions of US channels. Either of these international career pathways offer the prospect of a senior role in the London (or New York or Hollywood) office of a large American or European company.

This means that executive producers now working for the main British channels are increasingly dependent on American and European companies in two ways. There certainly is some anxiety among UK executive producers that Americanisation, or Globalisation, or Internationalisation is going too far. But many executive producers are both ambitious and insecure; few are keen to criticise potential future co-producers or employers.

CHAPTER 4

Drama and Soap: Most Popular Genres

Drama and Soap continue to attract British television's largest audiences. Soap and drama together provide about half of the 50 highest ratings for every week of the year. Data on catch-up viewing via repeats and various playback technologies show that drama and soap are again top of the ratings. But British television has often been accused of specialising in crime series, hospital dramas, nostalgic working class soap operas, and Victorian costume dramas.

'Drama' has always been preferred by BBC, ITV and Channel 4, as the most truly British genre. 'Drama' reflects the traditional close UK links between stage and television. Drama is a prestigious genre within television, because it tends to imply live theatre, good writing, talented acting, and public service broadcasting. Drama is also the most expensive genre to produce. 50 or 100, or even 200, people are involved in making one fresh hour of drama. The high audience and prestige 9pm time slot on the major channels is awarded to drama more than to any other genre. Drama is seen as deserving generous funding because it – more than any other genre – needs to confront, and to achieve better ratings than, Hollywood fiction imports. Hollywood produces fiction in a big way with the world's largest budgets for both film and TV fiction.

Non-soap UK drama typically costs between £500,000 and £1 million per hour. Only BBC1, BBC2, ITV1, C4 and Sky can afford to make much drama. These few channels collectively each year commission and transmit about 1,000 hours of fresh UK 'drama' and soap. The main channels way back in 1990, similarly produced about 1,000 hours of new drama and soap. But the big difference is that BBC1, BBC2, ITV1 and C4 now only attract just under half of all UK television viewing. The lesser UK channels mainly show drama repeats from the big channels plus imports from

Hollywood. The Sky/Virgin channels each year show thousands of hours of imported American TV fiction series and movies.

Britain's TV drama commissioners spend an average of £500,000 on a TV hour – less for a 'soap' hour and more for a 'drama' hour. This amounts to about £500 million for the 1,000 hours of new British drama and soap each year.

Hollywood has been advancing further onto the UK drama stage. Imports of American TV drama are increasing. BSkyB since 2010 has sharply increased its commissioning of new UK drama. Hollywood has bought up several leading UK independent producers of drama. UK drama often features American actors playing American characters. Moreover the financially stronger, and more prestigious, American cable channels – such as HBO, Starz, AMC and Showtime – have increasingly participated in 'co-productions' in which British talent is employed by American producers and commissioners.

A significant 2012–13 change was the British government's decision to award a significant tax break to 'high end' made-in-UK television productions with budgets of above £1 million per hour. This also applied to documentary and animation but mainly affects drama. The tax break was intended to encourage filming within the UK – rather than in cheaper foreign locations such as eastern Europe, Belgium, Ireland, Morocco and South Africa. It was supported by the London arts elite and the mass media in general. The tax break lobby was actively led by London's larger independent producers and by the London offices of several Hollywood companies.

This tax break policy of 2012–13 encouraged an existing trend towards a higher level of prestige funding above the usual UK ceiling of £1 million per hour. Some of this prestige funding involves twenty or so prestige UK drama projects funded mainly by the BBC and ITV1 each year. Other prestige projects are more likely to be 'event' or 'branding' projects of HBO, Starz or other American cable companies. These two types of prestige drama inevitably focus on topics likely to appeal to American audiences. Typically this means big authors and big themes, such as ancient Rome and Tolstoy's *War and Peace*. Or it may require portrayals of big characters such as Winston Churchill, Margaret Thatcher, Queen Elizabeth.

TV drama highs (1970s, 2000s and 2010s) and lows (1985–2000)

While there was a Golden Era of a kind in the 1970s, it is increasingly accepted that British TV drama performed better in the fifteen years after year 2000 than in the previous fifteen years (1985–2000). Better in what ways?

- The commissioning of drama, especially at the BBC and ITV has been more effective since 2000.
- Since 2000 there has been a bigger spread of TV drama – including artistically ambitious upmarket drama, quality-popular mid-market drama, and mass market popular drama.
- Since 2000 UK drama has used a wider range of filming locations – including Cardiff, Manchester, West Yorkshire, Northern Ireland and Scotland. More drama has been filmed in faraway places such as South Africa, New Zealand, the Indian sub-continent, the Caribbean and especially in the middle east/Moslem/Arab countries.
- Women have been more prominent, especially as drama commissioners, executive producers, and as lead actors.
- Since 2000 British TV has continued to do many costumed period pieces but these increasingly are about dark satanic mills rather than about elegant lords and ladies. There is more gritty or fantasy historical drama, and less comfortable history.
- TV drama producers have embraced new technologies such as high definition and have made significant use of the internet and social media.

Technology in general has played a leading role in turning UK-style dramas (of between three and ten hours) into a more established cultural product. Increasing numbers of producers, writers and consumers of fiction have come to regard the short TV series as a superior creative product to the new novel, the new movie or the audio book.

In the years around 1990 the BBC (non-soap) drama was attracting only about fifteen per cent of all UK viewing of fiction (drama/soap/movies). In most weeks during 1990–2 the only BBC produced drama in the week's top forty ratings was two half hour episodes of *EastEnders*. The BBC's lack of commitment to non-soap drama series was evident in its small total output. For example in the last quarter of 1991 ITV aired 120 hours of new British drama while BBC1 aired only 62 hours.[1]

For a number of years on either side of 1990, British, and especially, BBC, television drama was in a state of severe decline. In 1990 an extraordinary 66 per cent of all UK television viewing of drama-and-fiction was devoted to imports.[2] These imports included the traditional Hollywood movies, plus Hollywood TV series, plus two Australian five-times-a-week soap operas – *Neighbours* (since 1986) and *Home and Away* (from 1989). The BBC had only one or two non-soap dramas in each week's Top 40 Ratings during the year 1990. BBC drama ratings depended very heavily on two episodes of its own *EastEnders* and on five episodes per week of Australian *Neighbours*.

The two Australian soaps briefly exercised a remarkable dominance in the UK (BARB) television ratings. This dominance was greatest in the years 1990–1. During one typical 1990 week (ending 11 March 1990) five episodes of *Neighbours* (BBC) had a total audience of 94 million, while *Home and Away* (ITV) had a total week's audience of 65 million. Next came *Coronation Street* (ITV) with 60 million, *EastEnders* (BBC) with 36 million and *The Bill* (ITV) with 26 million. Since 1990, BBC drama has recovered, but this recovery was very slow and gradual. Today both BBC and ITV are relying for ratings on quality-popular serials and series, as well as on soaps.

Despite drama being British TV's most popular genre, the BBC from 1946 to around 1996 largely neglected popular drama. The BBC launched

1 'BBC in a home-made drama trap' (*Broadcast*, May 1 1992).

2 The 1990 ratings for both *Coronation Street* and *EastEnders* include a Saturday or Sunday repeat. The 1990 ratings for both *Neighbours* and *Home and Away* include a same day repeat.

its first soap, *EastEnders*, only in 1985 – almost 50 years after the BBC entered TV drama production (in 1936).

ITV in 1990 had plenty of UK Soap (*Coronation Street* and *Emmerdale*). ITV also made a very few prestige, or artistically ambitious, dramas. ITV by 1990 had decided to focus heavily on quality-popular drama. ITV drama such as *The Sweeney* (from 1975) pioneered the UK development of dramas filmed primarily outdoors and on the streets. ITV was moving away from the traditionally static studio recording approach.

Around 1990, the BBC and the new Channel Four were pursuing a strategy of some popular soap plus some prestige drama –with much less focus on middlebrow, middle market, popular-quality dramas. Many drama producers and performers, around 1990, were mourning the decline of the 'Single Play' or one-off drama. But, in fact, the BBC and C4 had retained the single drama approach, by now called 'Film'. In the year 1989 British TV made forty-two such 'films', which each averaged about 100 minutes. The BBC (Screen One and Two) made twenty-two such films in 1989, while Channel Four made twenty.[3] But thirty-three of these films were shown on the smaller audience channels of BBC2 and C4 where they duly achieved quite low audiences.[4] These 'films' typically had higher budgets and lower audiences than most drama. Per million audience members reached, these films cost about ten times as much as soap drama and several times as much as quality popular crime drama or comedy drama.

Meanwhile American television series were present in significant numbers at both high and low audience times. Hollywood TV series on British screens in 1989–90 included long-running popular series such as *Dallas*, *Knots Landing*, *Dynasty*, *Beverly Hills 90210*, *Star Trek*, *Quantum Leap*, *LA Law* and *Twin Peaks*.

In terms of drama finance and commissioning, ITV was much more active than the BBC. In 1989 63 per cent of all viewing of UK produced drama was of ITV drama. These ITV dramas were mostly being made by the 'networking' ITV companies – two in London, and one each in

3 John Pym, *Film on Four: a survey, 1982–1891* (London: British Film Institute, 1992).

4 William Phillips, 'Film One-offs That Prove a Turn-off' (*Broadcast*, July 27 1990).

Manchester, Leeds and Birmingham. We interviewed in 1990–1 four of the five people in charge of drama at these ITV locations – Lloyd Shirley (Thames) Nick Elliott (LWT), Ted Childs (Central) and Keith Richardson (Yorkshire). These regional executives were in charge of producing most of the UK's most popular drama of this period. For example Ted Childs in 1990–1 was executive producing *Inspector Morse*, *Boon*, *Soldier, Soldier* and *Chancer*. 1990–1 ITV drama production had already largely been farmed out to independent and freelance producers. Each ITV drama executive was commissioning drama through a small office team of about ten people.

The BBC continued to neglect drama throughout the 1990s. But when Greg Dyke became Director General in early 2000, he put more money into drama, with which to produce more middle-range drama. Both Dyke and his Director General successor, Thompson, increased BBC drama spending. Other big changes, especially since 2000–1, mean that UK television drama is in a very different situation from the catastrophic conditions which prevailed in 1990.

Both BBC and ITV now have a highly centralised commissioning system which spreads its finance and patronage across prestige drama, quality-popular drama and mass market drama. Soap drama continues its extraordinary ratings dominance. But the weekly ratings are no longer dominated by ten Australian soap episodes per week. Soap dominance is now exerted by fifteen British soap episodes per week.

In contrast to the situation in 1990, very few American movies, or drama series, get into the top hundred ratings of the week. *Dallas*, which had a commanding presence on British television across thirteen years (1978–91), has no present day equivalent. In 1990 the UK's four existing channels (BBC1 and 2, ITV and C4) all relied on a few long-running and high profile Hollywood TV drama series and on many movies. Today the presence of Hollywood drama and fiction on British screens is less obvious and less high profile. But Hollywood is still present and powerful on the UK drama scene.

Drama serials versus quality popular series

Most of the thirty-seven drama producers and executives we interviewed in 1990 already looked back nostalgically to the 1970s as the 'Golden Age of the Single Play'. But there still are each year a few one hour, and a greater number of two hour, dramas. A present day ITV 'two-hour' drama in fact runs for about 92 minutes – not greatly different from the common BBC single drama length of 75 minutes in the 1960s. Dennis Potter had fifteen singles produced in a six-year period (1965–71).[5] One of today's drama formats preserves the single drama to some extent; Jimmie McGovern has written batches of five separate one hour dramas, each of the five being linked by the same broad theme or location.

Today's most common short form drama is the 'serial' which typically runs for three, four or five hours and then terminates. These serials tend to be quite prestigious; they typically have only one writer, one director, and one producer. Serials tend to have generous budgets (at least £1 million per hour) and are able to employ top acting talent.

There have always been a very small number of high prestige and very high budget serials. Previous to 1990 ITV companies in general, and Granada in particular, did a few high profile prestige series in order to support their license-renewal ambitions. Most lavishly produced were two Granada serials – *Brideshead Revisited* (1981) and *The Jewel in the Crown* (1984).[6] These two serials were planned as unusually expensive projects and both went massively over budget. *Brideshead* was delayed by a major technicians' strike, which destroyed the filming schedule; *Jewel* involved sending a huge team of people to India for many weeks. The ratings were

5 W. Stephen Gilbert, *Fight and Kick and Bite: the life and work of Dennis Potter* (London: Sceptre, 1995), 323–64. Humphrey Carpenter, *Dennis Potter: the authorized biography* (London: Faber, 1998).

6 Lez Cooke, *British Television Drama: A History* (London: British Film Institute, 2003), 128–60. Nick Roddick, 'Brideshead Revisited', *Sight and Sound*, Winter 1981–2: 58–60.

just adequate, but weak in view of the big expense, big publicity and protective scheduling.

In more recent times the most expensive 'British' TV dramas have been UK/US 'co-productions' in which American cable channels supplied the bulk of the finance. An early example of this trend was *Rome*, an HBO-BBC production which aired on the BBC in 2005–6. *Rome* reversed the old tradition in which American public TV acquired BBC dramas for a token price.[7]

Some British serials today are still based on literary classics or are costume dramas set a century or more ago. These are addressed later in this chapter. One sub-type of period/costume drama can be called the Saga Serial – a drama format which follows individuals or families across several decades. *Our Friends in the North* (BBC2, 1996) was a pioneering Saga Serial. *The Village* set out on BBC1 in 2013 to recount, in grim detail, the family stories of one small village from 1913 onwards.

Other, partly overlapping categories of serial drama include Docudrama, Political Docudrama, Bio-pics and Political Fiction. A docudrama is defined here as based on real events, but largely or entirely presented by actors. One docudrama was based on the notorious event of five young prostitute women murdered in Ipswich; the drama, *Five Daughters* (BBC1, 2010) presented the five as ordinary young women who had strayed first into drug addiction and only then into prostitution.[8] Susan Hogg, the executive producer, told me how proud she was of the production which involved very extensive interviewing with relatives, police and witnesses, while still achieving a 'poetic' drama. Another multiple murder sequence was the subject of the impressive docudrama, *Appropriate Adult* (ITV1, 2011).

Political Docudramas have been numerous – often dealing with real events in Northern Ireland, South Africa, Iraq or Afghanistan. There has been a steady flow of at least one political Bio-Pic a year since the 1960s;

7 Basil Comely, 'Masterpiece Theatre: Oiling the wheels of UK drama' (*Broadcast*, 23 May 1986).

8 Simon Lewis, 'Five Daughters: Behind The Scenes' (*Broadcast*, 23 April 2010, 40–1).

the tenth TV bio-pic of Margaret Thatcher appeared in 2009.[9] There have been at least 40 television bio-pics of recent British Prime Ministers including Wilson, Heath, Thatcher, Major, Blair, Brown and Cameron. Other bio-pics focus on politicians with unusual views or medical conditions, or errant sex lives. Another bio-pic focus is on singers (John Lennon, Shirley Bassey), writers (Dylan Thomas, P.G. Woodhouse) and entertainers. Such people are suitable for single drama treatment, because these are public figures already known to millions of people in the TV audience.

TV serials about fictional politicians and political events usually attract the TV critics more than the TV audience. Two Westminster based serials, *The Politician's Wife* (C4, 1995) and *The Politician's Husband* (BBC2, 2013), both written by Paula Milne, had equally disappointing audience numbers. Another example, *Party Animals* (BBC2, 2007), was a high quality eight hour serial about young political staffers, working for Westminster Members of Parliament. There was some excellent acting and writing, with much emphasis on Westminster sex life. One unanticipated effect of *Party Animals* was to boost the career of Matt Smith. Eleanor Greene, the producer, told me: 'We struggled with the Danny Foster character, this nice guy – sort of geek chic – character.' From 40 auditions for this one part they eventually chose Matt Smith, who subsequently succeeded David Tennant in *Doctor Who*. But despite its quality, and despite extensive press coverage, *Party Animals* had poor audience ratings. Indeed during its BBC2 run on eight successive Wednesdays, the ratings fell quite sharply. About £4 million had been spent on the serial, but, towards the end it had only a little over one million viewers. A steep audience decline is precisely what the drama commissioners do not want. This example illustrates again why commissioners look for some high public profile element with which to hook and hold an audience.

'Series', which are typically planned to run for at least twenty episodes, and if possible for 200 episodes, are the other big category of UK TV drama. Many series are scheduled at 9pm and reach large audiences. These series typically lack huge artistic ambition; most seek to be 'quality

9 Michael White, 'The Lady's Not for Turning off', *The Guardian*, 17 February 2009.

popular' drama with a middlebrow audience of at least a few millions. These Quality Popular series account for some of the highest (non-soap) drama ratings each week.

There are three large categories of quality pop drama. Firstly the fantasy, science fiction, thriller, teenage category; secondly, crime and police drama series; and thirdly hospital and medical series. There is, perhaps, a fourth common category – family dramas (other than the established soaps). Additional common locations for quality pop drama are the closed communities of prisons, ships, the military and similar workplaces.

Crime and hospital settings attract documentary, as well as drama, producers. These drama series frequently feature a doctor or detective – who is professionally brilliant, while grappling with personal demons. These heroic doctors and detectives usually have to struggle against bureaucracy and hierarchy. Most ratings-successful crime and hospital series only produce perhaps eight or ten hours per year. But a few crime and hospital series have been awarded what some people call 'semi-soap' status.[10] Typically this involves producing over thirty hours per year. Series such as ITV's police drama *The Bill* and the BBC's *Holby City* were awarded semi-soap status; this included having permanent buildings with fixed indoor and outdoor sets, a biggish team of producers, writers and directors – plus a large team of actors. The longest running British dramas of this kind have been *The Bill* (ITV, 1984–2010) and *Casualty*. In 2010 the BBC's *Casualty* entered the Guinness Book of Records as 'the world's longest-running primetime medical drama' with over 700 episodes completed; it had averaged thirty one hour episodes per year. *Casualty* began in 1986 and was initially seen as yet another hospital series; however, it gradually expanded its annual number of episodes and came to be regarded by some BBC executives as their premier quality-popular drama. Geraint Morris, the top producer of *Casualty* in 1991, was then making fifteen one hour episodes for the sixth season of the series. He identified, for us, one key ingredient of *Casualty*'s success:

10 *Emergency – Ward 10* (ITV 1957–67) was the UK's first successful twice weekly drama. 1957 was three years before the launch of *Coronation Street*.

> It's because *Casualty*, like *The Bill*, has been so well researched … I've looked for young writers, because they are more prepared to do research. We have a nurse advisor and a doctor advisor; and I've insisted that all writers spend as much time as possible in a Bristol hospital or in one of the London hospitals we're friendly with … *Casualty* scripts are very difficult to write; some scripts go to five drafts.

'Classic and Costume' dramas are dealt with later in this chapter. One other important quality pop category is the Comedy Drama, which typically differs from situation comedy because it has a strong central narrative, a more cinematic style, and episodes which normally run for one hour. Examples of successful comedy dramas include *Doc Martin* featuring Martin Clunes as a brilliant but flawed doctor who fainted at the sight of blood. Another example was *Shameless* which featured a large family deeply committed to drugs, drink, crime, casual sex and long term unemployment. *Shameless* ran on Channel Four for a decade and closed in 2013, having done 139 one-hour episodes.

Drama commissioners

Writers, actors, directors and executive producers are key people. But the drama commissioner plays the leading role; this involves placing multi-million pound bets on new drama. British TV since 1990 has seen several successful drama commissioners – mainly at the BBC and ITV.

But the single most influential UK drama commissioner was Sydney Newman, a Canadian who revolutionised both ITV and BBC drama in the 1958–68 decade. Sydney Newman launched *Armchair Theatre* for ITV (ABC) in 1958 and became BBC Head of Drama in 1963. He wanted to combine the multi-episode American series with the best of current British live theatre. Sydney Newman developed four sub-categories of British TV drama – sub-categories which have broadly continued to the present day:

- Each *Soap* today does 200 or 300 half hours per year and airs before the 9pm threshold – meaning that soaps must be 'family', not 'adult' viewing. Soaps are the most working class of the main drama types, and have the lowest budgets per hour.
- *Series* normally air at 8pm or 9pm. These are mid-market products which typically do between six and thirteen hourly episodes each year. Many series run for two or three years, but some for many years. A very few do forty or more hours per year.
- *Serials* normally air at 9pm and tend to be more prestigious, and upmarket, than series. Serials are usually based on a book, and/or are written by a single writer. Most serials today run for between three and six hours and then terminate. Serials tend to be above average in cost, and often below average in audience numbers.
- *Singles* and *Films*. These were plentiful in the 1960s and 1970s but there are only a few TV 'films' or single episode dramas today.

Shaun Sutton succeeded Newman and was Head of the BBC Drama Group for twelve years (1969–81).[11] These Newman-Sutton years (1963–81) were the BBC's 'Golden Age' of drama – which included the main television output of Dennis Potter[12] and of Harold Pinter (Noel Prize for Literature, 2005). Pinter's work fitted TV and theatre equally well.[13] Mark Shivas was BBC Head of Drama for the 1983–93 decade. Even towards the end of this decade, Mark Shivas was still devoting most of his energy and much of his BBC finance to commissioning single TV 'dramas' or 'Films'.

Why was drama badly neglected by the BBC in the late 1980s and for most of the 1990s?[14] Neither the Governors nor the Director Generals in

11 Shaun Sutton, *The Largest Theatre in the World* (London: BBC, 1982).

12 Gilbert, *Fight and Kick and Bite: the life and work of Dennis Potter*, 323–64. Humphrey Carpenter, *Dennis Potter: the authorized biography* (London: Faber, 1998). Cooke, *British Television Drama: A History*, 128–60.

13 William Baker an John C. Ross, *Harold Pinter: a bibliographical history* (London: The British Library and New Castle, DE: Oak Knoll Press, 2005), 1–126.

14 'BBC in a home-made drama trap' (*Broadcast*, May 1 1992). David Graham, 'Extending the Dramatic Licence' (*Broadcast*, 9 April 1993). William Phillips, 'New Drama

this period were much interested in drama. Checkland (BBC DG 1987–92) and Birt (DG 1992–9) were concerned with management and finance. There was no single person in the BBC who was in charge of soap, non-soap drama and acquisitions from Australia and Hollywood.

In the late 1980s and the 1990s BBC Drama was short of finance, short of slots in the schedule and lacking in central direction. Alan Yentob, who was controller of BBC2 from 1988 and of BBC1 from 1993, was more interested in Arts programming and Documentary than in Drama. Yentob's most decisive drama move was to cancel BBC1's new soap, *Eldorado* (1992–3) which was set in, and filmed in, Spain. This was an unlikely location for a British soap, and its original commissioning reflected the weakness of BBC drama management. Will Wyatt, who was in charge of all BBC TV at this time, subsequently admitted the weakness of BBC drama and blamed the two channel controllers and Mark Shivas.[15]

Another very influential drama commissioner was Nick Elliott, the key decision-maker in ITV drama across two entire decades (1988–2007). In 1991, when Nick Elliott was only in charge of drama at LWT, he discussed with me his successful weekend ITV series, notably *London's Burning* and *Agatha Christie's Poirot*.

Senior BBC managers recognised Nick Elliott's success with quality popular series at London Weekend and invited him across to take charge of BBC drama series. He held this BBC post for one year (1994–5) but was shocked by the prevailing BBC drama management chaos. He went back to take charge of all ITV drama for twelve years. Across two decades Elliott commissioned at least twenty-five successful quality popular shows and at least a dozen prestige writer-driven drama serials – which Elliott called 'once-a-year shows'.

Georgina Born's book[16] on the BBC contains a colourful account of how BBC drama management continued on its chaotic path at least until

---

Series, 1983–1993' (*Broadcast*, 9 February 1996). William Phillips, 'BBC Drama Dives' (*Broadcast*, 15 May 1998).

15 Wyatt, *The Fun Factory: A life in the BBC*, 206–10.

16 Georgina Born, *Uncertain Vision* (London: Secker and Warburg, 2004), 302–72.

1996–7. Compared with both ITV and Channel Four, the BBC continued into the 1990s to be locked into an unchanging industrial system of television play production. Trade unions had a leading role in retaining the TV play industrial system.[17] This system continued to stick closely to the London drama pattern of a play with perhaps three sets. The TV play also often used about three built sets; then three clunky studio cameras moved back and forth between perhaps the sitting room, bedroom and pub sets. Many BBC senior executives in 1990 still preferred such static drama to the outdoor all-film style of *The Sweeney* (ITV, 1975–8), which some saw as a low status UK version of the Hollywood 'Action Adventure' TV series.

BBC drama continued during the 1990s to be at a scheduling disadvantage against ITV Drama. While ITV had its main *News at Ten*, the BBC had its main BBC1 TV news at 9.00pm. This meant that most drama on BBC1 had to be scheduled from 8.00 to 9.00pm, which was (and is) before the 'watershed' of 9pm, meaning that these BBC1 dramas must be suitable for family viewing. The other main slot for BBC1 drama was 9.30 to 10.30pm, but this suffered from the fact that all UK audience numbers on weekdays fall quite sharply after 10pm, as early risers go early-to-bed. Consequently the BBC's top dramas were placed either at 8pm or 9.30pm on BBC1 or on BBC2 at various times, including 9pm. But the scheduling impasse contributed to the common BBC assumption that most non-soap drama would attract lowish audiences at a high price-per-audience. With these constraints, it seemed logical to schedule low numbers of drama hours and to concentrate on high prestige.

All of this changed around 2001, when Greg Dyke, as the new BBC Director General, switched the main BBC1 news to 10pm, leaving the 9–10pm post-watershed hour available for drama. Dyke also put more finance into drama; and Jane Tranter arrived.

During 2000–8 Jane Tranter was the BBC's commissioner of drama and for two years of comedy as well. She played the lead role in transforming and updating BBC TV drama for the new century. She saw the need

17 Peter Seglow, *Trade Unionism in Television: A case study in the development of white collar militancy* (Farnborough,: 1978).

to connect with the internet generation and to advance into fantasy and time travel – while also re-emphasising literary classics and TV authorship across a range of drama sub-genres.

Ben Stephenson succeeded Jane Tranter as Controller of BBC Drama Commissioning, when he was aged 31. Two years later, aged 33, he told me:

> We do 450 hours of BBC drama of which 200 hours is soap and continuing drama. The BBC is a hungry animal. On top of our 450 hours, additional drama is made in Children's and Daytime. Soap is very much part of the BBC drama family. We all stand on *EastEnders'* shoulders. Soap trains a lot of actors and especially trains writers.
>
> Our task is to do some drama which wouldn't work anywhere outside the BBC. Some things are not ratings commissioned, but still do well. It's often the executive producer who's got the longest standing relationship to the project and the writer. Most exec producers today are embedded in an Indie; we work with about 50 Indies a year – thirty on screen and twenty in development. Today we get a much greater range of the very best actors – often these actors are attracted by the quality of the piece, not by the BBC money.
>
> We cherish the best writers. Single authorship remains the great defining element of UK TV drama. You want a writer to own that piece ... We work with over 400 writers a year. Most good writers prefer to do three brilliant episodes, rather than six not so good.
>
> Most of my week is spent in meetings. Much of my weekend is spent reading scripts – thirteen scripts this last weekend. I can read a full one hour script on my tube journey into work each weekday. We have a development team. I don't get involved until the script is complete. Individual development people can come to me with a script; I can say 'Yes', or 'No', or 'Yes, but'.

While the BBC decided to focus all of its new drama on BBC1 and 2 (with none on 4 and 3), Stephenson continued to commission across a big range of drama sub-genres. This included more crime-and-grime, and more literary drama (for BBC2). Historical and costume commissions for BBC1 included nostalgic realism (*Call The Midwife*), *War and Peace*, *The Three Musketeers* and *The White Queen*, which Stephenson called 'history for those not interested in history'.

ITV, after some dubious drama decisions in the early 2000s, returned to the strong drama commissioner role. Laura Mackie told me about her job as Director of Drama at ITV. She was responsible for commissioning each year nearly 500 hours of fresh drama, roughly half soap and half non-soap drama.

> What you want is to sit in a room and hear a brilliant idea, which is highly original but is going to garner you a huge audience ... Successful long form series are the Holy Grail ... But you always want new things. You must constantly renew the schedule. We cannot be governed by sentiment ... An hour of 9pm ITV drama normally costs £600,000 to £700,000 ... The audience is more promiscuous now. We have to make the shows unmissable ... Yes, writers read something in the paper; recently we had a spate of people offering us series about male nannies.

Laura Mackie told me in 2009 that she was 'slowing down' several established and popular TV series, and would soon terminate them. Three of these about-to-be-terminated series were *Heartbeat*, *The Bill* and *The Royal* – which together had been running for a combined total of 48 years. Mackie was confident that these were wise decisions and that ITV was developing plenty of good new dramas. She was proved right because ITV drama, from 2010 onwards, developed a number of commercially successful quality-popular series including *Downton Abbey* and *Broadchurch*.

Channel Four has also emphasised assertive drama commissioning in the 2000s and 2010s. Jay Hunt explained that Channel Four was using extra money (saved by withdrawing from *Big Brother*) to finance dramas such as *Southcliffe*, *The Mill*, *Babylon* and *Indian Summer*. Hunt was also proud of *Run* (C4, 2013) which began as an internet drama. Channel Four was intending to invest in two 'high-end global dramas' per year. The C4 Head of Drama, Piers Wenger, wanted projects 'that could sit comfortably on premium US cable networks'. This would involve Channel Four in competition with the BBC and Sky.[18]

18 Peter White, 'C4 takes aim at global drama' (*Broadcast*, 4 April 2014).

Drama exec producers and independent producers

The TV drama executive producer plays a prominent role in all the phases of production. Most of these executive producers are working within an independent production company. About ten or twelve indie production companies make most of the UK's output of non-soap drama.

The Kudos company has been since 1992 one of the UK's most influential drama production houses – with series such as *Spooks* (BBC1, 2002–11), *Life on Mars* (BBC1, 2006–7), *Ashes to Ashes* (BBC1, 2008–10), and *Hustle* (BBC1, 2004–12). Kudos has also produced *The Amazing Mrs Pritchard, Law and Order UK, Death in Paradise, Utopia, Hunted, Broadchurch, The Smoke* and *The Tunnel.*

The founder of Kudos was Stephen Garrett, who had been in charge of youth programming at Channel Four in the late 1980s. In a 1990 interview he emphasised to us the importance of cancelling 'old' series, and launching new ones. Two decades later Stephen Garrett told me how Channel Four had in 1997 rejected his spy series idea, but had funded extensive development work:

> In bookshops I kept being attracted to the spy books. The last Le Carré series, *Smiley's People*, had gone out in 1982. Anyhow, we did our research. We had a '100 Top Enemies' List. Half way down the list was Osama Bin Laden.
>
> In 2000 my current Kudos partner, Jane Featherstone, joined us at Kudos. I took her round to meet the then BBC drama team – Lorraine Heggessey at BBC1, Jane Tranter at drama commissioning, and Gareth Newman, the new BBC independents commissioner. Gareth said what we had was too Channel Four – we needed a higher octane, bigger action, bigger budget, show for BBC1. In early 2001 we went back to the BBC with a new script, which they green lit. We were halfway through pre-production when the New York twin towers were attacked on September 11 2001. *Spooks* launched on BBC1 on May 13 2002 – straight into the zeitgeist.
>
> We attracted very good writers and actors to *Spooks*. We went for a bigger, brasher, bolder, more cinematic look. We wanted to be brutal, to kill off characters. We deliberately promoted leading characters and then quickly had them killed. The message was that nobody is safe.

Normally the executive producer in the indie company is the only person who works on the TV serial or series from its first day to its last day. The executive producer's key initial role is to get the project funded by the relevant big commissioner. In many cases the initial funding is merely for 'development' of some, or all, of the scripts – or for a single 'pilot' episode. There are often big delays at this point – known as 'development hell'. Even when the full show has been commissioned, it takes several or many months to generate the final scripts. Only when the scripts are complete will the executive producer receive the main funding and will be able to allocate the other main tasks. A series producer is appointed and there may be other producers, or producer-directors, to prepare specific episodes. A director (or directors) works with the producers and a casting company to employ actors for perhaps 50 separate speaking parts. When the writer's work is nearly completed, the camera/lighting/sound team are employed, as are heads of costume, a production manager and so on. In the later stages, the chief editor plays a leading role, with the director and producers. Finally the executive producer needs to organise pre-transmission publicity and other significant details.

Inside the BBC, ITV and C4, a very small number of in-house drama executive producers each work with a number of hands-on executive producers. Susan Hogg, described to me her role as an in-house BBC executive producer:

> I'm responsible for about 25 to 30 hours of fresh drama per year. This means several projects in production and currently I have seven projects in development. I'm especially involved with scripts and the edit ... My job is about filling slots. It's about creating business and getting shows off ... I'm a creator-seller. You, as an exec, must have the confidence that you are going to create your own material. Which you are passionate about. We, in the BBC, can only sell to the BBC. Independents can sell to lots of buyers.

Drama (along with comedy) is a scripted genre, which means that script writing is especially salient. But the style and tradition of TV drama writing varies between different national traditions. Hollywood television grew out of movies and film-making, as Muriel Cantor reported in her classic 1971 work, *The Hollywood TV Producer*; Cantor described the transition towards the writer producer.[19] My late 1970s interviews included such Hollywood producers as Cy Chermak (*Ironside* and *Chips*), Gene Reynolds (*M.A.S.H.* and *Lou Grant*), Matthew Rapf (*Kojak*) and Leonard Katzmann (*Dallas*). Each of these men was a producer-writer whose main task was to commission and monitor the writing of about twenty three hours of television per year. Because each script went through about five versions this involved the executive producer in reading and editing over a hundred script versions each year. Gene Reynolds, for example, said that his most time-consuming task was scripts (written each year by several different writers); his second biggest task was casting non-continuing parts; and his third big task was working with his film editor.[20] In more recent times much has been said and written about the 'showrunner' – especially in the context of higher budget American cable shows. These larger budgets obviously give the executive producer more power; and some 'showrunners' like to see themselves as producer/writer/directors.[21] US cable dramas are key competitive commercial properties and aggressive commercial promotional tactics may have played a part in building super-producer images.

The British TV drama executive producer has, of course, emerged from a different tradition – not from Hollywood, but from live theatre, where the writer or author is key. In British television, nearly all drama executive producers have worked with writers since their earliest days in television. Of thirteen drama executive producers, interviewed for this study, all but one had been a script editor. The pattern has existed at least since the 1980s. Just as book publishers are deluged with the work of would-be novelists, drama producers and executive producers are deluged with many TV drama scripts. Junior script editors – often recently graduated from University or Drama School – sift through the piles of unsolicited scripts. Meanwhile more promising scripts – from known names and via an agent – are read by slightly more senior script editors. A senior script editor will work with the producer, or executive producer, on the most promising scripts. Many

19 Muriel Cantor, *The Hollywood TV Producer* (New York: Basic Books, 1971).

20 Tunstall and Walker, *Media Made in California*, 50–85.

21 Brett Martin, *Difficult Men* (London: Faber and Faber, 2013).

young script editors step onto the drama producer ladder as an assistant producer or episode producer.

Since independent production became well established around 1990, the leading companies have developed distinctive subject matter, distinctive filming styles, and distinctive ways of employing actors, writer and directors.

Two successful executive producers illustrate how different individuals can build up their own distinctive styles and subject matter.[22] Both Tony Garnett and Lynda La Plante around 1990 set up their own indie production companies. Both were already established senior producers. Garnett set up as an indie when he was aged 53, while La Plante was 49 at her indie launch. Both he and she had experience in professional acting; Garnett had been a script editor, while La Plante was a highly regarded writer of TV dramas. Tony Garnett had produced numerous TV shows directed by Ken Loach and he broadly shared Loach's famously leftish views. Lynda La Plante had her own career-long focus – namely feminism; she executive produced Helen Mirren in the *Prime Suspect* series and most of her dramas were actress-led.

La Plante produced mainly for ITV and Garnett for BBC. Both produced for Hollywood majors – but they were confined to 'pilots', mini-series and lower budget movies. Both indie producers, when back in London, fixed their attention, not on high end prestige projects, but on more mid-market quality popular TV drama. La Plante continued to focus on the superior crime series – notably *Trial and Retribution*. Garnett, in his later career, executive produced mainly crime and hospital drama for BBC1 and BBC2. Both La Plante and Garnett tended to employ and to re-employ people from their own largish group. For example Tony Garnett had three series running on BBC during 1996–2001, which together totalled 114 episodes. For a single series, *The Cops*, which did twenty-nine episodes during 2000–2, Garnett employed five writers, three directors and one producer.

Several successful drama independent producers worked on highly regarded dramas in their earlier years. Nicola Shindler (founder of the Red

22 Stephen Lacey, *Tony Garnett* (Manchester: Manchester University Press, 2007). Julia Hallam, *Lynda La Plante* (Manchester: Manchester University Press, 2005).

Production Company) worked as a script editor on *Cracker*; as an assistant producer, she worked on *Our Friends in the North* and *Hillsborough*. She was a producer on *Queer as Folk*. But Shindler, with her preference for North West of England dramas went through some lean years, before producing successful shows such as *Scott and Bailey* and *Last Tango in Halifax*.

Most drama indies depend heavily upon just one or two currently successful series. Lime Pictures has depended on *Hollyoaks* (C4), Shed has relied on *Waterloo Road* (BBC), and Carnival has relied on *Downton Abbey* (ITV). Some drama Indies seek to spread themselves beyond television: Neal Street is an indie which combines television with theatre and films.[23] Neal Street was formed by Sam Mendes (the prominent film director) and Caro Newling (a theatre producer) together with Pippa Harris, in charge of TV drama. Harris had previously held senior jobs inside BBC drama. After a lengthy lean period at Neal Street, Harris had two huge successes. She exec produced four Shakespeare plays for the BBC at the time of the London 2012 Olympics. Harris also unveiled *Call The Midwife* – babies, midwives and an East London period setting – which was a massive hit with both female and male viewers. Neal Street had also done work for such US outfits as Showtime and HBO; the latter show was *Stuart: A life backwards*, which helped to confirm a youthful Benedict Cumberbatch as a rising star.

Another reason why drama independent producers tend to be insecure is that both the BBC and ITV try to produce in-house some of their longest running drama series. A leading example of this tendency is *Doctor Who* which for twenty six year (1963–89) was a cheap BBC children's science fiction show. But in 2005 the BBC relaunched *Doctor Who* as a more expensively made 'family', early Saturday evening, show. *Doctor Who* stepped into, and helped to consolidate, the new British TV mainstream of fantasy drama.[24] Since 2005 *Doctor Who*, as a TV production,

23 Robin Parker, 'Neal Street Productions: From Stage to Screen' (*Broadcast*, 20 April 2012: 28–31). Andrew Billen, 'Pippa Harris: Crown Princess of Drama' (*Television*, April 2013: 19–21).

24 *Doctor Who* has attracted more books than has any other British TV series – at least 75 factual and fictional books, plus hundreds of articles in fanzines and academic

has faced many cliff-hanger challenges – somewhat like the good Doctor himself who jumps dangerously between plotlines and across continents and galaxies. *Doctor Who*, since 2005, has depended heavily on its current actor and actress stars, and on its chief writer/executive producers. Part of the fascination of *Doctor Who* has been the question of whether the BBC drama commissioners and executive producers can continue to keep the youthful-ancient *Doctor Who* popular with its family fan base.

Doctor Who has become part of BBC1's channel brand image. As such it receives much BBC support – including favourable scheduling (early Saturday evening), massive BBC publicity and promotion, as well as expensive casting, and a generous budget.

Independent drama production companies with their dependence on a few current successful shows inevitably experience bust as well as boom. It's not surprising then, that a currently successful phase may seem a suitable time to sell out to a bigger American or European company.

Writers, actors, directors

Soaps and semi-soaps – with their big number of hours – employ their main writers, actors and directors across the whole year. But, with that important exception, most writers, actors and directors operate in a freelance market which typically only employs them in short bursts of a few weeks or a few months. Most TV writers, actors and directors cannot find

journals. Even the academic literature on the *Doctor Who* fanzine literature is quite extensive: See: Miles Booy, *Love and Monsters: The Doctor Who experience, 1979 to the present* (London: I.B. Tauris, 2012). Russell T. Davies and Benjamin Cook, *Doctor Who: The Writer's Tale, The Final Chapter* (London: BBC Books, 2010). Kim Newman, *Dr Who* (London: British Film Institute, 2005). David Butler, ed., *Time and Relative dissertations in Space: critical perspectives on Doctor Who* (Manchester University Press, 2007). Matt Hills, *Triumph of a Time Lord* (London: I.B. Tauris, 2010).

enough work. But currently successful people can, and do, work on several projects within a single year. One consequence is that many writers, actors and directors are hugely experienced on a very wide range of projects. Another consequence is that many people have spent a long time going to auditions, writing proposals and doing work outside drama.

TV drama writing takes three main forms. Firstly a broad concept proposal (and perhaps a sample episode) are written usually by a senior producer and/or a writer. Secondly 'storylining' involves writing a detailed outline for each episode. Then, thirdly, each episode must be written in full scripted detail.

Nearly all TV drama is scripted well in advance; and British television has liked to proclaim itself as 'writer-driven'.[25] Most prestigious for the writer is to script an entire drama serial of, perhaps, five hours. But British TV only commissions modest numbers of these projects per year. One such scripting commission is comparable to, but much scarcer than, a commission to write one printed novel. So even the most ambitious and talented young writer must start elsewhere. Much the largest employers of TV drama writers are the soaps, each of which requires more than one feature film's length of writing per week. Many writers begin with writing episodes on *Coronation Street*, or another soap. The next largest entry gate to TV drama writing is work for the live London theatre – especially at the artistically inclined Royal Court or Donmar. Most middle ranking TV drama writers are writing episodes for one of the established long-running popular series. Newspaper TV critics often focus on the writer whose task is relatively easy for journalists and readers to comprehend. The newspapers pay special attention to well established drama writers whose previous writing achievements can be quoted. But most such writers – including Paul Abbott, Peter Bowker, Peter Kosminsky, Lynda La Plante, Jimmy McGovern, Paula Milne, Steven Moffat and Stephen Poliakoff – were born before 1965 and some were born before 1950. Some of these famous

25 Sean Day-Lewis, *Talk of Drama: views of the television dramatist now and then* (Luton: University of Luton Press and John Libbey, 1998).

writers may be involved in several film and TV projects; but others may be looking for fresh commissions.

Established TV writers tend to have well developed preferred ways of working. A *Doctor Who* executive producer (like Steven Moffat) can see himself as a 'showrunner' who also controls the writing. In *Doctor Who*'s twelve episodes of late 2014, Moffat was the executive producer and lead writer, but he was assisted by seven co-writers, six directors and thirteen one-episode 'co-stars'.

Some serials are partly designed around a particular writer's ability to script an established novel. Andrew Davies has scripted numerous fiction classics (Austen and Dickens) into TV serial form.[26] Jimmie McGovern has seen himself as a Liverpool-based writer. From 1982 he wrote for the then new Channel Four soap *Brookside*. John Yorke says of McGovern: 'He wrote about working class life with a rawness and intensity that stopped you mid-step.[27] McGovern scripted the much admired *Cracker* and other politically charged productions such as *Hillsborough*, *Dockers* and *Sunday*. Jimmy McGovern invented a new type of mini-series – several single dramas linked by an overall theme. *The Street* linked separate stories about people living on the same street; *Accused* linked several stories about people who had been accused.

The Director is another key player in TV drama. The precise scope of the director's task will depend upon the producer's and executive producer's status and requirements. But the director is in practice the main person in charge when most of the money is being spent; for perhaps eight or fifteen weeks the director is directing actors for five or six long days per week. He or she is usually prominent also in casting all of the actors and some other members of the drama team. Finally the director is normally the chief overseer of the editing phase. But the greater the number of hours and episodes, the more likely that two or more directors will be employed. Actors, especially, recognise and experience the power of the director. But

26 Sarah Cardwell, *Andrew Davies* (Manchester: Manchester University Press, 2005).

27 John Yorke, *Into The Woods: a five act journey into story* (London: Penguin, 2013), 190–1.

print journalists have more difficulty in discovering how significant a particular director really is. Directors seem to fare better in newspaper feature pieces than in newspaper reviews of specific drama episodes.

There have been few female drama directors in British television. This contrasts with the success of many women as drama commissioners, executive producers, writers and, of course, actors. Women who have worked, for example, as junior producer-directors, tend to choose the producer, not the director, career ladder. One observation is that the director must work closely with (and 'direct') both the drama's acting team and its technical team. If the lead male actor and the director of photography object to a female director, she will then be in a difficult position. A very few well-known female drama directors do exist. Susanna White is admired for her director work on a broad range of productions such as *Bleak House*, *Jane Eyre*, *Generation Kill*, *Parade's End* and *Our Kind of Traitor*.

The actors are the biggest single ingredient of TV drama – in terms of cost, numbers of people employed and audience impact. But the average UK television actor in fact is actively employed in TV productions for less than four months of his or her year. Nearly two-thirds of UK TV actors are aged under 45 and a similar proportion are based in London and South East England. Most TV actors also act in other media – especially on the London stage, in radio drama, in British movies, or in Hollywood. Many actors do things such as advertising and voiceovers. This propensity, of actors to work across more than one medium, complements British television's production of many short serial and series runs of between two and thirteen hours. A mature British actor may have performed in thirty or more stage, radio and movie roles as well as having played thirty or more large and small television roles. Actors who start work on a new TV series may initially be contracted for a maximum of three years (as opposed to seven years in Hollywood). Many moderately successful series run for about three years – thus generating a total of perhaps twenty episodes.

David Tennant exemplifies several aspects of British acting. Tennant attended drama school in Scotland and did small parts at his local repertory theatre in Dundee. He then combined a twin-track career of television roles plus much Shakespeare and other 'serious' stage acting. David Tennant was a major factor in the revival and success of *Doctor Who* on

BBC television. He played the lead role for about forty months. While his last *Doctor Who* episodes were still appearing on television, in late 2008, he was playing *Hamlet* in Stratford and London. Tennant played the lead in a BBC drama serial, *Single Father* (2010) and in *United*, a 2011 serial about the fatal Manchester United Munich air disaster of 1958; in 2011 Tennant also played a vampire hunter role in a Hollywood movie. In 2013 Tennant appeared in three TV serials, including *Broadchurch* which involved him, as the police detective, solving a single murder across eight hourly episodes. Also in early 2013 David Tennant appeared as Walter Scott in BBC Radio Four dramatisations of three Walter Scott novels. Tennant continued to do a lot of Scottish accented voiceovers in TV commercials.

BBC radio producers point out that many British actors are very happy to act in radio drama. Radio is neither well paid nor glamorous, but it is easy (no lines to be learnt) and quite fun to do. Radio enables 'resting actors' to keep in circulation in the profession. Even actors who are busy with stage and TV parts can find a couple of days in their schedule for a radio performance.

Most highly regarded and famous British male acting stars conform to the broad pattern of versatility, including the big Shakespeare roles, other stage drama, some film and much television. This is true of such David Tennant contemporaries as Rory Kinnear and David Simm. Sir Kenneth Branagh is another example of a famous actor who has performed in a vast array of both stage and television roles. Male actor versatility is also exemplified by the many British actors who do some Hollywood or movie acting. Versatility is further shown by British actors who sign seven year Hollywood contracts and play very American-seeming leading roles; examples have included Hugh Laurie (in *House*), Dominic West (in *The Wire*) and Damian Lewis (in *Homeland*).

Despite the lesser availability of big roles, Britain's female actors can also be remarkably versatile. Many women actors have appeared in Shakespeare or Ibsen roles as well as in crime and other popular series on television. Helen Mirren played numerous classical and costume roles both on stage and TV. Mirren starred in the television series *Prime Suspect* in which she played a female police officer battling against both murderers and policemen.

Another aspect of British actor versatility: in their senior years some well established actors choose to do less stage and more television. For the senior actor, television involves less stress and requires less energy than performing a big part night-after-night on the live stage. TV playwrights who write good older parts can anticipate the active interest of famous older actors.

Soaps: Truly British, truly popular

Ever since 1957 'Soap' has been Britain's most popular programming and much the highest rating type of drama. Three soaps (*Coronation Street*, *EastEnders*, and *Emmerdale*) still account for more millions of audience hours than all of the remaining drama on the main BBC/ITV/C4 channels. These soaps are early evening dramas – nearly always scheduled between 6.30pm and 9.00pm. There is no historic or current connection with any category of American soap drama. *Coronation Street* began in Manchester at Granada in 1960 as a once-a-week, low budget, TV drama. The American term 'soap' was only attached subsequently by print journalists. These shows are truly popular, truly British, and as near truly working class as anything on TV in the UK.

The year 2010 marked two UK soap anniversaries. The BBC's *EastEnders* had its 25th birthday and ITV's *Coronation Street* had its 50th birthday.[28] In 50 years *Coronation Street* had done over 7,000 episodes. By 2014 the *Street* had done 8,000 episodes.

Between 1990 and 2015 the total UK soap audience did not decline. The audience for each episode did indeed fall by about half. But the number of weekly episodes put out by the three major soaps doubled from seven to

28 Brian Viner, 'Fifty things you didn't know about The Street', *The Independent*, December 9 2010. William Roache, *Soul On The Street: An Autobiography* (London: Hay House, 2007). H.V. Kershaw, *The Street Where I Live* (London: Granada, 1981).

fifteen half hours per week. During 1990–2015 *Coronation Street*'s total millions of audience hours did fall; but *EastEnders* audience hours remained the same. *Emmerdale* went from two to six episodes a week and its total audience actually increased.

These soaps contain much humour, much melodrama and many episode-ending cliff-hangers. The soaps also include assertive female characters[29] and a selection of larger-than-life alpha male villains. These villains are allowed to pursue their evil ways for months, or a few years, but the Soap Gods decree that each villain's career must eventually be terminated, either by death or by a long prison sentence. Much soap time has been devoted to accidents, bigamy, crime, drugs, explosions, fires, gays, HIV/Aids, kidnapping, marital violence and rape. The first 50 years of *Coronation Street* included seven suicides, fourteen murders, thirty-nine births, 88 weddings and 114 deaths. Kieran Roberts, as executive producer, confirmed to me the importance of core family history and narrative:

> Yes, certain key families are the core of *Coronation Street* – especially the McDonald, Barlow, Webster and Platt families. These are multi-generational families with lots of complexity and decades of history on the show. Things unfold in real time. If someone gets pregnant, that pregnancy will last nine months. The viewer is able to follow how the characters' lives unfold. It's added value when you can remember a character's previous life, family and relationships. It's like belonging to a special club.

Each week about two hours of fresh drama are required both for four *EastEnders* and for five *Coronation Street* episodes; commercials make *Street* episodes several minutes shorter. These two long established soaps are produced on permanent sets; characters and storylines move between homes and down the street to the pub and shops. There are quite frequent offsite scenes mostly at locations near to *EastEnders*' home in Elstree (north London) and to *Coronation Street*'s new eight acre home in Salford/Manchester. Production at both soaps goes through similar phases, as described to me by Kieran Roberts, executive producer of *Coronation Street*.

29 Charlotte Brunsdon, *The Feminist, the Housewife, and the Soap Opera* (Oxford: Oxford University Press, 2000).

Longer term major storylines are developed by a small group of senior producers and storyliners. This group has a lengthy meeting four times a year. *Coronation Street* employs about seventeen full-time writers; they all attend a meeting every three weeks. Each meeting discusses a block of three weeks' storylines – this happens about four months before transmission.

> The writers are very passionate about *Coronation Street*. They work hard and care deeply about the show. Writers often stay with us five, ten or even twenty years.

A director normally directs one block of five shows. From picking up the scripts to completing post production of 115 finished minutes, it takes about six weeks.

> It's an immense achievement to plan, film and edit something the length of a feature film in six weeks. Our directors usually do two or three blocks of five episodes and then leave a gap.

Coronation Street (like *EastEnders*) normally 'doubles up' to use two camera teams, filming different plotlines. Because of holidays and occasional accidents or illness, both big soaps 'triple up' with three crews working simultaneously for some weeks each year. Each camera team uses three cameras for studio scenes, plus a single lightweight mobile camera.

Each big soap employs about fifty actors on contracts of various lengths (depending on storyline planning requirements). Casting of both big and small acting parts is a major activity. Soaps are attractive to many aspiring, and to some established, actors. Post production typically takes about two weeks. There is a massive editing task because today's soaps do big quantities of 'filming'. An experienced director and editor speedily reject most of the available 'film', which is not retained after the transmission of the finished edit.

The executive producer of a big soap is in charge of all of these phases for all of each week's episodes. The executive producer sees each episode at storyline stage (two or three times), at draft script stage (two or three times), during the edit, and also needs to view the finished product before it goes on air. Consequently the executive producer has between 80 and 100 separate episode versions under review at any one time and has to consider 700 or 800 episode script versions per year. Diederick Santer, when executive producer of *EastEnders*, told me:

> Storywise my head is in about eight or nine places at once. I'm thinking about the episodes, which are transmitting, about the episodes which are ready to transmit, and about the episodes that are in post-production. I'm also keeping an eye on the episodes that are shooting – and talking to the directors and cast; looking at the episodes which are due to shoot, and thinking about the episodes that are in script development.
>
> I'm thinking about episodes being commissioned, making sure that the script editors and writers know what we want from each storyline; thinking about the storylines that are being signed off. Then I'm thinking ahead to what storylines we should be doing next. Most publicity difficulties are short-term sudden fire fighting. As happened recently, a publicist comes on and says that a newspaper will be carrying a story next Sunday about one of our actors doing something naughty in a nightclub. We suspended the actor and issued a press statement before the piece was published. Then we had to rewrite the scripts to exclude his character.

In addition to an avalanche of script monitoring, the executive producer of a big soap is presiding over a £30 million budget and about 200 people, some of whom are quite insecure. Everyone knows that, while some soap characters last for two or three decades, the executive producer must continually freshen up the product, which may mean sacking people – especially actors, but also writers. Executive producers refer to a 'burn out' factor which leads to one individual typically taking the demanding role for only two or three years. Five executive producers were in charge of *EastEnders* during the 2000–10 decade, and a sixth took over in 2010.[30] Successful executive producers of big soaps are highly regarded in UK

30 John Yorke (2000–2); Louise Berridge (2002–4), Kathleen Hutchison (2004–5); Kate Harwood (2005–6); Diederick Santer (2006–10). Three of these people (Yorke, Harwood and Santer) were interviewed for the present study. Also interviewed was Kieran Roberts who was producer of *Emmerdale* and later of *Coronation Street*. In both of these latter ITV cases the 'producer' does the overall hands-on producer role which the BBC calls 'executive producer'. When interviewed in late 2010 Kieran Roberts was in charge of all ITV Manchester drama, including *Coronation Street*.

television and tend to move on to very senior positions in the BBC, ITV or independent production.

In recent years the big soap executive producers have been striving to maintain their ratings lead against newer competition such as *X Factor* and *Britain's Got Talent*. Back around 1990 the competitive position was quite different. 1982–92 was a period of considerable soap turbulence. In 1982 Channel Four launched its early evening soap, *Brookside*, which used a group of real brick houses and focused on issues currently running in the tabloid newspapers. Three years later the BBC launched *EastEnders*[31] and then ITV decided to relaunch *Emmerdale Farm* as a more competitive *Emmerdale*.

The 1991 producers were well aware that their soaps were much cheaper per hour to produce, and attracted much bigger audiences, than TV drama in general. Emily Bell calculated that the advertising revenue earned in 1991 by *Coronation Street* and *Emmerdale* was six times greater than these soaps' production costs.[32]

Each of the top producers of *EastEnders, Coronation Street* and *Emmerdale* in 1991 told us that he had spent some time as an actor. The 1991 soap producers were already only staying in the demanding job for about three years. A common pattern was a cull of actors, put into effect by the top producer after perhaps one year in the job. Much of the rest of that producer's tour of duty then involved integrating the new characters, fresh actors and new storylines. Michael Ferguson, the *EastEnders* executive producer, told us he had decided that there were too many regular actors and too many single (unmarried) parts:

> Previous producers had not had the courage. They added new cast members without also removing any. So I had to be quite ruthless.

31 David Buckingham, *Public Secrets: EastEnders and Its Audience* (London: British Film Institute 1987). Larry Jaffee, ed., *Walford State of Mind* (Weekawken, NJ: East End Company, 2010).

32 Emily Bell, 'Serial Killings on Channel Three' (*The Observer*, 5 April 1992).

All three 1991 top producers had certain attitudes in common, which may help to explain why these soaps have survived. Each of these three producers was aware of, and quoted, research data. The producers felt a little lonely in their positions of power (over actors, writers and directors). They found it helpful to discuss their problems with the top drama executive bosses.

Brookside, however, was an exception, although, in 1991, it was nine years old and was Channel Four's ratings leader. But *Brookside* eventually collapsed twelve years later (in 2003) and was closed down. Channel Four's top brass in London (both Jeremy Isaacs and Michael Grade) seem to have taken little interest in *Brookside* except as a cash cow and ratings cow. They left it to Phil Redmond, who successfully created *Brookside*, but kept it out of the mainstream of British TV. It was based in Liverpool, and heavily staffed with Liverpool people who (à la early Channel Four) had not previously worked in television. Mal Young,[33] the top 1991 producer of *Brookside*, had no experience of other TV companies or other TV programmes. He had been to both art and drama school and was 'prop man' when *Brookside* launched in 1982; this was his first job in television. He then worked his way up *Brookside* for eight years, until becoming the top producer in late 1990. Remarkably, for a successful TV series, Mal Young told us in 1991 that he had to struggle to motivate the *Brookside* team:

> Most of our people have worked on *Brookside* for eight or nine years. Motivating them is a problem for me ... In an industry which isn't normally demotivated, it's very nine to five for them; because they are Liverpool locals, some of them think of it just as a pleasant secure job. We get the continuity of staff, but the problem is just keeping them motivated and ticking over. We've never dropped out of Channel Four's top five, so ratings are no problem.

33 Mal Young had his 34th birthday in 1991. He subsequently held senior BBC drama positions, including Head of Drama and Head of Continuing Drama series.

This *Brookside* atmosphere was very different from the atmosphere prevailing at the big three ITV and BBC soaps. Success in soap drama seems to require eternal vigilance and continuing updating of all soap ingredients.

Soaps are seldom scheduled against each other. If *Coronation Street* and *EastEnders* are in exactly the same time slot, then both will get reduced audiences. Much research is available to drama producers and they know that many or most 'regular' viewers only in fact view perhaps three of the week's five episodes. But this enables such viewers to keep track of the major characters and current storylines. These big, long-running, soaps deliver dramatic narratives which are much longer and more detailed than the narratives of Tolstoy, Dickens, Trollope or Proust. Some 'regular' viewers of two, or three, soaps get to know a large number of fictional characters and to follow a huge flow of family narratives.

Back in 1990 many television people discussed the soaps as being the lightest of light entertainment. Today there is more recognition of the quality-popular strengths, and subtleties, of the soaps. For example, soap producers and writers must present gritty social reality, sexual promiscuity and violence; but, because the soaps are scheduled before 9pm, the soaps must be suitable for viewing by families and children. While their atmosphere is often aggressive and brutally confrontational, the UK soaps seldom use major obscenities, and show little violent physical detail. In terms of sex, the camera seldom gets past the bedroom door.

Are the UK soaps surviving the multiplatform era? Nobody can tell for sure, but the soaps have always been big in the press – especially in the daily tabloids and in the dedicated soap magazines. The soaps were quick to adopt High Definition (which required much redesigning and rebuilding of sets). The soaps are big on the smaller channels – *EastEnders* is repeated on BBC3. During 2007–8 the soaps (led by youth soap *Hollyoaks*) began appointing 'digital producers' and developing additional back-up internet material, aimed at such specific groups as young viewers and older super-fans.

Classics, *Bleak House* and costume drama

British television has since 2000 been producing about thirty-five hours per year of costume and historical drama. (If we include children's series, such as *Robin Hood*, the total is higher). Adult costume drama can be classic (such as Dickens), or freshly written literary drama, or saga drama (stretching over long time spans) or freshly written quality popular costume drama.

All of these types of costume drama are typically seen as prestige projects; the BBC does the most, ITV does less, and C4 does only about one per year. Most of these dramas are serials, often based on an old or new novel. A few successful costume drama serials are extended to become series, which may then run for several (but not many) years. Costume dramas are expensive to produce and often have budgets of above £1 million per hour. In recent decades a substantial slice of that finance has typically come from American and/or European broadcasters. Many costume dramas over the years have made heavy use of grand British country house locations. A large country house provides at modest cost, grand settings, large rooms, attractive gardens and plenty of space for cars, filming vehicles, catering buses, and mobile toilets.

In recent decades, classical British television has relied especially on Shakespeare, Jane Austen, Tolstoy, the Bronte sisters, Trollope and Dickens. Laura Mackie, when commissioning all ITV drama, told me that British actors love to do classical shows because there are so many good acting roles. There is prestige, including that of acting alongside big name actors. Dickens has been the favourite classical author of both actors and commissioners.[34] British television has produced, since the 1950s, an average of thirty hours of Dickens per decade. There were seven separate TV productions of *Great Expectations* between 1959 and 2011. *A Tale of Two Cities* and *David Copperfield* each had four productions, while *Oliver Twist*,

34 John Glavin, *Dickens on Screen* (Cambridge: Cambridge University Press, 2003). This volume claims to cover both television and film Dickens; but its main focus is on Hollywood productions, many of them from the silent film era.

Nicholas Nickleby and *Bleak House* each had three productions. Most of the productions were of between three and five hours.

The BBC's 2005 production of *Bleak House* was originally planned for ten hours, but was cut back to eight and a half hours, using half hour episodes. *Bleak House* was unusual in having such a powerful and decisive commissioner (Jane Tranter), and such an accomplished writer (Andrew Davies).[35] *Bleak House* also had a forceful and active executive producer in Nigel Stafford-Clark who oversaw all phases of the production and, in practice, performed the roles of both executive producer and hands-on series producer. He told me:

> As a writer, in that field of classic British novels, Andrew Davies has no peer. Nor, I think, ever will have ... He and I agreed that we would do a Dickens ... But it was Jane Tranter who chose the novel. She had been the reason why I had done so many BBC shows ... So I had a meeting with Jane to talk about *Bleak House*, and she said 'Look, we can't go on making these shows, four or six one hours on a Sunday night ... We need to find a new way to make them fresh, bold, original – and cheaper.' Jane said she'd commission it anyway, but could Andrew and I think up something new.

Nigel Stafford-Clark got *Bleak House* commissioned and ran the production through his own independent production company, Deep Indigo:

> Even when working for the BBC, I do everything – from all the contracts to the choice of special purpose filming vehicles. The choice of half-hour episodes was mine. I was leafing through my then sole copy of *Bleak House* and read, in the introduction, that it was originally published in twenty instalments. So why not twenty episodes? I chose an unusual (for drama) filming approach – of two cameras, both hand held. I watched several Latin American films which used this 'breathing camera' technique. It saves a lot of camera set-up time. Hand-held is usually associated with a lot of camera movement. We did it with little camera movement, except at the edge of the frame – literally the cameraman breathing. It helped the tension we needed and was perfect for *Bleak House*, which is all about secrets kept and secrets divulged.
>
> I also agreed to the BBC's HD request (not order). *Bleak House* was the first BBC costume drama to use High Definition, although HD might reveal too much of such things as wigs and make-up. I also decided to use a lot of Dirty Screen, where you only use half the screen.

35 Cardwell, *Andrew Davies*.

I was actively involved in story-lining each of the episodes – deciding, with Andrew Davies, the main narrative elements in each half hour.

I took the initiative in getting the leading actors, such as Charles Dance and Gillian Anderson, on board. Only after this, were the two directors, and the departmental heads of other specialist areas, chosen.

Andrew Davies had previously adapted plenty of classic novels. But he had seldom had to work so fast. Nigel Stafford-Clark told me:

The BBC already had an air date for it. Then I worked back from that date, telling Andrew that he would have to write two half hour scripts per month; initially there were to be ten hours, so he would need to keep this up for ten months. I supplied him with the storyline; he looked at it and came back with suggested changes. As soon as he finished writing the episode, I would give him the next storyline. We would give him notes on his completed episode. John Sutherland's[36] notes were often the best. The pressure on Andrew to keep writing was extraordinary.

We found we were going through the material faster than Dickens, who had a journalist's sense of what he could get away with. Dickens did some short cuts, left some holes in the plot, and sometimes contradicted what a particular character knew at a particular time. Some changes had to be made in what Dickens wrote. Generally speaking, when the final script is written, the writer's work is finished. Writers do not normally visit the set or discuss with the actors.

Only after a full year's work on *Bleak House* did I look for a director. Now you hand it over to a director, who's going to make the show. You hope the director will take over your idea and make it better. I asked a wonderful young director, Justin Chadwick, to come in and I told him the approach – HD, two cameras, dirty filming – and he just got it perfectly. Justin also brought in the director of photography. The last six half hours were directed by Susanna White who also directed *Jane Eyre* and *Generation Kill*. Coming in late, like that, is an extremely difficult task, but she made it look easy. On a big show like this, the director's work is very intense. While filming, each director only had time to glimpse the rough assemblies in the car going home and going back to work next day. We usually filmed six days a week, with planning discussions on Sunday.

With both the script and the director in place, Nigel Stafford-Smith was looking for the 'completely unsung but vital people – the departmental

36 John Sutherland, *Inside Bleak House: A Guide for the Modern Dickensian* (London: Duckworth, 2005).

managers.' These included the production designer, the make-up designer, and the set designer. In the British acting tradition, the *Bleak House* cast included plenty of actors whose careers had spread across theatre, television, and film. Nigel Stafford-Clark told me:

> As leading players, Charles Dance and Gillian Anderson made themselves available for quite an extended time. But you're also asking other prominent actors for not great money, to do, say, one week now and perhaps two weeks later, spread out over two months.
>
> About the forty or so principal parts – people who would have to carry the particular scenes they were in – there was enormous discussion with BBC executives. They always push towards the popular end; they want to attract a big audience. The director and I did the casting with our casting director. British actors like being part of an ensemble team ... Even the inevitable talented-but-difficult actors tend to become part of a virtuous ensemble circle. That helps when things go wrong. If you have a day when nothing goes wrong, you get nervous and superstitious.

Nigel Stafford-Clark said that, during filming, he always spent half the day with the filming and half the day in the production office – coping with what's happening tomorrow and what didn't happen yesterday. Post-production and editing took about as many weeks as filming:

> The director and I are looking at each day's rushes. The editor is assembling all the way through shooting. The director and I look at the first assemblies – initially edited as per script. Then you get a new idea. Andrew had written us very fast into scenes and out of scenes. It was the editor's idea to have that loud swoosh sound to underline quickly each cut between scenes. It conveyed immediacy; it was not in the original written script.

Freshly written literary dramas have often been set in the years between 1910 and 1939 and (even before the BBC's massive 2014–18 project) during 1914–18 in particular. They tend to appear on BBC2, or, less often, on BBC1. Three such serials, in 2012–13, were *Parade's End*, *Dancing on the Edge* and *Birdsong*. All were serials of three or five hours. All were written by celebrated writers – by Tom Stoppard (rewriting Ford Madox Ford), by Stephen Poliakoff and by Sebastian Faulks. All three scripts contained high culture and art history references. In each case the initial idea had come from the producers; there were then lengthy waits for commissioning and scripting. All three serials featured upper class characters played by prominent actors. All three made big demands on the Director. All three of these serials attracted American interest. Because *Parade's End* was an HBO/BBC co-production it had a budget (£12 million for 5 hours on air) well above normal BBC levels.

In *Saga Dramas* the writing is especially salient. Here the writer's task is to follow a group of characters over a very lengthy time span such as thirty or fifty years. The costumes might begin around the 1950s and alter as the characters age (in some cases being played initially by a young actor and later by an older actor). The most often quoted (and praised) example is *Our Friends in the North* (BBC2, 1996), whose nine episodes followed a group of friends over a thirty year period.[37] In *Any Human Heart* (C4, 2012) one character is portrayed across the decades by three different actors. *White Heat* (BBC2, 2012) follows a group of friends over 45 years. *The Village* (BBC1) set out to follow one village and its people from 1913 across the twentieth century.

A final costume category is the *freshly written quality popular historical drama*. These begin as serials on ITV or BBC1 and may advance into longer life as series. These serials often have a split level design with the posh people upstairs and the servants and lower orders down below. Such was the pattern established by *Upstairs Downstairs* (ITV, 1971–5) across 68 hours; it was about a grand Victorian London house and its inhabitants. This split level approach has continued into, for example, *Titanic* (ITV1, 2012) which was explained by its executive producer, Nigel Stafford-Clark, as: 'Like Dickens on a boat ... With the toffs on top, steerage on the bottom and the middle class in between.'[38]

Downton Abbey (ITV, 2010) is another upstairs, downstairs drama. This format provides for three major sets of plotlines – the upstairs posh people and their bizarre behaviour, the servants in the basement with their

37 Michael Eaton, *Our Friends In The North* (London: Palgrave Macmillan/British Film Institute, 2005).

38 Tim Dams, 'Raising ITV's Titanic' (*Televisual*, March 2012).

more respectable behaviour, and thirdly the relationships (of various kinds) between the posh level and the servant level.[39]

These quality pop historical dramas have typically been driven forward by a forceful producer and/or writer. Jon Hawkesworth, who produced *Upstairs, Downstairs* was an inventor of this drama format. Also extremely salient have been the writer/creators such as Jean Marsh and Eileen Atkins (*Upstairs, Downstairs*) and Julian Fellowes (*Downton Abbey* and *Titanic*). These dramas again deliver melodrama and fascinating detail (did they really wear/eat/talk that kind of stuff?). There are wonderful female roles for young and old, and an excellent chance of attracting some American funding.

Even before the outbreak of 2014–18 anniversary dramas, quality popular costume drama especially favoured the period around 1914–18; many contrasts were drawn between the idyllic Edwardian era and the immediately subsequent horrors of the war. There is also much emphasis on the years 1933–45. Recent TV drama has often dwelt nostalgically on eccentric-but-brilliant British efforts such as the Dambusters bouncing bomb raid and the brilliant code-breakers of Bletchley Park. More recently, nostalgia has been combined with gritty historical reality. *The Village* includes an element of upstairs-downstairs, but it is deeply, darkly, pessimistic. *Call The Midwife* offers several feel good elements – babies galore, gallant (well acted) midwives and nice nuns; but it also emphasises some of the hardships experienced by working class women in the 1950s.

So what conclusion on classic/costume/period drama? It remains one of British television's best and most prestigious outputs. But it seems to have become a luxury which British television can scarcely afford. British nostalgia increasingly depends on American cash and perceptions.

39 The servants are often presented more positively than are their employers: John Lloyd, 'Downstairs at Downton: saintly, stoic, morally superior' (*Financial Times*, November 6/7 2010).

Crime as story engine

In terms of total audience per week the most popular sub-category of drama on British television is soap; second is crime; and third is the medical/hospital category. The number of TV murders, available each week to British audiences, exceeds the national total of real murders. This is a country in which most police personnel do not carry firearms; meanwhile most real murders lack any element of mystery. So why does fictional crime in general, and murder in particular, attract such big audiences? An answer came from Kate Harwood, as production head of BBC drama series and serials, who told me:

> Crime has always been a staple of drama and literature. You can hang a million different things on a good crime story. It's a fantastic story engine. We divide it into cosy, or comfy, crime like *Morse*, or more gritty crime. John Thaw was a great screen actor who inhabited the part in *Morse*. But the trend is away from comfy crime and into more and more gritty crime.

Cosy crime played an especially strong role in the quality-popular TV crime of the late 1980s. Much of it was based on the work of two women – Agatha Christie and Ruth Rendall. Cosy crime typically happened in beautiful South of England locations (*Morse* in Oxford and *Wexford* in Hampshire). *Agatha Christie's Poirot* used Art Deco settings in London. The Channel Islands and Cornwall provided other cosy locations.

The switch towards more gritty crime occurred in at least three phases – around 1990–3, around 2001, and from 2008 onwards. 1990–3 gritty crime was exemplified by *Cracker* (ITV, 1993–6). This series was about a criminal psychologist attached to Greater Manchester Police, who was brilliant at understanding criminals and murderers; meanwhile the psychologist grappled with his own demons as well as his marital, weight, drink, smoking and gambling problems. *Cracker*'s 24 one hour episodes depended on three key people. Jimmie McGovern, fresh from being a lead writer at *Brookside*, had an Irish Roman Catholic and Liverpool working class background.

McGovern saw the working class as having been betrayed by Margaret Thatcher and other politicians; he was passionately resentful at the way in which the police had escaped responsibility for the deaths of 96 Liverpool football fans at Hillsborough. A second key player was Robbie Coltrane, a well established screen actor who delivered a spectacular performance as the troubled criminal psychologist. A third key *Cracker* player was Gub Neal, the series producer. Neal had the original idea, he chose McGovern as the lead writer, he chose the title, he cast Robbie Coltrane in the lead role and cast most of the supporting parts, he decided against a single musical theme, he chose the promotional stance and he recruited Paul Abbott and Ted Whitehead to write the one third of the scripts which were not written by Jimmie McGovern.[40]

Another wave of gritty crime occurred in the early 2000s, and against the background of events in New York, Iraq and the middle east. Crime series also followed the Kudos lead in conspiracy thrillers, of including terrorism and heightened violence. A third wave of gritty crime on UK television dated from around 2008, the outset of the banking crisis and the decline in UK household finances.

By the early 2000s both the BBC and ITV were transmitting crime series very different from those of the 1980s. One such series was *Waking The Dead* which transmitted 82 hours on BBC1 during 2002–11. This series certainly included perverse details – such as a body hung from the ceiling after death, or two dead bodies sexually conjoined. The series producer, Colin Wratten, told me:

> A dark agenda? Yes, proudly dark. Our niche in a busy market is that if it's dark and crunchy and visceral, then we're there. We try not to make it gratuitous. Something interesting comes out of that maggot-infested body or that person who's had their head nailed to the floor. Three or four bits of forensics will come out of it ...

Gritty crime on UK television since 2002, and even more since 2008–10, has had several distinctive characteristics. Gritty crime is typically located,

40 An outstanding book on this series is: Mark Dugvid, *Cracker* (London: British Film Institute/Macmillan, 2009).

not in the sunny south of England, but in the rain, fog and night of such northern locations as Manchester, Liverpool, Yorkshire, or Glasgow. If the location is London this tends to be multiracial East or South London. These gritty shows project a very distinctive sense of place, whether this be rural Yorkshire, Liverpool, urban Belfast or period Dublin.

Recent crime TV has increasingly focused on working class settings, stories and characters. There has also been some increase in black working class participation; some recent series portray working class criminal gangs as as being mixed black and white.

Ever since the 1980s television crime drama has been able to attract top male acting talent, including Kenneth Branagh, Benedict Cumberbatch, Idris Elba, Trevor Eve, Martin Freeman, Philip Glenister, David Jason, Martin Shaw, David Suchet, David Tennant, John Thaw and Stephen Tomkinson. A well-written crime series, which does perhaps eight hours a year, might require twenty weeks of filming. But that leaves room for the lead actor to engage in at least one other major project, and several minor projects, per year.

While the murder detective was traditionally a male, in recent years we have seen more lead police roles filled by detective policewomen. These include Gillian Anderson, Brenda Blethyn, Amanda Burton, Olivia Colman, Siobhan Finneran, Susanne Jones, Sarah Lancashire, Helen Mirren and Lesley Sharp. Most of the series, in which women played the big police roles, were also written and produced by women.

Not all recent UK crime dramas have been about the gritty present. Many crime series find some way of combining older with newer crime. *Inspector Morse* was followed by both a sequel (*Lewis*) and a prequel (*Endeavour*). Some series such as *Silent Witness* and *Waking The Dead* involve re-examining old cases. *New Tricks* featured old detectives brought back from retirement to help a younger female officer solve old crimes. Sherlock Holmes has been revived numerous times, not least by Benedict Cumberbatch in the modern dress *Sherlock*. Several series have been about, or have had echoes of, Jack The Ripper and the London East End murders of prostitutes a century ago.

Television drama dilemmas

Since around 2000, British TV drama has experienced a golden age. The best UK actors, playwrights, directors and producers are competing to make British TV drama. There is a broad range of drama output. The biggest category in terms of hours are the downmarket daily soaps. A middle category are the quality-popular drama series. A third category are the short drama serials – which are intended to be upmarket cultural products. The higher the brow level or target market, the greater the cost per audience member. It can be argued, that this three-way division reflects class, status and power in British society. However, the boundaries are quite fluid. Audience research suggests that many people view at least some drama from all three categories.

Meanwhile Sky with its numerous movie channels, Sky Atlantic, and other channels which carry some drama, is the only London operator which specialises in delivering mainly American fiction and drama onto British screens. (Sky does, of course, locally commission some drama in London).

However, much or most British-produced TV drama – other than the soaps – can be seen as 'Anglo-American' in one way or another. Much top-of-the-line serial drama – especially on the BBC – involves an American producer putting up some or most of the finance.

Many of those very British quality-popular drama series involve some American, or American leaning, element. Most UK quality-popular drama is now produced by American, or European, drama 'independents'. Many of these series have American actors playing leading roles. In such cases the producers have their eyes on the American market – from the earliest days of the commissioning process. In other cases the London producers do not have an American co-producer, but do give consideration to possible subsequent American interest. BBC, ITV and C4 commissioners, and London drama producers, often hope subsequently to produce a made-in-USA version of their UK drama. Certain drama projects, with themes likely to appeal to American audiences, tend to be favoured by London drama commissioners. This can mean dramas about British royalty, Israel, or international spy networks. Much filming is done in inner London, near to the British Museum and near to hotels favoured by American visitors.

For nearly one hundred years, the UK has lacked a policy for screen entertainment in general and for screen fiction-and-drama in particular. Also for nearly one hundred years Hollywood has participated in London lobbying.

On April 1 2013 new regulations came into force which gave favourable tax treatment to selected TV productions with budgets over £1 million per hour. Will this hazardous date signal yet more unintended consequences for ad hoc 'policy'? This 2013 tax break followed aggressive lobbying by 'The TV Coalition' – a London group made up of drama independent producers, Hollywood-in-London companies, regional bodies such as Creative England, and TV trade unions.

The golden age of UK television drama looks likely to continue. But much of the gold will be American.

CHAPTER 5

BBC News Dominance

News is, after Drama and Soap, the most popular genre on UK television. Every week News provides twenty or more of the 100 top ratings. News is the prime exhibit of public service broadcasting. News is unique also in its scheduling; the two most popular channels, BBC1 and ITV1, both 'strip' news across five weekdays at four times a day (breakfast, midday, early and late evening).

Since 1990 BBC News has surpassed the news efforts of its competitors; ITV has lost more than half of its news audience, whereas the BBC has lost only a quarter of its 1990 audience. With newspaper sales also in steep decline, the BBC has become the UK news leader on TV, on Radio and Online. The BBC News provides local, national UK, and world news; and BBC news has 24 hour all-news outputs.

Technology innovations such as satellite transmission, electronic news-gathering, and online news, were developed in the US and later adopted in the UK. American editorial innovations adopted by UK news operations included the newscaster or news anchor,[1] breakfast news, and 24 hour news. When adopting an American innovation, both BBC and ITV news executives tended to be wary of possible editorial and commercial implications.

1 Frank Magid, the leading American 'news consultant' gave this author an interview in May 1978 in Cedar Rapids/Marion, Iowa. Magid told me that he had done consulting work for ITV regional news operations in the UK. See also: Craig Allen, 'Sold American: US News Consultants and News Issues Abroad', in Robin Anderson and Lance Strate, eds, *Critical Studies in Media Commercialism* (Oxford: Oxford University Press, 2000), 84–100.

BBC News versus the competition

The BBC's present level of dominance in domestic electronic news dates only from the 1990s. BBC Online did not begin until 1997. In television news the BBC and ITV/ITN still competed in 1990 on roughly equal terms for both prestige and audience. Only in Radio news was the BBC always a clear leader, and in 1990 British commercial radio's news output still gave BBC radio news some competition.

In the 1980s ITV/ITN had slightly bigger audiences then did BBC TV news and ITV also competed with the BBC in the news coverage of prestige events. Today, however, as a news provider the BBC easily surpasses any newspaper and any other UK broadcaster. The BBC has over 60 per cent of all UK audience time devoted to television news. It has at least 60 per cent of the radio news audience; and BBC online is the leading UK net news provider.

The BBC employed 4,136 members of the National Union of Journalists in late 2010,[2] (before the cuts of 2011); and about 5,000 BBC employees were eligible to join the NUJ. The BBC broadcasts between 750 and 1,000 hours each week of television and radio news – or over 110 hours of news per 24 hour day. The biggest contributors to this total are the BBC's four separate 24 hour news services. These are the domestic *BBC News* and the international *BBC World* – both being 24 hour TV news services. Thirdly there is UK domestic BBC *Radio Five Live* and fourthly BBC World Service Radio in English; both the latter offer news and news talk, 24 hour radio services. These four broadcast a total of over 650 hours per week. In addition there are the 37 local and regional BBC radio stations, while BBC1 (TV) and Radio 4 together do about 100 hours of news per week. Then there are the language services of BBC World Service Radio. Finally there is BBC News Online which, of course, is available and is used around the 24 hours. Regardless of how news is defined and measured, the

2 Jeremy Dear, general secretary of the NUJ in interview with author, 11 November 2010.

BBC News today is clearly the UK leader in terms of reputation, audience share, number of journalists employed, and hours transmitted.

The arrival of competition in 1955 in the form of ITV (and the specialist ITN news company) led to three decades of duopoly or joint leadership between the BBC and ITV. In 1967 both ITV and BBC extended their main TV evening news to about 25 minutes; and in 1983 both the BBC and ITV introduced their breakfast news shows. Many individuals spent some years at ITV/ITN and some years at BBC TV news. ITV news audiences were typically about 20 per cent larger than BBC audiences. For example, in November 1985 the ITV early evening and late evening news had an average weekday combined audience of 19 million; the BBC's equivalent two evening news offerings had a combined audience of 15.5 million.

It was not until around 1990 that BBC TV news moved decisively ahead of ITV/ITN. In retrospect the years 1987–92 are widely known as the years of the 'Birt Revolution'. John Birt was Director General of the BBC for seven years; but it was Birt's time as Deputy Director General (May 1987 to December 1992) which was crucial for BBC News and current affairs.

Satellites hugely expanded the possibilities for foreign reporting from the late 1970s onwards. Visnews (the partly BBC owned TV news agency) began daily satellite news feeds to Australia[3] in 1976 and by 1980 London TV news had access to same day satellite stories from around the world. 'Electronic News Gathering' (ENG) was also well established for domestic newsgathering by the mid-1980s. ENG used microwave, satellite, and videotape technologies to speed location reporting onto the evening news. The years 1987–92 also saw the increasing success of Channel Four (launched 1982) as a third force in UK television journalism. In 1989 Sky launched its Sky News channel.

The 1980s decade had been an awkward one for BBC news; there were clashes with the Thatcher government over coverage of the Falklands war and over the Northern Ireland 'troubles'. The Governors' 1987 appointment of John Birt as Deputy Director General specifically gave him the task of

3 Jeremy Tunstall, *The Media Are American*, 48–49.

reforming BBC news.[4] Birt was awarded a rapidly increasing news budget. He was primarily a TV manager and scheduler of entertainment. He was genuinely startled (as an engineering graduate from Oxford) by the lack of basic numeracy in the BBC and in BBC news in particular.

John Birt in 1987–8 quickly decided to sack several of the top BBC news executives. Birt replaced some of these people by promotions from within the BBC. Some, like Tony Hall[5] and Samir Shah (from London Weekend), were astonished at how high up the new system they were promoted. John Birt's shy, but flamboyant and assertive, personality attracted much attention, as did his inability convincingly to explain his 'Mission to Explain' the news.

The thirty-four BBC and ITN news producers and news executives interviewed by this author in 1990–1 split into three roughly equal-sized groups.[6] Some were against, and some were for, Birt. A third category were more neutral; yes, they said, Birt had moved in with his own people and his own management ideas, but this kind of change was normal, both in the BBC and in organisations elsewhere.

Despite the somewhat chaotic reforms and ferocious antagonisms, BBC TV news had in 1989 a year of stellar success. But the stars of BBC coverage in Tiananmen Square in Beijing, and of anti-communist uprisings in eastern Europe, were old (pre-Birt) BBC hands such as John Simpson[7] and Kate Adey.[8] However location coverage of revolution-on-the-streets is expensive. During 1987–9, the ITV/ITN news surrendered its audience lead to BBC TV news – a lead which the BBC News has retained ever since. BBC TV news has continued to outspend the ITV/ITN news by a huge margin.

4 John Birt, *The Harder Path: the autobiography*, 247–304. David Docherty, *Running The Show*. Chris Horrie and Steve Clarke, *Fuzzy Monsters: fear and loathing at the BBC* (London: William Heinemann, 1994).

5 Claire Barnett, 'Tony Hall', *Broadcast*, August 17 1990.

6 Tunstall, *Television Producers*, 52–9.

7 See below (page 171) for more details on John Simpson.

8 Kate Adie, *The Kindness of Strangers* (London: Headline, 2002), 356–70.

But, in the longer term, at least three of John Birt's changes were real achievements. Firstly BBC News became less badly managed. Secondly Birt encouraged numeracy – in terms of money amounts, audience numbers and the explanation of numbers in news stories. Thirdly, Birt successfully encouraged the BBC to be an innovator in the new digital age.

Since 1990 BBC news has become more of a non-stop 24 hour service; also more international; and more specialised. Two key 24 hour news service developments were the arrival of *Radio Five Live* (in 1994) and the all news TV channel, which when launched in 1997 was called *News 24* – but is now just *BBC News*. A third 24 hour development was, of course, *BBC News Online*, which in 1998 employed about 140 journalists; in 2010, when the Online Service was merged into the combined TV and Radio newsroom, there were over 1,000 BBC online journalists. As with many big BBC changes, news twenty-four-hourisation took some years of awkward development. A critical independent report in 2002 (when the BBC 24 hour TV Service was already five years old)[9] led eventually to the 24 hour service being awarded the leadership role in breaking fresh stories. The old tradition was that specific BBC programmes and individual correspondents kept any exclusive stories for their own next transmission. But today a BBC journalist, who discovers something new during the morning, will give it immediately to the 24 hour TV and radio services. BBC correspondents are also now required to blog.

BBC News has, since 1990, become more international in several senses. In particular *BBC World* is a 24 hour television service aimed at foreign audiences; it is closely linked with the domestic *BBC News* TV channel, which thus now has more foreign stories available for UK use. There are also now other foreign facing, news led channels, such as *BBC America*. However, there has been a big contraction in the number of radio language services from BBC World Service radio; this has been partly balanced by TV services in Arabic and Farsi.

9 Richard Lambert, *Independent Review of BBC News 24* (London: Department of Culture, Media and Sport, December 2002).

BBC News and current affairs employs much greater numbers of specialist correspondents – particularly in political, business, foreign and social news – than was the case in 1987. Another big change is in the number of broadcasts per day or per week which these specialists may be asked to make. Because of the increased number of channels and outlets – plus the speeded up preference for getting the story quickly on air – a correspondent may do ten, twenty or even thirty separate TV and radio broadcasts in a single day.

ITV/ITN news had a much less happy story from 1990 onwards.[10] News is, per hour, one of the cheaper genres; the problem has been that news is only moderately popular and, in commercial terms does not justify the large slices of the high audience evening times which regulators have traditionally required. Commercial broadcasters prefer to fill their evening hours with more high audience entertainment and want to carry fewer hours of news and current affairs.

From 1990 onwards, the 15 ITV companies began their long series of mergers, leading very slowly to a single ITV. These ITV owners, together with the regulators, developed a structure which was poorly designed to compete against the expanding BBC. In February 1991, Sir David Nicholas, then editor-in-chief and CEO of ITN, gave me an interview. He had just moved the successful ITN operation from one much-too-small building (near the BBC HQ) to a much too large, new glass palace (200 Grays Inn Road). This new building effectively bankrupted ITN which was rescued by Carlton. David Nicholas had deliberately constructed a building too big for ITN's current needs; he was unable to rent out the surplus space because the market for London office space nosedived in 1990–1. During our interview, David Nicholas chatted away happily; outside snow fell silently and inside the glass palace there was a lot more daytime silence than is normally found in a building where journalists work.

10 Richard Lindley, *And Finally …? The News From ITN* (London: Politico's, 2005). Andrew Montgomery, *ITN: 50 Years of News* (Long Hanborough: ESP Publishing, 2005).

ITV was competing with a stronger BBC news and with such new entrants as Channel Four News and Sky News. The ITV/ITN management searched for profitable diversifications and other changes. Several of these efforts proved to be disastrous failures.

- Another ITN (1997) investment was in Euronews, where ITN briefly provided the commercial management – but Euronews was a very non-commercial enterprise. Mark Wood, when chairman of ITN, told me that working with the other European participants in Euronews was 'like negotiating with the Austro-Hungarian Empire'.
- ITV executives insisted in 1999 that the main ITV news should no longer be *News At Ten* but should move to 10.30pm or 11pm to make way for entertainment programming.[11] The national press named this confusing move 'News At When?' and by 2000 the late ITV news audience was less than one third of the *News At Ten* audience number in 1985.
- Another big ITV/ITN mistake was the July 2000 launch of an ITV 24 hour news channel. By this time both the Sky and BBC 24 hour news channels were well entrenched in the market, but heavily subsidised. When it collapsed in 2005, the ITV News channel had a UK audience share of 0.12 per cent, while Sky News had 0.55 per cent.
- The newly consolidated ITV in 2007 made huge financial cuts in its provision of local TV news in the ITV regions. The single centralised ITV management no longer saw either regional news or regional advertising as significant.

The BBC and ITV are the two big players on the UK television news scene. Channel Four and Sky News are small niche players by comparison. Channel Four News had a chaotic opening in 1982. But by 1990 it was well established as ITN's upmarket alternative to the more downmarket ITN/ITV news. The one hour (really 45 minute) Channel Four News at 7pm

11 Howard Tumber, '10pm and all that: The battle over UK TV News', in Michael Bromley, ed., *No News is Bad News: Radio, Television and the Public* (Harlow: Longman, 2001), 96–108.

has usually had a weekday evening audience below one million. It long depended on a small team of senior correspondents and in particular on Jon Snow as lead presenter. It makes a virtue of its small team and hour length by running many political and other stories for over three minutes – with major stories running for ten or twelve minutes. But Channel Four News is in competition with BBC2's late evening *Newsnight* rather than with the full blast of BBC News.

The only other important niche news player is the 24 hour Sky News, which competes mainly with another 24 hour news channel, namely BBC News. Sky News was launched in 1989 by Rupert Murdoch as part of the initial Sky offering. It struggled (like the rest of Sky) and initially served up much live American breakfast news to midday UK audiences; it also used a lot of Euronews. But by 1991 Sky News was present in all national newspaper newsrooms. Sky News developed a small number of high profile journalists – such as Jeremy Thompson and Adam Boulton – and some excellent correspondents. As with other Murdoch enterprises, Australians were prominent in the early years. However, Sky News was required by law and regulation to follow the British public service tradition of neutral and balanced news. This meant that when the 24 hour BBC news channel began in November 1997, the UK had two somewhat similar public service all news channels. It took the BBC News channel eight years to overtake Sky News in audience numbers. From 2006 onwards BBC News pulled ahead.

BBC leads UK press and broadcast news agenda

The BBC has become the main leader of the entire UK news agenda – not only across TV and Radio, but also across the press. The UK, like comparable countries, has five main categories of news service – television, radio, online, the printed press and news agencies. BBC strength is obvious in its leadership of television, radio and online news. BBC Online is a very clear leader in its field; it has become a major rival to the traditional

UK domestic news agency, the Press Association. Not only can all journalists use BBC Online for repeated updates on the day's news, but so also can members of the general pubic. The BBC is quoted as a source by newspapers more frequently than in the past.

As broadcast news in general, and BBC news in particular, has grown in both depth and breadth, the UK newspapers have been losing circulation. National UK daily newspapers sold about 14.7 million copies in 1985 but this number approximately halved in the next three decades.[12] Compared with the 1960s, newspapers now cover fewer political stories and facts. TV and Radio, however, now carry increased numbers of political stories and facts within their greatly extended number of news channels and hours. Newspaper political coverage in the 1960s (when the *Daily Mirror* and *Daily Express* were sales leaders) was relatively serious and balanced compared with the more tabloid and partisan coverage since the 1980s.

Since the 1960s, even the upmarket dailies have forsaken comprehensive political coverage and tend to focus on their own 'exclusive' stories. TV and Radio in effect increasingly decide which of these press exclusive stories to follow up and thus to place centrally on the national news agenda. How broadcast news operations follow up selected newspaper political 'exclusives', was well illustrated by the *Daily Telegraph*'s 2009 revelations about the dubious expenses claims of many Members of Parliament. On May 7th 2009 the *Telegraph* team had finished their investigative work; the first round of the expenses scandal bombardment was due to be fired in that night's newspaper. Following standard practice, the main broadcast media were given advanced access to the imminent revelations. The *Daily Telegraph* journalists waited:

> The broadcasters' reaction to the story would be critical. Although the investigation team knew they had uncovered a massive scandal, the impact of the story would be severely dented if the hugely influential TV political editors played down its significance …

12 The numbers are not precisely comparable because of changed definitions affecting cut price copies, free copies, and the like.

> The answer was emphatic. All three channels led their news bulletins on the expenses story ... The BBC devoted almost ten minutes of the programme to the story and Nick Robinson's verdict was unequivocal. It was, he said, a 'disaster' for the government.[13]

This expenses scandal story ran and ran – on TV and Radio and in the newspapers – for many days and weeks. The scandal led directly and indirectly to the end of many political careers.

Financial sleaze stories have great media and public appeal. This *Daily Telegraph* story dealt with sleazy financial behaviour by elected politicians. Another crowd pleasing category of political sleaze news story deals with sexual sleaze, often a male Politician being unfaithful to his wife.

In addition to 24 Hour 'BBC News' and BBC Online, BBC agenda setting scheduled outputs continue through the 24 hour news cycle:

- At breakfast millions of people still look at newspapers, but many follow TV or radio breakfast shows. The BBC Radio *4 Tod*ay programme follows up the newspapers and maps out the new day's agenda.
- At midday there are again several BBC television and radio outputs, which – journalists say – shape the news agenda well into the afternoon.
- From 5pm to 8pm there are numerous big news outputs – notably BBC Radio 4 and BBC1 TV at 6pm, ITV news at 6.30pm and Channel Four TV news at 7pm.
- From 10pm to 11.20pm there are the BBC1 and ITV1 evening news shows, plus *Newsnig*ht (BBC2).

On a typical weekday all of these outputs have a collective audience of over 30 million (some, of course, are the same individuals following more than one radio/TV output). Among those millions each day are nearly all print journalists.

13 Robert Winnett and Gordon Rayner, *No Expenses Spared* (London: Bantam Press, 2009), 138.

Fast track careers and news bureaucracies

Television news has its own star system. Leading news presenters (or anchors) appear on national television, in high audience slots, at greater length than anyone else, except possibly the Prime Minister. Senior correspondents, such as Political Editors are typically on national TV and radio at least several times a week. But these star individuals and their junior presenter and correspondent colleagues are operating within a complex bureaucracy.

Classic bureaucratic features, found at the BBC News, include the following: a specific work role, or literally one working desk, may be occupied by two, three or more people around the 24 hours; BBC News uses lots of 'meetings', since journalists don't like 'committees'. There is typically one early, and one later, meeting for any major news output – meetings in which probable stories, running orders, length and strength, are briefly discussed and quickly decided. The BBC news operation is very highly specialised: groups of people only do online business news, or specialise on graphics and maps, or work for the Hausa or Swahili language services. Another classic aspect of bureaucracy is a Rule Book: the BBC has its own *Editorial Guidelines* rule book; most pages of this 350 page book offer 'advice' to news producers.[14] However, the big news bureaucracy is often quick, accurate and comprehensive; it covers some stories 'which only the BBC would ever look at.' Moreover huge amounts of practice have improved performance. Many BBC correspondents and news presenters – on the BBC News channel and on many other news outputs – have accumulated large numbers of flying hours. As a result, most BBC correspondents and presenters seem calm, confident and competent.

The BBC, ITV/ITN news – and their news competitors – depend heavily on their teams of senior correspondents. Three correspondent categories – Politics, Foreign and Finance – are discussed later in this chapter. The BBC has a team of about twenty domestic UK political correspondents,

14 BBC, *Editorial Guidelines* (London: BBC).

about ten Business and Economics correspondents and about fifteen correspondents who cover 'social' areas including Education, Health and Crime.

The 'Presenters' of the main news outputs are even better known to the audience. Millions of audience members observe these TV news presenters more frequently and more closely than they observe their next-door neighbours. Several controversies have lengthy histories. Do these people just read stuff from an autocue? Are male news presenters allowed to be middle aged and crumpled, while female presenters must be young and attractive? Do news presenters reveal their personal political opinions? In recent decades the news presenter role has expanded well beyond merely 'reading the news from an autocue'. News presenters now interrogate politicians and discuss stories with correspondents; and they appear across a range of non-news programming. Women have, very gradually, become more prominent as TV news presenters; male dominance has been somewhat diminished.

News presenters, like most presenters in UK television are freelance, employed on short-term contract. But they tend to have very long careers as news presenters. A 2009 report on seven top female and seven top male news presenters noted that the majority had been presenting TV news outputs for at least a decade. There was a big age difference – the women had an average age of forty-three, while the men had an average age of fifty-four.[15] The most significant difference was that these women typically began news presenting around age thirty, when they had had only limited journalism reporting experience. The men had tended to start news presenting around age forty, after having spent their thirties doing high profile journalism – often as foreign or political correspondents.

Back in the 1950s and 1960s most news presenters really were news-reading autocuties. They were, however, male autocuties – good-looking men who typically had experience in stage acting and/or in radio. In the 1960s the state of technology was such that the news presenter's main task was to read out words written by others. Film processing was slow and the

15 Patrick Foster, 'Situation vacant at the BBC: a woman to read the news (must be over 59)'. *The Times*, September 25 2009.

evening news preferred to cover morning (not afternoon) events and press conferences. Film inserts were fed into the bulletin via telecine which had to run for several seconds before the pictures appeared. This meant that the telecine operator and the news presenter had to follow the text and timing to within half a second. In 1967 I spent a day at the BBC's then TV news location (Alexandra Palace); reading the TV news was Robert Dougall. He was relaxed, charming and slightly ex-military. He took me for 'a turn outside the Palace' and only one person asked for his autograph. Dougall presented BBC news for nineteen years; his colleague, Richard Baker, presented the TV news for twenty-eight years.[16] Both men started in 1954 – the year in which BBC television ceased merely to replay the Radio news. Two decades later, in 1973 Angela Rippon was the first woman to present the main BBC TV news.

By the late 1980s satellite costs had fallen sufficiently for transatlantic, and other long-distance, interviews to be relatively cheap; and thus routinely available. Nigel Ryan (Editor of ITN, 1968–77) told me in 1991:

> The role of the presenter has increased out of all recognition. I think the quality of Channel 4 News and Jon Snow is extraordinary ... We used to have very nice fellows, but just actors, who read the news nicely; they wouldn't be able to do the news today. I like to think I had a hand in this, in having a newscaster (like Sandy Gall) who also still reported from Vietnam and Afghanistan. The newsreader today has to do live interviews with ambassadors and foreign politicians who are going to challenge everything – and then he must get onto the next item. I have the highest admiration for Jon Snow and Jeremy Paxman.

Jon Snow and Jeremy Paxman became members of a select group of men who acquired major reporting experience before moving across to presenting leading news output for two decades or more. Another member of this all-male presenter group was Trevor McDonald. Alastair Burnet was able to present the main ITV *News at Ten* while also Editor of *The Economist*. Over a glass of Scotch, Alastair Burnet told me that this was not difficult, because his *Economist* editing gave him the current news background with

16 Robert Dougall, *In and Out of the Box: an autobiography* (London: Collins and Harvill, 1973). Richard Baker, *Here is the News* (London: Leslie Frewin, 1966).

which to do the news presenting. It was also important, he joked, to read out the Scottish Football scores with some authority.

The pattern continued of the long-serving woman news presenter, who began news presenting without extensive experience as a political, foreign or other correspondent. Some youthful women presenters began presenting regional TV news – perhaps in somewhere remote from London such as Aberdeen or Bristol. Several women news presenters, however, initially worked on London and South East regional news shows. But this old pattern has largely faded.

Meanwhile the pattern continued of the male foreign or political correspondent who became a long serving news presenter. Huw Edwards, who presented BBC main news from 1999, was a former political correspondent. Mark Austin did eight years as a correspondent in Africa and Asia before becoming the lead presenter of ITV news. Jon Snow described himself as having 'reported from Afghanistan to Zimbabwe; interviewed Mandela, Reagan, Gorbachev, Thatcher, etc – 'before becoming the main presenter of Channel Four News in 1989, when aged forty-two'.[17] In 2007 he told me:

> This job is rare. Provided you stay in one piece, the older you get, the more you know. You've done most of these stories before. I was in Iran in 1989 covering the American Embassy hostage crisis; I covered the Iran-Iraq war. It's not just the places, but it's the situations, leadership struggles, the intrigue. You've done them before …
>
> Live interviewing several different people in different countries? I was dreadful to begin with … It takes a long time to get into it. But now it's just like any interviewing. I feel at ease and don't think about the miraculous technology. I best like the foreign visits – Baghdad two weeks ago, and Washington next week. It's important to keep getting your feet wet. It's expensive; on the last trip we took sixteen pieces of baggage. But if you've just got back from Iraq or Afghanistan, you have the advantage over the politician or interviewee who's not been recently.
>
> It's quite a long day when in London. Two big meetings at 9.30am and 2.15pm. I don't have an office or a secretary – I sit out on the editorial floor. I write (or rewrite) about half of what I read. Often I do a late afternoon interview down in Whitehall or Westminster; I usually go on my bike. At 6.50pm it's make-up and on air. We don't rehearse.

17 Jon Snow, *Shooting History* (London: Harper Perennial, 2005).

> George Bush's policy in the Middle East has created something worse than Vietnam; American newspapers have declined; CNN is crap. Abroad is just not covered by the US media; the average American is even more ignorant now than previously. But, ever since being a Washington correspondent, I feel close to America; have been to Cape Cod each summer for the last twenty-five years.

24 hour television news has been one key factor in greatly expanding the number of news presenters; the arrival of the BBC News channel in 1997 eventually led to a new BBC strategy for news presenters. The BBC today has at least forty regular presenters for its domestic UK daily TV and Radio outputs. Each main output – such as the 6pm or 10pm TV and Radio news has its own three presenters. Each of these three typically does the job three times a week for about forty weeks per year; a presenter may go out to report stories in person a few times a year and this can involve reporting from a war zone. The presenter typically does some other news presenting and also presents some non-news output. This mix of activities goes far beyond reading-the-autocue.

Today about half of all BBC domestic daily news presenters are women. A new group of talented BBC and ITV women presenters emerged after 2000, including Fiona Bruce, Andrea Catherwood, Katie Derham, Julie Etchingham, Mishal Husain, Emily Maitlis, and Cathie Newman. These women are as well qualified as their opposite number male presenters – not least in terms of their reporting experience and language skills.

There are now at least 50 prominent BBC and other presenters and senior correspondents who regularly perform across three or four separate platforms; some perform across all six of: television, radio, blogging and online, press, books and paid public speaking.

Television is the key platform, as John Simpson, in particular, emphasised to me; were he not the BBC's top foreign news journalist, other media would be less interested in him. Prominent television news presenters also present a range of series, including quiz shows and classical music. Numerous long-established BBC factual series are presented by top television news presenters.

Radio is an obvious platform for prominent broadcast journalists. Because the BBC controls most UK radio journalism, it's mainly BBC journalists who are able to combine radio and TV. The BBC actively conducts cross-channel promotion, not only of its programmes, but also of its journalists.

Blogging/online has become a standard duty, or activity, of most broadcast journalists. Some broadcast journalists are very enthusiastic; others complain that it takes too much time and can attract hate mail, especially from the Middle East.

Book writing attracted some broadcast journalists in the past. But this has expanded in recent years. By 2006 at least twenty-eight currently employed broadcast news journalists had (on average) each published three books.[18] (This did not include any crime, sports, or fiction) The complete total today is likely to be nearer 50 authors. Broadcast journalists write these books for several reasons – to enhance their careers, to make money and to evade the 90 seconds conventions of much TV. Several journalist authors complained about the demands of book-writing at 6 am.

Newspaper writing tends to be discouraged, especially if it might be politically partisan. But some of these broadcasters do nevertheless write for national dailies and weeklies.

Paid Public Speaking is yet another platform. Several broadcast journalists insisted that each year they only did a few paid after dinner, or commercial conference, speeches. Journalists in general have excellent anecdotes which they recount with skill. Some of these journalists are probably better suited to after dinner humour than to book length autobiography. Some believe they could have been successful actors.

Most prominent news presenters and correspondents had fast track early careers; their career typically reaches a high plateau in their forties and fifties. Many enjoy substantial later careers after the age of 55 or 60. Presenters, who once did the main evening news, may now present the midday TV news or appear on the BBC news channel. Several prominent journalists redefine themselves. Both John Sergeant (former political editor)

18 *Who's Who In The Media* (London: Media Guardian, 2006).

and Jeremy Vine (former BBC Africa/Johannesburg correspondent)[19] have written perceptive autobiographies and redefined themselves (in different ways) as song-and-dance raconteurs. John Humphrys (who as a Washington correspondent covered the Watergate saga) became, on the BBC *Today* programme Britain's most famously high profile political interviewer; he also became a belligerent defender of 'simple, clear and honest' English.[20]

News executives in charge and in crisis

Traditionally in Britain the news has been separated from other BBC and ITV genres. From 1987 onwards the John Birt reforms involved bringing BBC News and current affairs closer together. When Tony Hall spoke with me in 1992 he had been Head of BBC News and current affairs since 1987:

> Last year we combined radio and TV newsgathering into one organisation. But News is still outside the broad sweep of radio and TV.
>
> My main task was to push the news programmes consciously upmarket ... ITN increasingly see news as a commercial business; ITN is chasing the ratings, using more feature material, pulling out of foreign bureaus and firing people ...
>
> When I started as a producer, I had no control over the studios I used or how long I used them. Since 1990 BBC producers control their own budgets. This ensures that producers run the place and it gives back to producers some powers that the unions previously had. That's made major savings to put back. Newsgathering is stronger since we're now in more places than we were, and we have more specialists.

Two decades later, ten present or former senior BBC news executives gave me interviews. All ten had been to university – four to Cambridge, two to Oxford and two to Manchester. Their median age was 48 years, and they

19 John Sergeant, *Give Me Ten Seconds* (London: Macmillan, 2001). Jeremy Vine, *It's All News To Me: How I Got Locked inside the BBC for 25 years* (London: Simon and Schuster, 2012).

20 John *Humphrys, Lost For Words* (London: Hodder and Stoughton, 2004).

were typically in their second or third senior executive level job; each of these ten executives had had an average of nine separate jobs in television. There had been sideways job moves as well as vertical one. Such sideways moves are favourably regarded, as broadening the executive's experience and skills. All ten of these senior news executives had worked on, or been in charge of, one or more of the BBC's most prestigious news and current affairs programmes. Six out of ten had been in charge of either the BBC's early evening or late evening, news. Five had been on the BBC Radio Four *Today* programme; five had been on *Newsnight* and four on *Panorama*.

Because of its three-times-three character (TV, Radio, Online and Local, National, International) BBC News presents many possibilities for internal moves. ITN, which predominantly supplies TV News to ITV and Channel Four, offers only two news operations. The BBC has enticed a number of ITN news executives straight across to the main BBC early and late evening news outputs. Craig Oliver joined the ITN training scheme in 1993; and 13 years later was Editor of the BBC *Ten O'Clock News*. He told me that he was seeking to change more than just the appearance of the BBC News and the use of the 'Studio Wall' behind the News presenter:

> I arrive here five days a week at 8am and try to leave by 8pm. On the *Ten* we never just repeat the *Six*. News today is cheap or free and tastes much the same wherever you go. You've got to have some added value.

Craig Oliver was subsequently promoted several times, within BBC News, and in 2011 he moved to 10 Downing Street to become David Cameron's top media person.

While BBC News is a rather closed world, ITN News is an even more tightly closed island. ITN has always been located away from the rest of ITV. It is now much smaller than its 1991 peak. ITV – providing news to both ITV and C4 – has tended to be dominated by a few long-stay news executives. Since the launch of *Channel Four News* in 1982, ITN's leading news executive was Stewart Purvis; he spent nineteen years first as deputy editor and then as Editor of ITN (1990–2003). Purvis rescued Channel Four's News from its disastrous 1982–3 start. Purvis played the lead role in deciding how ITN would supply news to two competing outlets – ITV and C4. For example, he told me in 1992:

> Sometimes an exclusive can be a problem. If *News at Ten* has an exclusive which the BBC *9 o'clock* will almost certainly get, then I force *News at Ten* to give it to Channel Four at 7pm. I'm the referee on such things.

Another forceful personality at ITN was Deborah Turness who was Editor of TV News for nine years (2004–13). She told me:

> News is the best drama on TV, because it's real. It has a tangible impact on the viewers' lives. Every day I come to work, it's exciting. I don't know what's going to happen ... I'm a control freak, very hands on. I can put my fingers in all the pots. I see my main role as keeping ITV News a distinctive brand, looking for exclusives and excellent breaking news. You've got to be distinctive. It can't just be an update. I'm constantly telling the team that we need exclusive content. My role is to be a dynamo, pushing, pushing. You're not in these jobs very long – compared to your career or your life span. The key to this job is: Don't ever, ever, stand still. You've got to keep innovating, keep challenging everyone around you. Keep risk taking.

In 2013 Deborah Turness made an unusual sideways move – into a senior post at NBC News in New York. Turness was appointed Editor of ITV News when in her late thirties. Television News, like television generally, is a youngish person's business. A few long-serving presenters are the main exceptions. Alongside top news executives, mostly in their forties, goes an institutional memory which stretches back only about 25 years. By 2015 it was already obvious that most senior British news executives lacked a clear memory of the first Thatcher Prime Ministerial term (1979–83), the Carter Presidency (1977–81) and the Iran Revolution (1979). Some of these news executives probably had a clearer recollection of *Jim'll Fix It* (1975 on), but only because they had watched Jimmy Savile while they themselves were children.

Political editors: Top agenda setters

> The BBC political editorship is an odd job, which makes some politicians clearly uncomfortable. There is an element of sketch writing, trying to add humour and colour from the day's events; and there's also an element of commentator, saying 'This is how it seems to me'.

Nick Robinson was talking to me about his job as BBC political editor.

In July and August 2005 three new chief Political Editors were appointed by the BBC, by ITV and by Channel 4. Within the broader circus of British national politics, such political editors perform on a political tightrope – a tightrope from which most journalists would quickly fall. Day after day, these political editors must report on the nation's high politics within short popular news bulletins. The reports must be legally correct and party political neutral. Some of their reporting consists of a pre-edited package, but part of many reports is a live segment typically delivered without a prepared text. Despite the inevitable complexities of events, of party and of law, the whole report must fit within a brief, pre-arranged, time slot.

The three new political editors of 2005 were Nick Robinson (BBC), Tom Bradby (ITV) and Gary Gibbon (Channel 4). Their average age on appointment was 38 years. All three had extensive previous political TV journalism experience – both as producers and reporters. Political editors focus primarily on the early evening and late evening 'main' news. A fairly big political report might include a 90 second edited 'package' surrounded by another 90 seconds of 'two-way' in which the correspondent speaks live to the news anchor. Political editors spend much of the day, often including lunch, gossiping with politicians and other sources in person (around the 'Westminster Village') and by telephone. This merges into interviews recorded in the afternoon. By the late afternoon these interviews, plus perhaps brief film clips of Parliamentary Questions, are edited into a package. A ninety seconds news package normally requires ninety minutes of editing in the edit suite. The correspondent consults on this editing process with the film editor and the producer and adds some extra words of linking commentary.

The job of the television political editor has greatly changed in recent decades. They are leaders of the national agenda. On days of big political news, the political editor can often be doing several high profile performances in a day. The BBC political editor can sometimes be on both TV and radio many times in twenty-four hours. The BBC's political editor is the most senior of a team of twenty national political correspondents. But back in the late 1960s there were only three BBC political correspondents.

Peter Hardiman Scott was the BBC's very first 'Political Correspondent' (later: 'Political Editor'), during 1960–75. In 1968 he gave me an interview and also completed (in green ink) one of my lengthy questionnaires. Hardiman Scott typed out his own news stories and read them to camera in 'televised radio' form. There was very little accompanying visual or film input. Hardiman Scott sometimes worked a long day, starting with an 8am radio appearance and finishing with a 9pm TV news appearance. He did much of his work on the telephone – averaging, he told me, twelve calls in and twelve calls out per day. He consulted regularly with another top journalist, David Wood of *The Times* – they often shared their choice of the day's top political story. Hardiman Scott, as a political insider, gave political advice to incumbent BBC Director Generals and he persuaded Hugh Carleton-Greene not to resign in 1967, when Prime Minister Harold Wilson appointed Lord Charles Hill as Chairman of the BBC Governors. Scott was (quietly) recognised by the BBC, and the salary he revealed to me was high by 1968 journalist standards. Hardiman Scott anticipated more recent BBC correspondents in yet another way – he was the author of several novels and several books of poems.

Hardiman Scott was a pioneer interviewer of Prime Ministers on television. It was only during Harold Macmillan's Prime Ministership (1957–63) that the big political Interview first emerged on British television. Hardiman Scott did a number of big interviews with Macmillan and with

Harold Wilson (Prime Minister 1964–70).[21] The two most direct pioneers of today's TV political editor role were Michael Brunson and Andrew Marr. Michael Brunson was ITV's political editor during 1986–2000. Brunson was a man of theatrical stage presence, who always seemed to be wearing the same raincoat; Brunson provided adroit touches of political humour with mischievous smiles and the occasional dramatic silence. Andrew Marr openly broke several of the then established rules during his 2000–5 term as the BBC's political editor. Marr set out to make politics both serious and entertaining. He seemed to be breaking the established rules of non-partisan neutrality. He was borrowing from the old press tradition of the amusing Parliamentary sketch. The viewers were sometimes treated to outlandish imagery; it was rather like – the viewers were told – a huge pile of termites in Downing Street or two monkeys trying to scale Big Ben. Sometimes this imagery was bizarre; but often it successfully combined gravitas and authority, seasoned with revealing witticism. This was supported by top BBC news executives, who could claim that Marr was merely updating and remixing public service information-education-entertainment.

Andrew Marr had one special advantage; as a national newspaper Editor,[22] he had learned to be a news polymath. But he lacked television experience. He had to learn the techniques of the prepared 'package' and the live 'two way'. Initially he wrote and learned his 'live' pieces, but this was too wooden. He then went too far in the opposite direction of no pre-planned points. Meanwhile the *Daily Mail* and other newspapers were jeering from the sidelines and reminding their readers of Andrew Marr's left-liberal views and his disastrous editorship at *The Independent*. He told me:

> But the BBC knew that when they appointed me. They knew I'd get a bit of stick. When I came in at the BBC, there was a great debate, initiated by Greg Dyke. Was

21 Michael Cockerell, *Live From Number Ten: the inside story of Prime Ministers and Television* (London: Faber and Faber, 1988).

22 Andrew Marr, *My Trade: a short history of British journalism* (London: Macmillan, Pan 2005).

> anyone still interested in the news? One solution was to fill your bulletins with saccharine tabloidesque stories of the softest kind.
>
> You've got to do the serious news agenda – the same as you'd have done in 1965 or 1975. You have to speak human – put it in clear, vivid, English. Your duty is to draw in those people who don't know the Westminster jargon and to persuade them that they can understand it. Which they can.

Most comments by political editors – such as 'The government will have to respond next week' – will seem undramatic. But some comments and opinions may contribute to a major political event such as the emergence of a new party leader and subsequent Prime Minister. Tom Bradby, told me of his early months as ITV's Political Editor:

> Often you have the journalistic credibility of your organisation riding on your judgements. One of the first things I did as Political Editor was the autumn 2005 Party Conferences. We took a very tough line on the fact that David Davies (who was a leading contender for the Conservative leadership) made a poor impression at the Conservative Conference. The delegates seemed incredibly disappointed with him. We reflected that very strongly in our unique way. It caused a lot of heat from David Davies' supporters and, of course, he didn't win the leadership. David Cameron did.
>
> Politics is so often the lead story. We are no-holds-barred. But, at the same time, I've got to sit opposite Cabinet Ministers at lunch. When you're also giving them a hard time on air, it's not always the most comfortable lunch …
>
> Many times you're in the thick of it – lots of aggression, obscenities, angry texting. Critical blogs are very much easier to take. When Brown was Prime Minister I was absolutely monstered by Brown's people and by Brown himself. Direct intimidation – if you carry on like that, we'll never co-operate with you again.
>
> We try to take a hard line – no bullshit from anyone. New Labour controlled the message more vigorously and more prominently … So this more aggressive news coverage has happened … Now the political editor is expected to say 'That's what they are saying, but this is what really matters.'

Just as blunt, tell-it-like-it-is, Tom Bradby was a good political editor for no-holds-barred, ITV News, so Gary Gibbon's gentler and more thoughtful approach was a good fit for Channel Four News and its longer, one hour, news at 7pm. On Channel Four, three-and-a-half minutes is a common length for a political story, with a bigger story running to perhaps six minutes. On October 20 2010 (when big government expenditure cuts were announced), Channel Four News devoted 22 minutes to the story.

When Nick Robinson succeeded Andrew Marr as BBC political editor in summer 2005 he became the UK's next high profile journalist – the senior person in a BBC team of thirty national political correspondents, Scots/Welsh/Ulster 'national editors' and 'Parliamentary' correspondents (who cover debates and committees in Parliament). The political editor is an elite reporter, not the producer or executive producer of a particular output or strand. On a politically busy day he is in demand from TV, radio and online. The BBC political editor is in practice the UK's most followed political blogger.

After Oxford, Robinson was a BBC trainee, and worked as a producer on a succession of BBC factual series; he was deputy editor of *Panorama*. For another lengthy period (1996–2005) he worked as a BBC political journalist, and then crossed over to become ITV/ITN's political editor. He told me:

> Coming from ITN, I found the BBC pretty hard to take. The biggest change is the scale. ITV is relatively small and very focused – often mainly just on the 6.30pm news. At ITV I needed to talk just to the editor of one bulletin. But the BBC's scale creates a lack of simplicity – so many outputs and so many bosses. Andy Marr used humour and engaged with the audience in a different way. I wouldn't have got this BBC job, nor previously the ITV job, if it hadn't been for Andy Marr.
>
> Yes, it's a long day, but I normally only do four days each week. I can be on the *Today* radio news at say 7.10am or 8.10am from my home on my ISDN line and I can do this at very short notice. On my way home in the taxi from the 10pm news, I usually call the *Today* programme. The only way to make this long day tolerable is that having done the *Today* programme, you don't need to go in early. A problem is spending too much time in the office at Millbank. I try to spend some time every day in the Commons. I prefer to watch a big debate from the Gallery.
>
> Phoning is a huge part of it. With quite a few Ministers you can get through directly on their mobile at any time. I tend to have a rush of political lunches, maybe two or three lunches a week and then none. Lunch is more about getting to know the politician, and getting that mobile number. Lunch is less alcoholic and is shorter than it was.

The increasingly assertive political reporting style of Andrew Marr and others, from year 2000 onwards, was linked to an increasingly assertive style of Prime Ministerial media secretaries in the 1990s.[23] Alastair Campbell was the Downing Street media secretary for the first six years (1997–2003) of the Tony Blair Prime Ministership. Alastair Campbell had previously worked for Tony Blair as the Opposition Leader's media secretary. Many commentators suggested that Alastair Campbell's assertive-tabloid approach to his job was without precedent; but this was incorrect. True, back during the Harold Wilson Premiership of 1964–70, both political publicity and political reporting were shrouded in secrecy. Daily 'Lobby briefings', in which the media secretary talked to the lobby (political) journalists, took place twice a day on a 'for use but not for attribution' basis.[24] Initially in charge of these briefings was Harold Wilson's 'press secretary', Trevor Lloyd-Hughes who performed his role in a very gentlemanly, correct, and rather neutral civil service way. The political journalists themselves behaved in a gentlemanly way (over 90 per cent were male). In those days embargoes were respected; the text of a key speech was often given to journalists in advance but they did not use it until the embargo time. There was, however, one important exception to this – in the latter part of this Wilson government, Lloyd-Hughes was replaced by a journalist, Joe Haines, who was a dedicated supporter of Wilson.

Joe Haines' time as press secretary, before the June 1970 General Election, was quite disastrous. The Pound Sterling had been devalued against the dollar (in November 1967) and in early 1968 Harold Wilson was receiving massively critical coverage in most newspapers (but not, of course, on radio and TV). A number of press journalists expressed to me not only contempt but hatred for the British Prime Minister; none of this was a surprise, if you were reading what they were writing in their newspapers.

23 The best historical account of the 'Downing Street Press Secretary' role is in: Colin Seymour-Ure, *Prime Ministers and the Media: issues of power and control* (Oxford: Blackwell, 2003).

24 Jeremy Tunstall, *The Westminster Lobby Correspondents* (London: Routledge, 1970).

Joe Haines talked with me when he was still a junior lobby man on *The Sun* (pre-Murdoch). He was one of the very few lobby journalists who still had anything positive to say about the Prime Minister, Harold Wilson. Soon after this (June 1969–June 1970), Joe Haines was Harold Wilson's media spokesman. Wilson at this point was very low in the opinion polls, and was soon to lose the June 1970 General Election. But Haines avoided the previous 'non partisan' media spokesman role and adopted a belligerent pro-Wilson publicity stance. The press journalists responded with their own belligerent criticism in their newspapers. Joe Haines replied by stopping both daily briefings. This episode provided an early taste of what was to happen to Tony Blair's publicity machine some three decades later.

For most of her Prime Ministership, Margaret Thatcher's press secretary was Bernard Ingham.[25] Throughout the 1980s Ingham had a reputation for pro-Thatcher belligerence. But, unlike Joe Haines, Ingham's style was a mix of partisan assertion plus some civil service neutrality. Thatcher used Bernard Ingham to badmouth her own Cabinet members; this Ingham treatment was often followed a few weeks later by the particular Cabinet Minister being sacked. Ingham became known as 'the sewer but not the sewage'. Ingham (who had worked as a *Guardian* journalist and as a government press officer) remained on goodish personal terms with most of the political journalists.

When Tony Blair appointed Alastair Campbell he was either unaware of, or chose to ignore, the Joe Haines precedent. Alastair Campbell became 'more than just a media spokesman'. He played an active role in gaining the support of *The Sun* and other Murdoch newspapers. Alastair Campbell had been political editor of the *Daily Mirror*. When still at the *Mirror*, Alastair Campbell gave me a very helpful and interesting interview; he was clearly an exceptionally able tabloid journalist. But less evident then was that Campbell could be aggressive and obsessively belligerent. With the two largest UK dailies – *The Sun* and *Daily Mirror* – supporting the new Blair Premiership, Alastair Campbell became over confident and

25 Robert Harris, *Good and Faithful Servant: the unauthorized biography of Bernard Ingham* (London: Faber and Faber, 1990).

excessively belligerent: Adam Boulton, the well-informed political editor of Sky News, wrote:

> By the second half of the first term, relations between the media and Campbell had curdled. Contempt and hostility manifested themselves on both sides. Campbell delighted in mocking the mannerisms of individual journalists (Robert Peston, then political editor of the *Financial Times*, was a favourite target) and would on occasion hand out 'Garbage Awards' for stories he judged to be particularly inaccurate.[26]

The belligerent Campbell style, was continued by his successors, when Alastair Campbell departed in 2003. This belligerent style probably exacerbated the blowback when Blair's ratings nosedived.[27] Many political journalists and politicians can smell blood and some became merciless hunters, keen to finish off a wounded leader. All British Prime Ministers since Eden and Macmillan received vicious press criticism in their closing months in office.

Alastair Campbell not only attacked individual journalists; in 2003 he also took on the BBC. Campbell won the battle against the BBC and achieved the sacking of the BBC Director General. But he lost this war and knew that he had to resign. An indirect consequence of Alastair Campbell was that the blowback and press hostility continued against Gordon Brown during his Prime Ministership (2007–10).

When David Cameron became Prime Minister in 2010 he chose Andy Coulson, a former Murdoch tabloid Editor to be his media secretary. Cameron was probably influenced by the Alastair Campbell example. But Coulson was not a wise choice because his paper, the *News of the World* was at the extreme end of the tabloid spectrum; and Coulson was already mired in phone hacking and illegality. David Cameron's second choice was the senior BBC television news producer, Craig Oliver. This was an interesting innovation. But the ideal Downing Street media secretary should have both print and broadcast experience. However, the rare person who

26 Adam Boulton, *Tony's Ten Years: memories of the Blair Administration* (London: Simon and Schuster, 2008: 191).

27 'Tony Blair's Legacy: The great performer leaves the stage', *The Economist*, 12 May 2007: 23–5.

has had senior experience in both print and broadcast reporting would probably not want the job.

Financial news

For at least four decades, BBC News executives had been trying, but failing, to establish Finance as a serious broadcast news field. However, all of this changed in August and September 2007, when Robert Peston, the BBC's new Business Editor, reported the problems of the Northern Rock bank. These problems led to a then seemingly impossible event – the collapse of a significant UK bank. Robert Peston became virtually overnight a national figure, hugely admired, derided, discussed and caricatured.

How did Robert Peston and BBC News manage to do this? Only a decade earlier it was obvious that TV/Radio had failed to challenge the newspaper advantages in financial news of 'depth, detail and numbers'.[28] Several newish factors had by 2007 hugely increased the potential for broadcast financial news. The internationalisation of banking and finance now meant that, more than ever, speed was of the essence. The BBC, with its many bulletins, its 24-hour news and its online presence, could now, like the banks, move numbers onto screens – in London and around the world – within seconds or minutes.

Another key factor was the BBC's increased presence in news against the now smaller, more partisan, and 'my-exclusive-against-your-exclusive', newspapers. The BBC had an established reputation for very seldom getting basic facts wrong. So, people (including bankers and other journalists) assumed that if Robert Peston and the BBC say it's a fact, there's a 99 per cent chance it is a fact. If Peston said a bank was going to collapse, that bank was indeed going to collapse – probably today or next weekend, at latest.

28 Jeremy Tunstall, *Newspaper Power* (Oxford: Oxford University Press. 1996), 354–73.

Robert Peston had an impressive track record. He had occupied four senior reporting posts at the *Financial Times* – Political Editor, Banking Editor, Head of a Special Investigations Unit, and finally 'Financial Editor'. He had worked for several daily and Sunday newspapers and done columns for two political weeklies. He had also worked for an online financial analysis service. His two decades in financial journalism meant that he already knew many senior politicians, including Gordon Brown, the 2007–10 Prime Minister. But (like Andy Marr) he had not previously worked in television or radio, and he had an uncomfortable start. Peston told me:

> It's vital to get to know people who know stuff. Establishing relationships of trust – so that they'll talk to you frankly, but without your being beholden to them. I've seldom been given a scoop all neatly wrapped up. You need to work out what the big themes are and what might happen. Then talk to many different people. Each person may give you one small thing, which you then put into a jigsaw, which turns out to be a decent story. Twenty-five years as a political and business journalist means you get to know lots of people who know you well enough to talk on the phone. Yes, much of it is on the phone. But I try to have lunch or a cup of coffee periodically with people, to catch up and renew.

When in late 2005 Robert Peston began work at the BBC, he was surprised at how ignorant most senior BBC people were of most things financial. He told me:

> Most senior people in this vast BBC News organisation simply didn't know what was going on in business. So I started sending internal emails in summer 2006, and it became a formal published blog in January 2007. I still think the informing-the-BBC role is as important as informing outside people. The best thing is to get the blog out pretty early each day …
>
> Back in 2003 I noticed that the Northern Rock bank was growing very fast. So I thought, hang on – they must be taking big risks. I wrote the story initially when I was *Telegraph* city editor. I looked like an idiot for several years, because Northern Rock's share price continued to rise. It was a star performer. But I continued to give my view, which differed sharply from the City view.
>
> Then on 9 August 2007 the markets, in which the Rock raised the money, suddenly stopped lending. I knew that, if this continued, Northern Rock would be in severe difficulty. I also determined that this would be the biggest story of my career. I immersed myself in the story. I wrote on my blog about it being a defining moment. All through August 2007, the financial media reported the Rock story as of little

> significance to the wider world. Then I disclosed that the first British bank casualty would be Northern Rock. I broke the scoop that Northern Rock was going, cap in hand, to the Bank of England for financial support. I broke that story on the BBC News channel at 8.30pm, September 13, 2007. I was accused by a lot of people of killing Northern Rock. But the Rock was hugely reckless in both its borrowing and its lending. There were 120 per cent mortgages and so on. In fact what I at first said was too kind to the Rock. After the Rock, the biggest stories were the Lloyds TSB-HBOS merger; Royal Bank of Scotland being rescued by the Treasury; Bradford and Bingley being nationalised; and Gordon Brown as Prime Minister as a running story. I was consistently attacked by economists, by commentators, and by some politicians, who saw me as scaremongering.
>
> From August 2007, when the credit crunch began, through to early 2009 – about eighteen months – I was working six and seven days. There were days when I did more than thirty separate TV and radio broadcasts, plus two or three blogs. In 2008 I was often working seven days a week. The really big decisions were taken by politicians and bankers at the weekend – when the markets were closed. That meant more weekend work.

How did the BBC – traditionally super cautious and uninterested in financial news – manage to lead the charge for many months in delivering these big bad tidings?[29] The BBC executives who chose Robert Peston in 2005 made a wise and courageous choice. He was variously accused of being too friendly with bankers, too close to Labour in general and to Gordon Brown in particular, and too personally weird. Peston does indeed have a mildly idiosyncratic personal style. He knows that he is not such a polished TV performer as some of his colleagues. He uses old-fashioned words like 'Crikey'. But he is a tough and resilient character. When Robert Peston was the FT's political editor, Alastair Campbell regularly insulted him: 'He would accuse me of being partisan in front of these other journalists. We had endless rows. But I've never let truculent people stop me doing my job.'

The BBC has had other outstanding journalists in this area – notably Stephanie Flanders who performed the near impossible task of making not just Business news but Economics news, seem comprehensible. The BBC now has a substantial group of people generating Business and Financial

29 Robert Peston and Laurence Knight, *How Do We Fix This Mess?* (London: Hodder and Stoughton, 2012), 179–99.

news. A collection of separate news desks supply the distinctive requirements for BBC domestic (and BBC International) TV, radio and online. Separate desks supply Radio Five Live and BBC World Service Radio. Another desk provides business news for the UK regions and for BBC local radio.

Before Robert Peston's appointment in 2005 there was a forty-year period during which the BBC handled business, financial and economics news with extreme caution. The BBC, in fact, appointed its very first 'Economics Reporter' in 1964. He was a then young man (born 1932) called Graham Turner, who had little background in economics but had published an excellent book *The Car Makers* (1964), which correctly took a pessimistic view of UK car manufacturing.[30] Turner subsequently told me that the BBC used him primarily to report the UK's monthly official trade figures. Once a month he did a batch of up to ten BBC radio and TV appearances to talk about these official trade numbers. In the 1960s and 1970s business and economics news was sharply divided between two specialisms – 'Labour and Industrial' and 'Financial'.[31] The Labour-Industrial correspondents focused heavily on prominent trade union leaders and only secondly on the details of the then prevalent strikes and disputes.[32] 'Financial' journalists worked mainly for the upmarket newspapers, each of which employed a team of journalists, located not in Fleet Street but in a separate 'City' office, about one mile away. The BBC covered business and economics through several quite senior 'Industrial-Labour correspondents' (not 'reporters'). ITV/ITN followed this BBC pattern.

In the 1960s both BBC and ITN executives (mostly themselves not very numerate) thought that business and economics news was too difficult and dangerous. It was dangerous, not least because it was controversial and political. Most political of all was the Pound, and the devaluation of the Pound against the Dollar; on 18–19 November 1967 the fixed Pound rate

30 Graham Turner, *The Car Makers* (Harmondsworth, Penguin, 1964).

31 Jeremy Tunstall, *Journalists At Work* (London: Constable and Beverly Hills: Sage, 1971), 190–8, 105–12, 139–46.

32 Denis McQuail, *Analysis of Newspaper Content*, a report for The Royal Commission on the Press (Chairman: O.R. McGregor). (London: HMSO, Cmnd 68104), 1977: 29.

against the Dollar was devalued from $2.80 to $2.40. BBC news executives at that time wanted to keep very well away from such political dynamite. The BBC was only following the then cautious, patriotic and gentlemanly standards of the City and the newspaper financial journalists. From my interviews (shortly after the Devaluation) with sixteen senior financial journalists, including Sir Gordon Newton, Editor of the *Financial Times*,[33] it was obvious that they had not wanted to be accused of 'talking down the pound'. So they had chosen largely to ignore the strong rumours that the devaluation of the pound was imminent.

In 1990 there was still not much finance/economics/business news on British television. Its advance was further delayed by the appointment of Peter Jay as the BBC's 'Economics Editor' (1989–2001). Peter Jay had been the youthful Economics Editor of *The Times*, where he argued for Monetarist theory and policy. Jay was a presenter on the, John Birt produced, *Weekend World*, which sought to explain policy to a very small Sunday mid-day audience. Peter Jay then served as UK Ambassador in Washington. On his return he led the disastrous opening of ITV's breakfast company, TVam. The appointment of Peter Jay to be BBC Economics Editor was one of John Birt's worst decisions. Peter Jay, now aged fifty-two, was simply not suited to the task; he appeared infrequently on the BBC news to deliver very articulate, and very brief, economics lectures. Peter Jay presided over a small 'Business and Economics Unit' group which covered industry, business, aviation and transport, in addition to economics. Peter Jay stuck largely to the economics and was widely referred to as the BBC's Economics Editor.

The BBC's gap between Peter Jay's 2001 departure and Robert Peston's 2005 arrival was filled by Jeff Randall, who had had extensive experience at the *Sunday Times* and other newspapers as a Business and City Editor. Randall became an excellent broadcaster, despite having little previous broadcast experience. But he was perhaps a little too Murdoch-populist for the BBC. Jeff Randall subsequently became a prominent performer at Sky News.

33 Jeremy Tunstall, *Newspaper Power* (Oxford University Press, 1996), 356–8.

How could the BBC have been so inept in its appointments of financial journalists for forty-one years (1964–2005) and then so adroit in appointing Robert Peston in 2005? Perhaps three factors contributed. Firstly, the BBC timing was right in 2005, because the big BBC news machine had recognised a new need for a few, high profile, star journalists. Secondly, Robert Peston had just enough time to get TV/Radio experience before the bank bombshells of 2007. Or perhaps that's the wrong metaphor. As with the foreign correspondents who said 'a massacre helped my career', Robert Peston's career was helped by the financial massacres of 2007 and after. Thirdly the BBC had some good luck; or fortune favoured the brave executives who chose Robert Peston.

London's four decades as world TV news hub

London was the world's television news hub across four decades (1967–2007). The key news organisation was the Visnews-Reuters video news agency – across two distinct phases.

Firstly, during 1965–90, the Visnews-Reuters combination was the dominant leader in world foreign news film. Secondly during 1990–2007 the United States APTN (Associated Press TV News) shared the lead with Reuters; but London remained the sole TV news world leader. London was the chosen editorial HQ location for APTN. From 1990 the BBC greatly expanded its foreign TV news provision. Meanwhile Reuters (unencumbered by US foreign policy) was seen around the world as the more established and less biased, world TV news agency.

From 2008 onwards London ceased to be the leading world hub for foreign TV news. Reuters is now a Canadian owned company based in New York.

Visnews was, of course, a wholesaler which sold newsfilm to retail news customers, national television networks, around the world. But Visnews was selecting from the world's events each day and in 1975 sending quite a small selection to each customer. Visnews was both choosing the news stories, and also editing down each story to two or three minutes. During 1967–90 even TV stories about the United States were heavily edited in London for world consumption. This included events such as the Watergate scandal of 1973–4, and the Iranian Revolution and US Embassy siege of 1979–80. Visnews was also the main provider to the world of TV pictures of the collapse of Communism in eastern Europe and the collapse of the USSR.

Most TV viewers and many journalists around the world do not fully comprehend how dependent almost all TV news operations are on agency news film. Even the BBC, with its exceptionally large team of full-time foreign correspondents depends heavily on agency news film. We often see 'our correspondent' clearly at the disaster, close to men shooting bursts of automatic gunfire, or interviewing local people and politicians; but these 'our correspondent' clips are often edited together with other footage, other shots of other fighters and clips from other interviews conducted by other journalists. The majority of TV networks across the world have two or less foreign correspondents or bureaus; so they must rely heavily on agency news film. During 1967–90 Visnews was always stronger than current American competitors. This was primarily because the three old American networks (ABC, NBC, CBS) did not want to cooperate with each other, and because the leading American news agency, Associated Press, was primarily a newspaper and radio news agency which did not want to be involved in TV news. There was a succession of US efforts in which the second American news agency, UPI, did participate.[34] UPITN, for several years, operated as a London-based TV news film agency which drew on British ITN news film and UPI's international bureaus and communications. But UPI was fast sinking into ultimate collapse.

Reuters experienced many changes in its main ownership and its main competition. Visnews was a creation of the older Commonwealth countries and was intended to encourage the flow of TV news within the 'old' Commonwealth and the then growing Commonwealth of 'new' nations in

34 Oliver Boyd-Barrett, *The International News Agencies*. (London: Constable, Beverly Hills: Sage, 1980), 238–41.

Africa and Asia. A decade after its 1967 birth, Visnews was one third owned by the BBC, one third by Reuters and one third by the public broadcasters of Canada, Australia and New Zealand.

The business strategy of the initially public service Visnews was to engage in the expensive collection of fresh daily news film from around the world and then, after editing, to sell much the same batch of film each day to almost all of the TV broadcasters in the world:

> Visnews in 1975 claimed that its news was seen on 'some 99 per cent of all the television receivers in the world'. It had network customers in all of the world's most populous nations – including China and the Soviet Union ...
>
> In addition to its core of BBC, NBC and NHK news-film, Visnews has is own staff of television reporters and stringers around the world. On any day it has about 30 video stories of which 8 or 10 are sent to any individual television client. At the Visnews headquarters in ... west London ... it is possible to see set out on just two sheets of paper a table indicating which of today's video stories are going to which of 193 customers in 98 countries ... of the 12 or 15 minutes sent each day to each client, the typical television network uses 4 or 5 minutes each day on its news bulletins, whilst some poorer television networks use the full 12 to 15 minutes day after day.[35]

From 1975 Visnews began to move from air freighting its edited film out of Heathrow airport to using satellite distribution.

Reuters' involvement as a one third owner of Visnews dated from the 1960s and enabled Visnews to use Reuters news agency offices around the world. But in the 1960s Reuters began to invest heavily in computerised financial data services.[36] Quickly this became a larger and 'higher margin' business than the 'lower margin', or unprofitable, world news service. By 1985, when Reuters was the 55 per cent owner of Visnews, Reuters itself had become primarily a large (public) data company. The general news service and the TV news film service each now represented only 5 per cent of Reuters revenue and no per cent of profit. Visnews had hitched its wagon to a Reuters which was, indeed, the star of international financial

35 Jeremy Tunstall, *The Media Are American*.

36 Donald Read, *The Power of News, the history of Reuters, 1849–1989* (Oxford: Oxford University Press, 1992) 283–369.

data. But the success and profits of Reuters attracted aggressive competition from two other data companies, Bloomberg and Thomson; and this three-way competition eventually led to the Thomson-Reuters takeover.

Paradoxically, while during the 1970s and 1980s Reuters-Visnews was the world leader in TV news, the BBC and ITN were very small players in terms of domestic television foreign news for the UK audience. In 1990, Margaret Eales, as ITN foreign editor told me:

> We have correspondents in Washington, South Africa, the Middle East and Hong Kong, but Moscow is the major bureau for us now – it's where the story is. In Moscow, we have a correspondent, Tim Ewart, a producer, two technicians and two local Russian staff, who act as secretary/translators. In Europe all we have is a small Paris office with a producer, but no reporter and no crewing; we can fly a reporter in quickly. It costs about £1 million to run a foreign bureau with one reporter, one producer, local staff, air travel in the region, and getting equipment around. We have very small resources compared with the BBC.

Throughout the 1970s and most of the 1980s, the BBC's provision was quite similar. The domestic BBC TV news operation in 1987 had only five foreign bureaus. BBC Radio had a bigger team of at least twenty foreign correspondents who supplied stories to domestic BBC radio. Thirdly, there was the entirely separate BBC World Service Radio which in 1979 broadcast 230 hours a week in English and an average of 13 hours a week in each of another 37 languages.[37]

But for television foreign news film the BBC – like nearly all other TV broadcasters around the world – was relying on the London-based Visnews-Reuters news agency. Like the BBC, Visnews was a Public Service Broadcaster, not-for-profit, news organisation.

When in 1987 John Birt became the BBC Deputy Director General in charge of News, he began a major reform, especially of TV foreign news. Until 1987 the assumption was that weekly current affairs, and not daily News, was the appropriate location for foreign television reporting. John Mahoney was in charge of the small, but expanding, BBC foreign TV news when he told me in April 1990:

37 Birt, *The Harder Path*, 288.

> To my left, that's the foreign-editor-of-the-day, who is working two 16-hour days, before having several days off. The Satellite Desk, with five people, pulls in all of the satellite stuff. Our Foreign Affairs Unit is led by John Simpson – we've been working him to death. John Birt has beefed up the foreign affairs unit wonderfully. Now we have not only people with amazing experience, like John Simpson, but also some absolutely first class youngsters; Jeremy Bowen is one, Ben Brown is another.
>
> We bring in pictures especially from Visnews but also from Eurovision, NBC, CBS and CNN. Nothing goes by plane now – Visnews do twelve or fourteen satellite feeds a day to clients around the world. Our main BBC satellite contract is with BrightStar.
>
> Crewing is a mixed economy. We have permanent staff crews in Moscow and Paris and contract crews in Washington, Johannesburg, Hong Kong, and Nicosia. Or I can go freelance. Or I can send a crew from London – a correspondent, a cameraman, a sound man, a producer/fixer, an editor, and frequently an engineer. That's six people, travelling often with gear, so it's expensive. In this business, the logistics often are bigger than the story.

Television foreign news has generated its own star system. One of the top BBC correspondents can expect to be recognised, not only on the streets of London, but across the country and region on which he or she is currently reporting. During the rise of BBC TV foreign news (from 1987 onwards) the biggest single correspondent/personality was John Simpson. He worked under various titles, latterly 'BBC World Affairs Editor' but he was a reporter, not a producer. John Simpson was the BBC's number one fireman specialist always covering the top world story of the moment. He told me:

> I was the only reporter in the world who was present at, and reported on, five great events of 1989: the Soviet withdrawal from Afghanistan, the massacre in Beijing's Tiananmen Square, the collapse of the Berlin Wall, and the anti-communist revolutions in both Czechoslovakia and Romania. I agree with the W.H. Auden poem, 'Leap Before You Look'. You've got to be sensible, but not timid. It's a delicate one. I've been lucky. Dangers, explosions, angry riots, or shootings on the street – they all tend to work according to laws. Sometimes you can get up and walk about. Frankly I would not stand out in the open with a television crew in Gaza if the Israelis were doing the shooting. And I'd be careful nowadays, when I did it with the Americans. But most other armies won't shoot you if you've got a camera.
>
> I'm deeply against wars. I don't like the notion that civilians are regarded as unfortunate but inevitable targets. I've seen a lot of civilians getting hit by people who thought they had high motives. But my job is not to share my opinions. As someone

> who's been to Iraq a great deal since 1985, I have strong opinions about it. But so does every single British general I've spoken to and every single British ambassador. Not one of them thought the invasion was a good idea, or has worked out well.
>
> The domestic United States doesn't now interest me greatly. I've spent a lot of time there, especially at elections. I was there when Bill Clinton was facing impeachment. I was there for General Petraeus's report on Baghdad (September 2007). But it doesn't present much of a challenge. Americans are such good speakers. You can film pretty much anything. I like places that are more difficult. It's the same with France; it's a bit too easy. I speak good French, and have a flat in Paris, but it's too staid, not interesting enough.
>
> In my first forty years at the BBC (1966–2006) I interviewed 130 presidents, prime ministers and monarchs. These big interviews are usually booked in advance. Otherwise you can hang around for weeks. These people are fickle and often not well organised.

In addition to John Simpson, two other star foreign correspondents gave me interviews; these were Jeremy Bowen, the BBC's long-time Middle East Editor and Bill Neely of ITN/ITV. Simpson, Bowen and Neely all started young in broadcast news and did not work in newspapers. Reporting the Northern Ireland conflict was an early career experience for these three journalists. 'Reporting a massacre helped my career;' from their early reporting years, all three journalists saw a lot of dead bodies. All three had not only done many TV appearances; all three had done time as a main news presenter. Jeremy Bowen, for example, presented BBC Breakfast on TV for two years (2000–2). This extensive and intensive experience of live television helped all three men to appear cool, calm and collected on live TV, despite, perhaps, having witnessed gruesome happenings earlier in the day. All three men had covered many countries and numerous wars. All three had reported from Afghanistan, Central America, Iraq, Lebanon, Kosovo and Yugoslavia. John Simpson told me that in 40 years he had reported from 118 countries and had covered 36 wars.[38] All three of these men had

38 John Simpson, *A Mad World, My Masters* (London: Macmillan, 2001). John Simpson, *Strange Places, Questionable People* (London: Macmillan, 1998). John Simpson, *Not Quite The World's End* (London: Macmillan, 2007). John Simpson and Jana Bennett, *The Disappeared and the Mothers of the Plaza: the story of 11,000 Argentinians Who Vanished* (New York: Saint Martin's Press, 1985).

lost close colleagues or assistants. Jeremy Bowen's Lebanese driver was killed on the Lebanon/Israel border by an Israeli tank shell in May 2000.[39] Bill Neely's ITV foreign correspondent colleague, Terry Lloyd, was killed by US marines on March 22 2003 near Basra in southern Iraq. John Simpson's interpreter was killed in Northern Iraq in 2003 by an American air force bomb; 15 other people were killed in the same incident and John Simpson was hospitalised. All three of these men who were killed had been travelling in civilian cars.

In the 1990s the BBC's World Service Radio continued to be a serious force in the international flow of news. But the news agencies continued to be enormously important across the 1990s and into the 2000s. For example, a study of television coverage of the war in Bosnia-Yugoslavia commented on 'The continued power of the news agencies to define much of the news agenda from the war itself.'[40]

The Associated Press of New York from 1994 onwards became the other half of a Reuters-AP duopoly.[41] Visnews, majority owned by Reuters since 1985, became Reuters Television from 1992. Associated Press established APTN (AP Television News) – based in London. The London APTN worldwide operation was set up by Stephen Claypole,[42] a former head of the Visnews editorial operation in London. For another decade, 1995–2005, Reuters TV and APTN dominated worldwide television news. These two agencies must have played a big part in painting 'the pictures in our heads' as to what the world looked like. As predominant text-and-numbers agencies both AP and Reuters provided both the big TV pictures and the detailed small print. As Anglo agencies they surely helped to select the short snappy words and phrases which also go with the Big Pictures. Robert Fisk has suggested that many snappy news phrases – such as Spike, Surge,

39 Jeremy Bowen, *War Stories* (London: Simon and Schuster, 2006), ix–xx.

40 James Gow, Richard Paterson an Alison Preston, eds, *Bosnia By Television* (London: British Film Institute, 1996), 4.

41 'World News Duopoly' in Tunstall and Machin, *The Anglo-American Media Connection*, 77–90.

42 Stephen Claypole gave this author two interviews – one when he was still at Reuters TV, and one when at APTN.

Back-on-Track, Road Map, Fence or Security Barrier, Foreign Fighters, Armed Activists and Af-Pak (Afghanistan-Pakistan) – originate from Washington's Department of Defense and State Department.[43]

Since 2008: Decline of London as TV news hub

The decline of London as a world news hub has been evident in both television and radio news. BBC World Service Radio played a prominent part in the world flow of news until 1990. But it then fell back before the advance of satellite and internet. The Portuguese Service for Brazil was one of the first BBC language services to switch from radio to internet only. Brazil – like all of the other big population countries – hugely expanded its domestic TV news provision during the 1990s.

BBC World Service Radio was directly funded by the UK government's Foreign Office. The mantra always was that the FO selected the target list of countries, while the BBC decided what should be said. But as UK (and US) foreign policy focused on Iraq, Iran, Afghanistan and Pakistan, the 'neutral' reputation suffered considerable damage. BBC World Service Radio reached a weekly audience peak of 182 million listeners in 2007, but declined thereafter.[44]

The BBC could claim that its total foreign audience numbers were still increasing after 2008; this was because of the increasing total audience for online news, for the English language *BBC World* TV news channel and for the new high profile TV services in Arabic and Farsi (for Iran). After 2010 the Conservative government removed the BBC's World Service efforts from Foreign Office funding. The BBC, now itself having to fund the World Service radio and TV efforts, folded these services into the

43 Robert Fisk, 'Fighting Talk', *The Independent*, 21 June 2010.

44 Author interviews with Nigel Chapman, Director of BBC World Service in 2007; and with his successor, Peter Horrocks in 2010.

single, centralised, BBC London News operation. By 2012 all three previously separate foreign news teams (TV, domestic radio and world service radio) were working as a single BBC team.

Several categories of newer technology – from satellites and satellite phones to smartphones and lightweight cameras – have contributed to a transformation of both TV newsgathering and TV news worldwide distribution. John Clarke, as editorial head of Reuters Television talked to me in April 2007 about such changes occurring at that time:

> In 1995 we began 24-hour, non-stop, distribution to our customers. Now we're moving to file delivery; Reuters TV now has 80 bureaus and one thousand clients worldwide. Most clients are TV networks, but we have increasing numbers of big Online clients – Yahoo was the first. We now use smaller crews and we no longer need to take two tons of equipment into the field; things like satphones and the Internet mean that we can get a reporter or stringer sending stuff back much more quickly. Watermarking enables us to know what Reuters material our customers are using.
>
> A lot of satellite architecture used to focus on London, but less so now. People in the Middle East want news about, and supplied from, neighbouring countries. Increasingly we have focused more on Asia. Our United States clients are less and less interested in foreign news. Lifestyle, bizarre, stories – polar bear and whale stories – these get monstrously big American audiences.

Some years previous to 2007, Reuters had been giving added emphasis to financial news within both its text and TV services. Mark Wood (Reuters Editor-in-chief, 1989–2000) told me that he had increased the proportion of bureau chiefs who had a financial journalism background.

Satellite news, which in the 1970s and 1980s was a Euro-American phenomenon, had by 2007 established a major presence, especially in the big population countries such as China and India. By 2005 India already had thirteen national all-news TV channels (mainly in Hindi and English) and fifteen regional all-news TV channels (mainly in big regional languages).[45] Against such overwhelming competition, the BBC radio services in Hindi and Urdu were attracting only very small audiences.

45 Tunstall, *The Media Were American*, 189.

The BBC in practice decided in recent years to focus its foreign television effort on just a very few countries. There are targeted BBC channels in Arabic and Farsi (for Iran). The other main TV effort, led by BBC World, is in English and is targeted especially at the United States. The BBC's language radio effort now focused especially, not on the largest languages (such as Hindi and Mandarin) but on more middle-sized languages such as Hausa (Nigeria) and Swahili (East Africa). Meanwhile there is active foreign news competition in English and Arabic from Al Jazeera, as well as from Russia, from China (CCTV and Xinhua), and others.

'Are Foreign Correspondents Redundant?' was a question posed in 2011 by Richard Sambrook,[46] on the basis of his experience as a senior BBC news executive. Sambrook discussed in some detail the new technologies which generate video from non-traditional sources such as smartphone-wielding eyewitnesses to wars, disaster and other extreme events. But staff foreign correspondents are still needed for the traditional reasons. A staff correspondent from a established news organisation can broadly be trusted by the audience to be telling the truth as he, or she, sees and hears it.

The huge growth of pubic relations in the last few decades is another reason why – despite new technologies – foreign correspondents are even more essential. It is said that public relations in the UK employs more people than does journalism. New technologies now allow large companies to launch what seem to be specialist travel, documentary, or entertainment TV channels, but are in fact 100 per cent commercial propaganda. Governments put out ever larger flows of 'information'. It's also noticeable that some senior TV news executives make sideways moves into highly paid public relations work for American companies.

Today BBC News has about 120 full-time staff foreign correspondents. The largest locations are Washington, Brussels, Paris, New York and Jerusalem. Other important BBC bureau locations are Beijing, Berlin, Delhi, Dubai, Los Angeles, Mexico City, Moscow, Mumbai, Rome, Seoul and Singapore. Of the BBC correspondents based in Africa, the Middle

46 Richard Sambrook, *Are Foreign Correspondents Redundant?* (Oxford: Reuters Institute for the Study of Journalism, 2011).

East, Asia/Pacific and Latin America, about 40 per cent have local names and about 60 per cent have Anglo names. These foreign correspondents provide stories both for BBC international and BBC domestic services. A typical BBC foreign correspondent will only get onto the main BBC domestic TV or radio bulletins a few brief times a month, at most. However BBC World and the News channel can accommodate more and longer pieces.

What John Mahoney old me in 1990 is still true. The logistics can still be bigger than the story. Moreover the story (such as a complex war with a lengthy historical background) may seem too large to fit into a one, two or three minute report. Especially in war reports, there is an obvious problem of either too much 'breaking news' or too much history, statistics and facts. There are some very familiar story components – our correspondent striding down a war-torn street, a military officer interviewed, the hospital full of wounded and dying people. Such ingredients must somehow be edited into a distinctive 'news story'.

An important change in recent years is that more foreign correspondents are women. They tend to be less flamboyant than the male correspondents; they don't dress in all-white suits. But several leading women foreign correspondents in recent times have had their own distinctive styles and extensive experience. This includes Lindsey Hilsum (Channel Four) and Sue Lloyd-Roberts. Orla Guerin of the BBC reported for lengthy periods from Islamabad in Pakistan – one of the most difficult, delicate and dangerous reporting locations in the world.

Lyse Doucet spent three decades reporting for the BBC from West Africa, Kabul, Iran, Jordan, Jerusalem, Gaza, Egypt and Syria. Doucet made an impressive 2014 documentary about children in Syria. Lyse Doucet and others have shown how, by focusing on extended families, a journalist can tell a compelling story and can show how civil war impacts on an entire nation state.

The Arab spring and the Moslem winter of the 2010s have presented foreign correspondents with exceptional challenges and dangers. But some things stay the same. The Arab middle east[47] and the United States were

47 Peter Partner, *Arab Voices: the BBC Arabic Service, 1939–1988* (London: BBC, 1988).

leading foci of BBC and London foreign news in the 1930s, 1940s, and 1950s – as today. This news concern, of course, parallels the focus of successive British governments.

Greg Philo and his colleagues have researched and written at great length about British news coverage of Israel and in particular about BBC and other television coverage of the Israel-Palestine conflict. Philo and colleagues believe the British media, and BBC TV in particular, to have been biased in favour of Israel and again the Palestinians.[48] Not all will agree with Greg Philo; some will suggest that dead Palestinian children always win against smiling Israeli government publicity people. Another way of looking at reporting from Israel/Palestine is to see this as extreme example of corporate propaganda – exercised by Washington and Israel. Yet another comment is that the complexity and turbulence of the middle east can remind us of the vital role of staff correspondents on the ground.

Television news: Growth and decline

For British television news, the 1990s was a decade of growth. BBC television news greatly expanded and London-based Reuters was a leading world supplier of fast foreign news film. But since around 2008 British TV news has been in decline. BBC news has been slowly shrinking; and Reuters, no longer the world's top news agency, is now one of two New York based world news agencies.

In the 1990s the BBC's senior management encouraged BBC News to expand, and provided increased funding. But since 2008 BBC news leadership has been tentative and finance has been reduced.

New technology favoured BBC News from 1990 onwards. In particular the BBC became a British leader in online news, and in 24-hour news services. In the 2010s new technology developments have been less

48 Greg Philo and Mike Berry, *More Bad News From Israel* (London: Pluto Press, 2011).

helpful to BBC News. In particular a commercial lobby has successfully cut back on BBC online news.

Around 1990 BBC TV provided remarkable coverage of the collapse of the Soviet Union and the end of the cold war. But BBC foreign news has been more hesitant and cautious in its coverage especially of the middle east and the various Arab springs and winters. BBC World now has to compete with many more 24-hour news offerings across the world.

Back in 1990 Public Relations activity was still relatively modest and was seldom quoted by TV journalists as constituting a major problem. But in the 2010s TV journalists are more likely to see Public Relations activity as inhibiting news reporting. Both governments and commercial companies are taking image management ever more seriously. Commercial companies now operate 'TV Channels' which may look like objective news, but are PR propaganda.

One of the biggest declines since 1990 has been in weekly 'current affairs' journalism. This is the subject of the next chapter.

CHAPTER 6

First Casualty: Current Affairs

> We're doing 150 hours a year of BBC current affairs. Most of that is made in-house. We use a few independents but most indies are not interested in current affairs; the price bracket – £150,000 to £175,000 an hour – is too modest for most of them.
>
> Legal issues consume much of my time. Legal firms are much more aggressive. We want to deal properly with complaints. But when a complaint is accompanied by a legal action or legal threat, it all becomes much more cumbersome ... Every item has to be checked and double checked before it goes back to the lawyers each time. Everyone realises that litigation can work, can exert pressure. They're spending more money on it. The whole thing is becoming much more legalised, from beginning to end.
>
> We no longer see it as the audience's duty to watch us. We have to bring them in. Today we're doing short series of various kinds. These used to be five or six parts; now it's usually two or three parts – journeys for BBC2, youth things for BBC3.
>
> Online isn't in direct competition for us – It can't do the depth and length which we do. But online has increased the ways we can get our story out. This evening's *Panorama* was on Radio 4 *Today* this morning, and also on BBC Online.

Clive Edwards, who had been BBC Commissioning Editor for current affairs since 2008,[1] was speaking to me in 2011.

1 Clive Edwards was in charge of both current affairs commissioning and in-house production – an unusual combination in recent BBC history. See Katherine Rushton, 'The Commissioner, Clive Edwards: Broadening The Appeal', *Broadcast*, 12 February 2010: 14–15.

'Current Affairs' was pioneered by BBC Radio and was organisationally located in Radio 'Talks'.[2] Current Affairs moved across into both BBC TV and ITV during 1955–60; and ever since 1960 there have been debates as to how old-style radio 'talking heads' should be combined, on television, with on-location film and dramatic pictures.

TV current affairs around 1960 still had an advantage over TV News. The BBC then wanted its daily news to be mainly on Radio, while weekly current affairs would use arresting film to explain events and to track longer term trends 'behind' the daily news. But, ever since 1960, current affairs Television has, more than most genres, repeatedly been redefined, reorganised, and rethought. What should be the balance between Education, Information and Entertainment? Can popular video technology really help to explain complexity and the longer term? Current affairs – like all TV – requires a theme, a story, a narrative; but how can this be combined with the legal and regulatory requirement for political neutrality?

As the Clive Edwards quote indicates, BBC current affairs offers several sub-genres. My classification will focus on three sub-genres. Firstly, big *Filmed Investigations* such as *Panorama* have been provided on BBC1 since about 1960. Secondly, *Specialist Current Affairs* are series which focus only on UK Politics, or only on Foreign Affairs, or only on Social Social Policy. Thirdly there is *Policy Talk* – these series tend towards 'talking heads' and 'televised radio'; they account for a lot of hours – but these hours are typically at low audience times, especially around midday or late at night.

Most people who claim that TV current affairs has been, and still is, in decline are referring to the big Filmed Investigations in the *Panorama* style. Since the termination of ITV/Granada's *World in Action* (1963–98), the provision of classic filmed investigation current affairs has been dominated by the BBC's *Panorama* and Channel Four's *Dispatches*.

Since year 2000, Channel Four's *Dispatches* has been the main example, across all UK commercial television, of current affairs on the filmed

2 Grace Wyndham Goldie, *Facing the Nation: Television and Politics, 1936–76* (London: The Bodley Head, 1977).

investigation model. In the years from 2004 to about 2007, *Dispatches* made a special commitment to explaining the Middle East/Arab/Moslem world. The *Dispatches* output expanded from ten hours to thirty-three hours per year in 2006. Channel Four's then Director of Television, Kevin Lygo, told me:

> Iraq? Yes, when I joined Channel Four in 2003, well we realised how important it was. We all felt – just instinctively, as nice middle class, middle-aged, liberalish sort of people – that this Iraq thing wasn't quite right.
>
> So, it seemed to us, this was an open door for Muslims – let's get in there, let's portray them. It was awkward territory for the BBC – they can't be partisan ... I also had a personal interest. After two years as a BBC trainee (1982–4), I left television and travelled around the Islamic world a bit; I speak some Arabic and a bit of Turkish.
>
> 'What is Islam?' we wanted every aspect of that. So we did hours of 'Although they don't teach it in our schools, Islamic-art-is-wonderful'. And right on through to the cult of the suicide bomber. Retrospectively, I think you'll find there's this sort of mosaic; an impression of Muslim countries as the good, the bad and the ugly.

My check on 155 editions of *Dispatches* across the years 2007–14 showed that twenty-five per cent dealt with Muslims and the Arab world or with Muslims in the UK. In 2013 *Dispatches* moved from one hour to half hour output; Channel Four continued to rely heavily on a small group of four independent production companies to make at least half of the total *Dispatches* output.

The BBC's commitment to *Panorama* did waiver in year 2000. But *Panorama* in 2007 was returned to the popular BBC1 slot of 8.30pm on Monday – with thirty minutes as the normal length (one hour for specials). However of my non-random sample of 62 *Panorama* programmes, only fifteen per cent were about foreign countries and some of these were on 'Only in America' topics such as 'Gun Addiction' and 'Kill at Will?' But *Panorama* did offer a few productions on more demanding topics such as the civil wars in Syria and Somalia and the secret drone war in Pakistan. The senior *Panorama* reporter, John Sweeney, was reporting from inside North Korea.

Both *Panorama* and *Dispatches* since 2007 have focused very heavily on the human story, or consumer element, in politics and public affairs. There has been very little on the government in power or on what's happening to each of the major political parties; very little on any European nation or on Brussels/European Union. There has been almost nothing on national politics in the USA, India, China, Japan or Russia. Those few serious 'foreign' programmes that are offered tend to have a strong British connection such as illegal people-smuggling from Africa into the UK. A 2012 *Dispatches* programme on Syria was called 'The Real Mr and Mrs Assad' and focused on the well known fact that the Syrian President Bashar al-Assad's wife, Asma, had a British background.

Very little attention was devoted to the activities of large multinational companies from the UK, USA, Europe, China or Russia. One rare exception was an April 2012 *Panorama* half hour on 'Billionaires Behaving Badly?':

> Commodities giant Glencore, which trades in wheat, coal and copper, stands accused of reckless greed in the Democratic Republic of Congo and Colombia. John Sweeney investigates ...[3]

In this Glencore investigation we, the viewers, saw John Sweeney in Colombia interviewing a man who had killed villagers whose mistake was to have been living over a newly discovered coal mine. We saw Sweeney interview the multi-millionaire Glencore chief executive Ivan Glasenberg; and we also saw a film of Congolese teenage boys, and a ten-year-old, working illegally in deadly conditions. But why are there so few traditional Filmed Investigations of this kind? Surely we are used to national politicians, print journalists and others telling us that these giant corporations are more powerful than most national governments?

3 *Radio Times* on 16 April 2012 *Panorama*.

Big strong stories and small weak current affairs

Current Affairs television makes only modest and quite weak attempts to cover the Big Stories of the day. The main reason is that current affairs is very modestly financed; the BBC, ITV and the other main channels have chosen to spend their money on news rather than on current affairs. Meanwhile current affairs producers have decided to spend what money they do have on programme-making and not on legal fees or court cases.

The conventions and professional practices of current affairs are more demanding than those of News. In News reporting – for example, about the misbehaviour of a government, a political party, a multinational company or an entire industry – it is quite acceptable to quote one expert's research, two conflicting political opinions, or our government against their government. News of this kind is acceptable, especially if it's only 30 seconds of critique, 30 seconds of response, and 30 seconds of scene-setting film. But in a current affairs output, of 25 or 55 minutes on a single topic, more evidence is conventionally expected – such as a revealing letter or text, some secret filming or some other significant and weighty, but previously secret, evidence. Current affairs is expected actively to investigate, to reveal, and to provide space for a 200 or 300 word 'Right of Reply'. Meanwhile the Right of Reply alerts the company or organisation in question, and gives it time to launch a legal challenge. These conventions and professional practices provide very favourable opportunities for company lawyers and public relations people, employed by large international corporations.

War is often seen as the biggest and strongest running story. But current affairs must proceed with caution if 'our boys', our British service men and women, are being killed. British military involvement and over 400 British army dead in Northern Ireland (1971–90) led to major clashes between current affairs TV producers and Mrs Thatcher and other Prime Ministers. The extensive BBC television coverage of war in Afghanistan, and Iraq was largely left to News and Documentary, not to current affairs.

What about Big Stories other than War? Why so little current affairs coverage of Climate Change? Why so little criticism of big multinational companies in Energy, Pharmaceuticals, and Silicon Valley/High Tech? Each of these industries has huge companies and big consumer interest. An even bigger consumer interest prevails in food, but why so little current affairs coverage of the agricultural subsidies paid to already wealthy large farmers by both Washington and Brussels?

The consumer angle must commonly present in current affairs seems to be journalism's traditional 'Human Interest'. Victims of big business, big government and big policy, generate strong narratives and are often cheap and easy to film. This applies most of all to Children-as-Victims.[4]

Another current affairs series which often focused on children was Channel Four's *Unreported World*; its output included 'Burundi: Boys Behind Bars', 'Ukraine: the teenagers who live underground', 'Honduras: The Lost Girls', and 'China's Lost Sons'. *Unreported World* introduced its viewers to child soldiers in Africa who had been required to kill adult prisoners; young children were shown for example working in open cast copper mines in Congo (DR). *Unreported World* was remarkable also in devoting at least one 25 minute programme during 2006–13 to over 50 separate countries from Abkhazia (Georgia), Afghanistan, Angola, Bangladesh, Benin, Bolivia, Brazil, Burma, Cambodia, Cameroon, China, Colombia, Cote d'Ivoire, Darfur (Sudan) and Eritrea through the alphabet to Trinidad and Tobago, Turkey, Uganda, Ukraine, Venezuela, Vietnam, West Bank (Palestine), Western Papua, Western Sahara, Yemen and Zimbabwe. *Unreported World* also reported from some of the world's most tense international borders, including China-North Korea, Israel-Palestine, Mexico-USA, Russia-Georgia, Somalia-Yemen and Congo-Uganda-Rwanda-Burundi.

Unreported World was covering not just the world's poorest countries, but the poorest people within those poor countries. Remote rural areas of many poor countries were shown to be experiencing large-scale violence or small-scale civil war. Rural ethnic minorities both within big countries

4 For example: 'China's Stolen Children', 'Congo's Forgotten Children', 'Pakistan's Taliban Generation', 'Orphans of Burma's Cyclone', 'The Lost Girls of South Africa', 'Return to Africa's Witch Children', 'Children of Gaza', and 'Iraq-the Lost Generation'. These were all titles of *Dispatches* programmes.

like India and in smaller countries across Africa, Latin America and Asia were shown by *Unreported World* to be fighting to the death in defence of their traditional lands and forests, against the aggressive incursions of national governments and multinational companies.

Sometimes *Unreported World* programmes issued far-sighted warnings. For example, a programme transmitted on December 10 2005 far-sightedly focused on Pakistan's North West Frontier province. The youthful woman reporter, Sharmeen Chinoy Obaid, presented compelling evidence that the operations of the Pakistan Army were already in 2005 antagonising the local population. Aidan Crawley, an East Africa expert who speaks Swahili, presented several *Unreported World* accounts of Kenya's rapid growth of population, corruption, violence, and urban poverty. Kenya, said Crawley in one programme, is a human time bomb; both population and inter-tribal violence are escalating, because Kenya's larger ethnic groups are deliberately boosting population growth in order to dominate in terms of electoral politics and violence.

Ed Braman, as series producer in 2007 told me about *Unreported World*'s style of breathless words thrown back over the reporter's shoulder at the shaky handheld camera following close behind:

> The breathlessness is often because we really don't know what's going to happen. We assume that the viewer is one metre behind the reporter, and the reporter knows nothing more than the viewer ... Yes, it clearly is a style and a format – but it derives from a particular attitude to reporting, not to selling.

The two-person team (a reporter and a producer/cameraperson) were often hurrying down dubious streets, being driven to secret late night meetings, or walking through the jungle to meet the rebels. There is no time for a reporter's measured tread in front of a smoothly retreating cameraperson. Eamonn Matthews, then executive producer of *Unreported World*, told me:

> After the decision to go ahead we take about eight weeks to make our 24 minute film. The first two weeks are preparation by our reporter and producer-director. We prepare a safety protocol which is often 40 or 50 pages long. Then three weeks are spent on the ground, moving and filming; we talk with the team on the phone every

single day. They then return and spend three weeks in the edit. We get £1.5 million for 20 films or £75,000 for each half hour film.

We're looking at the world's poorest people, the 'Bottom Billion' as the economist Paul Collier[5] says. Why do they live like that? Why do they have no justice, no police force, and perhaps no medical care, no education for their children? So we're looking at the reasons for failed states: pressure on the environment, demand for commodities leading to mining in forest areas, culture clashes and cultures adapting to modernity.

Eamonn Matthews was the series producer at Mentorn of *Unreported World*, when it launched on Channel Four in autumn 2000.[6] Subsequently Matthews broke away to set up his own independent company, Quicksilver, and took *Unreported World* with him. He told me in 2010:

I worked at *Panorama*, *The Money Programme* and *Assignment*; but I often felt – not least when I spent six months in Afghanistan – that we were leaving out the best bits. Most 1990s filming was too tightly directed, and now seems desiccated. I realised that the best bits were spontaneous things, like a mortar bomb exploding. TV is best at taking you there. Most of our stories are not accessible to conventional methods. We find out how the local people get in there. This can mean walking for several days; our team walked through the Burmese jungle every day for three weeks to do Inside Burma's Secret State.[7]

The pictures do the prime storytelling. We do start with tightly argued scripts. But we always cut the film without the script; we're strongly against telling the film editor to cut back to the original script. You must be well informed and rigorous; you must also do what TV is good at – putting the viewer into a different culture. We also interview local spokespersons on the ground. But we reject the British current affairs habit of sprinkling in a lot of talking heads; we also reject the American preference for the expert-in-an-office. That's televisual illiteracy.

Whilst most *Unreported World* programmes dealt with rural areas, some looked at the position of the poorest people in some of the world's large

5 Paul Collier, *The Bottom Billion* (Oxford: Oxford University Press, 2007).

6 Christopher Dunkley, 'Even poor current affairs is better than none', *Financial Times*, September 16/17 2000.

7 The team was: Seyi Rhodes and Simon Phillips. See Simon Phillips, 'Unreported World: On a mission to expose Burma's hidden crimes', *Broadcast*, 1 May 2010: 34–5.

cities – such as Cairo, Caracas, Delhi, Kinshasa, Los Angeles, Mexico City and Rio de Janeiro – and revealed truths-stranger-than-fiction. For example, in a hospital in Caracas, Venezuela, 80 per cent of the patients have gunshot wounds. The bus service in Guatemala City has had over 100 bus drivers murdered in the previous nine months.

Unreported World was a big success in terms of press comment. But it suffered from the small audiences which are typically attracted by specialised current affairs output. Channel Four had scheduled *Unreported World* into the 7.35pm slot after the then Friday shorter, half hour, *Channel Four News*. But its audience was always smaller than the quite small News audience. It was decided that a regular audience of about 500,000 was not enough, and in 2013 *Unreported World* was relaunched with less emphasis on the rural poor. The new focus was on urban poverty, crime, corruption, injustice and squalor in such cities as Caracas, Dakar, Delhi, Mexico City, Mumbai and Pretoria.

Policy talk and ten minute current affairs

Current affairs has come to be defined in British television as having low audience numbers and receiving low financing-per-hour of output. The most expensive type of current affairs is the Filmed Investigation traditionally made by *Panorama*. Secondly specialist current affairs such as *Unreported World* is more cheaply financed. The third and cheapest category is 'talking heads' political/policy television with little location filming.

Most Policy Talk on British television is done by the BBC. *Daily Politics* (and *Sunday Politics*) consists of midday political talk supported by film clips from the Parliament Channel and elsewhere. The most prestigious outputs of this kind are on BBC1 on Sunday morning. Policy talk normally transmits only for about 34 weeks each year; these shows then follow Parliament by taking some 18 weeks of summer and other vacations. These shows, including *Newsnight* and *Question Time*, total 500 hours per year of BBC1 and BBC2 television policy talk. BBC Radio does some 200 hours of policy talk, such as *Yesterday in Parliament* and *Today in Parliament*. These outputs are quite convenient for the BBC (which can put out hundreds of hours of cheap programming) and are popular with the many politicians who like to air their views even to the small audiences involved. The BBC controls and monitors all of these shows from its political journalism location at 4 Millbank, very close to Parliament. Sue Inglish was appointed BBC 'Head of Political Programmes, Analysis and Research' in 2005. She told me that she presided over a team of about 150 people – producing political TV and radio as well as doing research.

The most popular BBC TV Policy talk show has been *Question Time* but the most prestigious, since its birth in 1980 has been *Newsnight*.[8] John Morrison, who was the then Editor of *Newsnight* told me in 1989 that 'What we do is Policy Controversy'. *Newsnight*'s weakness is too often to say at length what the daily news has already said. Many government Ministers and shadow Ministers are interviewed but these politicians can choose whether to appear; they are typically well briefed on how to defend their department's policies. There is quite a lot of frustrated 'Minister, that was not my question'. *Newsnight* has its own high quality journalists, who make some foreign trips and can talk about 'when I was in Syria/Egypt/Afghanistan just a few weeks ago.' *Newsnight* is not entirely lacking in film from outside London and from foreign places; these short pieces of film can be called 'Ten minute current affairs'. There is in fact a long tradition of short current affairs because the big current affairs shows, especially *Panorama* in the 1960s, used to do several items.

Arguably *Channel Four News* is at least as good as *Newsnight*, both in ten-minute-current-affairs and in policy talk. But neither of these shows carries as much prestige, or has such a large audience as BBC Radio Four's *Today* three hour breakfast news offering. *Today* has some advantages: it covers numerous items and also gives extended time to its chosen topics of the day. *Today* calls quickly on the reporter and correspondent strength of

8 An interesting account of *Newsnight* in and around 1997 is: Born, *Uncertain Vision*, 412–30.

BBC News. *Today* is widely acknowledged as setting the UK's daily political agenda. The fact that *Today* is both more serious and more popular than the TV breakfast shows, indicates that, at this time of the day, the audience prefers straight talk rather than talk-and-pictures.

Much the most popular of the Policy Talk programmes is *Question Time*, which began on BBC1 in 1979. *Question Time*'s once-a-week audience number is nearly as big as *Newsnight*'s total five-times-a-week audience, even though both begin at the late evening time of 10.30pm. Many of *Question Time*'s viewers evidently prefer TV political talk once, rather than five times, per week. They like the significant element of audience participation; audience members from the general public ask the questions. Politicians enjoy the rare opportunity of speaking on BBC1 television for about two minutes on each of the evening's four topics. Each *Question Time* panel normally includes three politicians, one journalist/media person and one other. Edward Havard, the then series producer, explained to me the production sequence, which is more elaborate than might appear. The audience arrive early and are carefully coached into generating the questions. The participants also arrive early (at the sometimes quite remote location) and are supplied with dinner. Skilled chairmanship – by David Dimbleby since 1994 – is also important.

To list the strengths of *Question Time* at 10.30pm must also be to indicate some of the weaknesses of *Panorama*, the classic current affairs investigative show which is on the same BBC1 TV channel at the much more audience friendly time of 8.30pm. From a producer's viewpoint, *Question Time* does have a clear format – five participants, four topics, questions from the audience about current political controversies. But within this loose framework, *Question Time* is an unscripted show which offers some spontaneity, much audience involvement, some surprises and some humour. For BBC executives the relative success of *Question Time* is yet another reminder that today's audiences prefer the quality-popular, and are less attracted in large numbers by political expertise when deployed by specialist journalists and 'experts'. Audiences prefer something more rough-and-tumble, quicker, more varied and more populist. Such as the News.

Decline from current affairs golden age?

It is commonly asserted that British current affairs TV went through a Golden Age of high profile filmed investigations in the 1960s and 1970s. Certainly British current affairs TV was then in a comparatively healthy state compared with now. Then (1960–80) BBC television News had not yet had its big expansion. Then neither British government nor big business had succeeded in vetoing certain types of critical programming. Then commercial television, especially ITV, was willing generously to fund loss-making current affairs in order to please the regulator.

Panorama celebrated its 60th birthday on BBC1 in 2013. But *This Week* did only 36 years and *World in Action* only 35 years on ITV, while *Weekend World* did 16 years on ITV.

It was only for 29 years (1963–92) that *Panorama* was on the BBC together with *World in Action* and *This Week* on ITV. It's easy to forget that all three of these series were mainly quality-popular, rather than highbrow, series. Even the excellent histories of these three series tend to emphasise a smallish proportion of the total output.[9] Certainly all three series did some high profile foreign reporting, did relentlessly investigate some miscarriage of justice cases, and did make some programmes which angered the main political parties. A few programmes became national, and even international, political events. *This Week*'s October 1973 programme (presented by Jonathan Dimbleby) showed shocking images of the Ethiopian drought – dying children, dead animals, grieving parents. But such a programme was, and is, remembered precisely because it was so exceptional. Similarly exceptional were *World In Action*'s six editions on the 'Birmingham Six'

9 Richard Lindley, *Panorama: Fifty Years of Pride and Paranoia* (London: Politico's 2002). Patricia Holland, *The Angry Buzz: This Week and Current Affairs Television* (London: I.B. Tauris, 1996). Peter Goddard, John Corner and Kay Richardson, *Public Issue Television: World in Action, 1963–98* (Manchester: Manchester University Press, 2007).

miscarriage of justice case. But *World in Action* and *This Week* together did over 2500 half hours during their lifetimes.

Brian Lapping was Executive Producer of *World in Action* during 1976–8 and made 84 half hour programmes. He had previously worked on the Daily Mirror, The Guardian and the Financial Times. *World in Action*'s output under Brian Lapping can be loosely divided into four roughly equal-sized categories. One quarter were foreign based; one quarter were domestic public affairs about UK national politics, policy and politicians; one quarter were human interest items with a serious (often consumer) angle; one quarter were human interest stories with a crime, sex or sensational theme. But not all even of the foreign stories were very serious. Eleven foreign stories reflected Brian Lapping's own interests and were highly critical stories located in Africa, Latin America and the Soviet Union. Four programmes were located in the United States; one was a critical account of Jimmy Carter's 1976 Presidential election campaign; three were imported programmes about Police forces in large American cities and were presented with a shock-horror 'only in America' framework. No less than six Foreign episodes were about groups of British businessmen on trips to foreign countries from Japan to the Netherlands; these 'export' programmes adopted a jocular serious-comic approach, focusing on bizarre confrontations, cultural misunderstandings and British self-mockery. Some of these *World in Action* stories were difficult to make, critical of governments (UK, USSR, Chile) and the kind of programme which is admired by both politicians and journalists. But some of these programmes would fit within the 'Reality' or 'Shock Doc' categories of today. Similar populist themes were present in *This Week*, which when it briefly changed its name to *TV Eye* in 1978 quickly became known by some critics as 'TV Eye, Ear, Nose and Throat', because of its obsession with medical stories.

The 1960s decade has perhaps the best claim to being a golden decade of current affairs. In particular the then three big current affairs shows were allowed to take the lead in carrying filmed reports on big foreign stories. Many big stories covered then newly independent African states – such as Congo and Nigeria and their civil wars. Vietnam provided opportunities for dramatic picture stories of Communist victory and American defeat. America itself in the 1960s provided much filmable drama and melodrama

– the assassinations of President John Kennedy, Martin Luther King, and Bobby Kennedy; the election of Richard Nixon to the Presidency in 1968 and the subsequent Watergate saga. None of these dramatic events led to serious conflict with the British government; and current affairs was still getting enough finance to take its still large film crews abroad.

The 1970s were a decade of current affairs consolidation. *Weekend World*[10] arrived as a third major weekly ITV current affairs output; the genre was well established in ITV as essential to impressing politicians, regulators and advertisers. In the 1970s these four current affairs series were together attracting a collective audience of about 20 million per week.

A big single UK current affairs topic during the 1970s and 1980s was Northern Ireland, although the number of civilian deaths peaked in the years 1971–6. Especially prominent in the resulting conflicts between politicians and journalists was Roger Bolton, as Editor of the BBC's *Panorama* during 1979–81. Subsequently Roger Bolton was Editor of Thames/ITV's *This Week* in 1988 when it put out the famous *Death on the Rock* programme which accused British Special Forces soldiers of killing unarmed IRA men in Gibraltar. Some newspapers and politicians denounced this programme, which subsequently won awards for investigative excellence.[11]

In 1992 the ITV decision was taken to close down *This Week*; Paul Jackson who as director of programmes at Carlton was the relevant commissioner, said in May 1992 that any primetime ITV series with an audience of less than six million was in danger. In fact *World in Action* and *This Week*'s combined weekly average audience had been rising from 10.4 million in 1986–7, to 11.1m in 1988–9, 11.55m in 1990–1 and 14.1 million in the first quarter of 1992.[12] These rising numbers were probably caused by several factors such as interest in the collapse of Communism in the USSR and Eastern Europe as well as some more populist commissioning (especially

10 Michael Tracey, *In The Culture of The Eye: Ten Years of Weekend World* (London: Hutchinson, 1983).

11 Roger Bolton, *Death on the Rock*. (London: W.H. Allen/Optomem, 1990).

12 Rod Powell, 'Network out of date on Current Affairs'. *Broadcast* May 15 1992.

by Paul Woolwich, the last Executive Producer of *This Week* (which duly terminated later in 1992).

1988–93 was a turbulent period also for BBC current affairs. John Birt arrived from London Weekend at the BBC in 1987 in charge of News and current affairs. Birt soon obtained more BBC money and more hours for these genres. Birt believed strongly in *Panorama* and tried to make its producers use more of the expertise of the news correspondents. Birt had another favourite project, namely specialist current affairs. In 1990–1 the BBC had four high profile specialist current affairs shows. The *Money Programme* had existed since 1966. *Public Eye* specialised on UK social policy. *Assignment* was about foreign affairs. *Taking Liberties* was about the law and miscarriages of justice. This collection of specialist current affairs shows blossomed around 1991, but soon declined.[13]

Yet another contribution to the prevailing current affairs turbulence around 1990 came from Channel Four, which from 1982 onwards launched, and then closed, a number of specialist current affairs shows. Jeremy Isaacs who had previously been in charge of both *This Week* and *Panorama* wanted to do something different. But these 'different' shows tended to have too much 'Youth', too little production and not enough audience. One early show *The Friday Alternative* started with an audience of 671,000 in November 1982 which fell to 188,000 in July 1983.[14] Channel Four did develop and sustain one successful specialist current affairs show, namely *A Week in Politics* which did studio political talk, well spiced with political humour. *A Week in Politics*, ran for Channel Four's first 15 years (1982–97); it did a total of 360 programmes, or 24 per year. The producer, and later executive producer, was Anne Lapping.

A steep decline in the quantity and quality of current affairs TV between 1977–8 and 1997–8 was reported by Steven Barnett.[15] During

13 The *Assignment* title was changed to *Correspondent* and then to *This World* which continued as a part documentary, part current affairs, foreign series – doing a few hour per year on BBC2.

14 Brown, *A License To Be Different*, 84–97.

15 Steven Barnett, *The Rise and Fall of Television Journalism* (London: Bloomsbury, 2011), 159–66.

the ensuing years, 1998–2007, mainstream current affairs nearly disappeared from the larger British TV channels. ITV closed down *World in Action* in 1998; Ray Fitzwalter[16] (who succeeded Brian Lapping at *World in Action*) had already told me in 1991: 'We're no longer doing current affairs, we're doing audience share'. Worse was to follow. *Panorama* was now the only remaining broad spectrum major current affairs series and it was demoted in 2000 from Monday mid-evening to Sunday late evening. However, the year 2007 saw the start of a modest revival. *Panorama* returned to Monday 8.30pm on BBC1; it became a half-hour series but with a few one hours each year.

For more than a decade after the 1998 end of *World in Action*, ITV had no high profile current affairs. In 1999 ITV launched the *Tonight With Trevor McDonald* series, which (without Trevor McDonald) as *Tonight* became a consumer watchdog series rather than fitting the tradition of high profile ITV current affairs. A non-systematic sample of 45 editions of *Tonight* during 2009–11 showed that three quarters of the output dealt with personal finance, health/medical, internet issues and the local environment (e.g. rubbish collection). Nevertheless ITV did, from 2011–12, cautiously tiptoe back to doing some more traditional and more investigative current affairs.

Its production system survived but will current affairs?

Despite the many changes in the decades since 1953, the broad production system of UK current affairs has changed comparatively little. The viewing public is mostly aware of the reporters who present the particular episode and the overall series anchor-presenter (if there is one). Two other key roles are those of the episode producer and the executive producer or Editor.

16 Raymond Fitzwalter, *The Dream That Died: the rise and fall of ITV* (London: Matador, 2008).

The *Panorama* presenter slot was famously occupied by Richard Dimbleby (1955–65)[17] and more recently by his son, David Dimbleby. This presenter, although vital to the overall image, is in fact a part-timer who only appears in the studio one day or so before transmission.

Each separate story is put together mainly by two people – a producer and a reporter-presenter. On a foreign story these two people travel together, accompanied by a small team including a camera person, perhaps a researcher and normally at least one translator/local fixer/driver. Usually the reporter-presenter is the senior in age and experience; these are prominent positions in television reporting. Some reporter/presenters, having worked up through the reporting ranks, are now associated with their own characteristic type of big story. Some of these people have extremely personal styles and may even be referred to as 'authors' doing 'auteur current affairs'. Julian Pettifer became a TV star with his 1960s reports on the Vietnam war. Peter Taylor achieved fame as an expert reporter on Northern Ireland and subsequently on terrorism–and–security. John Pilger was famous/notorious for his devastating critiques of American policy in Cambodia and elsewhere. Pilger became part of a new concept of 'balance' which allows one partisan leftwing output to be balanced against a subsequent partisan rightwing output.[18]

Michael Crick, the author of several exposé books and biographies, developed what he called 'Middle Distance Current Affairs', also known as ten minute current affairs. Crick focused on bye-elections and detailed political investigations; his secret weapon was humour – he excelled at revealing comic and entertaining elements in important but superficially dull political happenings.

Senior current affairs reporters tend to be in their forties or fifties and may be visiting this particular country or topic for the fortieth or fiftieth time. The accompanying episode producer is typically much younger and much less experienced; but it is the producer who is in charge. Obviously

17 Jonathan Dimbleby, *Richard Dimbleby* (London: Hodder and Stoughton, 1975).

18 Anthony Hayward, *In The Name of Justice: the television reporting of John Pilger* (London: Bloomsbury, 2001).

some of these relationships work smoothly while others generate a lot of anecdotes. The typically young producer has to organise the team and to fix up interviews – if possible on both the government and the opposition or 'rebel' side. Fixing the interview can often be more difficult than actually conducting the interview itself. Normally the reporter-presenter and the producer will jointly oversee the editing of their film into the required shape and final length.

But the executive producer or 'Editor' is the key person. He or she carries even more power and responsibility than do most executive producers. The Editor must try to defend (or expand) the annual budget, to maintain a favourable slot (such as Monday 8.30pm). The Editor is in charge of attracting and rejecting personnel – both reporters and producers. The Editor decides which topics will be covered; and then has a 'casting' problem – which producer will work amicably with which reporter? The Editor is in charge of the finances and knows that some foreign projects will be much more costly than average as well as more difficult to complete than average.

The Editor must know how to deal with commercial and political pressure. Kevin Sutcliffe, who as a Channel Four executive was for several years in charge of commissioning independent producers to make *Dispatches* programmes, told me it was important to select an independent producer who had some legal knowledge. He added:

> When you go to court you want to go with someone you know and trust. Reasonably often we are put to the test legally. You need people who know how to conduct themselves.

Another concern for the Editor is the suddenly high profile fresh topic. Editors like occasionally to produce a programme in just three days, rather than six weeks; this may require all-night working, special quickie legal advice, publicity changes, and so on.

Most Editors of major current affairs shows have been aged in their thirties when appointed, and a few were still in their late twenties. Most Editors (and especially of *Panorama*) have stayed in the job for less than three years. The BBC has in practice used the Editorship of *Panorama*, and of a few other news and current affairs outputs, as a professional training ground for subsequent senior managers. Several *Panorama* Editors kindly answered my questions over the years. The first of these was Jeremy Isaacs (*Panorama* Editor, 1965–7) who was trying – and failing – to change *Panorama* from a multi-item to a single-item-per-week programme. Brian Wenham (Editor 1969–72), like Isaacs, came from the ITV system. Peter Pagnamenta (Editor 1975–7), who was still doing two items a week, gave more prominence to his young producers and less to the famous reporters. Roger Bolton (Editor 1979–81) focused on Northern Ireland and had a turbulent time including being sacked by the BBC and then reinstated. Peter Ibbotson (Editor 1983–5) was especially concerned with decisions on foreign programmes, which were expensive and sometimes difficult to complete. Tim Gardam (Editor, 1988–90) had to absorb the Birt Revolution; Birt wanted *Panorama* to use the BBC senior news correspondents – an innovation which was subsequently discarded. Steve Hewlett (Editor 1995–7) handled the famous Princess Diana interview, in which she described her marriage to Prince Charles as involving a third person. Peter Horrocks (Editor 1997–2000) faced a difficult inheritance; despite many rumours as to its imminent death, he kept *Panorama* alive. All of these Editors had several things in common. They were all university graduates with non-science degrees mainly from Oxford and Cambridge. Nearly all of them could have been successful academics or print journalists. They had typically spent only about ten years in television before being put in charge of the BBC's flagship series.

The Executive Producers (or Editors) of ITV's *This Week* and *World in Action* were equally able and somewhat more varied. *This Week's* 1960s and early 1970s trio of Editors – Jeremy Isaacs, Phillip Whitehead and David Elstein were probably unsurpassed in terms of intellect, general television talent and urge-to-innovate. Later Editors of the ITV current affairs shows – such as Jack Saltman (*This Week*) and Ray Fitzwalter (*World in Action*) – struck me as much more cautious individuals. Jack Saltman told me in 1991:

> I'm worried that current affairs may be coming to an end. Politicians are getting much more choosey about appearing – like Chris Patten recently. Big organisations are trying to heavy us.

Roger Bolton was a unique talent who as Editor at *Panorama* and at *This Week* – was utterly determined to fulfil the historic role of revealing the truth about public events; this brought him into conflict with the IRA, the British Army, Mrs Thatcher's British Government and the BBC and ITV systems. It was widely thought that the termination of Thames TV's licence to operate in 1992 was partly due to Roger Bolton's Northern Ireland coverage. If so, this was an extreme example of the potency of the Editor/ Executive Producer role in current affairs. After the 1992 closure 'nobody offered me a job'[19] Roger Bolton told me. The Editor went down with the ship. Roger Bolton describes what it had felt like to become Editor of *Panorama* at age thirty-three:

> For me, the period of 1979 to 1981, when I was editing *Panorama*, was a golden time. I had the length of programme – fifty minutes – the staff, resources, and freedom from undue ratings pressure, to explore basic and fundamental issues and to do original journalism ... We established that Pakistan had obtained the capability to make nuclear weapons and discussed how that had been done ... Peter Taylor and Jonathan Holmes discovered the politics of hunger: the way in which food aid to the Third World was often misused on arrival ...
>
> One day I was stuck for a producer to go with Jeremy Paxman up the Khyber Pass to Afghanistan ... So I turned to a researcher just twenty-three, not long out of University ... So Robert Harris, now a distinguished author and political columnist ... got his plane ticket to Pakistan ...
>
> When Reagan came to power in 1980, I popped over the water, listened to what the new incoming administration was saying and came back to commission another Tom Mangold programme called 'The Rearming of America'.[20]

Current affairs in British television has experienced a big decline since the 1960s and 1970s. But those previous peaks were much less golden than

19 Roger Bolton subsequently established a successful independent production company and he presented many programmes on BBC Radio 4.

20 Roger Bolton, *Death on the Rock*, 112–14.

selective memory may suggest. Current affairs has even been experiencing a modest revival since 2007. Current Affairs will probably continue to do some mini-series on selected topics. It may also continue to stretch into such border areas as History, Documentary and Travel. But each of these Genres will be trying to take bites out of what used to be the protected territory of current affairs.

CHAPTER 7

Traditional Public Service BBC Genres in Decline: Education, Natural History, Science, Arts, Children's and Religion

Six broadly 'Public Service', and mainly BBC, factual genres have been in decline – especially since the loosening of public service regulation around 1990. These declining genres are Education, Natural History, Science, Arts, Children's and Religion.

Three other factual genres – Documentary, History and Travel – have succeeded in sustaining strong, and idiosyncratic, British identities, and have broadly prospered since 1990. These three successful and prosperous genres are discussed in the next chapter (Eight).

Many people in the 1990s believed that the present chapter's declining genres would be able to benefit from major TV industry changes, especially the multi-channel and online-digital revolutions. But such optimists failed to note the competitive threat from the USA, from BSkyB and from commercial British online and digital companies. American companies such as Discovery targeted these genres in general and Natural History in particular. BSkyB has targeted the Arts genre with two entire Arts channels. In Education, British and American companies combined to oppose and to terminate the BBC's digital curriculum, JAM, project. In other cases British companies such as HIT moved successfully into the American market; but HIT, which began as a producer of British children's programming eventually became a toy-and-rights subsidiary of the leading American toy company, Mattel.

The six genres discussed in this chapter have struggled to justify themselves, especially since the heavy financial cuts from around 2008 onwards. While they carry some prestige, these six genres are seen – by both politicians and the great British public – as less essential than News and Drama.

These six public service genres have mostly attracted only middling-to-low audience numbers. Executive producers and commissioners within these genres increasingly struggle to justify themselves in terms of cost-per-audience-member; they also struggle to achieve the 'slot average' rating for their particular scheduled time and channel. This often results in a continuing series being rescheduled onto a smaller channel and/or into a lower audience time of day.

These six genres – Education, Natural History, Science, Arts, Children's and Religion – loosely share a common public service history:

- After three decades of existence on BBC Radio, these genres achieved a strong 1960s and 1970s television presence on both BBC and ITV.
- During 1982–92 these genres were less likely to be on BBC1 and ITV, but more likely to be on smaller audience BBC2 and Channel 4.
- Since 1992 these genres now appear much less on any of the five major channels.
- BBC Radio (especially Radio 4) has continued to be a, or the, leading location for some of these six genres.

Meanwhile other more formatted factual genres – Cooking, Homes, Quiz/Game, and Reality – have performed well in terms of lowish cost and high-ish audience numbers. These four genres are discussed in Chapter Ten.

Fragmentation into numerous production subgenres, as well as fragmentation across numerous audience segments, characterises the six declining public service genres. Natural History involves thousands of species and locations. Science, of course, is numerous Sciences, each one highly complex and specialised. Both Arts and Music are fragmented into their own numerous styles, generations and markets. Children's programming must grapple with numerous subjects and numerous age levels within childhood. Education overall is hugely fragmented and specialised. TV Religion also has had somehow to grapple with many religions and faiths plus their internal divisions and sects. This fragmentation of subject matter and audiences obviously makes it difficult to achieve strong audience ratings. That in turn leads to diminishing budgets and a common need to look for additional coproduction finance (which can mean yet more fragmentation).

The 'public service' genres have difficulty with trying to remain in the public service mainstream. In the last few decades the tendency has been to mix all three of education/information/entertainment within a single genre and a single series. Much factual programming – including the News, Documentary and History – incorporates some humour and some entertaining detail. But humour and entertainment fit less comfortably into Science or Religion.

While these genres are not greatly favoured by licence fee or advertising finance, their fragmentation makes them highly suitable for the providers of large bundles of subscription channels. This is an especial strength of the major American companies. Discovery, Disney, Nickelodeon, and National Geographic, each spreads its programming across several channels. These American companies make Natural History, Science, Children's and Arts/Music programming on a huge scale. They distribute this output around the world and across a large collection of local national channel versions. Most of these genres can be easily dubbed or subtitled into other languages. This is especially true of cartoon/animation; some genres are broadly picture led, rather than word led, including Natural History and Art.

These big Hollywood players tend to locate their EMEA (Europe, Middle East, Africa) hub in London. They also commission some original programming from local London producers. In addition the BBC and other London producers often buy American episodes or co-produce with American producers. Consequently the BBC's or Channel Four's Natural History, Science or Arts series may include some wholly or partly made-in-USA episodes.

Channel controllers and top genre commissioners quickly recognised that the BBC's 2008 policy of 'Putting Quality First' (PQF) meant bigger than average cuts for Natural History, Science and other factual genres. In 2010, Kim Shillinglaw, the then BBC Commissioning Editor for Science and Natural History, made clear how she planned to respond to these big budget cuts. She wanted independent producers to avoid big expensive 'landmark' series, but to offer the following:

> More … Health ideas; 'real-world' Science; female-skewing shows; female talent; new natural history presenters who don't look like the same old faces; BBC1 specials

> with a big experiment or stunt at their heart; BBC4 ideas with some wit (especially in science) and a different shape to the presenter-led three-parter.
>
> Less ... Big 10-part natural history landmarks, marine science shows and medical docusoaps.[1]

Two years later, in 2012, Kim Shillinglaw was sounding still more populist:

> I'm not sitting here worrying about Science's place in the ecology of channels ... I am sitting here thinking 'we have less money, the media landscape is crowded, we do have to work harder to make what we do cut through' ... We are really restless in looking for the next new thing ...
>
> It's more the approach than the subject that I'm interested in.[2]

Kim Shillinglaw was no BBC maverick. In 2014 she became Controller of two TV channels – BBC2 and BBC4; these are the very channels on which not only Natural History and Science, but also Arts and Education mainly appear.

Education television: Boom and bust

'Education' on British television expanded during the 1960s and 1970s. But, from the mid-1980s onwards, it was driven off television by the big expansion of commercial and BBC daytime television.

During its first decade of the 1920s the BBC developed two kinds of educational output – firstly 'National Lectures' lasting one full hour and delivered by famous writers, intellectuals or scientists. Secondly, BBC Radio offered small batches of 20 minute 'Talks'.[3] In the 1940s the Radio talks took on a wartime flavour and in 1944–5 there were talks intended to assist returning service personnel in re-entering civilian life and work.

1 Katherine Rushton, 'A wider spectrum of Science,' *Broadcast*, 22 January 2010.

2 Catherine Neilan, 'The Science Innovator', *Broadcast*, 28 April 2012.

3 *The BBC Yearbook, 1932* (London: BBC, 1931), 153–81.

The 1950s saw the first big effort to take BBC Radio into schools, with the active support of the teachers.[4] Television for schools grew quite slowly; in 1962 most schools still did not have even one TV set, and TV sets were too small for effective classroom use.[5]

If there was a golden era of British educational television, it was the 1970s.[6] But in 1974–5 both primary and secondary schools had three times as many Radio as TV hours. 60 per cent of all television Education was now devoted to the Open University, while OU plus 'Further' (adult) education had 77 per cent of all education TV hours.[7]

The Open University effectively used its BBC television programming as a shop window and publicity device; scores of prominent academics appeared as visiting performers.[8] But even by its third year, there were not enough TV slots to enable each OU course to have one (25 minute) TV output per week plus one repeat. So, by the mid 1970s the Open University was already facing a TV crisis; this worsened as the BBC rapidly extended its hours to compete first with Channel Four (1982), and then with ITV's breakfast company and with the new Sky channels.

However, from the later 1980s onwards, Open University and Schools broadcasting could increasingly reach their target audiences with video recorders and subsequent technologies. The Open University developed its own YouTube channel and also put co-production finance into some mainstream BBC TV series in such genres as Art and History. But the BBC was prevented by commercial opposition from making programming for schools and schoolchildren.

After Lord Tony Hall left the Royal Opera to become BBC Director General he announced his support, in October 2013, for three big BBC projects or seasons. These were to be about the Great War (2014), Digital

4 Asa Briggs, *Competition, 1955–74* (Oxford: Oxford University Press, 1995), 932–6.

5 Harry Pilkington (chairman), *Report of the Committee* on *Broadcasting, 1960* (London: HMSO, Cmnd 1753, 1962), 104–12.

6 Anthony Bates, *Broadcasting in Education* (London: Constable, 1984).

7 Lord Annan (chairman). *Report of the Committee on the Future of Broadcasting* (London: HMSO, Cmnd 6753, 1977), 301–15.

8 Jeremy Tunstall, ed., *The Open University Opens* (London: Routledge, 1974).

Creativity (2015) and in 2016 the ultimate BBC anniversary, of Shakespeare's death in 1616. But these and a few other special projects were really all that was left of BBC TV's general education genre.

ITV and C4 have largely retreated from anything like formal education; they can argue that some of their factual output is both 'educational' and popular. But more formal or traditionally educational broadcast output is now mostly to be found on BBC Radio Four, which broadcasts on the Arts, Books, Current Affairs, Documentary, History, Natural History, Religion and Science. BBC Radio Four now devotes about thirty hours a week or 1,500 hours a year to these genres. This programming relies heavily on professors and other experts; the audience, inevitably, is somewhat upmarket and oldish.

Natural history: Genre in decline

The Natural History genre has been in decline since around 2008, despite the Natural History Unit at BBC Bristol having long been seen as a jewel in the crown of British television. From 2008 onwards the BBC allocated less money to commissioning big Natural History series. In 2008, David Attenborough, the BBC's star natural history thinker and presenter, had his 82nd birthday. Meanwhile BBC producers continued to pursue traditional 'objectivity' which ruled out any campaigning on Climate Change or other controversial public issues. Also from around 2008 onwards American channels such as Discovery,[9] Animal Planet and National Geographic Wild achieved greater strength on BSkyB and Cable.

British natural history television had its most spectacular years of success between 1979 and 1990. The leading series were: *Life on Earth* (1979, 13 hours) on Evolution; *Living Planet* (1984, 13 hours) on Ecology (organisms'

9 Ole J. Mjos, *Media Globalization and the Discovery Channel Networks* (New York: Routledge, 2010), 73–95.

relations with one another and their surroundings); *Trials of Life* (1990, 12 hours) on Ethology (animal behaviour). These more conceptual series were followed by, or overlapped with, other series, including *First Eden* (1987, 4 hours) on the Mediterranean and *Lost Worlds, Vanished Lives* (1989, 4 hours) on Fossils.

All of these series, which were both presented by and 'authored' by David Attenborough, marked the ascent of BBC Natural History. The subsequent period – 1991 to 2008, marked a plateau and included these Attenborough-authored series: *Private Life of Plants* (1995, six hours) on Plants; *Life of Birds* (1998, ten hours) on Birds; *Life of Mammals* (2002, ten hours) on Mammals; *Life in the Undergrowth* (2005, six hours) on Invertebrates; *Life in Cold Blood* (2008, five hours) on Reptiles and Amphibians.

Between 1979 and 2008 David Attenborough had completed an oeuvre of some 83 hours of authored and presented top-of-the-range natural history. Before 2008 he had already begun a new pattern by which he presented, but did not author, the series. This included three Planet Series: *Blue Planet* (2001), *Planet Earth* (2006–7), and *Frozen Planet* (2011).

Between 1990 and the downhill year of 2008, BBC natural history programming adopted numerous new technologies, such as *time-slice* which moves viewers around a scene, while time remains stopped. *Mini-cams* were being hidden in piles of dung or in pretend boulders. *Time Lapse* photography showed 24 hours of plant life in a few seconds. *High speed* shooting at several thousand frames per second revealed previously unseen movement. *Helicams*, carried by small helicopters, could now film herds of running animals from above. *Infra-red* technology improved night filming. *High Definition* (and its successors) generated better detail and allowed filming in poor light. *Underwater* technology allowed cameras to film at much greater ocean depths. *Frozen Planet* developed new techniques for filming at very low temperatures.

Previous to 1990, natural history producers used prodigal quantities of expensive film; subsequent 'film' technology was dramatically cheaper, allowing producers to use just one minute from several hundred minutes shot. Pre-production became more sophisticated, with scenes being planned and 'storyboarded' in advance. Narrative became a central concern. Natural history could no longer just show a succession of film clips; it must now have a 'story arc' with which to hook the viewer. Music became ever more central to the story-telling. Natural History, like other genres, developed a range of series categories:

Top of the Range Series, with a minimum budget of £1 million per hour. Such a series normally appears on BBC1, has at least one major co-funder, will film in multiple locations and countries and will take perhaps three years to complete.

Top BBC2 Series with a more modest budget such as £300,000 per hour is normally made in-house by BBC Bristol and typically focuses on one main country or region and one main theme. This could be *Galapagos* (BBC2, 2007), *Madagascar* (BBC2, 2011), or *Wild Brazil* (BBC2, 2014).

Variants on this were two BBC in-house anthology series, *The World About Us* (1967–86) and *Natural World* which both were a collection of single hours, each devoting one hour to a very specialised topic such as one animal in one location.

BBC3, BBC4 and the BBC children's channels are more open to independent producers, such as those located close to the BBC Natural History Unit in Bristol. Here the budgets are much smaller, such as £120,000 an hour on BBC4.

Especially since 2003 most British made natural history programming has been made by, or for, the BBC. In 2003 ITV terminated its (Anglia) *Survival* series which made more than 900 editions over a lifespan of forty-two years (1961–2003).

Channel Four, looking for something with a highish profile and lowish cost, discovered *Inside Nature's Giants*. While the BBC might spend many months pursuing one animal, Channel Four commissioned the dissection of the dead bodies of large animals. *Inside Nature's Giants* was a slightly odd mixture of horror movie and school science lesson. It favoured such 'Giants' as Elephant, Shark, Giant Squid and Polar Bear.

These self-same species also appealed to BBC programme makers, whose list of favourites included other big creatures, such as Whales, Tigers, Lions, Gorillas, Eagles and Crocodiles. BBC producers favoured the spectacular annual migrations of huge numbers of fish, birds and large mammals.

Yet another favoured category were small cute creatures such as Meerkats, Monkeys and Frogs. Big BBC series are typically edited to have a rapid pace. One episode called 'Hunters and Hunted' in the *Life* series (BBC1, 2009, 10 hours) showed mammals hunting (often in packs) in Kenya, Jordan, Belize, the UK, Florida, Alaska, Ethiopia, India, California and the Falklands. Each of the 11 hunting sequences averaged four or five minutes of spectacular and bloody action. A subsequent *Natural World* one hour ('Africa's Giant Killers', BBC2, 2014) was made by Icon Films and showed a pride of young lions in ferocious mortal combat with elephants.

BBC Bristol, in its high profile and big budget series always wanted to innovate – by using the very latest technology to film in ways which had not been previously possible. The approach also was to pursue animals across distances not previously attempted, to get close up to birds migrating over huge distances, to get close up to whales and sharks swimming in the ocean. Another expensive device was to cut quickly from one continent to another – one moment we're in the Brazilian rain forest, but a few seconds later we've switched to the Indonesian rain forest and then we switch to the Congo. Behind these few TV minutes lie hundreds of flying hours and hundreds of filming days.

All of this required a bigger organisational effort than almost any other television genre. Effectively two people were in charge of the landmark series – David Attenborough and an executive producer. Alistair Fothergill, who worked as executive producer alongside David Attenborough on several series, told me:

> David is a very special man and at every level; much more than people realise. The bit of him that's obvious is the tip of the iceberg. There's much more beneath.

On the classic or 'landmark' (in Bristol NHU speak) series, David Attenborough was effectively the 'creative' executive producer alongside a more managerial person officially designated as the executive producer. Attenborough himself played seven roles; he had the basic series idea; he determined the main theme for each episode; he was the on-site presenter, filmed close up to the target animals and speaking his own words; he then wrote (or re-wrote with the episode director) the commentary; next he spoke the commentary onto the edited film in the dubbing suite; he also wrote the quite lengthy book-of-the-series; and finally he led the publicity effort in a flurry of TV/radio/press interviews.

David Attenborough told me about the production sequence on the ten series in which he played many parts:

> When doing the original pitch, I've usually written just one sheet of A4 for each one-hour programme. Sometimes the controllers say 'No' to this idea, but ask 'Why don't you do that?' Subsequently the designated executive producer takes my summaries and presents a formal costed document. Then we are looking for co-funders. When we get the okay, I normally (but not always) review the main filming for each episode. The executive producer allocates episode producers for each of the episodes. We don't want more than one filming trip to, say, Australia. So you designate one producer to do all of the Australian filming.
>
> We use academics who know the science and where to go to, and when and how to film. There are guys out there who've spent 35 years looking at a bee or an orchid or a worm that no-one else has heard of. When you come along from the telly, they're delighted. Then if you behave in the proper way and give them credit, they're overjoyed.

David Attenborough reminded me that, while he was early into the writing, he himself was relatively late into the filming phase. Filming was broadly of two kinds. Firstly some filming was slow and could span two years. For example, the focus might be upon a specific animal at springtime when the ice is melting and the females are giving birth. Perhaps two specialised Canadian cameramen (one who films below water and one who films above water) would be employed for two spring seasons. Then there was a second phase of filming. This was when David Attenborough had flown in to perform his presenting role – to be filmed near the selected species, perhaps below ground level, or on a glacier, or high up in the canopy of a tropical rain forest.

Because the book of the series had a long lead time, Attenborough started writing the book before the filming was completed:

> I dislike writing the book. The first of these big TV book tie-ups was for Ken Clark's *Civilisation* series. He used his TV script almost verbatim. But when VHS tape came in, the function of the book changed – it was no longer to tell you what you'd seen,

> but now the book was to tell you things the TV series had not told you. The book's photographs are different, they have nothing to do with the TV series; they nearly all come from photo agencies. Writing the books doesn't take that long. I do only one draft. I start writing while the later filming is still going on. I try to leave it as late as possible.

David Attenborough was not involved in the detailed film editing but he did look in – and comment – during the lengthy editing process. Only when the film had reached its final (or almost final) edited stage did he swing into action again. This was the commentary which he both wrote and spoke:

> Commentary is a demanding kind of writing, which I enjoy much more. You don't use any adjectives; writing commentary is like joinery or carpentry. The precise word must be spoken at exactly the correct point in the film. I could easily spend an hour on one sentence. Then I'm looking at the film and my script. You try to tell the story in pictures. You only add commentary where it's absolutely necessary. Yes, in natural history we have stronger pictures (than in much other TV) so we need to say less.

At his fiftieth birthday in 1976 David Attenborough had been hard at work on his first landmark series, *Life on Earth* (BBC2, 1979). Attenborough was the right man at the right time. Attenborough had already had a distinguished career as a young 'Talks' TV producer, including working as producer of Sir Anthony Eden's key late 1956 Prime Ministerial announcement of UK war against Egypt. Attenborough had played both a producer and presenter role in *Zoo Quest* (BBC, 1954–61). Attenborough had also become Controller of the new BBC2 channel soon after its disastrous 1964 launch. He subsequently occupied still more senior BBC posts. Since BBC2 introduced colour TV in the UK, Attenborough became a colour TV expert. But the colour sets had not sold well. As late as 1975 only 43 per cent of UK television licences were for colour TV. After Attenborough left the BBC in late 1972 (aged 46) his former senior colleagues hoped that a big Natural History series would help to boost BBC revenue for the more costly colour licence. Subsequently the fact that Attenborough personally knew most of the top BBC executives was helpful to the BBC Natural History Unit in Bristol.[10]

Most British natural history programming is produced in Bristol by the BBC and some independents. This fact gives the natural history genre a unique atmosphere. The natural history genre and its active members are ahead of the TV industry in several respects – not least in their levels of scientific, as well as technical, expertise. But the danger also exists of their being out of touch with the national TV industry in London. Not only is Bristol removed from London, but natural history producers and personnel are abroad for many months at a time, working in remote parts of remote countries.

The head of the BBC Natural History Unit in Bristol needs to co-ordinate the far-flung filming teams with the Bristol-based researchers, editors and other technicians; meanwhile the NHU head must spend time every week in London talking with BBC commissioners and with visiting co-producers. Four people who had headed the NHU since 1988 gave me interviews. All four were concerned about finance. All four were aware of the need to combine scientific objectivity and political neutrality with 'passion'. People who spend weeks and months in extreme climates, waiting for animals to perform, inevitably develop strong emotional attachments to their particular species. These producers and camera people are unlikely to be cool and calm on climate change issues; and they are likely to be anxious about their next work assignment and their career prospects.

Andrew Neal was the NHU head during 1988–92 and, when he spoke with me, he was especially worried about finance. This was the time of John Birt pushing more money into BBC News; Andrew Neal complained that NHU finances were being reduced, and he was being forced to cut staff numbers. Neal told me that he favoured sponsorship finance from oil companies such as Shell; but the BBC did not go down that sponsorship path.

In 1992 some passionate Bristol disagreement led to the appointment of a new head of the NHU; he was Alistair Fothergill, then aged thirty-two.

10 David Attenborough, *Life On Air: memoirs of a Broadcaster* (London: BBC Books, 2002).

During 1993–8 the NHU roughly doubled in size and total production budget. This was probably due to a combination of Fothergill leadership, impressive big budget productions, and some luck – by the mid 1990s the BBC was putting more money into genres other than News. Alistair Fothergill, who worked on numerous projects with David Attenborough, was insistent that natural history programming should be strongly authored; he advocated close attention to audience research, to a strong main narrative plus a 'jigsaw storyline', and a conclusion in which all of the pieces come together. Alistair Forthergill has also been an advocate of making feature film versions of successful TV series. He has a long working association with Disney. Much of Alistair Fothergill's 1990s success was shared with Neil Nightingale, who was the NHU head during 2003–9.

Andrew Jackson took charge of the NHU in 2009. He had worked there previously in the 1970s, but had also built up a Bristol independent producer, Tigress. He told me:

> Natural History has a seven-year cycle; it only pays back in seven years. So BBC yearly budget rounds are a problem. But we have advantages. Our programming sells better than big frocks-and-bonnets drama, which only sell to English speaking countries. We sell to 72 countries most of which are not English speaking. Animals don't speak and our commentaries are easily translated. Foreign buyers can, if they wish, edit out our presenters and insert their own. We do extra bits of linking film to assist in this.
>
> The NHU could never have grown up outside the public sector. Our people are knowledgeable and passionate. You could make *Top Gear* without being able to drive a car. But you need to know what an animal is going to do before you can film it. Cameramen and producers get to know things about the animals which even the scientists don't know.

But, in retrospect, 2008–9 marked a turning point in UK and BBC Natural History TV. In 2008 David Attenborough completed his last all-seven-roles performance in *Life in Cold Blood*. Also in 2008–9 BBC Bristol's Natural History Unit experienced budget cuts, meaning that it must focus more on cheap-per-audience programming.

Since 2008 BBC output included more mid-priced productions about single species and single locations such as Galapagos (yet again). There were some fresh twists to single location series; *Countdown to the Rains* (BBC2,

2013) used 75 fixed rig cameras to observe large animals along a one mile stretch of a river in Zambia. Another innovation involved ten minutes to explain 'how we filmed' the other 50 minutes of a 60 minute episode. An asset here are some extremely knowledgeable and experienced camera operators. One BBC production showed a BBC cameraman going back to re-film a particular Polar Bear; another production featured a cameraman returning to India to film a specific Tiger he had previously filmed some years earlier. These productions tend to feature a rather long and slow narrative before we – and the cameraperson-presenter – say farewell to the large animal for the last time.

The *Springwatch* series developed a seasonal format which seemed to have plenty of stamina; here the focus was on the UK's smallish animals, birds, insects and trees. *Springwatch* has taken advantage of new technologies, such as multiple remote controlled cameras, and in May/June presents a live and near live daily commentary on British birds, badgers and other modestly sized creatures. *Springwatch* achieved respectable BBC2 early evening audiences such as 2.5 million; and this magazine-style format was applied to other seasons of the year.

A series like *Springwatch* employs many editors, many cameras and huge distances of cable. It then transmits a quick daily sequence of 'live' output (and some which 'we recorded earlier'). This approach generates a highish total cost but a lowish cost per-hour-broadcast. It has other advantages, such as strong storylines and narratives, as we see baby birds developing from one day to the next. These shows allow a significant element of audience participation, as members of the audience tweet and email in their comments. *Springwatch* has an element of soap appeal because it's happening in real time – those same bird species may be active in our own gardens. A huge managerial attraction of such series is that these are potentially *long running series*; they are not in the serial mode of the landmark outputs which run for six or eight hours and then stop.

Some other series have departed further from the demanding and expensive standards of the 'landmark' Attenborough series of old. Some critics assert that too much Natural History programming has become less real but more like a 'reality' entertainment format. More series now involve animals in captivity, either on farms or in animal sanctuaries, or even in zoos. One 'pioneering' series, *Hidden Kingdoms* (BBC1, 2014) showed what a mouse (or other tiny animal) would see when it looked up at an elephant. Small running animals were filmed, as if from a track-side car race camera. Another series involved cutting open and then rebuilding a hillside rabbit warren (*The Burrowers*, BBC2, 2013). Such camerawork can be seen as part of a wider Disneyfication, which includes comedians as presenters. The animals are shown almost as toy creatures or as anthropomorphic mini-humans, 'orphans' or 'plucky little chaps'.

BBC Natural History has successfully developed a group of post-Attenborough stars such as Chris Packham and Kate Humble. These presenters in fact already had decades of previous experience and expertise. Presenters are now increasingly required to mix impressive expertise with fun, games and unscripted humour.

From 2008 onwards, David Attenborough presented several short series for Sky and other commercial broadcasters. While the BBC could afford less finance for natural history, Sky and Discovery/Animal Planet commissioned more such programming from independent producers in Bristol. One such indie producer was Icon Films whose *River Monsters* series appeared on Animal Planet (Discovery) from 2009 onwards. Discovery now provides much less co-production financial support to BBC natural history. This must be worrying for the BBC NHU, because several of its most popular series – such as *Planet Earth* (2006), *Frozen Planet* (2011) and *Africa* (2013) – had Discovery co-production financial support.

The Bristol location of the BBC Natural History Unit may now be a disadvantage. It must mean that natural history is less plugged into the higher reaches of the BBC than are some other genres. ITV executives may regret the disappearance of *Survival* in 2003, while Channel Four executives may regret that they focused on merely cutting up the dead bodies of large beasts. BBC natural history producers may regret that a combination of scientific caution and BBC caution, prevented them from centrally addressing such key issues as global climate change, global population growth and the extinction of species. Subsequent generations will still be able to view the astonishing series of Attenborough and others. In some cases these will be the best available surviving pictures of animal species which did not survive.

Science: Another genre in decline

Since 1990 Science programming has been in decline on British television – especially in terms of hours of programming broadcast and total audience hours of viewing.

But much has stayed much the same. Science programming tends to focus on two extremes – at one extreme on astrophysics and its millions of light years, and at the other extreme on human bodies, human biology, and human psychology. *Horizon* has been British television's major Science series since 1964. The human body was already *Horizon*'s favourite topic in 1990 and this has been even more true since 2010. A non-random sample of 124 hours of 2007–14 *Horizon* programming involved about half of the total output being devoted to such human interest and body interest topics as: Ageing, Alcohol, Allergies, Autism, the Human Body Clock, Brains, Car Crashes, Children, Cosmetics, Diet, Decision-Making, Dead Bodies, Disaster Survival, Dogs, Dreams, Drug Abuse, Exercise, Fat, Fracking, Genius, Heart Disease, Long Life, Meat, Memory, Murder, Obesity, Organic Foods, Pain, Personality, Placebos, Pregnancy, Sight, Storms, Sugar, Surgical Mistakes, Superbugs, Talk, Taste, Violence and Weather. Several topics – such as Allergies, Fat, Meat, Personality and Sugar – have been addressed several times by *Horizon*.

Both before 1990 and after 2010, BBC Science programming depended heavily on astrophysics. By 1990 Patrick Moore had been presenting *The Sky At Night* for 43 years. When Moore died in 2012, the BBC had already anointed Professor (and former pop musician) Brian Cox as its new star of astrophysics programming. Another new academic star from a remote Science was Iain Stewart, a Geology professor.

At the other extreme, medical series in general, and surgery series in particular, were always prominent. *Your Life In Their Hands* was a medical science series, which began on BBC in 1958 and ran in short bursts until 2005. It explained common surgical procedures but it also featured two categories of contrasted humans – the anxious patients and the intrepid surgeons. These medical science series required charismatic doctors and professors. One such who began on TV before 1990, and continued after 2010, was Robert Winston – scientist, surgeon and expert on human reproduction and fertilisation. He was also an excellent performer on television, not least as presenter of *The Human Body* (BBC, 1998) which used dramatic film to track human life from conception to death.

In 1990 Robin Brightwell, who was the then Editor of *Horizon*, told me:

> We are continually having problems, if we do anything at all critical connected with pharmaceuticals or those big chemical companies. That's always very difficult and creates legal problems.

What was already 'very difficult' in 1990, was even more difficult in 2010 and after. Very little science television deals with big pharmaceutical or big chemical companies. Indeed very little Science television deals with Big Business, Big Industry, Big Government or Big Military use of Science and Technology. Nor does much programming today deal with the large overlap between Big Science and Big Technology.

British science television tends to ignore not only British companies, but it also does little to critique huge American and European multi-national companies. Any mildly sceptical person is bound to wonder whether there is any connection here with the fact that British TV science has traditionally relied on American co-producers, often from politically insecure American Public Service Broadcasting (PSB) stations, such as WGBH (Boston).

While much has stayed the same since 1990, there has been much change – mostly changes indicating decline. In 1989–90 there were six major science series running on mainstream British television – against only one or two (depending on definition) today. The Editors of all four of the BBC's then continuing Science series gave me interviews in 1989–90. *Horizon*, on BBC2, was the BBC's top-of-the-genre prestige series, then doing 18 one hours per year. Also on BBC2 was *Antenna* doing 10 one hours per year, and addressing Science from a more current affairs/policy angle. *Antenna*'s Editor was Jana Bennett.

Two somewhat more popular series, *Tomorrow's World* and *Q.E.D.*, both appeared on BBC with the mission of delivering Science and Technology topics to a large mid-evening audience. *Tomorrow's World* (BBC1, 1965–2003) eventually broadcast over one thousand 25 minute programmes. It was a feel-good, have fun, quick mix of several items. *Tomorrow's World* producers were proud of giving the great British public its first information about such new gadgets as the hole-in-the-wall ATM (in 1967) and the Barcode Reader (1983). Richard Reisz, the Editor in 1990, told me that *Tomorrow's World* did 38 episodes in 1989 with an average audience of 10.2 million. Half of *Tomorrow's World*'s five minute items were pre-recorded, and half were 'experiments' filmed live. One live item had involved setting a car on fire in the BBC Car Park in order to demonstrate a new fire extinguisher.

Q.E.D. (BBC1, 1982–98) was a more popular version of *Horizon*. David Filkin, the Editor of *Q.E.D.* in 1990 told me:

> At *Q.E.D.* I've got a loose brief to do science, medicine and technology. We're doing fourteen *Q.E.D.* 30 minute programmes a year; five of these fourteen are now being done by independents. I'm most proud of three separate programmes we've done on the soldier Simon Weston – how his face was destroyed in the Falklands War and then reshaped by surgery. These were not strictly science programmes but I'm allowed to do that. I do populist treatments on loosely science-based subjects; it overlaps a bit with BBC Documentary. We're averaging an audience of seven or eight million. A couple of years ago we got fourteen million viewers for 'The Science of Sexual Attraction'.

In the 1980s and 1990s both ITV and Channel Four offered long-running science series. ITV transmitted several medical science series, mostly presented by Doctor Miriam Stoppard. Channel Four's *Equinox* did some 200 episodes during 1986–2006. But after 2001 neither ITV nor C4 had a science series. As *Equinox* faded, Channel Four found rating success with its *Bodyshock* series.

The definition of science television has grown increasingly uncertain. But, depending on how some medical series are classified, the total UK audience hours achieved by Science programming are a little above or a little below one third of 1989 levels. Andrew Cohen, the then Editor of *Horizon*, told me in 2009 that the Science genre faced big challenges, not least the recently imposed reduction in its finances:

> People claim endlessly that *Horizon* is dumbed down. But it's an eclectic mix. It has always been an experimental strand … Getting young females, any young audience actually, is incredibly difficult. But 'How Mad Are You?', a two parter on mental illness, did well with young women …
>
> *Horizon* used to follow the science agenda, to tell the story from the perspective of science and scientists. We now try to tell it from the perspective of the audience. But audience numbers are not everything. If I commission a consumer science programme with Professor Regan, we're aiming for three million. But when I commissioned the film about CERN, 'The Six Billion Dollar Experiment', just over half a million was okay.

Perhaps 'telling it from the perspective of the audience' may make Science programming seem rather full of gloomy health advice and similar to – but less entertaining than – hospital semi-soap drama. Science programming had in the 1960s and 1970s been able to do huge coverage of Space – mainly American Space and astronauts – and fresh kinds of filmic spectacle.

The years before 1990 saw much domestic British Science programming being presented by popular professional TV presenters. *Tomorrow's World* regularly achieved audiences of over 10 million during 1965–77 when Raymond Baxter was the leading presenter. He was not a Scientist but had been a wartime Spitfire pilot and had done commentary on grand prix and other car racing. He covered such stories as the first flight of the supersonic Concorde. He combined old world charm with boyish enthusiasm for technology and speed.

Producers of Science programming subsequently preferred their presenters to be youngish professors who could combine expertise with television charisma. But in recent years there has been a tendency to allow the charismatic youngish male and female professors to share the presenting duties with comedians and actors. Meanwhile *Horizon* especially has favoured selected super colossal topics such as Asteroids, the death and depth of the Oceans, Pandemics, Solar Storms and the Earth's hot core. An especially favoured approach has been the youngish physics professor, seated on a mountain top, and discussing our distance in millions of light years from various remote galaxies. But despite numerous short series of two, three, or four hours, Science producers continue largely to ignore many, or most, established branches of both Science and Engineering.

The difficulties which confront BBC science producers were illustrated by the 200th anniversary of Charles Darwin's birth in 2009. Charles Darwin, probably Britain's (and possibly the world's) most televised great Scientist was certainly not ignored. But BBC top management allowed producers in several genres – including Science, Natural History and History each to do their own Darwin programming. In this situation Natural History (with David Attenborough) and History (with journalist Andrew Marr) took the lead. Science struggled to avoid third place in terms of publicity and audience numbers.

Science is very marginal indeed inside ITV and Channel Four. In the BBC, Science is established as a necessary, but smallish, genre, that attracts only about one per cent of BBC expenditure. Typically successful science producers – even of *Horizon* – do not advance out of science into the broader uplands of the BBC. Only one former Science producer and Editor of *Horizon* has ascended into top BBC management; this was Jana Bennett, who when she gave me an interview in 2009 was the BBC's Head of Vision (i.e. Television). At an earlier interview in 1990 she had told me:

> A lot of people in this country have a blockage about science and technology. That's sort of why Britain is in the position it's in in terms of the world's economy.

Arts on TV: Dilemmas and decline

Having peaked in the 1980s, British Arts TV went into a long decline. In 2010 *The South Bank Show*, ITV's main Arts offering, was closed down after thirty-two years and 740 episodes. Meanwhile the BBC, ITV and Channel 4 together cut their collective Arts TV expenditure from £72 million in 2006 to £44 million in 2011 – a cut, including inflation, of about half. In recent years factual entertainment formats have been cheaper.

The BBC now accounts for about three quarters of all BBC/ITV/4/5 Arts programming. But, whereas in the past the main Arts channel was BBC2, today small audience BBC4 is the main Arts TV provider. BBC4 typically has more than half of each week's top rated Arts and Music programming. A key difficulty for Arts producers is the scarcity of middlebrow or quality/popular material; there is no easy Arts equivalent of quality pop Classic FM radio, which mainly transmits small bites of famous classical composers. Nor is there much obvious equivalent to, for example, 9pm drama on BBC1 or ITV1, which typically combines popular material with quality acting.

Often the art show episode focuses on a single artist, musician or author; it consists of an extended interview plus some kind of filmed site visit – for instance to the artist's place of birth, home, studio or favourite subject matter. These art episodes offer several of the television producer's preferred ingredients – including strong visual, and often musical, material. There may be an interesting and attractive personality with a strong life story narrative. The art episode also offers appealing movement, around the art gallery, around the artist's home and hometown, or around the artist's preferred landscape. Often there is additional archive material – such as film of the artist as a young man or woman. However, the famous artist tends to be an older artist, who may not deliver a lively interview. The potential audience is fragmented. Different members of the TV audience possess very different levels of cultural capital and cultural appetite. How to compromise between posh/highbrow and pop/lowbrow? Opinion and interest are fragmented even within one art form; and Art is fragmented into numerous art forms. Books and their authors often make dull television; Opera is expensive and difficult to present; old pop music – like The Rolling Stones or The Beatles – attracts bigger TV audiences than does today's pop music.

This discussion will largely ignore pop music. But, even if TV pop music is included, it does not alter the broad picture of Arts and Music decline. There is today much less pop music on the main TV channels, compared with the 1980s. Pop music has retreated to the fringes of the television schedule, but is big on BBC Radio and on several other technology platforms. There remains a significant output of TV pop music nostalgia; BBC4 devotes many hours to pop music stars of the 1940s to the 1980s, but most of these shows typically get very modest (for pop music) audience numbers. Present day repeats of *Top of the Pops* (originally on BBC1) only get audiences of 300,000 or 400,000 – less than one tenth of their original audience numbers in the 1960s or 1970s.

When in 2010 ITV terminated the *South Bank Show*, it did launch a modest replacement show, *Perspectives*, with a small annual number of episodes. This left the BBC during the great bulk of Arts programming:

- BBC summer 'Events' – notably the classical Promenade Concerts and the pop music Glastonbury Festival.
- *Imagine* launched in 2003, with Alan Yentob as presenter-producer; it did about thirteen hours per year on BBC1.
- *The Culture Show*, on BBC2, is a several-item 'magazine' series.

But it is low audience BBC4 which now does the bulk of BBC TV's Arts hours.

BBC4 is not only unusual in specialising in Arts programming. It spends most of its money on commissioning programming into one hour a day – 9pm to 10pm. It goes on air at 7pm with BBC news and continues with many BBC repeats, which it gets almost free. BBC4 also acquires programming cheaply from the US and Europe. But within its key 9–10pm hour, BBC4 spends some £20 million a year or £400,000 a week on arts programming. Within this key hour BBC4 specialises in short runs of three or four hours described as 'series', 'seasons' or 'evenings'. About one hundred separate titles appear in the 9–10pm slot within a single year. Perhaps one third of these titles are straight arts and some are music competitions (such as *Cardiff Singer of the World*). About another third are short series – about Japan, or Brazil or the year 1965 – which are part art, part history and part documentary. Richard Klein, when Controller of BBC4 told me:

> Most channels get 50 or 60 per cent of their audience from their top ten shows; they strip and strand. We do neither. BBC4 is the Goldcard channel for the Arts. We do six or eight 'Seasons' a year. The idea is often mine. I'm a single father, who's German and loves cycling and the sea. It turns out we're doing series on Germany, fatherhood, the great outdoors, and the sea. But we've also had seasons on The Edwardians, Israel, Iraq, Modern Beauty, Japan, Rude Britannia and several on Pop Music. You need to match names with the right subject matter, such as Stephen Fry on Wagner. BBC4 wants to empower people to understand the Arts. We seek to unpack, give context,

> and explain about a wide range of art and artists ... How does a tenor sing that way? There's a huge range. Very few people want only absolutely highbrow arts. My job is to appeal to a lot of people. Yes, we use old-fashioned BBC and PSB 'hammocking'. Our 9–10pm arts programming is often hammocked between popular BBC repeats at 8pm and 10pm.

BBC4's Arts programming, despite its low audience numbers, is much written about by the TV critics in the press.

The current Controller of BBC4 is inevitably a key figure in British television Arts programming. The entire Arts TV field has been dominated by a handful of producer-presenters or writer presenters ever since 1960. The first such dominant figure, Huw Wheldon, was the producer-presenter of *Monitor* (BBC1, 1958–65) who introduced the concept of single topic one hour 'films' about artists and musicians; Wheldon later became managing-director of BBC television.[11]

Alan Yentob has been the most influential single person in British Arts TV programming. Yentob occupied a series of top BBC jobs from Head of BBC Music and Arts (1985) to Controller of BBC2, then of BBC1 and then Director of all BBC Television. Alan Yentob gave me two interviews, one in 1990 when he was BBC2 Controller and another in 2009 when he was producer-presenter *of Imagine*, the BBC's premier Arts series. He told me:

> I split my time in half. Only half my time is spent as co-executive producer of *Imagine*. If I'm on location in America, or Europe or elsewhere, I can still be doing my other BBC work. The smartphone helps. One hour of *Imagine* takes about four months, so individual producer-directors normally won't do more than two in a year. I like using freelancers who are specialists. I also greatly like some of our essay-style subjects – such as 'Are You Sitting Comfortably?' about chair design; or the recent 'Love Story' about the evolution of the love story. It reminds me of my old one on the Ford Cortina car. I've always had broad tastes which include our recent hour on a hot rapper.

11 Paul Ferris, *Sir Huge: the life of Huw Wheldon* (London: Michael Joseph, 1990), 115–62.

Alan Yentob is known for a few two and three hour specials such as *Orson Welles* (1982), *Leonardo* (2003) and *Philip Roth* (2014). Yentob added:

> When Mark Thompson arrived as BBC Director General, he made me the BBC's Creative Director. Until 2007 I was also Director of Drama and Entertainment. Now it's just two jobs – *Imagine* and BBC Creative director. I'm engaged on BBC strategy and involved in all major creative appointments.

Alan Yentob successfully maintained Arts series which were perhaps 60 per cent 'quality' and only 40 per cent 'popular'. But Yentob had had the advantage of much of his career output being heavily promoted on BBC1. Meanwhile Melvyn Bragg, as producer-presenter of the *South Bank Show* on ITV, needed to select topics which were perhaps 40 per cent 'quality' and 60 per cent 'popular'.

Ratings research has always shown that strong Arts presenters attract audiences. These presenters have often had a background in art history and as arts critics in the heavier newspapers. Robert Hughes, an established newspaper Arts critic, wrote and presented eight BBC hours of *The Shock of the New* (1980) – still said by some people to be the most influential TV Arts series ever made. Another newspaper critic who developed a no-nonsense assertive style in a long succession of TV series is Waldemar Januszczak.[12]

Yet another press Art critic, turned TV presenter, is Andrew Graham-Dixon, who has often presented *The Culture Show* as well as short, three hour, series on the art of single countries. A variation on this approach was introduced with several short Art-plus-Food series co-presented by Graham-Dixon and an Italian chef, Giorgio Locatelli. These latter shows were produced by Wall to Wall, the format specialists. This indicated the potential attractions of visiting a succession of countries with a combined Art/Food/Travel format.

Gareth Malone is another very prominent Arts presenter – of a remarkably successful BBC quality-popular format. Malone has specialised as the

12 'How I became an art critic', Waldemar Januszczak, *Sunday Times*, Culture section, 2 February 2014.

boyish-looking creator and choirmaster of groups of untrained singers. The TV audience can learn something about choral singing, but may also get some entertainment from a choir knockout contest.

In retrospect it's obvious that Arts programming has declined steeply since the late 1980s when all four then existing TV channels had a significant Arts output. BBC1 had *Omnibus*; BBC2 had *Arena* (scheduled 9.30–10.30pm) and *Bookmark*. BBC2 also offered *The Late Show* (at 11.15pm) four nights a week for most of the year. In 1990 the producers of *Omnibus*, *Arena*, *Bookmark* and *The Late Show* all told me that they had an obvious ally in their colleague, Alan Yentob, who was Controller of BBC2.[13]

In 1988 ITV had *The South Bank Show* which was still popular and was doing some 25 episodes a year at around 10pm on Sunday night. *South Bank* had actually been conceived by John Birt and the original advocate of 'quality-popular', Nick Elliott. The very first interviewee was Paul McCartney, and James Bond stars became favourites; but *South Bank* also profiled some Nobel prize winning writers, opera singers, and youthful painters and sculptors.[14]

The biggest change has been at Channel Four, which today has very little Arts output (apart from late night pop music). Back in the 1980s, Channel Four was transmitting substantial quantities of high art (and low audience) programming.[15] Because Jeremy Isaacs (C4's first CEO) was passionate about Opera, C4 was putting out twelve full length Operas per year; the normal practice was to film current theatrical Opera productions. One C4 Opera was in Sanskrit. C4 also offered several television versions of

13 These producers who gave me interviews in 1990 were: Andrew Snell, Nigel Finch, Roger Thompson, and Michael Jackson.

14 Penny Perrick, 'A far cry from Wigton', *Sunday Times*, 31 May 1992. Ciar Byrne, 'And the award for longevity goes to …', *The Independent*, 4 February 2008. John Lloyd, 'Art for everyone, not just insiders', *Financial Times*, 16/17 May 2009. Rosie Millard, 'He's going down with the flagship', *Sunday Times*, 10 May 2009 'The South Bank Show', *Private Eye*, 28 May 2009.

15 Jeremy Isaacs, *Storm Over 4: A Personal Account* (London: Weidenfeld and Nicolson, 1989), 168–70. Michael Kustow, *One in Four: a year in the life of a Channel Four commissioning editor* (London: Chatto and Windus, 1987). Dorothy Hobson, *Channel 4: the early years and the Jeremy Isaacs legacy* (London: I.B. Tauris, 2008), 72–4.

Theatre productions, including a National Theatre production, in masks, of *Oresteia* (Aeschylus) and a Royal Shakespeare Company theatrical *Nicholas Nickleby*. There was also the Indian epic, the *Mahabharata*. When Jeremy Isaacs left C4 in December 1987 to go to the Royal Opera House at Covent Garden, all of this changed. The new CEO of C4, Michael Grade, wanted less high culture and more quality popular.

Sir Jeremy Isaacs was subsequently involved in a new Arts channel (Artsworld) which in 2003 was acquired by Sky and became Sky Arts 1. Sky's Arts channels now offer a huge range of old BBC, old European and old American Arts programming – plus a small, but increasing, quantity of new, original, Arts programming. BSkyB is now using Arts programming for prestige-building purposes, and to attract upmarket advertisers – just as ITV and C4 did in the past.

Children's TV: A story of Hollywood dominance

Children's Television is unique within British TV as the only genre in which American programming has more than half of the genre's total viewing audience. There is today almost no specifically 'Children's TV' on any of the BBC's main channels or on any of ITV's four main channels, or on any of Channel Four's main channels. There is a very small audience for specifically children's TV in the form of Channel Five's 'milkshake' breakfast. In the 1970s and 1980s, children returning home from school were offered large blocks of late afternoon 'Children's' TV on the two, then dominant, channels – BBC1 and ITV. But no longer.

The BBC still produces a significant quantity of children's TV for its two dedicated children's channels; CBeebies targets pre-schoolers and CBBC targets schoolchildren. CBeebies can claim to be a big success. CBBC does quite well with children aged between four and nine, but most children aged between ten and fifteen do not want to view a TV channel which they themselves may have viewed when they were aged five, six and seven. UK children aged between ten and fifteen today devote about 80 per cent of their viewing not to children's television, but to teenage, family, and other mid-evening TV, including soaps.

Some 30 American 'Children's' TV channels are available to UK satellite or cable households. Hollywood KidVid is hugely larger than anything available in Britain. The BBC is the sole and lonely British player against the top American channel-groups, such as Disney, Nickelodeon and Warner. The American channels mostly operate on twenty-four hour schedules – in competition with the BBC's two children's half channels (which cease transmission at 7pm). ITV's Children's offer, CITV, is another half channel, which stops transmission at 6pm.

So one obvious reason for UK weakness and US strength is that the US channels, unlike the UK children's channels, are on air during the favourite children's viewing times – after 7pm. The favourite series of younger children (five to nine) are on air between 7.30 and 9.00pm. The favourite series of older children (ten to fifteen) may begin as late as 8pm or 9pm.

Children want familiarity (my favourite old series) as well as novelty (my new favourite series). Precisely what viewing actually occurs depends upon many variables including the preferences of parents and of siblings. But just as children do fresh school work each year, their TV preferences change numerous times between their second and sixteenth birthdays. If we hugely simplify by assuming that children change their TV preferences, once every eighteen months, then TV producers must provide for about nine separate 'generations' or cohorts of children. Two BBC channels, which close down at 7pm, clearly cannot match such a target.

Research by OFCOM and others has shown the increasingly large amount of time which children and teenager devote to social media and to non-television screens. Nevertheless the total viewing of television productions has not much altered, and most UK children still view some fifteen hours of TV productions per week. But producers of children's TV need to work hard, and to compete hard, in an era of multi-channel TV, of many handheld devices and of several competing screens. A child who is viewing TV may, today, also be looking at a second screen and/or using a phone.

So what do producers of children's TV and video need to have on offer? Necessary ingredients include good quality production, plenty of choice, channels not limited to daytime, plenty of programming repetition, strong marketing and publicity, and – last but not least – generous financing. However British children's TV is defeated by Hollywood kidvid on each of these necessary ingredients. Hollywood offers much more top-of-the-range programming including thousands of hours of animated cartoons; several of the most popular and longest-running children's series on the BBC are made-in-Hollywood series. In terms of choice, American kidvid offers a wide range (such as animation, 30 minute series, 'classic' movies, 11 minute series, junior drama, science-fiction and game shows). Hollywood-in-the-UK offers numerous 24 hour kidvid channels against the BBC and ITV channels which are not available after 7pm. American kidvid does huge amounts of repetition (facilitating catch-up viewing). Hollywood's publicity and marketing are somewhere between aggressive and triumphal.

Hollywood kidvid operates a business model very different from that of UK public service broadcasting. In particular, a dozen Hollywood kidvid channels each has more money than does the whole of BBC and UK children's television. The American kidvid channels are part of the major Hollywood movie/TV conglomerates. Revenue comes from several sources. American kidvid channels are in the toy business on a huge scale; general advertising (to children and parents) is crucial; the kidvid channels charge cable operators carriage fees for the right to show the channel and some are Pay channels for which subscribing households must pay extra.

The pioneering American kidvid channel was Viacom's Nickelodeon, which began its European operation in 1993. Three other big Hollywood companies, Disney, Fox and Time Warner (Turner) followed hesitantly, and not until around 1999 was the full strength of Hollywood kidvid in Europe becoming fully apparent. Viacom had begun in 1987 with MTV Europe, based in London, and playing (initially) UK and US music videos. Only after MTV Europe's increasing success with Dutch, German and British teenagers and twenty somethings, did Viacom launch Nickelodeon.[16] This was followed by pre-school Nick Junior in 1999 and Nick Toons

16 Bill Roedy, *What Makes Business Rock: building the world's largest global networks* (Hoboken, NJ: John Wiley, 2011).

(animation) in 2002; Viacom now had four London-based channels aimed across the European children's and youth market.

These American children's TV channels all derive from cable television. The US cable TV system developed in the 1980s. Cable operators, who needed to persuade the American public to pay, for the first time, to receive new TV programming, emphasised that cable channels had appeal for all family members – parents and children. In 1984 the two cable channels extracting the most fee income from local cable operators were CNN (News) and Nickelodeon (Children's).[17] Ever since the 1980s huge quantities of subscription dollars have flowed into Hollywood's Cable TV children's programming.

One final Hollywood financial advantage is that American children's television is highly suitable for exporting around the world. Much British children's TV emphasises its Britishness and its most successful export markets are Australia, Canada and Northern Europe; these, and a few other markets, are a main focus of the BBC's commercial arm, BBCW. But the American children's TV output is exported on a more genuinely worldwide scale. Animation and cartoon series travel well and can be easily revoiced into the local language or cheaply provided with subtitles. In some countries some American children's TV is available via Pay (extra) channels.

All of these financial special Hollywood features mean that British children's TV producers are competing against a Hollywood kidvid juggernaut which has not just several times, but many times, as much money. Meanwhile the BBC remains the sole significant funder of original UK children's programming. Although its present combination, of pre-school CBeebies and school-age CBBC, derives only from 2002, the BBC's broad approach has never greatly changed. The BBC's approach to children's television has always been to provide a limited daily ration of high quality children's TV, which offers some public service education and information, combined with some entertainment and humour.

Until 1990 UK Children's Television depended heavily on public service regulations. Both the BBC and ITV agreed in practice to allocate

17 Tunstall, *Communications Deregulation*, 128–32.

particular genres to specific time blocks. These included Education before 4pm; Children's programming was salient in the 4 to 6pm time slot; from the (around) 6pm News to 9pm was Family viewing time; after 9pm was adult, or unsuitable for children, programming. Suitability, or lack of suitability, for children played a big role in the whole system. Another assumption of this fairly stable system was that only a modest minority (such as fifteen or twenty per cent) of UK children's TV programming would be of Hollywood American origin.

In the decade (1955–65), after the arrival of British commercial television, there was, of course, competition between a conservative BBC and the newly arrived ITV. In some of these years, ITV did rely very heavily on inputs of *Popeye*, *Mickey Mouse* and other Hollywood classics. This period saw the publication of some pioneering social science studies of children and television.[18] In the 1960s, pop music and American westerns were very popular; some research suggested that many British children regarded American shows with horses and cowboys as similar to British shows about animals in zoos.[19] At this time children's programming was strong on BBC Radio; but the BBC Radio Children's Hour slot was abolished in 1964.

From 1965 to about 1985 specifically Children's TV had its British golden era. Throughout these two decades the two leading TV channels, BBC1 and ITV, together offered over 20 hours of designated Children's TV per week. Most of this was during 4–6pm, but both the BBC and ITV also offered children's programming on Saturday morning. The BBC offered about 60 per cent of these hours, while ITV did about 40 per cent. BBC children's programming suffered very severely from ITV competition, especially during 1958–62. But by 1964–5 the BBC was fighting back successfully with less severely educational TV and with more child-friendly fun

18 Hilde T. Himmelweit, A.N Oppenheim and Pamela Vince, *Television and the Child* (Oxford: Oxford University Press, 1958).

19 D. Harper, Joan Munro and Hilde T. Himmelweit, 'Social and Personality Factors Associated with Children's Tastes in TV Viewing' in Jeremy Tunstall, ed., *Media Sociology* (London: Constable, 1970) 363–71.

and games. Children's TV producers in the BBC grappled, over a lengthy period, with the competing demands of education and entertainment.[20]

In 1961 BBC children's TV executives decided not to show the pre-school series, *Sesame Street* which had launched on American public service TV in 1959. Monica Sims, as head of BBC children's TV, rejected *Sesame Street* because of its hectic pace, and lack of real life and topical children's experience, as well as its orientation to exports and timeless repetition. *Sesame Street* was designed for the advertising saturated US market; it was aimed at the US urban ghetto; it was too American; and it would not encourage British kids to strive towards British middle class values. These reasons, explicit and implicit, led to a BBC veto; however, ITV and Channel 4 subsequently showed the series.

The BBC's own favourite children's series was *Blue Peter*, a 'magazine' multi-item show, which launched in 1958 and transmitted over 4,000 editions across the next five decades. *Blue Peter*'s Editor for 26 years (1962–88) was Biddy Baxter,[21] who insisted that the show must go out live. This meant that the child audience could enjoy such unscripted events as a young Elephant leaving a large pile of pooh, and large puddle of urine, on the studio floor. Children were encouraged to paint, write, draw, sing and make their own small toys out of kitchen rubbish. *Blue Peter* had its own pets (cat, dog, tortoise, parrot) and its own Blue Peter Garden (complete with lawn, vegetable patch, goldfish pond, and greenhouse). Children were encouraged to write letters to *Blue Peter* and some letters were read out on air. Biddy Baxter had access to BBC research data, but she seems to have preferred the children's letters; she even claimed that the majority of new editorial ideas came from the children themselves. But all of this stress on live TV, active participation, gardens, pets, and letter writing, obviously contained an element of middle class bias. The child audience was being

20 David Buckingham, Hannah Davies, Ken Jones and Peter Kelley, *Children's Television in Britain* (London: British Film Institute, 1999), 14–44.

21 Jane Martinson, Biddy Baxter: 'I never wanted to do anything else,' *The Guardian*, 25 November 2013.

trained by *Blue Peter* for middle class British suburban life, and not for *Sesame Street*'s urban, working class, American ghetto.

Senior people in British children's television have often tended to use their own children as a test market. Lorraine Heggessey, who headed BBC Children's TV (1997–9), told me that her own children became useful advisers. This could be seen as introducing another element of middle class bias.

British children's TV series were often child versions of successful adult series. *Blue Peter* (1958) was itself a child version of *Tonight* (BBC, 1957). *Newsround* (BBC 1962) was launched by the BBC as News for the 6 to 12 year old market. *Horrible Histories* (BBC, 2009) was a children's version of *Blackadder* and *Monty Python* history. *Horrible Histories* was hosted by a rat puppet, Rattus Rattus, and leapt from one horrible history era to another, including the Groovy Greeks, the Terrible Tudors and the Vile Victorians. Favourite characters included such colourful folk as Charles II, Henry VIII and George IV. Many of the jokes were aimed at the parents as much as at the children; and, some would say, *Horrible Histories* was horribly upmarket and Cambridge Footlights.

The 1965–74 decade saw British children's TV aimed mainly at children aged between about four and fourteen. But from 1974 onwards more attention was paid to teenagers. This teenage trend began with *Tiswas* which, during 1974–82, occupied much of ITV's Saturday mornings. The BBC replied with several of its own teenage series – such as *Multi-Coloured Swap Shop* (1976–82), *Grange Hill* (1978 on) and *Byker Grove* (1989 on). These teenage series were very much in the mainstream not just of children's, but of family, television. Several youthful presenters of these shows – including Chris Tarrant, Noel Edmonds and Ant and Dec – subsequently became star presenters in major entertainment formats. In the teenage shows, some sixteen and seventeen year olds were played by actors who in fact were perhaps a few years older. The teenage show (sometimes an expensive drama) appealed to channel controllers, because it attracted not only teenagers but their younger siblings; parents also could look in to learn more about today's youth.

The boundaries of the children's genre were further eroded, or squeezed, by the UK arrival of two Australian youth-plus-family soaps, namely *Neighbours* (from 1986 on BBC1) and *Home and Away* (on ITV from 1989). Moreover *Neighbours* was soon given a 5.35pm start time (plus a lunchtime, same day transmission). This meant that BBC1 lost 20 per cent of its previous 4pm–6pm children's time slot. A decade later, in 1998, *Neighbours* was still starting on BBC1 at 5.35pm while *Home and Away* started on ITV at 5.10pm.

By 1990 British Children's programming on British television was already in decline. After 1990, the less regulated, and much more competitive, system saw British Children's programming not only squeezed out of key times like 5.30–6.00pm, but exiled to the fringes of the schedule. Then, as the number or Sky Satellite homes increased, so did the numbers of American child-dedicated channels. In 1993 four American kidvid channels in the UK accounted for 56 minutes of viewing per week in satellite and cable homes; by 1995 this had doubled to two hours. By May 1998 the most popular US show was *Sabrina, The Teenage Witch* showing on Nickelodeon; the Cartoon Channel offered several familiar cartoon titles; the Disney Channel's most popular 1998 UK offering was *Teen Angel.*

In and around 2002 the UK children's TV scene was transformed. ITV had already largely retreated from this TV genre. Meanwhile the BBC decided to remove much of its Children's programming from its main, BBC1, channel. The BBC would now designate its BBC3 as a 'Youth Channel', targeting the sixteen to thirty-four age bracket from 7pm onwards. Meanwhile the BBC launched two 7.00am to 7.00pm channels – one aimed at pre-school children (CBeebies) and another (CBBC) aimed at schoolchildren.

CBeebies can claim to have been a big production success.[22] But even the most popular CBeebies show of the week is very seldom viewed by more than seven per cent of the 0–4 age group target. Even the most popular CBBC programming is seldom viewed by more than 4 per cent of its five to fourteen target audience. Major domestic UK channels (BBC, ITV, C4 and C5) attract a child audience which is collectively about twice as high as CBeebies and CBBC combined.

22 Jeanette Steemers, *Creating Preschool Television: a story of commerce, creativity and curriculum* (London: Palgrave Macmillan, 2010).

But the BBC can claim that, by exiling children's programming from its main channel, it has been successful in terms of overall BBC market share. When children's programming was finally removed from BBC1's late afternoon schedule, BBC1's 3.00–5.15pm audience share more than doubled (+116 per cent) from 2012 to 2013.[23]

Does it matter that the UK children's television scene is now dominated by Hollywood product and companies? This is, of course, one recent example in a much longer story of Hollywood products on British screens. It is, however, an extreme example. Despite advocates of Public Service Broadcasting having, since the 1920s, emphasised the key importance of Children's broadcasting, the Children's genre is now the UK's most Hollywood-dominated TV genre.

Some people will see such an outcome as unimportant or inevitable, under conditions of free trade and scale economies. Others may see US dominance of the UK child TV market as a mechanism by which Hollywood can train up UK child consumers to become adult consumers of Hollywood's mainstream product. In many other countries the use of dubbing or subtitling into another language may mean that half the original jokes and references are missed. But British children – with no intervening translations – are more likely to comprehend many of the Hollywood references to US schools and grades, to basketball, baseball and pop music, and to the various levels of US Police forces. UK child viewers of Hollywood TV are more likely to grasp American spellings, abbreviations, regional accents and ghetto slang. By their sixteenth birthdays many young Britons are probably getting most of the references in Hollywood's adult comedies and crime sagas.

23 Stephen Price, 'PSBs: A Tough Act to Follow'. *Broadcast*, 2 August 2013.

TV religion: From worship to factual fragments

Since 1990 TV Religion has been fragmented between numerous different religions, and numerous genre approaches. This contrasts sharply with the position previous to 1939 when broadcast Religion was dominated by Protestant Christianity and BBC Radio. Fragmentation today encompasses several forms of Protestant Christianity, plus Roman Catholicism and Judaism. TV religion in the UK now embraces Muslims and Hindus in particular, but also Buddhists and Sikhs. The focus on these latter religions is an attempt to reflect patterns of immigration into the UK since 1950.

TV Religion has been fragmented not only across a dozen Christian and non-Christian faiths, but also across a range of factual genres. The prevailing approach could be described as Comparative Religion or the Sociology of Religion. But TV Religion's top-of-the-line product consists of short series produced within the genre traditions of History, Documentary, Art, Current Affairs, or Travel. Many short series dealing with religious topics have been produced within one of these various factual genres, but could have been commissioned under the 'Religion' labels of the BBC or Channel Four.

TV Religion now mainly appears in short series which are often historical accounts of religious happenings of four, ten or twenty centuries ago. The approach is picture-led and presenter-led. The focus is often on Cathedrals, Mosques and Temples, or on illustrated holy books and early documents of Christianity, Islam and Judaism. Another picture-led focus is on such holy cities as Istanbul, Jerusalem, Mecca, Rome and Varanasi. These short TV religion series are typically led by presenters who have achieved TV prominence in previous History, Documentary, Arts or Current Affairs programming. The producer and the presenter neither dogmatically defend one religion nor attack another religion. As elsewhere in television, the main intention is to tell an appealing story with an adroit mix of education, information and entertainment. But in contrast to much factual TV, producers of TV religion do not pursue the exposé approach or use secret filming. The entire enterprise of TV religion itself resembles a 'right-of-reply'. All religions today (not only Asian religions, but also the Church of England and Roman Catholicism) can be seen as minority faiths, riven by internal conflicts. UK TV Religion mostly seeks to avoid internal conflicts within specific religions; it also seeks to avoid doctrinal conflicts between Protestants and Catholics, or between Sunni and Shia Muslims.

BBC and broadcast Religion have always had elements of eccentricity. The heavy emphasis on Protestant religious worship in the 1920s and 1930s reflected the personal eccentricities of John Reith[24] as BBC Director General. Eccentricity has long characterised the BBC's breakfast religious slot, before the 8am news on BBC Radio. This breakfast religious slot had its 70th anniversary in 2009. At first called '*Lift Up Your Hearts*', it changed its name in 1970 to '*Thought For Today*'. In 1982 it was reduced from 4½ to three minutes. Since there is no religious right of reply, and since the BBC does not want religious antagonisms, 'Thought For Today' must avoid controversy and belligerent advocacy; but it can be eccentric. The BBC Radio audience has often heard the 'thoughts' of an English Bishop or a Muslim journalist. But the popular Rabbi Lionel Blue in the 1980s and 1990s was something else:

> Blue also never shrank from sharing with listeners his own inner turmoil: his mental breakdown, his homosexuality, his years in therapy, the deep arguments with his mother, their reconciliation late in life and the way, as a Jew, that he had actively considered Christianity while an undergraduate at Balliol.[25]

Thought For Today is representative of BBC Religion not only in being eccentric and non-dogmatic, but in being on BBC Radio, not TV.

The dominant broadcast partnership of Protestant religion and the BBC survived across three decades until 1955; but this was always a Radio-based dominance. From 1955 (and the arrival of ITV) the monopoly

24 Marista Leishman, *My Father: Reith of the BBC* (Edinburgh: Saint Andrew Press, 2006). Asa Briggs, *The Golden Age of Wireless* (Oxford: Oxford University Press, 1965), 227–49.

25 'The Breakfast Pulpit', in Paul Donovan, *All Our Todays* (London: Jonathan Cape, 1997), 149–73.

transformed into a broadcast duopoly which now focused on television. From 1962 to 1976 there were about five hours of TV religion per week – evenly divided between the BBC and ITV. BBC network Radio, with eight hours of religion per week still did more hours than all of television.[26] BBC Radio continues to broadcast more religion than does BBC TV.

Channel Four, in its early years, did little religion; so the (BBC + ITV) duopoly years effectively spanned 1955–90, a total of 35 years. While BBC Radio continued to do worship in the form of church services, both ITV and BBC television focused primarily on Entertainment, Spectacle and Hymns. Spectacle was provided especially by annual events at Christmas and Easter as well as the occasional royal or state marriage or funeral. Singing and Hymns were to the fore, while TV coverage focused on movement, and spectacle outside the Church building; even the November Armistice Day event has had a patriotic, rather than a religious, emphasis. The routine televising of religion depended on long-running hymn-focused series. *Songs of Praise* (BBC1) which began in 1961 celebrated its 50th anniversary in 2011.

Commercial TV ran its own version of early Sunday evening 'religious' entertainment in the form of *Stars on Sunday* (ITV, 1969–79) which focused on singing and Bible reading by Hollywood stars (such as Bing Crosby and Howard Keel) and by British stars such as Gracie Fields and the singer-comedian Harry Secombe. A subsequent 25 minute religious series, *Highway* (ITV, 1983–93) used Harry Secombe as the regular singer-presenter who also interviewed interesting local personalities, mostly from around ITV's remoter UK regions. This ITV series also did much European and world travelling, with Secombe miming his songs and hymns from Rome or Latin America, while the real recording was always done in London.[27]

26 Pilkington (chairman) *Report of the Committee on Broadcasting*, 87–92. Lord Annan, *Report of the Committee on the Future of Broadcasting*, 316–24.

27 Harry Secombe, *An Entertaining Life* (London: Robson Books, 2004).

These early Sunday evening shows, both BBC and ITV, used celebrity singing and amateur (free to TV) choirs, while providing attractive pictures of churches large and small, plus human interest interviews with worthy local personalities. But, while the BBC continued with *Songs of Praise*, the ITV companies increasingly saw *Highway*'s audience as too small, too old, and a drag on subsequent Sunday evening ratings. *Highway*, no longer required by the regulator, was demoted to Sunday morning in 1992 and terminated in 1993.

In 1990 the then *Songs of Praise* producer, Roger Hutchings, pointed out to me that the series was an Outside Broadcast with film inserts. In choosing from the many available offers, the producer needed a largish church building which could hold a largish congregation and (usually) a combination of local choirs; also required were wide aisles to allow space for cameras-on-wheels. *Songs of Praise* has not changed hugely since 1990 – but it has been somewhat speeded up; there is no sermon, few long prayers and the Bible lessons are spoken rather than formally read. There are rapid cuts and more inserts from various sources, including feature films. More (expensive) lighting is today used to great effect – so much so that in some Cathedrals two separate editions of *Songs of Praise* are produced on a single day. Another change is that the TV audience number is much smaller than in 1990.

By 1990 the BBC had already broadened its definition of TV Religion. In addition to *Songs of Praise* on Sunday evenings, BBC 'Religion' offered two series which it described as 'Religious Documentary'. These series, *Everyman* and *Heart of the Matter*, shared the 10.15pm Sunday night slot on BBC1. Both series could be described as Documentary (or Current Affairs) first, and Religion only second. Jane Drabble, the producer of *Everyman* was a rising star in BBC TV at the time; she had a Current Affairs background and told me in 1990 that she was a non-believer. But Drabble moved on to higher things (in BBC Education) and the producers at BBC Religion had difficulty in maintaining their documentary series.

From 1990 onwards there were two new pressures on TV Religion in the UK. One pressure came from events in Iraq, Afghanistan, and Pakistan which were receiving big news coverage, not least on TV. Additional pressures resulted from the growing numbers of Pakistani and other Muslim immigrants in some areas of London, Leeds-Bradford, Greater Manchester and Birmingham.

During the latter part of his (2001–4) spell as C4 chief executive, Mark Thompson approved a strong Muslim-Iraq programming emphasis across several genres. When Mark Thompson became BBC Director General in 2003 he took with him some of this enthusiasm for explicating Muslims and Muslim belief. Other people pioneered more original styles of TV Religion at Channel Four and then moved across to the BBC. One such person was Aaqil Ahmed who described himself in 2013 as 'a working class, Pakistani boy from Manchester.' Ahmed had been in charge of Religion at Channel 4, before in 2009 becoming the BBC's Head of Religion and Ethics.

Against a background of war and civil war across the Muslim and Arab worlds, BBC Religion has paid increased attention to international religion in general and to Muslim religion in particular. But BBC Religion has not attempted to rival News and Current Affairs reporting of religious war, terrorism and genocide. There is a marked reluctance to consider religion and domestic religious conflict within Iran, Israel, Pakistan, Saudi Arabia, Turkey and Yemen. Moreover while some Irish[28] and United States media investigate their domestic religious controversies, British TV Religion avoids any deep investigation of Paedophile Roman Catholic priests. British producers of TV Religion seek to reduce, not to exacerbate, conflict; and, even more so than News producers, they do not want to put their own people's lives in danger.

At the BBC both Religion and History producers make short series about religion and history. Favourite topics include the story of the Christian Bible. *Around the World in 80 Faiths* (BBC 2009) was a short series which gave about five minutes to each of 80 faiths. A favourite documentary topic has been the small but exotic community of Orthodox Hasidic Jews in Stamford Hill, North London. Other documentaries have focused on religious retreats. A documentary series which neatly encapsulated the Church of England was *Cathedrals* (BBC4, 2013); it focused on the small

28 Gordon Lynch, *The Sacred in the Modern World* (Oxford: Oxford University Press, 2012), 54–86.

numbers of active believers and clergy inside the huge cathedrals of Wells, Southwark and Wakefield.

Channel Four has continued with its slightly more edgy coverage of religion. Ramadan in Britain has been a focus for C4. This has included a prize winning 2012 two-parter, *Make Bradford British*, which adopted a 'reality' approach to encourage a brief life-swap between Muslims and non-Muslims in Bradford. A feel-good positive account of Muslims and their religion was also present in *A Very British Ramadan* (2013) in which a Muslim Rugby League professional, Rashid Khan, explained some of the problems of seasonal fasting. Channel Four also used its familiar dead body approach by allowing its Dr Death (Gunther von Hagens) to present 'The Crucifixion' on Easter Day (2012) with the help of a reconstructed human skeleton.

Producers in both BBC and C4 television share the common position of not wanting to be seen as anti-American in general or politically anti-American in particular. Issues which are seen as too political for TV religion include the possible role of Boston Roman Catholic clergy and congregations in helping to finance IRA terrorism during the Northern Ireland 'troubles'. Also seen as political, not religious, would be the issue of whether US-originated Pentecostal theology, money and televangelism, may have contributed to large scale Muslim versus Christian violence in Nigeria.

Similar anxieties carry over into domestic UK coverage of religion. Producers and editors in the News genre (TV, Radio, Online and Newspaper) do address controversial Religious topics; but all British TV Religion programming deliberately avoids certain 'controversial' topics, including these:

- Atheists, Humanists and non-believers are allowed almost no Religion broadcasting time.
- Conflict within major religions – including the Church of England, Roman Catholicism and Judaism – is avoided.
- While diverse groups within the Muslim tradition receive some Documentary, Current Affairs and Ethnic coverage, little 'Religion'

television time is devoted to internal Muslim doctrinal disputes about such issues as cousin marriage and bomb violence in the UK.[29]

- British Education policy in recent decades has provided big financial support for Religious Schools. But TV Religion has devoted little attention to what religious doctrines are taught in these schools, and what Science is censored out.

TV Religion has been ambitious and creative in picturing and presenting religious history. But it has done little to outline or explain the doctrines and beliefs which lie behind major current religious conflicts and current issues, such as personal and sexual conduct. Despite massive TV coverage of dramatic events across the Muslim world – from Africa to South East Asia – how many TV viewers (or TV Quiz participants) could distinguish between Sunni and Shia beliefs? Despite the importance of Religion in the world today, Religion has largely ceased to be a distinctive genre in British television.

Six traditional public genres in decline

The change from a few channels to hundreds of channels has involved UK television in an awkward compromise. Despite the BBC, ITV, C4 and C5 each having a number of channels, there has been neither enough time nor enough finance adequately to fund and maintain twenty-one genres.

Hollywood's and BSkyB's hugely increased channel provision has led to fragmentation beyond twenty-one genres, and into a much larger total of many sub-genres, many small audience numbers, and much scheduling repetition. UK policy has failed to analyse, or significantly to shape, this fragmented picture. Consequently we can anticipate that:

29 Robert S. Leiken, *Europe's Angry Muslims: the revolt of the second generation* (New York: Oxford University Press, 2012), 117–216.

- The six genres in this chapter – Education, Natural History, Science, Art, Children's and Religion – will continue in a downward spiral of lower audience ratings, leading to less finance, leading to still lower audience ratings.
- Meanwhile these six genres will continue to be squeezed by the relative success of Documentary, History and Travel – the subject of the next chapter.
- Another squeeze will be exerted by three major categories of Entertainment involving eight genres and dealt with in Chapters Nine, Ten and Eleven.

CHAPTER 8

Flourishing Public Service Genres: Documentary, History, Travel

Compared with Natural History/Science/Arts/Children's/Religion, the genres dealt with in this chapter have flourished in recent years. Documentary/History/ Travel have prospered for several reasons:

- Like the declining genres, these are broadly 'Public Service' genres. But these three genres – Doc/Hist/Travel – tend to offer a bigger Entertainment element. They are not quite as serious and educational.
- These genres are especially suitable for BBC2, 3 and 4 and Channel Four.
- Documentary/History/Travel score prestige points with politicians, the press, the regulators and the advertising industry. From 2000 onwards, Channel Four spent some of its profits from its *Big Broth*er reality show to finance the more prestigious and upmarket genres of Documentary, History and Travel.
- Last, but not least, is finance. These genres tend to require only modest budgets. The Doc/Hist/Travel genres are relatively cheap per audience member reached.

Audiences tend to like strong 'real life' material. These series often focus on the human *rites de passage* of birth, sex and marriage, and death. Back in 1990 a TV baby birth was unusual. But two decades later, scores of baby births were being shown on TV each year. The successful C4 *One Born Every Minute* did 4 one hour birth shows in 2012; it was competing with BBC2's *The Midwives* and other baby birth programming. BBC3, with its youth mission, takes a very active interest in sex and sexually transmitted diseases, with such entertainment-plus-education series as *Unsafe Sex in the*

City. There has also been increased factual interest in Death – in History and even in Travel, as well as in Documentary.

Amongst these genres there is an especial interest in the full life story. A classic Granada series began as *Seven Up* with 14 seven year olds in 1964. The same individuals were filmed again at seven year intervals; the eighth filming, *56 Up* (ITV) was in 2012. There is a unique audience appeal in being able to see what has happened to these individuals over half a century. This series is a triumph of Documentary but it also becomes History and has some of the appeal of art or poetry. Several other series have adopted this 'full life' approach which obviously places special demands on the producers and researchers.

Most of the major technology developments of recent years have assisted the factual series. These include online back-up and audience participation. Archive, the reuse of old programming, provides an extra depth of material for all of these genres, and not least for History. The trend towards using large numbers of fixed cameras has greatly expanded the potential of factual filming.

A completely different camera trend is towards the single person or self-shooter model. One individual, acting as both director and camera-person, can be relatively unobtrusive. Nichola Koratjitis told me how she had used this approach to make You're Not Splitting Up My Family (C4, 2008) – a single 70 minute documentary. Two twelve-year-old boy twins were being bullied by their alcoholic father. Koratjitis told me:

> For twelve weeks I filmed the family … Often I went in and sat opposite the Dad, or I would kneel on the floor to film. Both Gran and Dad were bitter, because they felt their authority was being undermined by the Social Services. Dad was drunk a lot and didn't fully understand how much he was knocking the boys about.

In recent years people in the UK and elsewhere have become more accepting of pervasive video, filming and fixed cameras. CCTV in public places is widespread in the UK. Cameraphones, smartphones and other mobile devices are commonplace. These additional video resources have made the general public more accepting of real-life filming.

Factual genres have – in recent years – attracted independent producers, large and small. Single programmes – from documentary, history or travel – are cheap to commission into anthology series – and can be seen as pilots for potential multi-part series.

These factual genres all require access of various kinds. The documentary maker requires permission to film inside a family or a prison; the history producer may need access to historic buildings; the travel producer needs similar access, plus the assistance of local experts. But, in recent years, access has become easier to obtain, as highly placed gatekeepers increasingly see filming as a public relations opportunity. In these genres there tend to be extensive discussions as to what access will, and will not, include.

Some series have no presenter. But even if there is a prominent presenter, who needs to be well paid, this person's pay-per-day is probably lower than in most other genres. Often the filming and presenting is quite quick. The research, permission seeking, and editing take longer, but are done by the modestly paid production staff.

Storyville single docs[1] often deal with US topics and about half focus on the rest of the world, including Asia, Africa and Europe. In many cases the BBC has bought the UK rights from the original producer in the country in question. Another BBC series, *Timeshift*, relies heavily on old archive film, plus interviews. It specialises in twentieth-century social history topics such as smoking, food, drinking, health before the NHS, trams and trains, the circus, ocean liners and fashion.

Channel Four's documentary flagship since 1990 has been the *Cutting Edge* series. *True Stories* appears on the More Four channel and specialises in UK 'stranger than fiction' stories, including some theatrically released documentary films of two hours. *First Cut* is a Channel Four/More Four series for directors who have not previously made a 60 minute film for TV.

These single documentary series are now less high profile, and get much smaller audiences than was the case back around 1990. Then the

1 Nick Fraser, *Why Documentaries Matter* (Oxford: Reuters Institute for the Study of Journalism, 2012).

BBC's main documentary effort consisted of an anthology one hour series on BBC1, namely *Inside Story*; and BBC2 had its own *40 Minutes* series. The executive producers of these two series (Paul Hamann and Caroline Pick) gave me interviews in 1990. These two executive producers were spending much more money on each single doc in 1990 than is the case today. In 1990 the single doc was surviving better than the single drama. Indeed in 1990 documentary in general, and the single doc in particular, was experiencing its very own golden period.

In 1990 BBC, ITV and Channel Four documentaries all had more money to spend than is the case today. In 1990 a documentary team of four or five people would travel around in a 'film bus' which typically would be carrying lighting and sound equipment as well as large cameras. A one hour documentary might have twenty or thirty filming days. Most of the people involved were securely employed on staff status; when one documentary was completed, they moved on to the next.

Today the audiences for single documentaries are much smaller. The finance in real terms is also much smaller. A typical filming crew is now often only two people and sometimes only one. Less money is spent on travel and subsistence; the crew (often one freelance producer-director and one cameraperson) may well already live near to the story – perhaps in the North of England or in North America.

Weaker in some respects, today's single documentary is stronger in other respects. Typically today's quantity of filming is much greater (perhaps 100 hours to generate one transmitted hour). The camera often goes further into intimate human areas, because the one or two person team has more time and gets better access. Often the authorship element (already strong in 1990) is stronger now. Today's producer-director, or self-shooter, may be filming a very personal theme or may be conducting a one-on-one biographical story.

But some other aspects of single docs have changed little since 1990. There is the same search for the extraordinary-within-the-ordinary. Today, as in 1990, this often is a documentary about family and children. Now, as in 1990, the newspaper critics tend to love single docs and to give them rave reviews.

In 1990, London was a favourite location:

> Rather than film in Liverpool or Newcastle, it is cheaper to concentrate on London prisons and mental hospitals, on race in Brixton, rats in Hackney and sleeping-on-the-street in the West End. Considerations of filming costs have led to massive documentary coverage of present-day Dickensian low life in London.[2]

Today this is even more true.

Observational documentary series: Hospitals, war, prison, school, family

Since summer 2011 the leading form of British TV documentary has been the traditional 'observational' (one location) doc converted into extended series form. A key obs-doc series was *24 Hours in A and E* which launched in 2011 with 14 hours of Channel Four coverage in the Accident and Emergency department of one London hospital. During 2011–13 this series completed 48 hours of fresh C4 transmissions.

24 Hours in A and E was unusual, in UK television history, in delivering so many highly intimate (and emotional) hospital happenings in close-up and in series form. The key new technology consisted of many fixed cameras, located close to doctors, nurses, patients and their anxious families. By 2012 the production team had 92 fixed cameras in place, with 100 microphones and additional mics on people. This 'rig show' approach can begin with a camera looking straight down into the recumbent patient's face; then we can see the patient being wheeled along a corridor and operated on; next we see and hear the patient talking with bedside relatives. Each one hour focuses on just two or three individual cases. Since there are fresh stories each week, the many viewers who missed last week's offering do not miss developments in a master plot; nevertheless we do 'get to know' certain doctors and nurses.

2 Tunstall, *Television Producers*, 35.

This kind of rig show documentary actually uses on screen less than one per cent of the recorded filming, so there is a huge editing task. The role of the executive producer is, as ever, crucial; this *A and E* series was by 2012 employing 170 people on the year's 14 hourly episodes. This was and is costly by documentary standards; but Channel Four scheduled the series in the 9pm top slot and was rewarded with good audiences and big prestige.

In this style of hospital doc series the producers offer two kinds of veto. As a patient, a relative, or a hospital staff member, you can firstly refuse to be filmed; and secondly you can veto the filmed and edited material from being transmitted. Obviously senior people give approval, because they think the resulting TV output will be beneficial for them and their hospital. Access agreements consequently lead to an account of the hospital as a place where people do suffer, or die, and where mistakes can occur. But the worst kinds of hospital happenings and fatal mistakes are not shown. To some degree senior hospital people are hoping that this more positive hospital coverage may counter the negative accounts of TV news and other news media.

There had been much previous filming of British hospitals and in 2010 (one year ahead of *A and E*) BBC2 had begun transmitting *Great Ormond Street* about the London children's hospital. This series often told tragic stories – for example about children needing risky brain or cancer operations – which did not make comfortable viewing. The children's hospital series offered mainly information and education. The greater audience appeal of *24 Hours in A and E* was partly due to its use of some entertainment – such as young Saturday night drunks, nurses making jokes and relatives behaving badly. In 2012 British TV showed seven hospital series. In 2013 there were eight hospital/medical series – mostly on Channel Four and the BBC channels; and this included two short series on mental hospitals. In 2013 hospital/medical series transmitted some 50 prime time series hours. A new orthodoxy had arrived in UK observational documentary.

Around the same time as the emergence of the hospital multi-camera obs-doc series, partly similar advances were made in the War Doc series. War Doc movies were already commonplace during 1940–5. But *Our War* (six hours on BBC3 in 2011–12) delivered an extraordinarily intimate account of the Afghanistan war. The intimacy was achieved by heavy reliance on the helmet cameras of soldiers-in-action. In strong Afghan sunlight the mini-cameras delivered remarkably high quality film (but somewhat scratchy sound). The producers selected from many hundreds of hours of filming; after selecting film suitable for a story narrative, the producers then added retrospective interviews with the young soldiers. Resulting from this process were close-up accounts of war's lengthy anxiety, sudden terror, endless tedium, and overall chaos. We, the viewers, 'meet' young soldiers who are later killed in action. As audience, we can easily see the muddle and confusion but can also think the overall military purpose to be elusive or mistaken. British troops, who doggedly patrol through Afghan meadows and villages, tend to step on I.E.D. bombs and to get ambushed by the Taliban. These British soldiers suspect that they are being used as bait, designed to draw the enemy into the open for the American Apache gunships. So why did the British high command allow such a series? Because they themselves could see the futility, or at least wanted the difficulties and dangers to be better appreciated back home.

Colin Barr, executive producer of *Our War* wrote in 2011:

> There's something hauntingly intimate about a teenage soldier's strangulated panic as he tries to save his dying friend.[3]

And, again, Colin Barr wrote in 2012:

> we gather footage from those soldiers on hard drives and memory sticks. You're looking for blocks of material you think can be constructed into stories and once you hit these blocks, then that's the platform on which we'll build the story ... You realise how much you resort to classic doc techniques and storytelling devices.[4]

As the British Army prepared to leave Afghanistan, there were other television series and singles which showed the shock of war as well as the physical and mental aftershocks. But *Our War* was a leader in showing how to create

3 Colin Barr, '*Our War*: Revealing the Reality of life on the frontline', *Broadcast*, 3 June 2011: 32–3.

4 Colin Barr tells Jon Creamer, 'Back To The Front', *Televisual*, August 2012: 21.

an intimate doc series out of several different Army units, all operating in one small part of a dirty and disastrous war.

Cameras were also key to the transformation of another type of observational documentary. This was the series style introduced by Channel Four's *Educating Essex* in 2012. The series focused on a single school in Harlow (Essex); its 7 transmitted hours were edited from 1,500 hours of filming, using over 60 cameras. The focus was on a limited number of human stories involving a smallish number of teachers, children and parents. Education obviously has big appeal, because we have all been to school and many of us are still actively involved in school as parents, grandparents, or as teachers. This series approach offers extraordinary human detail; we, the viewers, can follow one child from the classroom, down the corridor and into a disciplinary meeting with the head teacher. We can also follow one troubled child from the classroom, into the exams, and then pondering on the exam results. Why did the educational establishment allow such intimate access? The head teachers and other senior teachers in question must have believed (correctly) that they would make a positive impression on the TV audience. Again, veto rights were extended to all participants. Again, *Educating Essex* was an attractive formula because it could be repeated with another school in another UK region – indeed as *Educating Yorkshire* and *Educating The East End* in the following years.

Prisons have traditionally attracted movie and television interest. However, *Holloway* (ITV, 2009) was unusual because, not only was it about 'The biggest female prison in Europe', but it was a short series, not a single doc. Paul Hamann was the executive producer, who back in 1989 had been the hands-on producer of *Fourteen Days in May* (BBC1, 1989) about the last fourteen days of a black Mississippi man who was being executed for a murder which he did not commit. This chilling experience led Hamann to found the human rights charity Reprieve with the lawyer Clive Stafford Smith. During 2009–13 Paul Hamann executive produced four separate short documentary series in prisons – *Holloway*, *Wormwood Scrubs*, *Strangeways* and *Her Majesty's Prison, Aylesbury*. Each short series involved many weeks and months of filming inside one prison. Why did the Prison Governors and their superiors allow filming which showed such things as prisoner suicide, and the prevalence of forbidden drugs? These doc series presented a broadly positive view of Governors and prison officers, who admitted that many prisoners were mentally ill. Here again the people in charge were granting access for their own good reasons. Meanwhile the obs documentary was showing elements of prison culture not previously available on TV or in movies.

Families have been another traditional focus for observational documentaries – usually involving one transmitted hour entirely about one family. But Paul Watson's *The Family* (for BBC1 in 1974) was a 12 part doc about a single family; Watson used a single camera crew continuously in the family home for three months. More recently the Firefly indie company, with *The Family* (C4, 2009), used the rig show approach to make significant advances. The first series used 21 fixed cameras in the family home and employed 40 full-time personnel (located in nearby buildings) who recorded over 50 hours per day for 112 days; this resulted in a total of eight transmitted hours. Next year *The Family* returned with a different family and 28 fixed cameras.[5] These series revealed, if not all, then much about the dynamics of family life with, for example, many confrontations between parents and children.

Arguably the human family has remained the prime focus of the observational documentary in series form. All of the previously discussed obs doc subjects include elements of family. In Hospital docs the relatives of the patients are usually central to the storyline. In all War docs the soldiers talk about their families and in After the War docs, about wounded soldiers, the family is central. In school docs the children are portrayed as moving between school and family. In Prison docs, again, the prisoners talk and think about their partners and children and about being with family after serving the prison term. Family themes similarly enter into other favourite obs doc locations such as hotels, workplaces, and housing.

Workplaces provide human interaction within a fixed group of fellow workers. Supermarkets, luxury retailers, antique dealers and betting shops as well as ships, airlines, banks and offices all provide distinctive settings,

5 Nick Curwin, 'The Family: Up close and personal'. *Broadcast*, 12 September 2008: 27.

with plenty of visible human interaction and narrative opportunities. Hotels attract documentary producers. With luxury hotels in London and Mumbai, we get some enticing glimpses of the international super-rich, including plenty of crown princes and expensive clothes, plus a small army of butlers, beauticians, chauffeurs, and other idiosyncratic servants (and dogs). Meanwhile *The Hotel* series (C4, 2011–13) was located in much more modest British family holiday hotels. *The Hotel* used its numerous fixed cameras – in the reception area, dining room, guest bedrooms, on balconies, in the kitchen, driveway and bar – to reveal to us, the audience, many small malfunctions of family and hotel life. It was unclear why these hotel managers had allowed the multiple cameras into their chaotic hotels. But one owner-manager seemed to be hoping (in vain) that the publicity would help him to sell the hotel at a good price.

Meanwhile, the Police are the UK's most experienced granters of TV documentary access. Around 1990 the Police were already allowing TV cameras into their helicopters to film stolen car chases.[6] More than two decades later, the BBC and C4 were showing such series as *Traffic Cops*, *Motorway Cops*, *Coppers*, and *999: What's Your Emergency?* By providing access to police cars and to helicopter film, Police managers realise that they are shaping the filming and providing TV producers with attractive ingredients. Filming from inside a police car provides car chases (often linked to helicopter film). Police men and women are portrayed as decent middle classish people, doing a difficult job quite well. Also the viewers get to meet many tragic-comical examples of low-life UK; we meet drug addicts, a man who's been in prison 25 times, and some very drunk drivers; but we also discover that many 'villains' have had horrible childhoods. In particular, these Police series are quite cheap to make (despite heavy editing) and offer the humour which UK audiences like. Needless to say we, the viewers, in these pro-Police series, see few cases of people who die while

6 For instance: 'Joyriders' (ITV, Central) which showed helicopter views of car chases in Oxford and Northampton; transmitted 4 October 1991; executive producer: Steve Clark.

in police custody and few examples of police refusing to investigate rape allegations in order to maintain their statistics of success.

Topic docs: America, Royals, Muslims

Favourite topics for British documentaries include 'Only in America' happenings and people, Muslim people and issues, and the British Royal Family in its numerous locations and manifestations.

More UK topic docs focus on the United States than on any other subject area. UK producers prefer extremes of various kinds – such as the seriously wealthy and the thirty million poorest Americans. Wealthy American documentary subjects have included numerous senior executives from Wall Street and Silicon Valley. Such billionaires as Donald Trump and Dick Fuld (of Lehmann Brothers bank, circa 2008) have been made to seem like characters out of a Disney cartoon. Looking at the other end of society, many British docs film inside American prisons, focusing on Death Row, and on huge prisons in places like Miami where thousands of prisoners experience a punitive and violent regime. Across America we meet a lot of poor people (black and white) with mental, drug, housing, and unemployment problems. Another focus is upon selected religious zealots attached to various Protestant sects. Why do British producers choose such extreme topics? An obvious reason is that, like Hollywood's TV-Movie-Video Game portrayals, these extreme and violent themes are popular audience entertainment. British producers film, of course, in California and New York, but also in such hinterland states such as Nevada and Arizona, West Virginia and Ohio. With so many local governments (state, city, county), access is often (but not always) easy to achieve. Usually the filming light is better, and the temperature warmer, than in London.

A leading maker of these British Only in America documentaries is Louis Theroux. He acts both as the presenter and co-producer of such shows. We, the British audience, know that Theroux is a man with a very sharp mind who exudes surface naivety and hesitation. The Americans, who are being interviewed by Theroux, tend to be rash and talkative. These people don't recognise that, while they might seem over-assertive even to an American audience, to a British audience, many of these Only In America Americans seem vain, obsessive and weird. Nevertheless the Theroux portrayals, while relying on his faux naivety, are not entirely unkind. Often there is some tragic-comic mix. In 'Twilight of the Porn Stars' (BBC2, 2012) Theroux returns to the Pornographic film branch of Hollywood (in North Los Angeles), but times now are bad compared with a previous Theroux visit 15 years earlier. Now the porn movie business has been ruined by the do-it-yourself free competition on the internet. We meet, and start to feel sorry for, Tommy who has been a reliable performer in 1,100 sex films; we also meet a cameraman who has filmed 3,000 porn epics.

We can feel additional tragic-comedy sympathy in a non-Theroux product such as 'The Queen of Versailles' (BBC4, 2013). Here David Siegel, a time share billionaire is building a Florida Versailles of 90,000 square feet and with 30 bathrooms. His wife is a former beauty queen. But as the documentary filming continues, Siegel's property business collapses, while the gigantic house is not yet finished. Suddenly the Siegels cease to be monsters and become sad characters with some endearing qualities.

The British Royal Family has been another focus of the topic documentary extremes of either dire deference or shock doc revelation. For about three decades (1947–77), TV coverage of the royal family was deferential both on the News and in occasional carefully controlled royal family docs with the emphasis on 'family'. But 1992 was what Queen Elizabeth called her *Annus Horribilis*, when the Prince Charles marriage collapsed, and other negative things happened. Since 1992 Grand Event, and deferential, royal coverage (births, marriages, funerals, anniversaries) and daily news coverage have continued.

Most of the increasing quantity of royal topic documentaries was deferential – with such titles as The Queen's Palaces, 'Philip at 90', Diamond Queen, and Our Queen. Those who arrange access for such TV royal docs must hope that the great British public will love what it sees. But there is an obvious alternative reading – that these docs reveal a royal family living in super wealthy luxury, including huge palaces at Windsor, Sandringham and Balmoral and a huge weekday office building (Buckingham Palace). The royals can be seen as a super-rich family, completely out of touch with the real concerns of the British people, and surrounded by super-rich friends, relatives and neighbours.

These royal docs have posed additional dilemmas, of which Charles was the most obvious. In 1977 Prince Charles left the Navy. For the previous decade he had been a student at Cambridge and then a military officer under military public relations wraps. In the year 1977 Charles suddenly ceased to be the silent service man, and quickly became the royal Issues Man. He began to make a succession of speeches in which he expressed strong views about architecture, medicine, the environment, organic agriculture, religion, education and many other 'non-political' public issues. This made Charles highly suitable for themed documentaries or topic docs. Charles was doubly suitable because the Issues Man was initially (1977–81) also the bachelor royal prince in search of a wife; then he was married to Diana; separated and divorced from Diana; and finally Diana was killed in the Paris car crash in 1997. For two full decades (1977–97) Charles-and-his-issues plus Charles-and-his-women, attracted very broad public interest. Documentary and Arts producers told me in 1990 that their most ratings popular topics were Ancient Egypt, Prince Charles and David Hockney.

Less deferential, or more shockdoc, topics of recent decades included the sex lives, finances and relatives of the core Windsor family. Andrew Morton reports that Charles once said to Diana: 'Do you really expect me to be the first Prince of Wales not to have a mistress?'[7] Charles (and his mother, Queen Elizabeth) were obviously well aware of this tradition, which, of course, included Edward VII, Queen Victoria's son and successor.

Another Charles dilemma concerned his rapidly increasing portfolio of property and commercial products, which passed the one billion dollar revenue mark in 2011–12. Charles as property developer and landlord, and Charles as supplier of organic food to supermarkets, was well suited for hostile documentary TV. Yet other dilemmas sprang from the Windsors' numerous cousins and in-laws. Documentaries have investigated

7 Andrew Morton, 'Tea, but little Sympathy', *Sunday Times magazine*, 27 May 2012.

the German origins of the House of Windsor. The Duke of Edinburgh's Greek and German relatives also made suitable negative material. Another documentary, 'The Queen's Hidden Cousin' (C4, 2011), looked at Queen Elizabeth's first cousins, two of whom lived out most of their lives parked in a Surrey mental hospital and were not publicly recognised as part of the royal family project.

Other potential royal dilemmas are posed by today's fast moving media. The royal princes may be encouraged to be cool and relaxed – which led to Prince Harry being filmed dancing nude in Las Vegas. The royal princes may want to hang out with sports and TV celebrities, but those celebrity careers are typically short, while royal careers are supposed to be lifelong. Yet other dilemmas are posed by the internet and social media. Not only can the princes make instant comments (in contrast to Charles with his handwritten letters) but thousands of private citizens can make instant and quotable comments about the royals.[8]

After Only in America and the British Royals, Muslims are a third favourite for the topic documentary. Once again the selection of topics tends towards the extreme or the bi-polar. Since 2001 and 9/11, Channel Four and BBC1, 2, 3 and 4 have shown many Muslim docs. Least favourably portrayed are selected super-rich males who tend to be based in Saudi Arabia, in the Gulf States and/or in West London. Also portrayed are young men (some British born) who are attracted to fighting, and perhaps dying as terrorist/freedom fighters in the middle east. However, very positive and sympathetic doc treatment is given to Muslim women suffering from oppression by their parents or their husbands. Such women may have been forced into an arranged marriage and may have seen their children abducted back to Pakistan, to the Gulf, or to Yemen. Some British Muslim topic docs are more gentle and subtle such as 'The Muslim Premier League' (BBC1, 2013) about Muslim footballers in the English Premier League; another example was 'Afghan Ladies' Driving School'. But there have been few topic docs about more ordinary members of the UK's 2.5 million Muslim community.

8 David Banks, 'Royal Plans have us in a Twitter', *Press Gazette*, December 2010: 37.

Many UK documentaries focus on one or more of several overlapping themes – namely Poverty and Disability plus the suffering of children, teenage girls and women. The majority of such topic docs operate on low budgets (such as £100,000 per hour) and achieve lowish audience numbers on C4 or BBC3 and BBC4; some reach BBC2. About half of these particular docs deal with the UK – begging on the streets of London, the 'hidden homeless' or children and adults with televisual disabilities such as Autism, Tourettes and Alzheimer's. An unusual Channel Four series *Born to be Different* chose six children born with disabilities and followed them through several subsequent rounds of interviewing.

About half of these poverty/disability/children/women docs are located in Africa or Asia. There are a few classics such as *Welcome to Lagos* (BBC2, 2010); the first part of this three part series was about a community of some 1,000 professional rubbish scavengers in Africa's largest city. Many of these docs show children living in horrible conditions, doing dangerous work (rather than attending school) and being exploited by adults. 'The Truth About Child Brides' (BBC3, 2011) was located in India, where child marriage is illegal; however, we were told, every three seconds a girl under 18 is married – which makes about ten million child marriages per year in the world. In these docs we also meet children punished as witches, kids with guns who have killed adults, and children living in refugee camps across the middle east.

At least twenty celebrated and experienced documentary producer-directors have achieved a substantial body of highly individual, and highly idiosyncratic, work. Typically they have been freelances or been attached to independent production companies. Between them, these leading producer-directors have won many BAFTAs and even more international awards. They like to call themselves 'filmmakers' although their output appears primarily on television. Examples:

Kate Blewett's output, primarily about children, included The Dying Rooms (1996, about Chinese children), and Bulgaria's Abandoned children. Her Ukraine's Forgotten Children (BBC4, 2012) described the smell of a live child's rotting flesh; one care institution was burying about 70 corpses per year.

Nick Broomfield's output includes two famous South Africa docs, and 'Battle For Haditha' about US Marines in the Iraq war; Sex: My British Job (C4, 2013) was about a Chinese brothel in Margaret Thatcher's old North London constituency of Finchley. Nick Broomfield has appeared in several of his own docs as producer-director-presenter-sound recordist.

Richard Curtis has specialised in short doc series which focus on macro-topics and giant leaps between intellectual gurus and billionaire businessmen. *The Power of Nightmares* (BBC2, 2004) saw parallels between US neoconservatives and Arab Islamists. *All Watched Over by Machines of Loving Grace* (BBC2, 2011) was about the computer takeover of world banking and politics. Curtis supported his giant leaps with flashy images and noisy sound.

Paul Hamann, a former head of BBC documentaries, continued to do short obs doc series about prisons and other topics.

Jezza Neumann made a succession of difficult docs, mostly about children, including China's Stolen Children, Undercover in Tibet, Zimbabwe's Forgotten Children, Children of Gaza, War Child, Poor Kids (UK) and Poor Kids (USA).

Paul Watson, who made the original *The Family* and was a top BBC drama executive, continued to make some disturbing docs about such topics as death and alcoholism.

All of these eminent documentary producer-directors have had the essential qualities (passion, determination) in trumps. They themselves exhibit the high quality, variety, and idiosyncrasy of much British documentary output.

History has a great TV future

History programming today occupies many more television hours than in the 1980s. In 1990 there were some history anthology series of separate one hour singles; and there had been a very few prestige special, expensive, series. But today there is a much larger flow of fresh History programming, mainly on the BBC and C4 channels. 'Yesterday' is one of the most popular of the UKTV channels and it specialises in reshowing old BBC History programming.

Technology has played its part. Computer Generated Images (CGI) now make it possible to show what today's ruined pyramid, palace, or bridge would have looked like centuries ago. Archiving is now on a much greater scale, meaning that much more black-and-white old film has been archived; also available are more decades of colour film and colour TV programming. Good archive film is expensive to procure, so producers tend only to use quite short clips of, say, London is 1910 or Berlin in 1920. But these short clips have become part of a broader speeding up of TV History, to suit the tastes of today's audiences.

History producers have developed a number of History formats which use similar material across many episodes. *The 1900 House* (C4, 1999), created by the Wall to Wall indie was a series which focused on a real family, in a real 1900 house, who lived, ate, and dressed in 1900 style. Other similar series dealt with farms in different periods of history. In some cases several history researchers dressed themselves in correct period dress and then acted as costumed guides around the farm and farmhouse. Similar series featured other historical workplaces.

Another formatted series, *Time Team* (C4, 1994), did archaeological digs. *Time Team* was led, not by a charismatic academic, but by Tony Robinson, a popular comic actor with no track record in archaeology. This was, perhaps, the secret of *Time Team*'s success. It demystified archaeology. The show consisted of Tony Robinson and his mildly eccentric archaeologist pals having a few fun days doing some digging on an established site and perhaps discovering something – a small Roman wall, some Tudor coins, or more recent relics of the railway age. The *Time Team* digs were very brief, so there was always a race-against-time narrative which avoided endless costly filming. Other cheapish techniques were aerial photographs of the site, and graphics-on-screen. *Time Team* achieved long life; Tony Robinson, with his nice-man-next-door manner undimmed, went on to present other series and specials.

Who Do You Think You Are? (BBC, 2004) was another format – a history series dressed up as a celebrity genealogy show – as its executive producer, Alex Graham told me in 2006, when the series was moving up from BBC2 to BBC1. This series included three key elements. Firstly, the celebrities used by the series typically had had successful on-screen acting or TV performing careers of one decade or more. Secondly *WDYTYA?* typically featured one or more particular family ancestors who had had a dramatic, melodramatic, or tragic life history. This ancestor was often a great grandparent. A number of these significant ancestors had been Jewish victims in the Holocaust, or had stories of extreme poverty in Ireland or Scotland or England, or had themselves been the children or grandchildren of slaves in the British Empire or the United States. *Who Do You Think You Are?* typically devoted 20 or 25 minutes to a popular history of some historical event, such as the Irish potato famine, the Gallipoli campaign of 1916, or poverty in the East End of London in the late nineteenth century.

Thirdly *WDYTYA?* also showed this week's celebrity setting about the genealogy search with the help of friendly local librarians and historians, census officials and other record keepers. These helpful people had, of course, been discovered in advance by the production team's researchers. But they added a pleasant touch of minor human eccentricity and they provided useful insights for amateur genealogists. In production terms, *WDYTYA?* relied very heavily on this week's celebrity, who became the star of the one hour show. The celebrity's own on-screen expertise was thus crucially important. From the point of view of the established actor (or TV cook or TV journalist) and his or her agent, this was a marvellous publicity opportunity. Consequently, it seems, the celebrity-presenter worked actively on the show for about ten days or two weeks, filming at quite a modest pay rate. This helped the series to become a highly rated factual show on only a middling factual budget.

History producers make many other non-formatted series, but still tend to look for familiar television ingredients such as narrative, events, and character/personalities. Producers seldom have enough money to create big battle scenes or other major events; some producers use battle scenes provided by amateur battle re-enactment hobbyists. More expensive are clips from Hollywood or other films about historic battles. British History producers have, since 2000, focused upon a largish number of favourite periods and idiosyncratic topics:

- *Egypt* – especially the Nile, temples and pyramids.
- *Rome* – focusing mainly on Rome, Naples and nearby locations, but also on more far-flung sites, including Hadrian's Wall.
- *The Tudors* – mainly the Tudor Monarchy, Henry VIII and Elizabeth.
- *1660–1780* – Charles II and his women are favourites as are the Slave Trade, Grand Houses and their interiors.
- *The Early Victorian* period (1837–61) which includes Victoria and Albert, the railways, Dickens and other writers, more Grand Houses and the Crimean War (1853–6) – the first major war to be photographed.
- *1900–20* which includes the Zeppelins, the *Titanic*, the 1914–18 War, the 1908 London Olympics, King Edward VII, personalities such as Kitchener and Lloyd George, and the 1918 Spanish Flu. This period also offers small amounts of colour film.
- *1939–50* has the 1939–45 war, Bombing of London and Germany, the Dambusters, Churchill, Hitler, the Nuremburg trials, the 1947 Partition of India (and independence), and the British withdrawal from Israel/Palestine.
- *The 1960s* are portrayed by British television as primarily a decade of pop music – Beatles, Stones and many others. Also featured: the Vietnam war.

India is the main exception to the paucity of British Empire material. India has TV history appeal in the UK because it offers massive televisual historical events and big personalities such as Mahatma Ghandi and the Nehru dynasty. India also has tragi-comedy appeal (posh chaps in very large hats shooting very large animals) and the nostalgic conceit of a happy-empire-despite-everything.

History is narrative, but which personality or character fits which narrative? If actors dominate, this is no longer TV history but TV drama. However history producers may use actors in back-up roles – perhaps to add to portrait paintings. Much history TV uses a presenter – who may be an academic historian, or a journalist or a professional presenter.

Another possibility is to reject the on-screen presenter and to rely on the leading characters in the story. Some history TV does straight biography. Phillip Whitehead made several short series, each devoted to one political dynasty. In the years 1991–7 six such dynasty series were transmitted: *Stalin* (1991) which dealt also with Svetlana Stalin, *The Kennedys* (1992), *The Windsors* (1993), *The Churchills* (1994), *Last of The Tsars* (1995) and *The Nehru/Gandhi Story* (1997). Phillip Whitehead, before his untimely death, told me:

> We try to focus on what seems a single central truth. So for the Joe Kennedy dynasty there had recently been several bad books about him. We decided to focus on how Joe Kennedy manipulated the careers of his sons. We used a lot of archive film, but we had the money to do fresh interviews. We found some marvellous Boston politicians and Kennedy cronies. The Kennedy series won an Emmy.
>
> For *The Churchills*, the family (especially his daughter, Lady Soames) were helpful; as were the historians including David Cannadine and Martin Gilbert, the Churchill biographer. A special strength of this series was being able to show the viewer so many different still and moving pictures of one individual (Churchill) over a long life. We also had nice stories such as how after Churchill's 1953 stroke, Christopher Soames ran Britain and forged his father-in-law's Prime Ministerial signature.

Phillip Whitehead formed effective partnerships with relevant historians and he agreed with them the major family/dynasty storyline. This procedure made for attractive and well-researched story-telling, but the dynasty focus played down other available (non-dynastic) aspects.

Phillip Whitehead's colleagues at the Brook Lapping company gave a biographical slant to some of their recent-history short series. Examples include the Norma Percy produced *Putin, Russia and the West* (BBC2, 2012, 4 hours).

History producers in British television often work with an Author-Presenter – such as Schama, Starkey, Beard or Ferguson. All four of these people were productive academic historians, before presenting their own TV series and using themselves as their own experts. As a historian Simon Schama specialised in Dutch art and the French Revolution. David Starkey specialised in the Tudor monarchy; Mary Beard wrote about ancient Rome. Niall Ferguson's specialism was imperial economic history. All four of these high profile historians were encouraged by their producers to be assertive. Paul Hamann told me that he was proud of having given BBC approval for Simon Schama's star role in *Simon Schama's History of Britain*. David Starkey was equally dominant in several Tudor monarchy series. Mary Beard had her own very assertive style – for instance, in trying to enliven short Latin inscriptions with humour and bawdy bravado. Niall Ferguson was perhaps even more assertive and politically partisan in his sweeping statements about the beneficial effects of the British, European and American empires. There are obvious tensions here.

Schama, Starkey and Ferguson in particular became involved in the Public Intellectual dilemma. As the Cambridge historian Richard Evans pointed out:

> Celebrity historians are especially likely to get into trouble if they desert their own field of expertise and enter the rough-and-tumble of political debate.[9]

These celebrity historians became active across four platforms – academe, television, newspaper writing and non-academic book publishing. The book-of-the-series (supported by several hours of TV publicity) can become a best seller. Newspaper editors sign up these historians to write opinionated columns. Television can become an historian's main source of income and of public intellectual prestige. Universities, especially American ones, like to have public intellectual celebrities on campus. One consequence is that these historians experience negative blowback through both the old and newer media. Simon Schama, having written many opinion pieces in many publications, became the victim of numerous other opinionated people. He was denounced as being ignorant about John Donne,[10] baseball, California, cooking, and other topics. A.A. Gill compared Niall Ferguson with B-movie publicity and accused him of monumental self-regard.[11] Internet comment can be even more negative. Mary Beard, after appearing

9 Richard Evans, 'Is history history?' *The Guardian*, 28 May 2012.

10 David Herman, 'Smallscreen', *Prospect*, July 2009.

11 A.A. Gill, 'There's nothing original under the skin', *Sunday Times*, 13 March 2011.

on a couple of TV political talk shows, was astonished at the ferocity of some online comment.

David Starkey's television performances had several of the familiar weaknesses of the professor-performer. He seemed obsessed with sex and other bodily details; he relished exaggerated tabloid language. He kept returning again and again to TV accounts of Henry VIII, Elizabeth I, and the other Tudors. But David Starkey had some advantages denied to the other big television historians. David Starkey's best achievements were firstly *Monarchy*, which ran on Channel Four for seventeen episodes across four years (2004–7); and secondly *Henry VIII: Mind of a Tyrant* (C4, 2009). Previous to these two series, Starkey served a lengthy media apprenticeship on television and on Talk Radio; he carefully developed his 'rudest man' image in *The Moral Maze* (BBC Radio 4). He did TV series on *Henry VIII*, *Elizabeth*, *The Six Wives of Henry VIII* and *The Unknown Tudors*. He used monarchy to establish the British/English monarchy as a vehicle for a general UK history. He was highly opinionated and highly speculative about the history and future of the monarchy.

With a mixture of luck and insight, David Starkey had focused in on one of the most melodramatic, most significant and most televisual periods of British/English national history. Henry VIII not only had a succession of six wives, but he developed a newly powerful and significant nation state; he defied the papacy; and he seized the wealth of the monasteries – thus enriching himself and the state. But how to dramatise all of this on television? *Henry VIII: Mind of a Tyrant* had the near-perfect answers. In addition to the buildings, there were paintings by, among others, Hans Holbein. Starkey was greatly assisted by a huge quantity of documents and objects which had big visual appeal. Starkey looks through these objects and documents, into Henry VIII's mind. How did the slim, scholarly and sensitive young Henry turn into the mature Henry who was a fat, brutal, monster? Between age 23 and age 48, Henry's waistline expanded by 16 inches. It happens that a large number of Henry VIII's personal possessions have survived including books, maps, and paintings. Above all, there are many letters in Henry's own handwriting and also many letters written to Henry by important politicians, and church people. Starkey and his team used all of these materials to great effect. Actors were employed to speak some of the words from the original letters and texts. These production devices bring Henry VIII to life with remarkable vividness for a man who died in 1547. Henry VIII himself – his pictures, his possessions, his handwriting, his mind, his precise words on many occasions – are to the fore.[12] David Starkey – Henry expert and enthusiast – plays only an important supporting role.

One of the weaknesses of the high profile TV historian is that he or she tends to have little grasp of the broad landscape of television genres. These TV historians, when invited onto other programming – political and entertainment – tend to make elementary out-of-genre blunders. Some TV historians, now resident as public intellectuals in American universities, tend to be out of touch not just with British TV but with contemporary British life. Consequently, some British journalists have seemed more scholarly as TV historians than have the academic historians. Jeremy Paxman has presented well informed TV history series. Andrew Marr, after retiring as BBC Political Editor, delivered several big TV series (and huge books) well suited to the requirements of television.

Producers of TV history have also relied on some presenters who offer a combination of history education and TV experience. Dan Cruikshank, an architectural historian, presented many singles and short series which focused on historical buildings. Lucy Worsley presented TV programming, often about the interiors of historic buildings and about the position of women within wealthy households; Worsley often appeared in correct period dress. Dan Snow, a member of the Snow TV dynasty, presented numerous short TV series – about battlefields, the two world wars, and many other topics. Cruikshank, Worsley and Snow were appearing mainly on BBC1, BBC2 and BBC4. All three were also writing plenty of books-of-the-series.

12 Susan Doran, ed., *Man and Monarch: Henry VIII* (London: British Library, 2009. Exhibition guest curated by David Starkey).

TV history's classics and TV future

> The key ingredient is passion. But TV History is a different genre from history ... TV is a link between the public and the experts. TV is not a medium for ideas or deep analysis, but it encourages people to look elsewhere ... The great danger is that TV demands narrative. Against your better instincts as a historian, as a TV maker inevitably you're drawn into constructing a narrative.
>
> — MICHAEL WOOD, in interview with author

The 'Archive' phenomenon is another major reason for TV history's strong future prospects. The BBC and ITV/ITN in particular have a long-term strategy of gradually making much of their past programming available to the public. Some of this Archive output appears, and will continue to appear, on the main regular channels; other Archive output has to be paid for by home consumers and/or by commercial channels. Nearly a decade before smart television sets became commonplace around 2012, the BBC, in particular, had been preparing itself to make huge amounts of Archive available on domestic TV sets. Obviously this Archive development includes programming from across the range of genres. But the History genre is especially suitable.

During 1969–74, TV History programming was largely dominated by four presenter-authors – Clark, Mountbatten, Cooke and Bronowski. With the higher licence fee for colour TV, the BBC had a strongly rising revenue. It spent some of this on three lavishly produced History series. Kenneth Clark was the 1969 author-and-presenter of *Civilisation* (BBC2, 13 hours). Clark wrote the script and presented a series about famous musicians, painters, philosophers and poets mainly of ancient Greece, Rome and Northern Italy. A common Clark device was a superior guided walking tour around churches, art galleries, piazzas and palazzos. But Clark also managed to fly round the world a few times.

An extreme case of strong authorship was Mountbatten: *The Life and Times of Earl Mountbatten of Burma*; this was twelve hours of prestige programming in 1969 on the ITV network. Mountbatten himself was the on-screen star. The TV series became an exercise in praise singing Mountbatten's own wisdom and virtue. Archive film was edited to praise Mountbatten's role as British commander in Burma fighting the Japanese, and to praise him as the man who subsequently oversaw the independence and birth of India and Pakistan. There was extensive fresh film of Mountbatten grandly returning to the scenes of his former triumphs.[13]

The thirteen-part Alastair Cooke's *America* (1972) was the premier 'authored' political history series of this period. He wrote what script there was and he presented the series on camera. He also wrote the series book, which (with the help of a forceful Hollywood agent) made him a rich man. The series spent a prodigal amount of NBC and BBC money. Alastair Cooke introduced his highly personal account of American history from his apartment, overlooking Central Park in New York City. Cooke covered 100,000 miles and stayed in eighty-six separate motels across the United States. The crew – numbering up to nine people – travelled in a caravan of cars; Alastair Cooke decided on daily starting and finishing times and presided over evening food and drink. A new director, on joining the travelling crew, was told by a cameraman: 'You'd better be a very articulate listener.'[14]

Yet another author-presenter prestige history series was Jacob Bronowski's *The Ascent of Man* (BBC2, 1973, 13 hours), which recounted the world history of technology. The series took four years to make and, again, involved much world travelling with large filming crews.

A second phase of TV history classics began in 1973. Jeremy Isaacs was the producer of two landmark series – *The World at War* (ITV, 1973–4, 26 hours)[15] and *Ireland: A Television History* (BBC2, 1980–1, 10 hours).

The producer-driven trend was evident in another landmark history series. Peter Pagnamenta executive produced *All Our Working Lives* (BBC2, 1984, 11 hours). The series looked at such twentieth-century British industries as steel, ship-building, car assembly, retail, cotton manufacture and the aircraft industry. The series, which used archive film and fresh interviews,

13 Philip Ziegler, *Mountbatten: the official biography* (London: Collins, 1985), 666–70.

14 Nick Clarke, *Alastair Cooke: a biography* (London: Weidenfeld and Nicholson, 1999), 419–41.

15 Taylor Downing, *The World at War* (London: Palgrave Macmillan, 2012).

forcefully expounded a historical theory that British industrial leadership was always followed by managerial and trade union decline.[16] *All Our Working Lives* had a highly distinctive style, because each episode depended on exceptionally rigorous research. In the case of each industry, for example ship building, the viewers were presented with matching archive film of the relevant bosses and workers. Moreover:

> There is an extraordinary power in the simple business of watching an old black and white documentary film, with a young man or woman working away, and then cutting to an interview in full colour with an elderly person who, you suddenly realise, is the very person who was wielding that hammer or stretching that cloth ... *All Our Working Lives* uses it repeatedly.'[17]

Peter Pagnamenta used the same technique in his *People's Century* (BBC1/ WGBH, 1995–7, 26 hours). This series spanned the world and the twentieth century, while again rediscovering and interviewing individuals who had appeared in archive film, shot several decades earlier. Peter Pagnamenta made other major history series about the USSR (*Comrades*) and Japan (*Nippon*). He told me:

> *All Our Working Lives* couldn't be made now. It was expensive and had no co-production moneys. But it made viewers think. There had never been an attempt to do a post-1945 industrial and social history on TV. It involved finding a set of people – car industry and steel managers, coalminers and other workers – who hadn't told what really happened in British industry before and after 1945. I sold *All Our Working Lives* to Brian Wenham (BBC2 Controller) on the basis of one sheet of paper. He just said 'Let's Do It'.

Brian Lapping is another leading example of an executive producer who developed his own distinctive approach to recent history. He did this as executive producer of four series – *End of Empire* (1985, 14 hours), *Apartheid* (1986, 4 hours), *The Second Russian Revolution* (1991, 8 hours) and *Death of Yugoslavia* (1995, 6 hours). His distinctive approach, which Brian Lapping

16 Arthur Marwick, 'Getting Down To It', *Times Literary Supplement*, 7 September 1984. Keith Harper, 'All Our Working Days', *The Guardian*, 23 June 1984.

17 Christopher Dunkley, 'The love and logic of work'. *Financial Times*, 13 April 1984.

initially developed for the end of the British Empire, also worked well with the ends of Apartheid, of the Soviet Union and of Yugoslavia. Each of these 'End of' series generated a strong main narrative, plus subordinate weekly narratives. The finance available especially for the two largest series was generous. *The End of Empire* was a money-no-problem prestige project from Granada, although it was eventually transmitted by Channel Four. *The Second Russian Revolution* was BBC funded, but the low value of the Soviet currency in 1988–90 meant that the Lapping team had virtually unlimited cash for buying archive film, and for employing Russian speaking researchers, translators, and camera crews. As a former print journalist who had specialised on the Commonwealth, Brian Lapping – in making *The End of Empire* – was determined to be his own expert. He personally chose the episode topics and themes for the 14 hours of *Empire* and the 4 hours of *Apartheid*. He was also sole author of both series books, one of 240,000 words, the other of 100,000 words.[18]

Subsequently fortune favoured the brave as Brian Lapping carried over his *Empire* and *Apartheid* production approach into the *Russia* and *Yugoslavia* series. The timing was especially fortunate. During the years 1985–95, both the USSR/Russia and Yugoslavia were in turmoil, while traditional restrictions on foreign television crews had suddenly disappeared. As the USSR collapsed into a sovereign Russia, top politicians were exploiting their new media freedom and had not yet established public relations caution and silence. In Yugoslavia there was TV competition, with politicians aggressively using television as a weapon of civil war. In both cases there were contending domestic media; energetic research discovered exciting recent news footage from across, and beyond, Russia. In Yugoslavia there were rival TV services in Serbia, Croatia and Bosnia. The Lapping system worked even better in *Russia* and *Yugoslavia* than it had in *Empire* and *Apartheid*. Brian Lapping was fortunate with his production teams and their language skills. As executive producer he was also fortunate in the support of Norma Percy as series producer for the Russia and

18 Brian Lapping, *End of Empire* (London: Granada and Channel Four, 1985). Brian Lapping, *Apartheid: A History* (London: Grafton Books, 1986).

Yugoslavia series; she had been an episode producer on both the *Empire* and *Apartheid* series.

Another classic History series of a very different kind, was the BBC2 anthology series, *Timewatch*. Roy Davies, its forceful producer, told me in 1991 that he was making eighteen *Timewatch* hours per year with a staff of ten producer/director/writers, each producing two one hour programmes per year. Davies said that he never gave one of his producers the green light until they had agreed a one sentence ('one full stop, one capital letter and no clauses') summary.

Timewatch continued under another Editor/executive producer, Laurence Rees, who subsequently made a remarkable collection of short series about the second world war. *Nazis: a Warning From History* was about the organisation of German forces on the eastern front; *War of the Century* was about the Soviet-Nazi war. *Horror in the East* considered Japanese war criminals. *Auschwitz: The Nazis and the 'Final Solution'* focused on the single camp where 1.1 million people, including 200,000 children, were killed. Laurence Rees devoted some fifteen years to his television and book coverage of World War Two and the Nazis. He says that he was helped by two accidents of timing. Firstly, he was able to conduct interviews with one hundred Nazi perpetrators and Auschwitz survivors. Dozens of killer-perpetrators were willing – now in their seventies – to be interviewed, on film, admitting and discussing multiple murders they had personally committed. Secondly, Rees says, he was fortunate that during the 1990s much war archive material – from Russia, and eastern Europe – became freshly available.

These series were not dominated merely by Laurence Rees as producer. He was, in effect, his own senior researcher; he was in a unique position:

> As the only person I know of who has met and questioned a significant number of perpetrators from all three of the major wartime totalitarian powers: Germany, Japan and the Soviet Union.

Laurence Rees points out that the support of the BBC was essential. Even the Nazi self-confessing murderers 'believed that the BBC would not distort their contribution.' Also:

> The research period for the projects was so long that only a public service broadcaster could have made such a commitment.[19]

Much classic History programming has, of course, been about the two world wars. Long before the centenary programming of 2014–18, the First War had received some classic coverage. *The Great War* (BBC2, 1964, 26 hours) was one such series.[20] Another series, *The First World War* (C4, 2003, 10 hours), was written by the Oxford historian, Hew Strachan, and produced by Jonathan Lewis. This series set new standards, not least in terms of scholarly authenticity.[21] In 2014 the BBC announced that it was commissioning 2,500 hours of first war programming to play across 2014–18 on BBC TV, Radio and Online.

The 'classic' history programming just discussed totals over 200 hours while the Beard-Ferguson-Schama-Starkey series bring the total to over 300 hours. Much of this programming concerns only the UK and Europe. Clearly there are big opportunities for more international and more worldwide programming. Michael Wood may well be seen as a key pioneer author-presenter of TV international history.

In The Footsteps of Alexander The Great[22] (BBC, 1997, 4 hours) is one of several series in which Michael Wood conceived the project, wrote the script, wrote the book, and was the on-screen star. He and his team followed Alexander's route of 334–23 BC; the route led from Greece to the borders of present-day China and then back – a 22,000 mile journey. We, the viewers, see Michael Wood following Alexander's trail sweatily across deserts and breathlessly over high mountain passes. The journey is by road, train, horse and mule; we often see Michael Wood marching forward on foot as he tells us about Alexander's stupendous difficulties and astonishing

19 Laurence Rees, *Auschwitz: the Nazis and the 'Final Solution'* (London: BBC Books, 2005), 6–18.

20 Emma Hanna, *The Great War on the Small Screen* (Edinburgh: Edinburgh University Press, 2009), 32–62.

21 Hew Strachan, *The First World War* (London: Simon and Schuster, 2003). Svetlana Palmer and Sarah Wallis, *A War in Words* (London: Simon and Schuster, 2003).

22 Michael Wood, *In The Footsteps of Alexander The Great: a journey from Greece to India* (London: BBC Books, 1997 and 2004).

military victories. Other Michael Wood series included *In Search of the Trojan War* (BBC2, 1985, 6 hours), *Conquistadores* (about the lost city of the Incas), *Saddam's Killing Fields* (the Marsh Arabs of Iraq) and *Hitler's Search for the Holy Grail* (Nazi myths).

The Story of India (BBC2, 2007) seems likely to be Michael Wood's most influential series. This series devoted a mere six hours to 5,000 years of Indian history. We see Wood, classical text in hand, striding around amazing buildings, temples and sites; the deep past, he tells us, is still visible and thrusts itself up into present day India. He also focuses on paintings, documents, religion, music and the local food; there are fabulous landscapes, an element of the art documentary. Local Indian experts are interviewed – not in a studio but walking around the temple or the site, with an ever-active camera. And always there is Michael Wood, in restless movement, smiling and laughing with boyish delight.

Michael Wood told me that he had long been wanting to make an India series. When the money finally became available from American PBS (with the BBC as the second and smaller funder), the team at Mayavision were determined to make a landmark series. The filming schedule was ferocious; filming was done in repeated intensive bursts, each of about three weeks. The crew moved relentlessly both between filming locations and at many sites. The three person team had worked together previously: Michael Wood was writer/presenter/interviewer. The sound man, Callum Bulmer, was important because of the centrality of sound and music in the series; he also took many of the stills in the book.[23] Jeremy Letts had an especially exhausting and demanding time; as director/cameraman he had to stagger forwards, backwards and sideways around Michael Wood, while carrying the high definition camera through the brutal heat of India. Wood added that:

> Western film crews are normally suspect; Indians are rightly fed up with films about the romance of poverty in Calcutta. But everyone was positive with us – from experts to bystanders. It's a very film-literate culture. On the street, people come over and ask 'Are you the hero?', and advise on where best to put the camera tripod.

23 Michael Wood, *The Story of India* (London: BBC Books, 2007).

> Our prime duty is to the general audience – you can and do meet your audience, especially on book tours. We got UK audiences of around 2 million – not bad for BBC2. The main weakness of the *India* series is that it's too dense, too much packed into the six hours. In half an hour I could write down titles for a 100-part history of India.

Surely viewers in Europe and the West can anticipate hundreds of fresh hours, not only of Indian, but also of Chinese, Muslim, Latin American, United States, African – and of European – television history.

Travel: Documentary and history journey

Travel programming arrived on British television at the same time as the arrival of jet aircraft and mass air travel in the 1960s and 1970s. From 1980 onwards Travel became part of a TV trinity which also included Documentary and History. Travel programming incorporates the documentary tradition of filming at the location. Travel usually includes some history – you cannot grasp much about any country from Afghanistan to Zimbabwe, without knowing a little of its history. Travel on TV typically involves some kind of journey (favourite TV term) within one country or world region. British TV travel producers tend to favour travel by train in general, and train-travel-in-India in particular.

Like History, the Travel genre has joined Documentary as one of a group of strong continuing Public Service genres. Travel provides education and information – about places far and near. Travel, as a PSB genre, also offers some entertainment. Travel is presented as being enjoyable as well as being serious. Travel TV gives you amusing surprises, beautiful landscapes and buildings, plus useful advice about where, and where not, to have your next holiday. Humour is potentially a strong entertainment ingredient, and this can mean using a professional comedian. Travel TV is neither investigative journalism, nor life-and-death documentary. But can the travel producer generate programming which is loosely feel good, without being bland and dull? British TV schedules have often placed their travel programming into slots such as Sunday at 8pm – something warm and feel good before Monday morning.

Most travel programming uses a prominent presenter, who is filmed making the journey – talking, walking, and interviewing. About half of all UK travel presenters have been comedians or comedy actors; the remainder have mostly been journalists, other actors, and a few professional presenters. The producer usually wants a presenter with a certain stage presence, who can broadly follow the production script while also exploiting spontaneous encounters with local people.

Travel TV has always been split into world, European and UK travel. World travel is the most ambitious, most expensive, and most likely to go out on the bigger channels, especially BBC2. A leading TV world traveller was Simon Reeve who during the 2003–13 decade presented 39 hours in ten separate short series. This included three separate trips around the world, *Equator* (2006), *Tropic of Capricorn* (2008) and *Tropic of Cancer* (2010); another Simon Reeve journey was *Indian Ocean* (2012) which visited East Africa, India, Bangladesh and South East Asia. These four journeys (total: 19 hours) covered many of the world's poorer nations in tropical Latin America, Africa and South Asia. These series did include some grim material, such as a cemetery full of dead drug traders in Mexico or Bangladesh villagers experiencing chronic and repeated flooding. But these Simon Reeve presented shows also offered lighter stories, feel good warmth, and gentle humour.

World travel producers have made short series with a wide range of themes. The extreme trek approach has involved the traveller-presenter in walking, or swimming, the length of the Amazon; long distance motor cycle trips have gone from West to East and from North (Scotland) to South Africa. Other world trips have focused on the world's gardens or tall buildings. But several comedy stars have illustrated the difficulties of themed long distance travel.

If the traveller-talk host is too busy with other things, the travel series may suffer. An example is *Victoria's Empire* (BBC1, 2007) in which the traveller was Victoria Wood. As one of the most gifted and successful writer-performers in British TV comedy (and drama) she was a busy woman who also was unwilling to be away from her children for more than 14 days at a time. This meant that the series – about places called 'Victoria' in the old British empire – had to rely on just three 14 day trips; each trip involved three different imperial locations and generated one hour of transmitted television. The first 14 day trip was to Ghana, Jamaica and Newfoundland. The next 14 day trip was (in August) to India, Hong Kong and Borneo; the third trip was to New Zealand, Australia and Zambia.[24] The Victoria theme was not strong enough to hold these far-flung places together.

British travel TV about Europe had, previous to 2012, dealt mainly with Mediterranean package tours. But in 2012 a new BBC2 series, *Great Continental Railway Journeys*, was launched and succeeded in focusing sceptical British eyes on Europe beyond the beaches. This series had been carefully derived from a previous *British Railway* version. The *Continental Railway* format offered several ingredients which BBC2 audiences found attractive. The series focused on rail travel and this included the use of photographs and silent film from before 1914. Travel by present day European train allows us to see how train stations have changed; we see, through the train windows, mountains, villages and forests pass by, and we meet assorted travellers providing snap interviews to the on-train TV team. Then we get some helicopter shots of high speed trains moving at 180 mph – shots helpfully provided by the train company. In *Great Continental Railway Journeys*, our presenter, Michael Portillo, carries a 1913 Railway Guide and he visits some of the same Cathedrals and Hotels as the guide suggested in 1913. We, the viewing audience, meet local 'experts', typically between six and twelve experts in one hour – mostly local historians, business leaders and tourist guides, all speaking English. The series is carefully designed around Michael Portillo – former Conservative Cabinet Minister and now active TV personality. He presents himself in colourful dress and with much stage presence; he speaks with brevity, clarity and a little self-mocking humour. He provides some personal family history (his Spanish father

24 Victoria Wood, Fanny Blake and Frank Welsh, *Victoria's Empire* (London: Hodder and Stoughton, 2007).

fought in the Spanish civil war).[25] The sixty year oldish Portillo enthuses over local food, local wine and beer, and hot-cold-and-mud baths. He bravely tries to play local games and to dance local dances. Portillo refers occasionally to writers, painters and singers, and more frequently to Wagner. *Great Continental Railway Journeys* used much advance work in setting up interviews and archive film; and it was heavily edited, with many hours of filming going into one hour on the TV screen. It was a presenter led, but producer driven, series.

The third main category of UK travel programme has focused on the British Isles. The long-running *Coast* (BBC2) series shows the strengths and weaknesses of domestic UK travel programming. There is a strong focus on South West England, Wales and the Scottish islands. Here we see many steep sea cliffs, many thousands of sea birds, and many fishing villages. Also, in UK travel, we glimpse smaller cities and towns with their castles, cathedrals, and often quaint-and-ancient industries. Other UK travel TV shows recount the deeds of famous Victorian engineers, such as Brunel, and offer details of major floods down the centuries. Some UK journeys involve small boats, bicycles, motor cycles, or walks along old canals.

Great British Railway Journeys developed most of the format ingredients which were later used in the *Continental* series. The *British* series, which gave an especially heavy emphasis to Britain's railways as the first national rail system, was initially scheduled into BBC daytime.[26] Later it transferred to mid-evening on BBC2 and was heavily repeated on BBC4. Other networks noted the success of TV travel. ITV began to take an active interest in counties such as Yorkshire, Northumberland and Shropshire. Meanwhile Channel 5 produced *The Railway: Great Western*, which seemed to be a 'sponsored film'; in this respect it was like *Night Mail* (1936) – a train film (with Auden and Britten) funded by the British Post Office.[27]

25 Michael Gove, *Michael Portillo: the future of the right* (London: Fourth Estate, 1995), 5–18.

26 Charlie Bunce, *Great British Railway Journeys* (London: HarperCollins, 2011).

27 Marsha Bryant, *Auden and Documentary in the 1930s* (Charlottesville: University of Virginia Press, 1997), 48–60.

Back in the 1960s there was fairly little travel programming – either UK or European – on British television. The main travel offering, especially during 1959–73, was provided by Alan Whicker, a former foreign correspondent and TV journalist. In *Whicker's World* he specialised in talking with super-rich and eccentric folks in such (then) exotic and faraway places as Australia, Bali, Beverly Hills, Brunei, Haiti and Hong Kong. Whicker also wrote newspaper columns and books[28] packed with anecdotes about his super-rich eccentrics. *Whicker's World* was still running on BBC1 in 1990, but with a reduced audience rating.[29]

In 1990 two specialised travel shows – which focused on package holiday (mostly European) advice had larger audiences than Whicker. *Holiday* (BBC1) ran from 1969 to 2007. ITV's competing offering, *Wish You Were Here* offered advice on slightly cheaper holidays and ran for thirty years (1974–2004). The producers of these two holiday shows both told me in 1990 that they had modest budgets; reporting teams had to work hard and fly economy – often visiting several separate resorts within, say, Portugal, Sicily or Tunisia.[30]

The years around 1990 were a period of change in TV travel programming; the BBC was discovering the global journey concept, but doing so rather slowly. In 1980 the BBC had launched *Great Railway Journeys of the World* with seven separate journeys; Michael Wood presented the Cape Town to Victoria Falls journey, and the comedian, Michael Palin, presented a London to Scotland journey. Nine years later in 1989 Michael Palin took the lead in *Around The World in 80 days* (1989), followed by *Pole to Pole* in 1992. Then in 1994, 1996 and 1999 BBC2 did three additional sets of (now shortened title) *Great Railway Journeys*.

These world journeys seem to require a strong guiding theme, strong production and a presenter suitable to the theme. *Around the World in 80 Days* had the Jules Verne fiction classic to hold its shape. *Pole to Pole* was

28 Alan Whicker, *Journey Of A Lifetime* (London: HarperCollins, 2009 and 2010).

29 For example, four *Whicker's World* weekly episodes in March 1990 averaged an audience of 5.9 million, but averaged only 71st place in each week's ratings.

30 Des Lynam gives an account of briefly working on *Holiday* in Des Lynam, *I Should Have Been At Work* (London: HarperCollins, 2006), 146–53.

fortunate in 1991–2 to be travelling through Russia, Ukraine and Africa just after the Soviet Union collapsed. One other Palin-fronted voyage, *Himalaya* (2004) – on Pakistan, India, Nepal, Bangladesh, Bhutan and China – had thematic coherence and very strong visuals.[31] But not all world journey TV has been so successful. Producers will continue to search for coherent themes and may also search for new travel TV formats.

31 Michael Palin, *Himalaya* (London: Weidenfeld and Nicolson), 2004.

CHAPTER 9

Comedy, Big Entertainment and Talk

Comedy, Big Entertainment and Talk all tend to involve studio audiences, whose members are encouraged to laugh, shout and interact. All of these genres lay claim to historic origins in Music Hall, Cartooning, Variety, Circus and Radio. These genres also have been recognised, since the 1930s start of British TV, as the third leg in the Education/Information/Entertainment combination.

Comedy, Big Entertainment and Talk are today focused mainly into about eight channels. BBC1, 2, and 3, ITV1 and 2, C4, More 4 and Five, between them, do a big range of comedy. But these genres, as Entertainment, are expected to be popular – to exceed the average audience rating for the particular time slot. These genres are mainly scheduled into Friday, Saturday and Sunday evenings – where the ratings competition is fierce.

But since year 2000 the Comedy, Big Entertainment and Talk genres have been primarily aimed at the mid-market, the mass market. Some of today's characteristic formats have been specifically designed for mass market appeal. Panel Comedy shows typically include several, currently popular, comedians – whose performance can be edited down to eliminate the less funny remarks. Big Entertainment shows, like *X Factor*, are similarly aimed at a big middle mass audience and are ruthlessly edited to avoid the duller material. Talk Shows also strive at a mass audience – often including both upmarket and downmarket guests in the same show; but, in general, Talk Shows seek to celebrate the popular new output of already established performers. Some of today's 'live' shows routinely attract large audiences which would have been exceptional in the past. Where once the studio audience was hundreds of people, today's live audience can be in thousands. This is the era of the large venue and the Arena Gig.

During the 1950s and 1960s these genres aimed mainly at working class audiences. Many of the performers had ended their education by age 15; most performers had started as pub-or-club comedians and/or as summer end-of-the-pier seaside entertainers. At Christmas they did Pantomime in a local theatre. This was the background of many comics who appeared during 1971–4 on Granada's *The Comedians*. Situation Comedies mostly featured working class characters. The big ITV and BBC Variety shows were TV versions of stage Variety and Music Hall. Much of the humour was very working class, mildly naughty and casually racist; for two decades the BBC's most successful entertainment show was *The Black and White Minstrel Show* (1958–78) whose obvious racism[1] the relevant BBC executives pretended not to notice. Some BBC producers also somehow failed to notice that Jimmy Savile and other top entertainers were sexually abusing teenagers on a massive scale.

But the 1980s and 1990s were an era of New Comedy. Many of the new comics were young graduates from the Cambridge Footlights or from Oxford. A number were writer-performers or writer-producers. From 1982 the new Channel Four became a home for new comedy and now there were at least four national channels commissioning comedy. But, of course, the more traditional, more working class, performers and series did not disappear. Around 1990 my interviews revealed much conflict and antagonism within the comedy and entertainment genres. Some of this was age-based as well as based on social class. In some cases an experienced working class comic was seen by his young graduate producer as ignorant, racist, sexist and – worst of all – unfunny.

1 Robert C. Toll, *Blacking Up: The Minstrel Show in Nineteenth Century America* (New York: Oxford University Press, 1974). Tunstall, *The Media Are American*, 86–90. During 1959–62, *The Black and White Minstrel Show* was the BBC's highest rating series: Briggs, *Competition: 1955–74*, 431–3.

There have been several other major changes since around 1990:

- Comedy in particular now has a much larger minority of female comics.
- British TV comedy is less racist than it was in 1990. In 1990 there was a small movement towards Afro-Caribbean comedy; recently there has been a modest amount of Anglo-Asian (Indian, Pakistani) humour.
- British TV comedy and entertainment are still somewhat social class polarised, but less so than in 1990.
- Since 1990 more comedians and entertainers have been to art, drama, or even music school or to North of England universities.
- Comedy writers continue to be important, but less so than back in 1990. Today there are more writer-performers and today also there is more semi-spontaneous, unscripted, funny talk.
- Back in 1990 both Comedy and Big Entertainment were shut off from most other genres. In 1990 much ITV Comedy and entertainment was made at one ITV company, London Weekend TV (LWT). The BBC was being run largely by journalists and documentary or arts producers, who were concerned that Comedy and Entertainment should maintain their big audience ratings. Jimmy Savile, who presented *Jim'll Fix It* (BBC1, 1975–94), was, we now know, molesting children on an industrial scale; and he was not alone among the Entertainment talent. This could probably not happen today, not least because of the greater presence of senior women executives and the more open conditions under which most of the comedy and entertainment shows are now made by independent production companies.

From stand-up to sit-down panel comedy

Until 1990 British TV offered four main comedy types – Stand Up, Sketch, Sitcom and Political Satire – all of which could trace their histories back to the nineteenth century. All four of these comedy sub-genres were heavily and expensively scripted. The comics needed to learn the lines and rehearse the moves – and a series run was typically short, such as six half hours.

But from 1990 *Have I Got News For You* quickly became the leader in a rising wave of Panel Show comedy. This panel humour was usually dressed up as a quiz, but was really several comics sitting around a table cracking jokes; some of the jokes were pre-written, but many were at least semi-spontaneous. Panel humour was popular and much cheaper to produce than were the other comedy sub-genres. Even when heavily edited (to eliminate the less funny sections) panel comedy was cheaper per audience. Panel shows could also do longer runs; and some panel shows could be endlessly repeated for a yet more commercially positive outcome.

Have I Got News For You was on BBC2 (1990–2000) before moving to BBC1; this show has five funny people making jokes about the previous week's news. The beauty of the format is that selected clips from the week's newspapers and television supply the cue raw material; the five people make the jokes and the less funny jokes are edited out. The show has proved to be very flexible, with many minor changes over the years. The team each week has consisted of two regulars (Paul Merton and Ian Hislop), two guests and (since 2002) a guest chairperson, who is usually either a politician, a journalist or another comedian. Richard Wilson (not the actor) who started producing the show in 1996, and later became its executive producer, told me:

> We did the 300th show in 2008. Paul Merton and Ian Hislop are the number one reason for *Have I Got News For You*'s success. When the show began in 1990, both were very young and newly famous. Paul Merton is an improvisation comic, he likes to react to stuff in front of him. Ian Hislop in 1990 was the new youthful editor of *Private Eye*; he had and always has the top inside political scandal stuff. For the first 12 years Angus Deayton was the chairman – until he was himself involved in his own scandal. The (now visiting) chairman's role is important. We like to balance the show with some amusing Conservative as chair. Boris Johnson admits that we raised his profile and helped him to become London Mayor. We work very hard on the autocue material which the chairperson delivers in newsreader style.
>
> HIGNFY is effectively the old BBC radio show, *News Quiz*, transferred to BBC television by Hat Trick. We show the panel members the questions about an hour before the filming begins with the audience. There is no rehearsal. We record about 90 minutes and cut it down to 29 minutes for the first showing. The show is quite

> heavy on research for the press and TV clips; and we employ several gag writers to do the autocue lines.
>
> Paul and Ian have insisted that we stick to two short annual runs, totalling 17 half hours on BBC1. These 17 shows are repeated each week in *Have I Got More News For You* at greater length, 44 minutes. Also a year or more later there is 17 × 29 minutes of *Have I Got Old News For You*. That's 51 transmissions on BBC1 and BBC2 each year ... The high quality depends on the heavy editing down. Each week we have about 90 written jokes for the chairman's autocue but only about ten survive into the transmitted show.

The success of *Have I Got News For You* as a panel news comment comedy led directly to a similar show about sport, *They Think It's All Over* (BBC1, 1995) and another show about pop music, *Never Mind The Buzzcocks* (BBC, 1996). Both of these shows were made by the Talkback indie with Peter Fincham as executive producer. Harry Thompson worked as a producer on both Talkback shows and on Hat Trick's *Have I Got News For You*. A later wave of new panel comedies included *Would I Lie To You?*, *QI*, *8 Out of 10 Cats*, *Mock The Week* and many others. The producers of long-running panel comedy shows need a regular flow of guest participants – and many of the comics involved in one or more of the established comedy sub-genres.

What we now call Stand Up comedy was present in nineteenth music hall entertainment and comedians were prominent in early twentieth-century Variety. Only in the 1970s did the North of England working-men's-club comedians get onto television in significant numbers. Granada's *The Comedians* (1971–4), launched the TV careers of more than twenty stand-up comedians including Frank Carson, Bernard Manning and Russ Abbott. The Granada producer (John Hamp) edited one-liners and very short bites of several different comedians into a half-hour show which (with music and commercials) ran for under 25 minutes.[2] Granada were following the stand-up success of Dave Allen who did 30 stand-up shows

2 Johnnie Hamp, 'Light Entertainment', in John Finch, ed., *Granada Television: the first generation* (Manchester: Manchester University Press, 2003), 172–6.

on ATV/ITV during 1967–9. Allen, who in fact sat down, attacked such sacred cows as Irish Roman Catholicism.[3]

Since 1990 Stand Up has remained the main sub-genre within which British comedians acquire their professional training. These live gigs tend to be more sexually explicit, more obscene and more adult than what's currently on TV. Most stand up television comedy still does short runs; but a return to anthology comedy – several comedians in one show – can stretch the scripted material across more weeks.

Sketch comedy's leading UK exponent from 1955 was Benny Hill. He was a writer-performer who delivered 109 hour- and half-hour- shows over a thirty-five-year career. But his bawdy humour and sexist sight gags were eventually terminated by Thames in 1989.[4] Two other sketch comedy superstars were *Morecambe and Wise* who were perhaps the most popular, and most influential, partnership in British TV comedy. These two comedians showed how Sketch Comedy could be a broader entertainment show, including some Stand Up and some guest stars. Morecambe and Wise also personified the shift in British TV comedy from a working class to a more middle mass focus. They began as child stars at seaside venues, and advanced via BBC Northern Home Service radio to their first BBC TV show in 1954. They continued to be TV comedians for three decades (1954–84). Their 1977 Christmas show had an audience of 28.7 million (51 per cent of the then UK population).[5]

As a sub-genre, Sketch comedy had one of its best decades in the 1990s. Cheaper production technology enabled short comedy sketches to be performed, and heavily edited, to a high standard. Harry Enfield was a leading writer-performer in successive 1990s *Harry Enfield* series. Enfield, Paul Whitehouse and Kathy Burke performed most of the leading characters. Loadsamoney, Tim-Nice-But-Dim, Wayne and Waynetta Slob, the DJs Smashey and Nicey, and other sketch characters, became national

3 Graham McCann, ed., *The Essential Dave Allen* (London: Hodder and Stoughton, 2005).

4 Dennis Kirkland, *The Strange and Saucy World of Benny Hill* (London: Blake Publishing, 2002).

5 William Cook, *Morecambe and Wise Untold* (London: HarperCollins, 2007).

treasures. Subsequent sketch partnerships have included Vic Reeves and Bob Mortimer,[6] Armstrong and Miller, Mitchell and Webb, and many others. These shows have had their passionate supporters, but audiences for sketch comedy have diminished. Typical audiences for 9.00 or 9.30pm sketch comedy on BBC1 are below 3 million and on BBC2 below 2 million. These low numbers have made ITV executives dubious about sketch comedy.

Situation Comedy has long been regarded in British TV as the most prestigious of the comedy sub-genres. Situation Comedy traces its UK history back to American radio and TV and to BBC radio. But Sitcom also derives from London live theatre comedy. Sitcom tends to be, by TV standards, rather static; many Sitcoms have, like live theatre, focused entirely on two or three built sets – such as the family kitchen and sitting room plus an office, or a pub. Situation comedy – as usually defined – is static also in largely lacking narrative, strong storylines, or melodrama. A typical sitcom episode shows the family or group confronting and solving some trivial problem; at the end of the episode everyone is smiling again and no melodramatic cliff hanger beckons. The 1970s and 1980s were the golden era of the British TV sitcom. Only about ten writers wrote the majority of the most successful sitcoms across these two decades. Sitcom is now generally regarded as a difficult comedy area. It's often said that a situation comedy needs two or three years to build a loyal audience – and today's commissioners and schedulers lack the necessary patience. Sitcom's preference for familiar characters, doing familiar small things, seems to lack the action and narrative most television now offers. This is reflected in a tendency for sitcoms to lapse into comedy drama, where there is more narrative, and more character development. However comedy commissioners, especially in the BBC, but also at ITV and C4, continue to commission new sitcoms, most of which complete about six or ten half hours and are then cancelled.

6 Ben Thompson, *Sunshine on Putty: The Golden Age of British Comedy from Vic Reeves to The Office* (London: Fourth Estate, 2004).

Most of the more successful sitcoms since 1990 have stretched the sub-genre a little beyond such conventions as the happy/unhappy family. *The Vicar of Dibley* (BBC1, 1994–2005) was a flirtatious woman. *Benidorm* featured British package tourists summer holidaying on the Spanish coast. *The Royle Family* involved a working class family who mostly just watched television and gossiped. *Miranda* featured a tall woman who kept falling over, and winking at the camera, as – slapstick style – she pursued her man. Two unusual features of *Mrs Brown's Boys* were that its foul-mouthed Mrs Brown was played by a man and the series was an Irish-British co-production. *Citizen Kahn* was not just an Asian sitcom, but a sitcom which featured a British-Pakistani family.

Political Satire, the fourth category of scripted comedy, made only brief TV appearances, until the 1982 arrival of Channel Four. Political satire did well on television around 1990. *The New Statesman* (BBC1, 1987–9) featuring Rik Mayall as Conservative MP, Alan B'Stard, achieved new levels of vitriolic denunciation of British politics and politicians. But *Spitting Image* (ITV, 1984–96) in its 141 episodes was probably even more effective in its merciless caricaturing of Prime Ministers Thatcher and Major and the royal family. In producing a puppet show of high complexity and technical quality,[7] *Spitting Image* provided work and training for at least 40 comedy producers, writers and voice artists; many of these people were leaders of British TV comedy in the 1990s and after. Bill Dare, the series producer of *Spitting Image* in 1991, told me that the then voice artists were paid about £2,000 per day for a few days work per year; the voice artist team included such names as Rory Bremner, Steve Coogan, Harry Enfield and John Sessions. Rory Bremner can claim to have been after 1990 the British political satirist with the widest range, funniest political material and most professional stamina. For over two decades since *The Rory Bremner Show* (BBC2, 1988) he did his own series and specials, mostly on BBC2 and C4. *Bremner, Bird and Fortune* – a one hour show on Channel Four – was remarkable for its relentless focus on politics; of 150 impersonation-sketches

7 Lewis Chester, *Tooth and Claw: the inside story of Spitting Image* (London: Faber and Faber, 1986).

performed by Bremner in 2008, 81 per cent were of politicians (with Tony Blair, Gordon Brown and George Bush in the lead). A fiercely comic and critical account of the Blair and Brown publicity operations was presented in *The Thick of It* (BBC4 and 2, ending in 2012).

Comedians and TV comedy

In TV comedy, more than in any other genre, a performer exposes his or her own personality, and own life history, in the performance. More even than actors in drama, comedians go through a harsh induction. The 'newly discovered' TV comedian, has typically been working in comedy for a decade or more. Most successful British comedians, before being discovered by TV, have performed hundreds of times in front of live audiences for not much money. They know what it's like to finance a career with second and third jobs, and to be repeatedly rejected at auditions. Many struggling comedians have dried and died, while being shouted down by audience drunks. Stewart Lee gives a marvellous account of this very protracted rite of passage; and Lee had the advantages of exceptional talent, an Oxford education, and some success in his early twenties. Lee performed 2,000 live stand-up gigs before he was discovered by television.[8] But if audiences are cruel and harsh, audiences can also be sentimental about their own favourite much-loved TV comedian.

Back in the 1980s the comedy writers were almost as important as the comedy performers. But since the 1980s, comedy writers have collectively become less salient – as a consequence of unscripted panel comedy and

8 Stewart Lee, *How I Escaped My Certain Fate: the life and deaths of a stand-up comedian* (London: Faber and Faber, 2010). Julian Hall, *The Rough Guide to British Cult Comedy* (London: Rough Guides, 2006), 78–9. Paul Whitelaw, 'Stewart Lee: No more sugaring the pill', *Broadcast*, 29 April 2011.

because more comedy is now scripted by writer-performers. Both performers and producers have become more important to comedy TV.

Television comedy has its own steep career ladder. Apprentice comedians have often started at school; as young adults, most comedians have performed in small pub-and-club or student venues. Those with comedy writing ambitions have often started their professional careers by selling one-liner jokes to BBC radio comedy shows. A second major level is reached when the aspiring comedian gets to play supporting roles on radio, or TV, or in live shows. A third level is reached when the comedian starts to play leading roles on TV and radio; at this point the comedian may get invitations to appear on TV panel shows. But all three of these levels are highly insecure. Comics from all three of these levels are likely to appear at the Edinburgh Fringe Festival where each year over one thousand comic acts compete for audiences, print praise and subsequent television employment. Only the well established comedians – typically playing a lead part in a continuing TV series and appearing on other shows at other venues – can afford to ignore the Edinburgh comedy cattle crush.

But comedy differs from other TV genres in that many, or most, established comedians also do live tours, often to twenty or thirty provincial cities outside London. These live appearances typically take place in venues which seat several hundred people, while some arena venues seat several thousand people. In stand up comedy live appearances, the lone comedian, who is the main attraction, can expect to receive a large slice of what the customers pay at the box office. Some comedians earn much or most of their comedy earnings by these big live appearances. They may see their TV appearances as publicity for their live touring shows. The touring show can use the same scripted jokes right across the 20 or 30 venues. These tours also ensure that British comedians are typically in touch with live audiences throughout their entire careers. Much TV comedy is performed 'near live' in front of an audience, and is then only edited before transmission.

Most comedians have found that their careers ascend during their thirties, level out in their forties, and descend in their fifties. Well established comedians are, however, able to extend their careers beyond age fifty in some obvious ways. Many senior TV comedians not only do panel shows, but they are employed on radio, or on travel TV, or as the lone entertainer on a political talk show. Some established TV comedians do a lot of TV advertising voiceovers and newspaper articles. A number have written more than one volume of autobiography.

British TV audiences seem to relish eccentricity and oddity, which many comedians are happy to supply. The comedians are encouraged by their agents to emphasise their peculiarities and amusing eccentricity. The mature comedian can become, not just a player in a series, but a freelance, a commercial brand. Ultimately a senior comedian can become the licensed wise fool in a crazy world, or even a Guru – the lone funny person who truly tells it like it is.

Male comedians, on a longer list of possible branded eccentric gurus, include the following: Rowan Atkinson was blessed with the rare ability to make audiences laugh at his sight gags without any words; he combined childish simplicity (Mr Bean) with highbrow humour in the *Blackadder* series. Russell Brand was the reformed addict (heroin and sex) with the silver tongue. Martin Clunes was the Mr Nice Guy (*Men Behaving Badly* and *Doc Martin*) who also made lovely factual series about horses, animals and islands. Steve Coogan was the comic who bravely and repeatedly denounced phone hacking and the Murdoch press. Stephen Fry was British TV's ultimate comedy polymath and guru-in-chief. Harry Hill, with an exceptionally eloquent face, was a former medical doctor, turned slapstick comedian. Ian Hislop was the ultimate comedian of political skulduggery. Transvestite Eddie Izzard, who set records for running many twenty-six-mile marathons in a single month, was also brave enough to do Stand Up in French in Paris. David Mitchell was the champion comic-on-many-platforms. Hugh Laurie was the very British comedy star who became seriously wealthy playing a very American TV doctor across 200 episodes of *House*. Paul Merton was the king of surrealist improvised comedy. Dara O'Briain was the Irish funny man who could talk excitedly about Science. Michael Palin was the non-stop traveller who smiled his way many times around the world. Griff Rhys Jones was the angry comic who, in *Restoration* became devoted to recovering decayed old buildings. David Walliams, the long distance swimmer, was devoted also to over-the-edge humour. All of these eccentric guru male comedians experienced successful later careers; and being an eccentric branded TV guru tended to be quite lucrative.

Big entertainment

Since year 2000 Big Entertainment shows such as *X Factor*, *Britain's Got Talent*, *Strictly Come Dancing*, *Dancing on Ice* and *The Voice* have been enormously popular on weekend evenings. These shows marked a return to some big entertainment themes of the 1950s and 1960s – when 'Variety' had included comedy, song-and-dance, family quiz and the amateur talent shows.[9] *Sunday Night At The London Palladium* (ITV, 1955–67) featured one current star entertainer with a supporting comedian-song-and-dance team, a quiz show and the Tiller Girls chorus. *The Black and White Minstrel Show* (BBC, 1958–78) was the BBC's top Variety show.

Secondly there were straight amateur talent shows – such as *Opportunity Knocks* (ITV 1956–78). A later talent show, *New Faces* (ITV, 1973–8 and 1986–8), 'discovered' several major comedy talents including Victoria Wood and Lenny Henry. *Come Dancing* (BBC1, 1950–95) was another talent show; it used mostly amateur dancers with some professional involvement. The old fashioned show was re-launched by the BBC in 2004 as *Strictly Come Dancing*; this was a knock-out talent competition, in which celebrities were coached by professional dancers.

So what's changed in TV big entertainment since the 1950s and 1960s? The current shows are sexier and more confrontational. The judges are more brutal. The competitive knock-out aspect is emphasised and turned (like a sports knock-out competition) into a narrative of failure for many and success for a few. Melodrama is deliberately heightened by music and, for example, by lengthy close-ups of contestants about to be told who's still in and who's out.

X Factor was produced in London by Talkback Thames/Fremantle and its first series producer, from 2004, was Claire Horton; she told me:

9 Louis Barfe, *Turned Out Nice Again: the story of British Light Entertainment* (London: Atlantic Books, 2008).

With the old talent shows, like *Opportunity Knocks*, each week's show was quite stand alone – more what we would today class as a 'heat'. We now have in each series – transmitted from August to December – a beginning, a middle, and an end. As a viewer, you become emotionally attached; you want to know what happens next. Everybody on the show has a journey.

X Factor starts transmission in August, but we start shooting auditions in April. We have 50 people on the road continuously from April onwards. We begin filming auditions in big cities outside London. The first ten programmes are recorded. Only for the last rounds in November and December do we move into the 750-seater studio in London. So our road team films auditions in places like Manchester and Birmingham. The 'boot camp' training phase is also pre-filmed. So are the shows from the judges' homes in Miami, Los Angeles and London. Then when we get down to our last twenty-four contestants (or acts), we take the cameras to their homes. We go to all twenty-four contestant homes.

When we're on air, we have a meeting on the following Monday. We're continually looking at what we could change. At the end of the run we each analyse the whole series. Then we go to Los Angeles for a week in March, because Simon Cowell is there doing *American Idol*. Everyone puts up their ideas for changes.

X Factor is a soap opera in its own right – from August to Christmas. The press are hungry for stories; we try to manage what the press get and don't get. There's a fine line between publicising the show, protecting the contestants, and protecting the brand. So we have four full-time people who deal with the press when *X Factor* is on air.

The broadcasters (ITV) are always interested in 'What Else?' What new media activity can they have? Any brand extensions that can go into ITV2? We have full-time people who are filming behind the scenes of *X Factor*, and we put this on the internet and the website. It's quite pricey to get something up, so it's then about audience traffic. With *X Factor*, as the series builds up, the audience grows, and the traffic going to the website grows. With a one-off show you can't do that.

Richard Holloway, who executive produced both *X Factor* and *Britain's got Talent* told me:

To get a mass audience, you must appeal to the whole family, teenagers, 16–34, old people, everyone. Get it right, and the rewards are huge. I exec both shows, but *X Factor* and *Britain's Got Talent* are made by totally separate production teams. The series producers, the APs and the researchers are different. *X Factor* has a 46 week production cycle. *Britain's Got Talent* takes about 43 weeks each year. It's the sheer weight of numbers. This year we've had 300,000 applications to audition for BGT. We do auditions in London, Manchester, Birmingham, Glasgow, Cardiff and one other big city. In each audition city we have sixteen or eighteen people who handle

> the initial auditions; they are people such as record producers. We see everyone that applies and shows up – many of them only for five minutes.
>
> The anticipation of *X Factor* coming on air is extraordinary. And this year, at launch time in August, we were on the front page of all five national tabloids for ten days in succession. The resource that goes into the show's editing is huge. We use much less than one per cent of what we shoot. But you don't want the public to think about the hundreds of hours we've spent in the edit suite. You want to create a story. Today you can record an hour's worth of HD pictures on a chip the size of my thumbnail. In the late 1980s an hour's worth of material would have been a huge reel of tape. Doing our present quantity on colour film would have been impossibly expensive. Yes, the Judges are extremely important – so also is the chemistry between them.

Richard Holloway confirmed that Simon Cowell[10] was a crucial performer in *X Factor* and *Britain's Got Talent* – as well as holding a portfolio of linked contracts as follows: one contract is between Cowell's Syco company and Talkback Thames/Fremantle. All contestants sign a form awarding rights in their performances to Cowell. Sony has a recording contract with Cowell. There are appearance deals between Simon Cowell, as a performer, and ITV in the UK and Fox in the US.

The BBC's most successful Big Entertainment show was *Strictly Come Dancing*. It had several features in common with *X Factor*:

- Both shows were expensive – each cost over £20 million for a full run of about 14 weeks. But because each week generated several hours of programming (on big as well as small channels) the cost per hour was below the cost per hour of drama.
- Both shows employed large teams of people, including some of the UK's best camera and lighting specialists.
- Both shows built up each week across more than three months. But each show is back-edited so as to help the audience follow the narratives of ultimately more successful contestants.

10 Chas Newkey-Burden, *Simon Cowell: the unauthorized biography* (London: Michael O'Mara Books, 2009).

- The Judges are as important as, or more important than, the contestants. Each show has a panel of four Judges who interact vigorously between themselves and with the contestants.
- In both shows there is a strong element of nurturing and training. The *X Factor* Judges sponsor individual contestants. In *Strictly Come Dancing* each contestant dances with, and is trained by, a professional dancer.

However there are some differences. *X Factor* starts out with unknowns, the great majority lacking any real singing experience. *Strictly Come Dancing*'s competitors are known mostly as television performers or sports people. Because the *Strictly* contestants are partnered by professionals, the overall performance of the *Strictly* dancers is of higher quality than most of the *X Factor* singing. In *X Factor* much of the entertainment in the early rounds derives from the lack of singing talent and the musical ignorance exhibited by most contestants. But the *Strictly* producers usually include only one or two hopeless cases – such as overweight middle-aged male broadcasters.

Both *X Factor* and *Strictly* generate huge audience enthusiasm and big emotional involvement amongst the studio audience. Both shows are quite harsh in terms of rejecting nearly all contestants. But ITV's *X Factor* is harsher and more brutal because the producers encourage contestants to discuss their hopes of pop music stardom; these high hopes are then quickly and harshly, or brutally, dismissed. The BBC's *Strictly Come Dancing* is gentler and more professional. A *Strictly* contestant who survives into the last ten is typically a professional performer who is extending his or her screen personality and competence across an additional genre platform.

These Big Entertainment shows differ quite sharply from each other. But *X Factor*, *Strictly Come Dancing*, and *Britain's Got Talent* all retained elements of the 1950s-to-1970s Variety and Amateur Talent shows. These Big Entertainment shows offered song-and-dance, comedy presenters, and celebrity judges. The producers of each show broadened the appeal by having contestants interviewed on the back-up shows on smaller channels. These shows have stimulated exceptionally high levels of YouTube, Facebook and Twitter activity.

The producers also invited super-star singers and dancers to do guest appearances. But both *X Factor* and *Strictly* remained talent shows, which demonstrated the continuing human appeal of genuinely amateur talent combined with genuinely slick professional production.

The talk genre

British TV offers three or four different types of entertainment 'Talk' – mostly on Friday and Saturday evenings. The biggest category is show business talk – typically hosted by experienced talkers such as Jonathan Ross and Graham Norton.

The UK Talk genre, like other TV genres, was copied – with significant modifications – from an American model. American TV Talk became a late evening 5-nights-a-week show hosted by a comedian. British talk initially was only once-a-week but in a high audience, evening, time slot. *Face to Face* (BBC, 1959–62) was a pioneering talk/interview programme in which John Freeman did non-political interviews with serious public figures, artists and writers. A few of Freeman's guests were American (Martin Luther King, John Huston) and a few were comedians (Tony Hancock) but most were big thinkers (Bertrand Russell, Carl Gustav Jung), and upmarket writers and artists. In keeping with minimalist British TV tradition, *Face to Face* only did just over thirty shows in total. There was little non-political Talk in British TV during the remainder of the 1960s.

Great variation within showbiz talk leads to several paradoxes. Talk has often been thought of as a cheap slot-filler, but some talk shows become more expensive and employ quite a large production team. The current top talkers may be dismissed as retired comedians or failed journalists; but these top talkers are bigger stars (to most of their UK audiences) than the movie, music and sports stars they interview on air. Several top talkers of recent years have in fact been polymaths with large knowledge hinterlands. There has been a common pattern of some talkers remaining at the top of the genre for about twenty years. Graham Norton, for example, became a top talker around 2000.[11] Top talkers have joined the ranks of multi-platform performers – not only on TV, but on radio, online, and in books. Top talkers are often accused, especially by younger viewers, of being bland and over-cautious. But some top talkers have big enough egos, and big enough bank balances, to deliberately court controversy. For example, when it became known in 2008 that Jonathan Ross had a three year BBC contract worth £18 million (or $27 million) he cheerfully claimed that one Ross was worth one thousand BBC journalists.

The most visible ingredients of the talk genre are the host and the guests. Another common ingredient is an accompanying music group. But behind the camera the major activity is booking the guests. Many of the most desirable guests are only willing to appear when they have a new product – movie, TV show, music tour, or publication – to plug. Talk show producers must orchestrate this booking exercise. Producers want to be the first show to book the currently hot guest. Publicists and agents, handling a new movie or TV show, negotiate to get into what they see as the most suitable TV show(s) and most suitable national newspaper(s). Talk producers have always been extremely well supplied with audience and rating data. The fixed format show, with different guests each week, has long made it easy to know which guests are most and least popular. Each talk show has its favourite, frequently appearing, guests; this pattern is based not only on host and producer preference, but also on hard data.

The first successful UK showbiz talk show was *Parkinson* which ran for 11 years (1971–82) on BBC1 on Saturday evenings; it specialised in big stars in general and Hollywood movie star guests in particular.[12] The golden years of British talk TV were, arguably, around 1990; the 1990 talk leader was Terry Wogan, whose half hour *Wogan* show was running three times a week at 7pm on BBC1. *Wogan* completed its 1,000th show in July 1991, with an extended interview with Madonna. The executive producer of

11 Graham Norton, *So Me* (London: Hodder and Stoughton, 2004).

12 Michael Parkinson, *Parky: My Autobiography* (London: Hodder and Stoughton, 2008).

Wogan was Peter Estall, who told me in 1991 that he had a production staff of twenty, made up of two teams; each team spent one week preparing next week's output and the second week putting those three editions on the air. Peter Estall visited Hollywood twice a year to trawl for star interviewees. The other leading talk show of 1990–1, *Aspel and Company*, appeared on LWT/ITV on only fifteen Saturday evenings per year. Michael Aspel had a long career history of presenting entertainment shows. Lorna Dickinson, the producer, told me of her pride at successfully stalking Elizabeth Taylor, who had recently been on the show.

A very few British talkers – and most notably David Frost – have successfully hosted both serious and showbiz series. When he interviewed ex-President Richard Nixon in 1977, David Frost had already hosted and interviewed many politicians. But Frost was better known – especially in the United States – as a showbiz figure and weekly commuter between London and New York. Perhaps Richard Nixon was not fully aware of Frost's 'serious' side, when he agreed to what became 28 hours of TV taped interviews.[13] Another British showbiz and serious talk host, Piers Morgan, was Editor of two Murdoch controlled tabloid newspapers, before becoming a TV talent Judge (*America's Got Talent*) and talk host on the American news channel CNN.

In the years after 2000, Jonathan Ross and Graham Norton became superstars of British TV. In 1990–1 *Tonight With Jonathan Ross* was running on Channel Four from November to June and doing three shows a week for 30 weeks (90 shows a year). The Ross show was live at 6.30pm. The producer (Mike Bolland) told us that Jonathan Ross was exceptionally active and involved:

> He reads the books, meet the guests in advance and attends the morning production meeting. The trick with a talk show is not to let it become purely a plug show.

For more than two decades after 1990, Jonathan Ross was the UK's top TV talker. When he was sacked by the BBC, after 'going too far' with Russell Brand in 2008, Jonathan Ross was snapped up by ITV at a fancy salary.

13 David Frost with Bob Zelnick, *Frost/Nixon* (London: Macmillan, 2007).

From year 2000 onwards the Ross and Norton talk shows were scheduled on weekend evenings alongside the Big Entertainment shows; current stars from the Entertainment shows often guested on the talk shows. The top talk show hosts were frequently chosen to present TV industry events for best TV, best Comedy and best Entertainment shows of the year.

Meanwhile the TV talk shows remain a special mix of TV Entertainment; many of the guests are indeed plugging their new shows, their jokes and their songs. The talk show is itself a small comedy-song-and-dance variety show. The channel's top talk show host is seen as one key ingredient in the channel's image and reputation. The talk show producer also expects to assist the channel controller by giving a publicity boost to certain selected channel stars and series.

Producers, agents, entertainment industry

British television has a tradition of very prominent entertainment executives. Lew Grade established this tradition when, as chief executive of ATV (the ITV company for the Midlands and London weekends) during 1956–68, he supplied much of the new ITV network's comedy and entertainment. Lew Grade and his two brothers (Leslie Grade and Bernard Delfont), controlled a 'Gradopoly' of British show business. The three brothers controlled numerous London theatres and clubs, and provincial touring companies; and the brothers were agents for much of Britain's top acting talent across live theatre, film and TV.[14] Subsequent top TV entertainment executives included Bill Cotton (junior) who over an 18 year period (1970–88) held a succession of top BBC jobs – from Head of Light Entertainment to Managing Director of BBC Television.[15] A more

14 'Gradopoly' in Hunter Davies, *The Grades: the first family of British entertainment* (London: Weidenfeld and Nicolson, 1981), 153–61.

15 Bill Cotton, *Double Bill* (London: Fourth Estate/HarperCollins, 2000).

recent example of the exceptionally dominant entertainment executive is Simon Cowell who found new ways to develop big entertainment brands, and to contract with the winners of knock out competitions; Cowell was additionally himself an Anglo-American performance star.[16]

A few key executive producers have each developed a long list of successful series. Across three decades from 1979 onwards, John Lloyd produced and nurtured five of British TV's most admired comedy series – *Not The Nine O'Clock News*, *Spitting Image*, all of the *Blackadder* series,[17] *Have I Got News For You* and *QI*.

Another exceptionally influential comedy producer was Paul Jackson, who produced key shows such as *The Young Ones* (BBC2 1982–4). Paul Jackson told me: 'Rik Mayall came to see me with a sitcom idea. It was biro-written on A4 paper with coffee stains. It became *The Young Ones*.'

Paul Jackson's 1980–5 'discoveries' included: Alexei Sayle, Keith Allen, Rik Mayall, Nigel Planer, Dawn French, Jennifer Saunders, Adrian Edmondson, Ruby Wax, Ben Elton, Lenny Henry, Tracey Ullman, Harry Enfield, Stephen Fry, Hugh Laurie, Julian Clary and Paul Merton. Jackson modestly told me that it was easy to discover these comedy talents. He just attended live shows on the then London club scene and also listened to BBC Radio 4. But Paul Jackson admitted that some proposals from these young comedians did need a lot of extra work.

Jon Plowman was another BBC producer who presented a modest persona, but who was enormously influential in the world of TV comedy. As BBC Head of Entertainment and then of BBC Comedy, Jon Plowman acted as the producer or executive producer of 46 separate BBC comedy series. Jon Plowman executive produced *French and Saunders*, *Absolutely Fabulous* and *The Vicar of Dibley*. One of his main difficulties with these star comediennes was, he told me, to persuade Jennifer Saunders to get the scripts written on time. About his experience of overseeing the production

16 Tom Bower, *Sweet Revenge: the intimate life of Simon Cowell* (London: Faber and Faber, 2012).

17 J.F. Roberts, *The True History of Black Adder* (London: Preface, 2012).

of *The Office* (BBC, 2001–2)[18] Jon Plowman told me that he made three contributions:

> We attached Anil Gupta as a third person because both Ricky Gervais and Stephen Merchant had so little TV experience ... My main contribution was nodding it through and persuading BBC2, who didn't want to do it ... Initially it came in very short – at 21 minutes and then at 24 minutes, instead of 29. I told them to shoot more office stuff.

The launch of *Little Britain* in 2003 was a different kind of case, Jon Plowman told me:

> I'd worked with Matt Lucas and David Walliams before. The main problems were of the 'Can We Really Say This?' kind. It's very difficult to make any comedy, and still more difficult to make a comedy for a general audience ... Research indicates that only about 5 to 10 per cent of the audience want the most edgy stuff. But this was initially destined for BBC3, where you can do stuff that would look dodgy launching on BBC1. I think you have to focus on the initial immediate audience. If it's the young BBC3 audience, then go for it. So we did. Later, of course, it ended up on BBC1.

Among numerous other BBC comedies, Jon Plowman executive produced *Goodness Gracious Me* (BBC2 1998–2001), the first comedy series on a main UK channel to be written and performed by an Asian team. He also executive produced the gothic–sketch–sitcom *The League of Gentlemen* (BBC2, 1999–2002). In an interesting book[19] on this series, the author devotes four sentences to Jon Plowman's contribution and not much more to the respected and experienced series producer, Sarah Smith.

Independent Producers have also played a prominent role in TV comedy since 1990. Key panel comedies were created by indie producers, including Hat Trick's *Have I Got News For You* and Talkback's *Never Mind The Buzzcocks*. Peter Fincham (subsequent BBC1 controller and 'saviour' of ITV) produced numerous comedies including *Buzzcocks* and *They Think It's All Over* when at the Talkback indie. While both Hat Trick

18 Ben Walters, *The Office* (London: British Film Institute, 2005).

19 Leon Hunt, *The League of Gentlemen* (London: British Film Institute/Palgrave Macmillan, 2008).

and Talkback are now part of bigger indie groupings and belong to the comedy establishment, there has been a steady flow of new comedy independent producers – some created by comedy performers, some by successful comedy producers, and some by comedy agents.

Both successful and aspiring comedians and singers seem badly to need the assistance and sympathy of a manager-agent. Michael Grade who was an apprentice agent, inside his family's show business conglomerate, has written:

> Good agents combine a wide range of skills: they need to be tough negotiators, shrewd talent-spotters, passionate lovers of show business ... The good agent must also be an agony aunt or uncle, prepared to nurse temperamental public performers through their personal and professional traumas. With some exceptions, the greater a star's talent, the more wildly his or her moods tend to oscillate between exhilaration and deep depression.[20]

Many comedians are both angered and enthused not only by their audiences and potential employers but also by their working colleagues. Many British comedians have conducted love/hate relationships with their writers and with their comedy partners. Most comedy partnerships involve one lead performer and one second banana. Should they both be paid the same? And should they both have the same agent? How much should the writers be paid compared with the performers? And so on.

One of the 20 or 30 currently top comedians may have a TV series, and appear in panel comedy shows, as well as doing some radio, some newspaper and book writing and some advertising. A successful stand-up comedian may in one year tour perhaps twenty provincial cities. There are also less publicised gigs such as performing for after-dinner-laughs at commercial gatherings. A successful (but not superstar comedian) might earn £500,000 (or nearly $1 million) in a good year. But he or she needs the expertise of a talent management agency (and its specialised departments) to handle the numerous bookings, contracts, scripts and proposals.

20 Michael Grade, *It Seemed Like A Good Idea At The Time* (London: Macmillan/Pan, 1999–2000), 69–70.

What soon became Britain's first specialised TV comedy talent agency was set up in 1954 by five comedy writers and comedians – Eric Sykes, Spike Milligan, Ray Galton, Alan Simpson and Frankie Howerd – and an agent, Stanley Dale (known as Scruffy). The lead agent role was quickly taken over by Beryl Vertue who began as secretary/typist but quickly became the chief agent at Associated London Scripts (ALS). Beryl Vertue provided these unique comedy talents with several services, starting with the fresh typing of scripts. The early ALS comedy writers and comedians tended to spend most of the day in the ALS offices – talking, trying out jokes, writing, eating and drinking; it was a surprisingly harmonious comedy college, or club, or family. Vertue was strong on sympathetic laughter over cups of tea, but she also quickly developed a comedy agent's business plan. She was a pioneer of merchandising comedy products. She retained all foreign rights, and later sold shows to northern Europe and the USA.[21] Vertue sold Johnny Speight's *Till Death Us Do Part* to the US, where it became *All in the Family*. She also sold Ray Galton and Alan Simpson's *Steptoe and Son* to the US, where it became *Sanford and Son*. Beryl Vertue subsequently extended into drama and movies and set up her own independent production company, Hartswood Films. Vertue was less successful with one of her star clients, namely Tony Hancock, widely regarded as British TV's best ever sitcom performer. In 1963 Tony Hancock broke away from his writers, Galton and Simpson, and from his agent, Beryl Vertue; and five years later he committed suicide.[22]

Addison Cresswell's death in 2013 marked the end of two decades in which Cresswell's agency and two other talent management agencies had exerted a remarkable grip on British comedy in general and on TV comedy in particular. The other two top comedy management agents were Peter Bennett-Jones (of the PBJ agency) and Jon Thoday (of Avalon). All three

21 Graham McCann, *Spike and Co: inside the House of Fun with Milligan, Sykes, Galton and Simpson* (London: Hodder and Stoughton, 2006).

22 John Fisher, *Tony Hancock* (London: HarperCollins, 2008), 393–422.

agencies began in the 1980s and signed up unknowns whom they helped to become successful. These agents became famous for a very few star contracts which paid sums such as £6 million (or $10 million) per year. Each of these three big comedy management agents tended to be close to one particular TV channel and/or comedy commissioner. Each of these agency companies also itself operated as a producer, through its very own independent production company. Peter Bennett-Jones had Tiger Aspect and Jon Thoday's Avalon was an important producer. Addison Cresswell's production wing was Open Mike Productions.

The emergence of these talent agency, plus production company, combinations was one of several linked changes which have transformed British comedy since 1990. Other linked changes included these:

- A few star hosts and comedy performers – such as Jonathan Ross, Graham Norton, Frank Skinner, Michael McIntyre and John Bishop – were each, in a good year, earning several million pounds.
- A dozen or more comedy panel shows generated a musical chairs game in which top comics circulated as guests and hosts around the same shows.
- The large live arena show emerged as a key comedy platform. This involved stadium gigs at the O2 and Wembley Stadium as well as at large venues, including the Albert Hall, *Live at the Apollo* (Hammersmith) and a few large halls in cities such as Birmingham and Manchester. In 2012 Michael McIntyre did 71 arena gigs, playing live to over 700,000 people. Many thousands of people were willing to purchase expensive seats in order to see in the flesh the star comics they had previously seen only on television.
- Television still reached much the biggest comedy audiences. Six episodes of a comedy series might reach a total audience of 20 million. Television was both the top comedy medium and the medium which built the star reputation and enabled that reputation to be spread across a range of other platforms.

Golden oldies: Everlasting repetition?

The 1970s probably generated more Much Loved British comedy and entertainment than did any other single decade. But most of the 1970s comedies had fairly short total runs. Nine 1970s comedy series – *Dad's Army*, *Are You Being Served?*, *Porridge*, *Sykes*, *Steptoe and Son*, *Till Death Us Do Part*, *The Fall and Rise of Reginald Perrin*, *Monty Python* and *Up Pompeii* – averaged just 47 episodes each (mostly half hours) – typically about six episodes per year, spread across eight years. Most much loved comedies were BBC shows and they are sometimes repeated in daytime on BBC1 and 2, and during the evening on BBC3 and 4. Many other comedy repeats are on the UKTV channels Dave and Gold.

But big repeat exercises – especially five episodes a week repeats – require long original runs, and British TV has had few of these. Very long-running 1970s British comedy consists mainly of *Morecambe and Wise*, *The Two Ronnies* and *Last of the Summer Wine*; these three shows together accumulated over 600 episodes. Another big series which began in 1981, *Only Fools and Horses*, took the collective total for these four series over the 800 episode mark.

So what other long-running sources are there for the channel controller who might like to run an old series, five days a week, for many weeks in succession? The Dave channel repeats a number of panel comedy shows – such as *Have I Got News For You* (and its variants), *Never Mind The Buzzcocks*, *Mock The Week* and *QI*. The Gold channel repeats some of the 200+ episode series and other more recent series such as *Harry Hill's TV Burp*, *Alan Partridge* and *Blackadder*.

We cannot know for sure what elements of past comedies will attract channel controllers of the future. But old comedies will probably attract producers in some other genres, such as History. Future producers and controllers may well regard the period from about 1985 onwards as a golden age of female comedy talents such as Caroline Aherne, Jo Brand, Kathy Burke, Bridget Christie, Jenny Éclair, Dawn French, Miranda Hart, Patricia Hodge, Joanna Lumley, Sarah Millican, Jennifer Saunders and Victoria

Wood. Most of these comedy stars were not just performers, but writer performers. However, while these women comedians have been original in some other respects, they have largely stuck to the traditional British comedy pattern of perhaps only six episodes per year.

What other sources are there of much loved comedy? Long running American comedy series are the obvious answer. American comedy series such as *Friends* and *Seinfeld* have indeed generated large numbers of episodes and have been heavily repeated on Channel Four and elsewhere. But the champion Hollywood comedy – in terms of weight of UK repeats – has been *The Simpsons*, which has been hugely repeated on the BBC, Channel Four and Sky. Additional much loved Hollywood comedy appears on Comedy Central and other UK versions of American channels.

In this era of hundreds of channels, the British public's comedy hunger, for more and more fresh-but-familiar entertainment, cannot be fully satisfied by the traditional British output of six or eight comedy half-hours per year. This is a reminder also that, while British comedy/big entertainment/talk seems very British, it is also quite American. The British public follows many low-audience American comedies; the UK Big Entertainment shows feature American judges, American music and Hollywood entertainers. The talk show's guest group typically involves one or more Americans plugging their latest greatest products.

CHAPTER 10

Factual Entertainment Formats Prosper: Cooking, Homes, Quiz/Game, Reality

The Cooking, Home/Housing, Quiz/Game, and Reality TV genres depend upon a fixed format, which can potentially be repeated hundreds of times. Formatted productions traditionally are unscripted and rely on 'ordinary people' to talk and perform spontaneously for little or no money. The formatted show aims to be cheap-per-audience; if successful, the format can be sold into export markets to generate extra finance and profits. The years around 2008 were crucial for formats. Independent producers, now with legally approved control over foreign rights, reacted to the TV financial crisis by focusing ever more strongly on trying to generate fresh cash from formats old and new.

Formatted Factual or Factual Entertainment are labels attached to about one third of all programming hours on each of the five main UK channels each weekday. The five big channels – BBC1, BBC2, ITV1, C4 and C5 – each devote, every weekday about four hours between 8.30am and 8.30pm to this programming. The key product-mix of the TV format is a combination of unscripted talk-and-activity within a fixed set of rules. These shows involve timing ('you have thirty seconds' or thirty minutes) and strict rules, presided over by hosts or presenters. These shows focus on human appeal – the contestants are determined to win the (sometimes large) prize, to win the contest, or at least to get through to the next round. The unscripted participants and competitors are placed in jeopardy, the fear of losing the prize, or not getting the house. Producers seek to develop a strong narrative as we, the audience, get to know more about the contestants.

In most format shows the audience sees the presenter as the star. Quite often two or three presenters are the main substance of the show, with the contestants in second place. But the format show, while presenter-led, is producer-driven. The format producer, or executive producer, plays at least four key roles. Firstly, the producer must select a potentially promising new format; the producer will probably choose one from a much larger number of possible formats which are being developed inside the production company. Secondly, the producer must seek to get the new format commissioned and financed by one of the TV channels; the channel may agree initially to provide some development finance, but the producer will seek to get a small batch (of perhaps six hours) commissioned. Even after this, the producer will still need to get an additional run commissioned. Thirdly, an executive producer must cast key roles – especially the presenter-host role, but also other important roles such as a senior researcher, a director and a series producer. Often the initial choice of presenter-host is rejected and another person is hired. Fourthly, an executive producer must choose the set, the camera system, and mechanisms for audience involvement.

Their fixed frameworks mean that formatted shows generate strong audience data, which the producers can utilise. From one season to the next, producers engage in a tweak-the-format exercise, such as dropping a particular round in the set sequence, or perhaps re-mixing the presenter team. Producers are well aware that the audience is attracted by villains, heroines, oddities, obsessives, eccentrics, larger-than-life characters, people with impossible dreams, and people who don't realise that they are bad at cooking, choosing houses, answering quiz questions or dealing with reality 'challenges'. The producers have to manage, edit, and finance all of this, while avoiding scandal or tragedy. Today's executive producer of a successful format tries to ensure that the success will continue into a popular and profitable future. A common device is to introduce a new celebrity version of the existing format.

Television formats have a long UK history, going back to early BBC radio and 1936–9 BBC television. Cooking advice was big on BBC Radio during 1940–5.[1] But the first real blast of formatted TV entertainment only arrived with advertising-driven ITV in 1955. Durable ITV American imports included *Double Your Money* (1955), *Name That Tune* (1956), and *Criss Cross Quiz* (1957).[2]

From the 1982 launch of Channel Four onwards, there was a steady expansion in formatted factual series. While leading star presenters typically hosted a succession of several formatted series, a small key group of executive producers each created at least twenty formatted series. The arrival of Channel Four in 1982 led to an early emphasis on an educational element in the formatted show. Naomi Sargant, C4's first 'Senior Commissioning Editor, Education' told me (in 1990) that she had commissioned 300 hours of Channel Four programming for each of six years (1982–8). These 1,800 television hours included *Take Six Cooks*, *Six Great Walks*, *Gallery* (a paintings quiz) and a consumer series, *For What It's Worth*. Sargant commissioned several gardening series; her most popular series was *Plants For Free*, which got an audience of 4 million on Friday night.[3]

The BBC has produced many formatted factual series but it has tended to follow at some distance behind the commercial broadcasters. The BBC has cultivated a different style of formatting – one which is public service oriented and deliberately advertiser unfriendly. Shaun Woodward[4] who in 1990 was co-producing *That's Life* (BBC, 1973–94) with the show's star, Esther Rantzen, told me that *That's Life* was like a sandwich; it always offered a slice of consumer watchdog meat between thick slices of light entertainment.

1 Starting with *Kitchen Front* in June 1940, BBC Radio broadcast about 240 food talks per year during 1940–5. Asa Briggs, *The War of Words* (Oxford: Oxford University Press, 1970: 36).

2 The US already had much experience of daytime, and other small audience, TV. In the three decades after 1948, US television transmitted nearly 700 separate quiz and game show formats, with the years 1949–52 being the peak. See: Maxene Fabe, *TV Game Shows* (New York: Doubleday Dolphin, 1979).

3 Andrew McIntosh and others, eds, *Lifelong Learning: A brave and proper vision. Selected writings of Naomi Sargant* (Leicester: National Institute of Adult Continuing Education, 2009), 105–82.

4 Later a prominent politician.

Peter Bazalgette during 1990–2005 was the UK's most important creator of factual formatted television. He was especially active in Food and Housing formats as well as being the key executive behind the British version of *Big Brother*; companies under his leadership also produced quiz programming. Peter Bazalgette was a producer who supplied several highly successful formats to BBC2 in the 1990s. Bazalgette's first major format was *Food and Drink*, an in-house BBC2 format which he was allowed to take outside into his new indie company, Bazal. By 1990 *Food and Drink* was often the highest rated BBC2 show of the week. It was a 30-minute show (8.30–9.00pm) which did several items. On 13 February 1990 it covered: Microwaves and food scares; Making a chocolate cake; Water filters; and Our-man-joins-wedding-revels and helps to cook the meal. Peter Bazalgette told me in 1990 that he had created a series which was so popular as to be embarrassing to his BBC2 bosses:

> It was genuinely in doubt whether *Food and Drink* would be recommissioned, for autumn 1989. The entertainment side of it – the bright, breezy, almost Blue Peterish side of it – is not totally beloved by the controller of BBC2, Alan Yentob, or by Colin Cameron of Documentary Features. But we've just had the number one audience on BBC2 two weeks running.

Bazalgette in 1990 told me that he was still learning his new job of independent producer:

> I've built this programme around audience research. Yes, the chefs are the stars of the show, but only because I've made them stars ... At present I waste time writing books and am too hands-on with *Food and Drink*.

Subsequently Peter Bazalgette was the executive producer of such influential series as *Ready, Steady, Cook*, *Changing Rooms*,[5] *Can't Cook, Won't Cook*, *Ground Force*, and the UK's version of *Big Brother* (for Channel Four). From the 1980s onwards, senior BBC executives wanted to expand their provision of formatted series, but this expansion was initially seen as

5 Annette Hill, *Reality TV: audiences and popular factual television* (London: Routledge, 2005), 93–7, 123–32.

developing from Documentary and Arts, while incorporating a significant public service element. Many of the new BBC format shows were commissioned by Michael Jackson as Controller of BBC2 (1993–6) and then of BBC1 (1996–7). Jackson relied quite heavily on Peter Bazalgette.

Daisy Goodwin was another executive producer who, during 2000–8, created at least twenty broadcast factual formatted series. Her commissions for BBC2 included *Would Like To Meet*, *Your Money Or Your Life*, *Life Laundry*, *Fame*, *Set and Match*, *Escape To The Country*, *Don't Look Down* and *Lipstick Years*. For Channel Four she executive produced *Jamie's Kitchen*, *Other People's Homes*, *Grand Designs*, *Property Ladder*, *She's Gotta Have It*, *How Clean Is Your House?* and *The Sex Inspectors*. Daisy Goodwin established her own Silver River independent production company in 2005. She told me in 2008:

> All my efforts are directed to selling programmes, which is what I like doing. In the end, people want to work with people they like. But a great idea helps. I'm good at thinking up ideas, and handing on the ideas to other people here. Then I think up the key sentences which need to be used to pitch the idea.

Stephen Lambert has been another leading creator of formatted factual series. At BBC Documentaries for 15 years, Lambert won many prizes. Only in 1998 did he move to the RDF indie company and start to create series such as *Faking It* and *Wife Swap*. Lambert had described his large output as Formatted Documentary; while some of his output has continued to be topic documentary, most of his post-1998 series have been at the high end of the Reality genre (as defined here). Lambert executive produced *Faking It* (C4, 2000–4); these 46 one hours were widely regarded in television as one of the most remarkable producer achievements in the history of British TV. The production team were involved in transforming, for example, a male naval officer into a convincing drag queen, changing a hamburger vendor into an up-market chef, or transforming a punk singer into a conductor of classical music. Stephen Lambert told me about the huge human effort and emotional investment which went into each *Faking It*:

> Both the faker and the mentor really cared. Only one specific performance had to be faked in front of a group of relevant experts. But this required huge commitment; in

> most cases the faker moved in to live temporarily with the mentor. We found excellent producer and performer talent, but we missed a trick in formatting. Each *Faking It* could have expanded into a format. We even failed to recognise the potential of a then unknown chef called Gordon Ramsay.[6] He was the mentor who transformed the burger seller into a chef.

Wife Swap (C4, 2003–9) focused on the family as the number one precinct for real human drama. *Celebrity Wife Swap* enabled well-known celebrities to be matched up for predictable conflict. In such shows, casting of the main characters was crucial. But the producers could also claim that the story often passed from conflict into some measure of agreement. Stephen Lambert told me in 2006, when *Wife Swap* was riding high:

> When we first thought of *Wife Swap*, we thought it's everything else apart from sharing the marital bed … With children and filming in the home, they are not easy programmes to make … We choose couples who have strong, and contrasting views. *Wife Swap* people are evangelical about their own way of doing the family; being on television reaffirms their evangelical approach …
>
> The challenge is to come up with new things. By about the third season you have the teams in place. Making the first few is very hard – the format has to evolve, as we do it. I discuss with them a lot, but the production team are the ones who must talk to the people involved.

Stephen Lambert in 2008 set up a new production company, Studio Lambert, under the wing of the large independent, All3Media. He obtained enough financial resources to employ several prominent TV producers. Five years later, in 2013, Studio Lambert's annual turnover was £47 million. This success had several components. Firstly, Lambert produced additional family-linked formats. One was *Three in a Bed* (C4, 2010 on) in which three (and later four) Bed and Breakfast proprietor couples stay one night at each others' B and B. Stephen Lambert told me in 2010:

> *Three in a Bed* is a combination of business show and domestic show. B and B is the most domestic kind of business there is. Outside criticism by the visitors is very

6 Gordon Ramsay, *Humble Pie* (London: HarperCollins, 2006), 257–60.

> personal, because it's your home. B and B people are good for TV, because they're used to performing for strangers. Casting allows you to put different characters up against each other ... It's a warmly catty programme, a comedy of manners.

But it was another series, *Undercover Boss*, which became Studio Lambert's big opening success; it launched on the American CBS network in February 2010 – immediately following the American football Superbowl final – and had a record audience of 38.6 million. The background to this astonishingly high audience number was that while still at RDF, Stephen Lambert had developed *The Secret Millionaire* (C4, 2006 on). Even before this, the RDF company had not merely sold format rights to American networks; RDF had itself made the American versions, employing (expensive) American personnel in Los Angeles. With his own independent, Stephen Lambert pursued the same policy after he sold the UK *Undercover Boss* to Channel Four. He told me:

> You need a pitch tape if you want to sell in the US market. As soon as we'd finished the very first episode of the UK *Undercover Boss*, we cut a five minute pitch tape; and I took this to the US. I was able to pitch it to the head of entertainment at the CBS network. She commissioned it and we made the American version in Los Angeles.

Studio Lambert continued to create new factual formats including in the US, *Million Second Quiz* and in the UK, *Gogglebox*, *The Great Interior Design Challenge* and *How To Get A Council House*. In 2012 Stephen Lambert became chairman, in the United States, of the UK super-indie, All3 Media which already owned Studio Lambert. Its Los Angeles office was now the US hub location for all nine of All3 Media's indie companies. Stephen Lambert was again one of the UK leaders in a powerful TV industry trend. Factual formatted entertainment was a key group of genres within UK television, but its most promising market was in the United States.

Formatted food and chef charisma

TV cooking has several obvious audience appeals. We all know a little about cooking and kitchen heat. TV Cooking series can deliver tension, conflict, humour, narrative and subplots. Attempts are made by producers to heighten audience involvement, to include both celebrities and ordinary people, and to offer some cheap and simple eating along with the posh expensive cooking.

But cooking has one big television disadvantage. The audience can neither taste nor smell the food. This is rather like the audience being unable to hear the music in a TV music series. Executive producers have in practice often decided to give their charismatic chef an exceptionally dominant role. These chefs are much more than mere Presenters of work done by a studio production team. Pat Llewellyn, who has probably executive produced more TV cooking hours than anyone else in Britain, told me:

> Chefs are workaholics, driven people. Most chefs are borderline personality disorder cases. We made a BBC2 series called *Mind of a Millionaire* – the psychological profile of entrepreneurs, people who make a lot of money; Gordon and other chefs fit it perfectly. Gordon Ramsay works like nobody else I've ever seen. I think Gordon's the bravest person I've ever met. Sometimes on *Kitchen Nightmares* people get seriously angry with his advice. People are very emotionally attached to their restaurant business. There have certainly been situations of simmering potential violence. But Gordon never backs off.

A small group of star chefs have been transformed into multi-platform performers. Some of these chefs appear on their own-name television shows; they operate and promote their own restaurants; they author the book of the series and collectively dominate the publishing of cooking books; they typically do newspaper and/or magazine cooking columns; they do paid public speaking; and some chefs do television advertising for supermarket chains and others. These star chefs preside over not only kitchen teams but also media teams; several top TV chefs have their own independent production company. TV chefs also campaign for good causes, such as more healthy eating and less reckless slaughter of fish and sharks.

Most of the UK's leading TV chefs have favoured especially the cuisines of France, Italy, Spain, South Asia, and of the UK (with locally sourced ingredients). But each TV chef has developed his or her distinctive personal image. Nigella Lawson, whose book *How To Be A Domestic Goddess* and whose TV series, *Nigella Bites*, both appeared in 2000, continued in the ensuing decades to present herself as sex kitten goddess of lusciously lovely food. Very different was Heston Blumenthal, who offered Kitchen Chemistry and the chef-as-scientist, along with outlandish combinations, weirdly colourful TV imagery, and historical cuisine scholarship. Jamie Oliver presented himself as the nice young man next door who hated fast junk food and had a mission to improve British children's diets. Oliver's company quickly became a leader in the food-and-restaurant industry. Hugh Fearnley-Whittingstall was the charming gentleman proprietor of River Cottage cuisine, using local farm produce and locally caught fish. Rick Stein was another west country chef who initially specialised in fish, but also did foodie journeys. Stein did eating-the-local-cuisine tours across Europe and then across Asia.

To compensate for the lack of taste and smell on television, cookery producers seek to deliver exceptionally high standards of lighting, colour, close-ups and deft editing. Producers also encourage their star chefs to deliver yet more conflict, tension, movement, aggressive criticism, and uninhibited praise. Music is used in large spoonfuls; some people comment that these are music shows with cooking accompaniment.

But the formatted charismatic chef cannot last forever. Star TV chefs, like stars in other genres, tend to shine most brightly for a decade or so. 'New' chefs are typically 'discovered' by television after they have already served perhaps a dozen years in the heat of the kitchen. The best TV chef years are their thirties and forties. By age 50 the top chef may be doing less television but will probably be still owning and running restaurants and writing cook books.

British TV's most successful cooking series has been *MasterChef*, which began in 1990. This series has been through several changes of format, chefs and producers. It has combined elements of charismatic chef and knockout annual competition, with much tweaking of the format. *MasterChef* has gradually established itself as the cooking equivalent of the *Mastermind* quiz and as a series which has almost semi-official status as the established voice of (previously much maligned) British cuisine. By 2011 there were four series – *MasterChef*, *Celebrity MasterChef*, *MasterChef: The Professionals* and *Junior Masterchef*. Like some other successful BBC franchises – or brands – *Masterchef* (as it was then spelt) began in a smaller way. From 1990, it ran for eleven years with Lloyd Grossman as the main presenter. Then, after a four-year gap, *MasterChef Goes Large* appeared in 2005; by 2007 it was, along with *Celebrity Masterchef*, at the top of the cooking TV ratings.[7] There were further changes in titles and formats in 2008 and 2011.

The *MasterChef* shows are quite cheap to make – at an average of something like £100,000 per hour, for an audience of between 2 and 5 million. These series get access to strong visual locations, not only in prominent restaurants but also in grand houses including Buckingham Palace. Production teams are quite small. One major cost is, of course, the two on-screen judges – usually John Torode and Gregg Wallace. Glenn Barden, who had series produced *Celebrity MasterChef*, told me:

> The judges' expertise is key to the integrity of the show. John and Gregg are the judges and it's always their decision. As producers we don't select winners or manipulate outcomes. Obviously the producers sometimes favour someone with TV appeal who's less impressive to the judges as a cook. But the judges always win.
>
> Whilst they are heavily formatted, it's the drama which really makes these shows work. It's all about looks, the expressions on the faces of both contestants and judges. The judge-presenters become the stars of the show. Inevitably they become slightly caricatured, a bit like cartoon characters. They know they've got to come up with that smile or that mugging expression. They're a comedy duo as well as a cooking duo.
>
> The pictures are key. We have great camera guys – some of them also work on *X Factor* and *The Apprentice*. We never work with more than two cameras; typically it's one cameraman, one sound man and the director, for filming in a kitchen. The camera guys still get their trade union tea breaks, but they face a long hot day. They earn their money.
>
> The edit is key. We take six to eight weeks to edit one hour. It's fine tuning the drama. Our executive producer, Karen Ross, always says and I agree: 'Less words. Let the picture do the talking. A look is best.' Also the music is massive. We heighten and

7 'Have viewers had their fill of food TV?' *Broadcast* 21 September 2007.

> lighten with music. We often use the theme music from one specific movie which we think fits the episode. There are whole message boards dedicated to the music of *MasterChef*.
>
> Filming is cheap, especially now with tapeless. So you shoot the shit out of it. You throw it into the edit suite, and say okay, sieve through the stuff and find the gold. It feels like panning for gold. I love it for that. I spend much of my life in the edit suite – just me and an editor locked into a room, ten hours a day. I'm in the edit suite all the time – at this facilities house – and hardly ever in the office. We have our team meetings here, not in the office.
>
> I also like a bit of art – a few arty shots give an added layer, another texture. I like working on a show which is never mean to people. *MasterChef* is not cynical. We'd never do something like *Come Dine With Me*, which is all about taking the mickey out of people. *MasterChef* has feel good running through it.

Following its *MasterChef* success, the BBC established other series with a strong 'British' as well as BBC imprint. The *Great British Bake Off* was remarkably popular with its bread, biscuits and cakes – including such tasks as a three decker wedding cake to be cooked in six hours. Another BBC success was *Great British Menu* on BBC2 five-times-a-week at 7.30pm; it relied on such British and patriotic themes as regional cooking challenges and dishes inspired by World War anniversaries.

Meanwhile ITV – despite the potential attraction of cooking to big advertisers – was less successful at cooking series than either Channel Four or the BBC. Channel Four's *Come Dine With Me* format was not solely about laughing at the participants; but it did focus on social combat in a cooking competition setting. This format involved four people, each person hosting a meal for the other three. Subsequently there were five people and then six (three couples). The show takes a week to film and is edited down to one hour. The cooks are seeking to cook a bit above their normal level but sometimes are cooking this dish for the first time. Hosting cooks gets marked by the other diners. The cameras are ever present – at the preparation, cooking and consumption of the three courses. The cameras also seek out the participants for their views before, during and after the meal. There is much point scoring, cooking snobbery and social snobbery. Clearly the casting of this show is important; the producers have chosen some outspoken people with eccentric views. Some participants tell the cameras that they are marking down their rivals; sometimes two women combine against an obnoxious male. The participants all aspire to be sophisticated cooks. All participants are from the same, often small, town or suburb; this adds an element of national television looking down on provincial pretension. In *Come Dine With Me* the casting is clearly crucial; so is the Editing, because these lengthy dinner parties, and the multiple individual interviews with the diners, generate big quantities of film.

Come Dine With Me generates much humour, intended as well as unintended. It does show a lot of cooking-in-action. Moreover, the diners can be generous as well as cynical. The cynical tactic would be for the participant cook-diner to give a low mark to each of the other cooks. But the typical mark in fact is quite high.

Much has changed in British (and British TV) cuisine since 1955, but some things have stayed the same. The first significant UK cooking series, *Kitchen Magic*, was launched by the BBC in February 1955; the chef was Fanny Cradock. Fanny and her (third) husband, Johnny, were quite weak on cooking but very strong on theatrical presentation and unscripted comedy chatter. He was the stumbling straight man, she the star presence. Fanny Cradock was the first British multi-platform cook; in addition to TV, she did hundreds of live theatre performances (and matinees). Cradock authored books, did commercial advertising, and wrote a Bon Viveur cooking column in the *Daily Telegraph*.[8]

Another deliberately eccentric cooking couple were Clarissa Dickson Wright and Jennifer Paterson, two upper class women who presented themselves as *Two Fat Ladies* (BBC2, 1996–9). They travelled around the country, by motorcycle, and cooked traditional hearty British food. Nevertheless the fat ladies advocated the use of fresh farm ingredients; and they prepared the way for the dedicated professional TV chefs of 2000 and after.

8 Clive Ellis, *Fabulous Fanny Cradock, TV's outrageous queen of cuisine* (Stroud: Sutton Publishing, 2007), 55–105.

House and home formats

Just as everyone is interested in food, everyone needs a home. Obviously millions of people were and are concerned with mortgages, rent, their next housing move, home improvement, and what's happening to the local housing market. Housing issues also relate to children, marriage, family, employment, schools and retirement. Moreover housing programming attracts advertisers of homes, household products, and do-it-yourself. Channel Four has the most housing programming of the UK's five main channels. The five main channels together do about 30 hours of housing programming per week, which includes repeats stripped across daytime.[9] Housing TV series are similar to Cooking series in giving prominence to their expert presenters. Housing shows offer advice, warnings, comedy, and tragi-comedy. Most of this emerges in the interplay between the series host-presenters and the people, usually couples, who are engaging in 'perhaps the biggest single expenditure in our lives.'

The presenters of housing series have not served lengthy kitchen apprenticeships, but most have had some previous involvement with real estate, construction or architecture. When *Property Ladder* launched on Channel Four in 2001, its main presenter was a nice looking 29 year old woman called Sarah Beeny. She quickly established herself as one of the stars of property/house TV in Britain. John Silver who executive produced *Property Ladder* and other Beeny series told me:

9 An incomplete list of such property series is: *The Building Inspector Is Coming, Country House Rescue, Crisis At The Castle, Don't Blame The Builders, Escape To The Country, Home, Homes Under The Hammer, The Hotel Inspector, House Doctor, How Clean Is Your House?, How Safe Is Your House? How To Be A Property Developer, Honey I Ruined The House, I Own Britain's Best Home, My Big Fat Property Fortune, My New Home, Our Home, Our House, Other People's Houses, A Place In The Sun: Home And Away, The Price Of Property, Property Prophets, Property Watch, Ruth Watson's Hotel Rescue, Sixty Minute Makeover, To Buy Or Not To Buy, The Truth About Property, Where's My Mortgage Gone?* and *The Wow Factor.*

> Back in 2000 we screen tested 120 property developers. Sarah Beeny was not only the best looking, she was the only property developer who listened to the people who were talking to her ... We only realised later that the drama was Sarah giving sound advice and the would-be property developers not listening to the sound advice.

By 2007 Sarah Beeny was pointing out that the property bubble would burst. The 2008 bank collapse seemed to be bad news for the property programmers, but they quickly came back with fresh approaches. By 2009 Sarah Beeny was fronting a new show, *Property Snakes and Ladders*. This was followed by *Help! My House Is Falling Down*, *Sarah Beeny's Double Your House for Half the Money*, *Sarah Beeny's Clicks and Mortar* and other Housing shows.

Following Peter Bazalgette's *Changing Rooms* (1996 on) there was a rush of new series about homes. *Grand Designs* began hesitantly in 1999 on Channel Four, but, from 2001 onwards, it became a huge ratings success. For a serious modern architecture series, this initially seemed astonishing. *Grand Designs* featured hopeful couples who were rashly building their own unique houses to match their own unique (and unclear) dreams. These dreams often seemed to be in deep jeopardy; but the narrative was appealing: Will the house ever be completed? Will it collapse while being repeatedly redesigned? Will the architect and the client couple be able to agree on the next expensive step? *Grand Designs* turned its presenter, Kevin McCloud, into a star. John Silver, who worked as a producer of *Grand Designs* for five years, told me:

> Daisy Goodwin had the idea and Peter Fincham (at Talkback) got Channel Four to change its mind and accept the series in 1999. We were defining ourselves against makeover TV – this was to be real people doing it, their dream, with their own money. As a TV series it was unusual because we had no producer control. It was also groundbreaking for a one hour factual show often to be two full years in the making.
>
> Kevin and I used to talk about *Grand Designs* being Aristotelian drama: Act One is Set Up; Act Two is Reversal; Act Three is Resolution. That was fine until Channel Four changed from three thirds to four quarters (with the extra commercial break). It was exciting. Kevin and I would laugh our heads off: 'And if they take this beam away wrongly, then the whole house will fall down.' One colleague called it 'Shakespearian slapstick'. As an executive producer now, I tell the producers that it's fireside storytelling, as with a children's story. The storytelling is totally in the editing.

Grand Designs devoted numerous hours to couples who had highly eccentric (ambitious) ideas about building house and home. The designs involved many unusual buildings – such as a ruined castle, a cinema or a Victorian water tower. Some sites were cramped and oddly shaped. The construction often involved large pre-built walls made of glass, concrete, or compacted wood. Many projects were planned for summer, but, because of delays, were carried out in winter.

Two plain and relatively simple formats were *Location, Location, Location* and *Relocation, Relocation, Relocation*. Sarah Walmsley, who executive produced both of these series, told me:

> Kirsty Allsopp and Phil Spencer do both *Locations* and *Relocations*. They both started as property search agents. They had expertise and brought that to the programme ... The key thing is to have interesting contributors who will talk and make a good story. What others call research we call contributor finding. It's easier than on some programmes I've worked on, because people like these series. People write and email in and ask to be on the programme ... The *Locations* production sequence involves on the shoot a producer, a director, an AP and the researcher. We only start this sequence two weeks before filming because the properties need to be still unsold and available. In the second week we look at a lot of properties and shortlist some. The next week is five days of filming; three days with Kirsty and Phil and the couple, usually filming at five properties. Then two more days are spent filming wide shots, plus shots of the area and nice ones of the house exterior ... We get signed permission from the vendor. We are inside the house before the contributor couple appear. What we show are their genuine spontaneous reactions to the house, and to the price negotiations.

In 2010 Kirsty Allsopp and Phil Spencer, together with Sarah Walmsley, set up their own independent production company called Raise The Roof. They developed additional series. *Phil Spencer: Special Agent* involved Phil helping home owners to sell their properties. Meanwhile *Kirsty's Best of Both Worlds* was about couples who often wanted to combine urban work with rural living. By now both Kirsty Allsopp and Phil Spencer – as leading presenters of house-and-property programming – also wrote books and newspaper columns; they spoke at industry gatherings and supported charities; they also pushed their boundaries into neighbouring genres; they guested on other people's TV shows. They had become multiplatform stars.

Quiz and game shows

Quiz and Game Shows have been the most heavily formatted genre on British television in each decade since ITV's 1955 arrival.[10] A quiz/game show can typically be produced quickly and cheaply. In production terms the quiz is a simple format which can be repeated many times by using fresh participant players. Successful quizzes eventually generate hundreds of episodes. More perhaps than any other genre, the quiz/game uses ordinary citizens to do unscripted talk – although there is a small group of individuals who have succeeded in several quiz shows.

The quiz/game format is often seen as too simple, too mercenary, too American, and too British working class. But senior executives and channel controllers see their top quiz or quizzes as an important part of the channel's output and image. The BBC likes to maintain its public service image with the difficult questions of *University Challenge* (began 1962 on ITV) and *Mastermind* (began 1972 on BBC). ITV has always focused on the quiz show as part of big entertainment. Channel Four has tried to have quiz/games which match its desired different-and-edgy image.

Some differences between quiz games of the 1980s and three decades later are:

- Today the majority of quiz-game shows are British or European in origin; in the 1980s most such shows were still based on American formats.
- Today's shows have larger studio audiences, use more on-screen technology and have slicker showbiz presentation – including more lights, music, cameras, action and more white space.
- Back in the 1980s successful quiz-game shows tended to transform into general variety and entertainment shows which included a quiz segment. Today's most successful quiz-games just do more episodes in better time slots.

10 Su Holmes, *The Quiz Show* (Edinburgh: Edinburgh University Press, 2008).

- Today's shows tell the audience more about each contestant's family, friends and personal history.
- Most quizzes today are more confrontational, assertive and unkind to failing participants.
- Bigger quiz-games have moved in a multi-platform direction with more repeats and back-up on smaller channels, plus linked material on web-sites.

Quiz formats expanded on British TV from the year 2000. For the next decade *Who Wants To Be A Millionaire?* was presented on ITV1 by Chris Tarrant and *The Weakest Link* was presented on BBC1 by Anne Robinson. Both of these quizzes achieved huge viewing audiences and huge press publicity. Both BBC1 and ITV1 were using quiz shows to build strong audiences before the main evening sequence of news, soap, entertainment and drama.

Another change occurred in year 2009 as BBC1 introduced *Pointless* and ITV1 introduced *The Chase*. Both of these shows were scheduled into the 5pm–6pm slot before the early evening News. Each was a quite traditional quiz show, with an unusual feature. *Pointless* required contestants to choose not just a correct answer, but an unusual answer. *The Chase* involved the contestants competing with a quiz expert. A quiz expert figure also appeared in *Pointless*. In addition both ITV1 and BBC1 used other quiz shows to anchor their weekend early evening schedules. The dominant early evening quiz presence on both BBC1 and ITV1 became still more salient after year 2010, as BBC1 ceased doing children's programming.

The rise and rise of quiz shows since 1990 has been matched by a decline in game shows. One leading example of a 1990 game show was *Beadle's About*. This practical joke format involved extremely complex planning of the 'joke' (such as blowing up someone's garage) – including much 'research' with the family, and the employment of a team of professional actors.[11]

11 Jeremy Beadle, *Beadle's About: a behind the scenes look at LWT's hit series* (London: Sidgwick and Jackson, 1989).

In 1990 the majority of UK quiz-game formats were still based on American originals. Since 1990 the UK, it is widely claimed, has become the world leader in developing new quiz-game formats and selling them around the world. There is indeed now less reliance on Hollywood, but several of the leading London-based independent quiz-game producers are in fact owned by such European super-independents as Endemol, Zodiak and Fremantle. German controlled Fremantle still owns a huge bundle of old American quiz-game formats, a bundle which was briefly British owned. But genuinely British developers of quiz-game formats include ITV and its acquired 'independents'. The financial attractions mean that since 1990 much more effort and money have been devoted to quiz-game development. These developers have focused on the features which attract audiences – tension, drama, the contestant's life-story-and-family, the what-will-you-do-with-the-money? Plus close-ups of twitchy faces and trembling hands. A big quiz-game developer such as Endemol (London) thinks up literally hundreds of possible new formats per year; but two or three new shows on air and one big success will easily pay for a year's development expenditure.

Many aspects of the quiz-game format business have changed little since 1990.[12] The audience still thinks the quiz presenter-host is dominant, although the presenter typically works many fewer days than do the producer and the production team. Some successful quizzes have had just one presenter-host, but others have had several. The main week-to-week production task is to find and check the contestants. The studio location and set tend to remain much the same; most quiz shows record several (up to five) editions on a single studio day. New teams of contestants and audiences are ushered into, and out of, the studio at perhaps two hour intervals.

The presenter or host of one successful show may have a second show (perhaps in a different genre). As a successful quiz becomes more established and popular, the producer tends to tweak the format to match this presenter-star's strengths and personality. The presenter's agent can demand and get more money. But while the presenter may be paid a lot per year,

12 Tunstall, *Television Producers*, 138–49.

he or she may be quite modestly paid per episode. A presenter who is paid £5,000 for each of 100 shows per year is earning £500,000 a year, for only a few weeks of full-time studio work. The presenter-host can earn other money for the remaining ten months of the year.

It was between 1955 and 1990 that quiz-games were transformed. In 1955–6 these shows were extremely simple. Contestants had to name popular tunes, and to do simple things with words and numbers. A wife might be asked to whitewash her husband in thirty seconds in order to win a new refrigerator. Most of these shows had been pioneered in America a few years earlier; but when peopled with working class British contestants, these formatted shows looked very British.

The Pilkington Report in 1962 was highly critical of TV quiz shows and the availability of prizes which could be won without much skill.[13] The long-term consequence was that the number of quiz shows was effectively rationed by the BBC and the ITV regulators; most shows did no more than twenty episodes in a year. But the huge expansion around 1990 in the number of channels, and of daytime television, led to an increase in the numbers of quiz shows and in the number of shows stripped five-times-a-week across daytime. Quiz-game shows – which Pilkington saw in 1962 as cheap, trivial, schedule fillers – have became salient, and are new leaders in the TV format business.

Compared with most other TV genres, the quiz format has changed in only modest ways over the last two and three decades. *Who Wants To Be A Millionaire?* was original mainly in being the first quiz to offer the (remote) possibility of such a large prize. *The Weakest Link* was original only in being 'the nastiest show on TV', with host presenter Anne Robinson routinely insulting the intelligence and appearance of contestants. *Deal Or No Deal* was original only as a 'quiz without quiz questions'. Even the new technology was not very high tech; ITV's *The Cube* involved a heavier use of computer graphics, but *The Cube* was original mainly in allowing family-and-friends to give detailed advice to contestants about the numbers, and the small balls-and-shapes manual tasks.

13 Harry Pilkington (chairman), *Report of the Committee on Broadcasting, 1960*, 57–65.

The BBC's *Total Wipeout* was described to me by a BBC Entertainment producer as a game show in which 'contestants large and small fall off very large, very soft, objects into clear or muddy water'. *Total Wipeout* is filmed on a purpose-built site in Argentina but otherwise is strongly reminiscent of *It's A Knockout* (launched on BBC1 in 1966) and *Gladiators* (launched on ITV in 1992).

Successful old formats, it might be said, never die. Four ITV quiz-game formats – *Family Fortunes, Surprise, Surprise, Through The Keyhole* and *Catchphrase* all launched in the 1980s or earlier; all four of these formats were terminated, before being relaunched into key slots (7–10pm) in ITV's Saturday and Sunday evening schedules.

Formatted 'reality' TV: Big Brother, business, dating

The term 'Reality TV' has been applied to a very wide range of programming. Here we will consider only *Big Brother*; two 'Business' formats – *The Apprentice* and *Dragons' Den*; and two Dating shows – namely *First Dates* and *Take Me Out*. These, and some other, formats share several common characteristics:

- These shows do indeed involve real people in non-fictional social situations. However, these real people have volunteered to take part; they all want to look good on television; and they are hoping to attract business finance, or a job, or a dating partner. The *Big Brother* participants were being generously paid.
- The shows are heavily formatted by TV producers, who provide the studio and other locations, and who operate a rigid system of rules and outcomes. The producers focus on casting – selecting, from a large number of applicants, a cast of characters who together will generate both real warmth and real conflict.
- The producers encourage audience involvement through tabloid newspaper publicity and through various electronic platforms. The

Dating shows, and *Big Brother*, use large numbers of cameras and huge amounts of editing in order to assemble human stories and narrative arcs.

- These shows provide small doses of information and education (how not to do a business presentation or how not to conduct a first date), but the entertainment goal is salient. These tend to be primarily Comedy shows. The real people participants try to be amusing; and the producer's editors edit the material for the amusement of the home audience. However, the authority figures – not only in *Take Me Out* but also in the business formats – provide much humour; they also reveal themselves to be people with huge egos and a tendency (as with TV chefs) towards personality disorder.

Big Brother had a bigger impact across British television than did any other single reality format. *BB* occupied hundreds of hours of Channel Four summer airtime during the 2000–10 decade. Especially in the first six years, 2000–5, it achieved C4's largest ever weekly audiences. Because it was broadcast seven days a week, and was viewed by largish audiences each evening, *BB* achieved huge total weekly audiences and huge weekly advertising revenue. *BB* became a running day-to-day story in the tabloid newspapers, which gave selected participants such labels as Nasty Nick, The Moaning Model, and The Incredible Sulk. The inhabitants of the *BB* House were deprived of outside contact, outside media and even their wrist watches. They did some tasks set by Big Brother, but otherwise sat around – talking, eating, interacting and squabbling. The viewing public could see 18 hours a day streamed on E4, as well as the (highly) edited evening highlights on the main Channel Four. The public also participated in each week's much anticipated 'eviction' of one housemate (selected from two candidates proposed by the housemates themselves). The then relatively new technology of multiple fixed cameras meant that the home audience saw some extremely explicit bedroom/bathroom/toilet detail.

Perhaps *Big Brother*'s biggest impact on the TV industry was to confirm Reality TV as an extremely popular and potentially profitable genre. Because *Big Brother*'s cameras operated 24 hours, and the streaming operated 18 hours a day, a huge team of over 300 people was required (for three months each summer). Each camera, editing or dialogue tracking, job needed to be done by more than one person. Both Endemol as the producer, and Channel Four as the broadcaster, were surprised at the huge margin by which advertising revenue exceeded production cost. Peter Bazalgette, when Chief Creative Officer of Endemol worldwide, told me that *Big Brother* had generated acrimonious contract renegotiations in several countries; this was inevitable if advertising revenue was double production cost. Tim Hincks, Bazalgette's successor as Endemol CCO, later confirmed to me that negotiations with Channel Four, over recommissioning *Big Brother*, were indeed 'rather difficult'. In 2010 Channel Four refused to pay what Endemol was now demanding. In 2011 *Big Brother* transferred to Channel Five, whose new owner, Richard Desmond, was shocked at how much Endemol wanted him to pay for *Big Brother*'s now depleted audience.

Perhaps the biggest sub-genre game-reality success of recent years have been business entertainment series. Here 'millionaires' are not just quiz contestants but are rich people trying to do something eccentric with some of their money. In *Dragon's Den* (BBC, 2005-on) we saw five rich people assessing the mostly weird inventions of mostly weird inventors. The humour lies in the wacky projects, in the wacky inventors and in the self-important pomposity of the millionaires, who seem not to realise that they are performing in adult entertainment, also known as unscripted comedy.

The leading UK example of business entertainment TV has been *The Apprentice* (BBC, 2005 on), a format developed by the expatriate Brit, Mark Burnett, for the comic American billionaire, Donald Trump. After two successful seasons on BBC2, *The Apprentice* (British version) moved to BBC1. Dan Adamson, who produced the second and third seasons, later told me:

> In buying the American format, we got a producer bible with twenty key points, which we ignored as much as possible. The US programmes were only 42 minutes, whereas ours were BBC and 58 minutes. We made the tasks much bigger – with more actuality and character. We Anglicised the format, made it less glitzy. We didn't want too much greed-is-good or Donald Trump's 'Look at my wealth'.
>
> Alan Sugar wasn't the BBC's first choice, but we producers wanted him. He's belligerent and grumpy and a street fighter. But he's also funny and genuinely London Cockney. The audience enjoys the obnoxious individuals and the belligerence between the candidates; the audience increases for 'You're Fired' at the end of each episode.

> Alan Sugar sticks to the broad format, but he's not pre-scripted. The Boardroom Session (which is about twenty minutes on the programme) takes up to four hours to film. We shoot about 1200 hours to get twelve hours. We have up to eight cameras filming the tasks on any one day, and up to six cameras for the Boardroom sequence ... In editing we play to what we see as the characters' strengths. What we learn later in the series we can use to edit the earlier rounds and to emphasise memorable characteristics of individual contestants. In series one, it was £250,000 per hour, some of which is hived off for overheads.
>
> Recruiting the candidates involves a long shortlist of 50 people put into groups and filmed doing tasks. Only then do we choose the final fourteen. We look for articulate people aged between about 24 and 35. We do checks with the Police and a Psychologist. We want articulate people who see themselves as alpha males or alpha females ... Yes, most of the weekly tasks are to do with selling. We need visual tasks like selling in a street market or a shop. We write rules for each task. All negotiations must be face-to-face, which creates scenes to film. The press coverage of the first three series was fantastic. Yes, we did employ a PR company for dedicated work on the series.

Dragon's Den is a business format which enables hopeful small entrepreneurs to solicit funding from a team of five successful millionaire businessmen and women. A few of the entrepreneurial ideas may be good; but the products tend to be eccentric consumer gadgets, children's toys and games, or bizarre retail concepts. The Dragons are mostly dismissive and seldom commit to significant investment. (Any possible losses will be covered by their appearance fee). Part of the entertainment value of *Dragon's Den* is that viewers get so much unintended humour from both the hopeful-hopeless entrepreneurs and the disputatious Dragons. What's really going on here is that both hopeful entrepreneurs and the wealthy Dragons are showing their craving for television publicity.

In Dating shows, the participants are not hard-selling their business ideas; but are, of course, soft-selling themselves. *Take Me Out*, which launched in 2010, and *First Dates*, marked a revival in the dating sub-genre. In the 1950s and after, American television offered at least 50 separate dating formats, alongside the quiz formats. Several of these dating formats transferred to the UK; the most successful UK show was *Blind Date* (ITV, 1985–2003), presented by Cilla Black: 'She was everyone's favourite aunt, lively and knowing, wanting the young folk to have a good time – but not too good a time.'[14] *Blind Date* achieved weekend evening audiences in the late 1980s of up to 18 million. Over two decades it did about twenty shows per year. Key to *Blind Date* was that the dating pair only spoke, but did not see each other, before the choice was made. Shows such as *Take Me Out* and *First Dates* reverse that situation; the initial selection is made largely on appearance with only the most basic further information provided (such as age). In *Take Me Out* four young men choose from, and are chosen by, a line-up of 30 young women; each young man must parade himself in front of the full assembly of 30 women in a large studio with lots of lights, cameras, audience and quick action.

First Dates is challenging for the production team; an entire London restaurant is hired for Saturday evening. No less than 40 cameras focus on about fifteen couples,[15] but the TV audience gets to see only about six couples. In a Channel Four hour of 45 minutes, this is only about seven minutes per couple. The focus is on the couple's initial meeting at the restaurant table and on their conversational openings. Some couples are gay, a few are middle-aged, and ethnic mixes are common. While the emphasis is upon across-the-table conversational gambits (filmed in close-up) we, the audience, also see the diners visit the toilets, from where they seek mobile phone advice from friends. Finally the couple tell each other – and us, the audience – whether they want a second date.

Apart from the more expensive production, today's dating shows – compared with *Blind Date* in 1990 – use somewhat less innuendo, but are more worldly wise, and are more relaxed in discussing (on a first date on TV) their sex lives, marital ambitions and work prospects. But at least one thing has stayed the same since 1990. A *Blind Date* producer in 1990 said that his show had succeeded in making Dating into a 'popular spectator sport'. That's still true today.

14 Birt, *The Harder Path*, 222–3.

15 Meredith Chambers, 'First Dates: How we turned the tables on dating shows', *Broadcast*, 14 June 2013: 28–9.

CHAPTER 11

TV Sports: Live, Formatted, Monetised

Since the 1980s, Sport has changed more, expanded more and been more commercialised than has any other television genre:

- British TV viewers in 1988 were offered about 55 hours of sport per week. That number of hours has grown thirty fold to about 1,600 hours of TV sport per week today.
- The BBC still has about five or six of the ten largest sports audiences per week. *Match of the Day* (BBC1, since 1964) is still the most popular single sports offering. But ITV in particular has ceased to be a sports TV leader.
- Sky Sport provides the bulk of the 1,600 sports TV hours; and has the great majority of the top hundred sports audiences each week.
- Sky Sports are quite happy for the BBC to have a few high profile sports productions per week. Increasingly Sky Sports sees its main competition as British Telecom – and this competition is as much about broadband as about TV sport.
- The Sports TV dominance of Sky and BT means that Sports is another Genre in which the public service broadcasters have been outplayed by commercial companies.

In 1990 Sky and BSB were together already offering a total of four sports channels. But the key development was the merged BSkyB's 1992 contract to carry large quantities of live English Premier League football. Rupert Murdoch (by 1996) saw sport as vital both to Sky's UK achievements and to his ambitions across the world:

> Sport absolutely overpowers film and everything else in the entertainment genre … Football, of all sports, is number one. Look at what we have done in Britain with our

> Premier League soccer, and now with rugby union and rugby league in the United Kingdom as well …
>
> [There is] one development which is very pleasing in our sports programming in India, which was beginning to get very expensive … We have now formed a partnership with our former sports programming competition, ESPN of the United States.
>
> We have the long-term rights in most countries to major sporting events and will be doing in Asia what we intend to do elsewhere in the world, that is, use sports as a 'battering ram' and a lead offering in all our pay television operations.

This was Rupert Murdoch speaking at the annual meeting of News Corporation in Adelaide, on October 15 1996.

Since the 1980s the sums of money involved in TV sport have hugely increased. TV sport has become monetised, while payments to players, managers and rights owners have been transformed. TV sport has become the key ingredient in a sports industrial complex which stretches across the continents. Other significant ingredients include numerous multi-million player salaries, pervasive advertising, aggressive merchandising of shirts and boots, gambling (legal and illegal), doping and cheating. Presiding over the sports industrial complex are a few dozen moguls, each with his many millions, or his several billions, available to place bets on teams, contracts and venues.

Competition, largely led by BSkyB, has forced the sports genre to be a technology innovator – especially in the use of multiple cameras, including Steadicam personality cameras, and in slow-mo and super slow-mo re-play technologies. Today's specialist slow-mo cameras can generate thousands of images per second. Much sports effort involves recording equipment which can track back and generate slow-mo pictures within seconds of the original incident. This, in turn, is now widely used in a number of sports as an official, or unofficial, check on decisions.

Television has also moved deeper into the game. Cameras are now allowed onto the edge of the playing area; players and managers give breathless interviews while still on the field of play. We, the audience, have increasingly been enabled to follow individual players in close up. Sports TV has moved further into the home; you can see many of your favourite team's games without having to buy an expensive season ticket and without having to travel to away games. Sports TV has also moved further into the pub;

and sports coverage is now available across the full range of mobile platforms. Sports TV can be always with you.

'Seeing it on TV is actually better than being there,' some claim. Certainly it's easier on TV to see a dark cricket ball, to judge which of two opposed players was the guiltier, and whether the ball crossed the line. Many sports stadiums acknowledge this by displaying the television replays on big screens. Even radio's live, at-the-venue, reporters seem to view the TV coverage as much as the contest itself.

Televised sport has become part format, part soap opera. Sports TV is a genre of unscripted formats. A television channel agrees with the rights holders a standard format for all the contests in an annual sequence. As with other formatted shows, the producers do not know the result in advance; the formatted live output, in this case, can be exported to other national markets and without major editing. Sport on television offers viewers several of the attractive features of soap opera. TV sport offers strong narratives (of players and teams through the season), and sustains emotional appeal for those millions of fans who follow one team loyally across decades. Televised sport offers heroes and villains and plenty of alpha males bursting with sporting charisma and flawed personality. Like TV soap opera, TV sport is not the full story; most of the best relevant scandal, shock and horror, appears online and in the newspapers. A typical British daily newspaper devotes about ten pages per day to sport. Much of this print coverage relates to contests shown on TV yesterday or due to be shown on TV later in the week.

Formatted football and short form sport

British TV channels in general, and BSkyB sports channels in particular, need two main types of sports coverage – short form and long form. Football is the UK's most popular TV sport and it is short form, with games typically lasting under two hours. Other popular short form sports are Rugby League, Rugby Union and Formula One, all of which have contests which typically last less than two hours. These short form sports are suitable for weekend afternoons and midweek evenings. But many TV channels, and especially sport channels, need some long form sports to stretch across the broad acres of daytime. The leading UK long form TV sports are Tennis, Golf and Horse Racing which typically spread across several long days or two long weeks.

Until Sky obtained its first big (Cricket and Football) contracts in 1991–2, the top sports offerings on UK television included once-a-year Events, such as the final of the Football Association Cup, the Grand National horse race and the Oxford and Cambridge boat race. These sports 'Events' continue but are no longer so salient or prestigious. Now the most salient 'Event' is the Olympic Games which came to London in 1948 and 2012. The BBC's television coverage of the 2012 Olympics Games is likely to be recalled as the BBC's last great sporting performance.

Meanwhile Football is Britain's most popular TV sport. Only about two million Britons play amateur football each week, but additional millions of men and women have played some football at some time in their lives. Football does have some obvious spectator advantages over several other games. Football offers movement and open play, while in UK professional football the ball is in play for about 70 per cent of the 90 minutes. These are big favourable points for TV coverage, as is the fact that commercial television is not allowed to invade these 90 playing minutes with advertising.

Football on television is formatted. There is no script and even the players (if there is no cheating) do not know the result in advance. Football TV producers do not need scripts, player rehearsals, special sets, or any of the other impedimenta of drama, comedy or big entertainment. Producers of football programming have typically produced hundreds of football games, mostly at a limited number of familiar venues. Each senior producer will have covered scores of games at (Manchester) United and City, at Liverpool, at Chelsea, Arsenal and Tottenham and at another few locations. A senior producer might go to a particular ground about five times a year. Each time the camera positions are much the same. The main camera position looks down the centre line; other important cameras look across the '18 yard line' (the front of the penalty area) to catch off-sides and penalties. Camera persons patrol the touchlines, focusing on specific players and on throw-ins and corners. The production team uses a substantial number of people to do what used to be called videotape editing – generating the super quick slow-mo images of the incident leading, for example, to a free kick.

Producers, directors and Outside Broadcast personnel become extremely familiar with the leading English football grounds. British teams go to a large number of separate locations across Europe both for nation v nation contests and for the two big European Football competitions – the Champions League and the Europa Cup. At these international games the host (German, French, or Italian) broadcaster supplies its own TV pictures; the visiting producers must combine this host service with their own cameras focused on the English players, angles, interviews and manager. Tony Pastor while head of Production at ITV Sport told me:

> We use the same Outside Broadcast company for the Champions League, which means going to Madrid, Moscow, Rome and so on. Our director, with a technical producer, does the recce. They review the camera positions and the studio set-up. The OB company drive the trucks out there a couple of days before – and then we fly in. It's expensive. For the whole production on a big match we're employing 60 or 70 people. The OB company hires the freelance people we want – at perhaps £300 a day. The UK has excellent OB people, who have become highly skilled by doing the same thing over and over again.

BSkyB has been the major force in changing not just British TV football coverage, but the entire UK football industry. English and Scottish football – once so insular – have been Europeanised, and a majority of the top Premier League players now are non-UK citizens. The top managers now are often not UK citizens; and the ownership too has been internationalised. Top players have become multi-millionaire celebrities. The English Premier League is awash with money (season tickets, TV, sponsorship, merchandising) and also awash with debt.

BSkyB's first contracts for large quantities of Cricket (1991) and of Football (1992) were key events. Another key development in this period was the arrival of the new Premier League to replace the old Football Association league structure. The 1989 disaster at Hillsborough (in which

96 fans were crushed to death) was also key, because it led to the government-supported and financed rebuilding of stadiums from mostly standing, to mostly sitting, venues.

Ten TV sports producers who gave me interviews in 1990 were well aware that this was a period of dramatic change. Both BBC and ITV producers were being offered jobs at doubled salaries, by BSB and then by Sky. Much else has changed since 1990. Previous to 1990 most Football TV coverage from both BBC and ITV was not live, but involved edited evening 'highlights' or magazine shows which had segments on several different sports. Edited series still continue on BBC and ITV. But the main Football provision today consists of several entire live games per week. Ever since 1992 the big majority of these live games have appeared on BSkyB with a much smaller number of live games mainly on BBC, ITV, and on competitors – Setanta, then ESPN (of the USA) and subsequently British Telecom.

In 1990 the small number of live Football broadcasts each deployed about ten cameras. Today about twenty high definition cameras are used; international matches use more and the very top matches, such as the European Champions League Final, use up to forty cameras. In 1990 British television focused firstly on games played in England, secondly on games played in Scotland and only thirdly on games played across Europe. Today the English Premier League has the biggest contracts with Sky and its competitors. But the interest in, and focus on, Football games played across Europe has hugely increased. By watching live television, British fans have become familiar especially with French, Spanish, German and Italian teams, players and managers.

Meanwhile the salaries of top footballers have hugely escalated. Already in 1990 the players' salaries were significantly higher than in the 1960s and 1970s. But today's player salary levels are several times higher, in real value, than in 1990. Since 1990 Football has attracted big sums of TV and TV-linked money. Another large revenue source is merchandising and advertising; this is not only sales of shirts and footwear but the commercial opportunity to embed advertising into the core TV output – with advertisements on the players' shirts, as well as on and around the playing area.

Television in general, and BSkyB in particular has also been central to changes in the other main British short-form TV sports – namely Rugby

Union, Rugby League and Formula One. Both forms of Rugby have been transformed during the Sky television era since 1990. Rugby Union, traditionally an amateur game for South of England gentlemen, has become a game for heavyweight professionals. Rugby League, traditionally a working class sport played in North of England winter mud, has confirmed itself as a summer sport. Today sports fans – largely deprived of TV football during June, July and early August – can view many summer hours of heavyweight Rugby League.

Rugby Union offers its TV fans some elements of intimate involvement. The fan gets a good view of large men high jumping in the line-out and of the set piece scrum, a strange creature with 32 beefy legs; the TV cameras also offer revealing pictures of loose scrums (or 'mauls'). The Rugby Union enthusiast can become familiar with a smallish number of national teams – for instance in the Six Nations competition which involves only England, Ireland, Scotland, Wales, France and Italy. French Rugby Union becomes especially familiar because some of the top UK talent plays in French teams. The Heineken Cup competition tends to be dominated by English and French teams.

But Rugby Union is less popular and achieves much smaller audiences than Football. Audiences may find Rugby Union less appealing because professionalisation seems to have led to better tackling and defence, and thus to less open play. Often the viewers have difficulty in seeing what's happening in both set piece and loose scrums, and may also puzzle as to which of the ever-changing Rugby Union rules the referee is enforcing. Much scoring in Rugby Union comes from long-range kicking, but this is slower and less dramatic than free kicks and penalties in Football.

Rugby Union internationalism has distinctive difficulties which seem to have been exacerbated by television. Obviously the TV advertisers are interested in the English audience which is bigger than the audiences in Scotland, Wales or Ireland. Meanwhile English Rugby Union, and its muddled macho managers, often allies itself with France and against not only Italy and Rumania but also against belligerent New Zealand, Australia and South Africa, as well as against Argentina, Tonga, Fiji, the USA and others. The arrival of British Telecom as a Rugby Union rival to Sky is contributing to the standard 'England problem' because BT are inevitably focused on reaching the big English market.

Rugby League avoids Rugby Union's loose mauls. Rugby League has done well with its summer focus and with its national and international competitions. But Rugby League success is focused into a small number of Yorkshire and Lancashire teams and locations such as Leeds, Saint Helens, Warrington and Wigan. Despite big efforts, the London Broncos have not achieved much success. Moreover, although a large minority of its players are from New Zealand, Australia, the Pacific Islands and France, Rugby League has continued to be largely a white, English speaking, and working class sport. Rugby League has introduced a salary cap which means that its top players earn around one million, but not several million, pounds per year. Nevertheless Rugby League's future and finances will depend heavily on decisions taken by television executives in general and by Sky and BT in particular.

Formula One car racing is a very different example of a short form and formatted sport. Each race lasts under two hours; the cars race for about 190 miles and reach speeds of up to 200 mph, while negotiating about 800 turns or bends. Cameras are located mainly at the numerous bends, in the pits and on the cars. Viewers also benefit from camera-in-helicopter and cameras-on-cranes coverage. Since the 1980s, Formula One has largely eliminated deadly accidents, but has managed to retain many exciting crashes from which drivers emerge unscathed. The safety regime has made passing-on-the-track relatively rare, but pit stop rules have been designed to maximise pit stop drama and linked changes in the race order. F1 race tracks have been largely standardised to a length of about 3.5 miles with about 15 turns.

Sponsorship and advertising generate more revenue for Formula One than do the world television rights. But the advertisers – of cars, tyres, fuel, countries and much else – are, of course, aiming at Formula One's national and international television audiences. Some F1 teams (Ferrari, Mercedes, Lotus) are advertising their cars. Some venues are deliberately advertising their glamorous home towns – the street circuits of Monte Carlo in summer or cool Singapore at night. Also central to Formula One is simple, old fashioned, advertising – at the track side, on the cars and on the drivers. The centrality of F1's television coverage is notable at the track. Even those who sit in some of the better seats only see each car about 50 times, for a few seconds each time. But from the grandstand one can also rely on a large screen TV picture, and a small screen hand-held device for basic race coverage and pit lane close-ups.

Its entrepreneurs have worked hard to package F1 as a sport. This means emphasising drivers, who, during the race, are lying down, largely out of sight, inside a low flying missile. It also means focusing on the team of supporting and managing personnel; and it involves emphasising glamour by allowing stars of stage, screen, politics and sport onto the starting grid just before the race begins.

While Formula One has worked hard at packaging itself as a television sport, several other sports are working hard at packaging themselves more like Formula One. Despite having to fly expensive cars and equipment between venues, Formula One has managed to establish itself on all five continents. Other sports are looking for opportunities to develop more and more world competitions which could fly teams to locations in perhaps twenty separate countries. Apart from the sports entrepreneurs, who really wants this? Well the TV fans, and, oh yes, the advertisers of global brands.

Long form sport on television

Long form sports – such as Cricket, Golf, Tennis and Cycling – suit television in general and specialised sports channels in particular. These sports offer endless supplies of events each of which lasts several days, two weeks, or, like the Tour de France three weeks of lengthy days of action. All of these sports have been packaged for television. However, some late nineteenth-century elements remain – including Tennis scores such as '40 Love' or Cricket terms such as 'silly mid-off'. But Television can reveal much from its many camera positions both close to, and far from, the action. Horse Racing and Golf spread across miles; coverage of Tennis tournaments spreads across numerous courts. The big cycle races stretch for many hundreds of miles.

But the TV cameras are also able to focus on the fine touch, close up, anxious moments of these sports. Tennis, Golf and Cricket all use small balls which means that inches count and nervous errors at key moments are often crucial. We can see, in close-up, top Tennis, Golf and Cricket players who 'freeze' and lose. These sports also feature dramatic one-on-one contests between Tennis and Golf players, or between Cricket batsmen and bowlers. Fans of some of these long form sports also recognise that participating players require plenty of quiet courage. Jump jockeys know that they can expect to fall off the horse once in every fifteen rides. Professional cyclists also must expect to fall onto a hardened road and hope not to fall while 'descending' at speed from a mountain pass. Nor is Cricket a gentle game; we, the viewers, regularly see a small, hard and bouncing ball striking the batsman's body at 80 or 90 mph. Moreover, close catching Cricket positions such as Silly Mid Off involve obvious danger.

All of these long form sports have been internationalised; and leading players clock up many thousands of air miles. Flat racing horses which perform in the UK and French summer are flown to the Gulf for the winter. Tennis and Golf have their Tours which circle the world, to pick up additional locations outside Europe and the US. Cricket has been internationalised around the old framework of the Commonwealth. But the key Cricket power is no longer England, Australia or South Africa. India, Pakistan, Sri Lanka and Bangladesh have made South Asia the centre of world Cricket. Cricket, with its eighteenth-century English origins has adapted itself to television more perhaps than has any other sport. A single Cricket match can today be of any length between five full days and about three hours. Quicky, Twenty 20, Cricket still often retains some long form elements because rapid fire, knock out, tournaments attract top international talent, and huge TV audiences in India, plus large audiences in England.

English Cricket has become dependent on the financial support of television in general and on Sky's massive Cricket output in particular. Sky – and the BBC, ITV, C4 and C5 over the years – have mainly been interested in international cricket; this means, in particular, games between England, and Australia, South Africa, India, Pakistan and Sri Lanka. Cricket, in fact, provided BSkyB with its first big sports contract in 1991. This was the first sports deal between the BBC and BSkyB. While the BBC retained all Cricket Test Matches in England, BSkyB acquired the rights to all Test Matches outside England. BSkyB's ability to provide huge quantities of live Cricket from the Caribbean and the Southern hemisphere was a great new step. Apart from the impressive commercial and production skills, overseas Cricket Test matches demonstrated the appeal of big quantities of one sport – in this case, a sequence of single matches, each of which generated up to 40 hours of live coverage and comment. For BSkyB, cricket had the major advantage of filling in British summer months – such as June and July – which lacked fresh live football. During the 1990s UK Cricket first found itself becoming dependent on BSkyB for the great bulk of its finance.

Highlights programming has usually attracted bigger audiences than the numbers watching any one hour of a six hour cricket day. The main cricket Highlights programming was on Channel Four until 2005 and then switched to Channel Five. In both cases the Highlights programming was made by the Sunset and Vine independent. Dylan Jane talked to me about his experience as the series producer of this programming:

> We do about 45 days of English-based international cricket each May to September. Sky do the live all-day transmission, and for our 7.15pm highlights show we can use all of their transmitted show as well as camera output which they did not transmit. We have one additional camera of our own which we use to make a specific point separate from Sky. We have our own commentary, our own graphics, own sound, and own music. We do our own interviews and 90 seconds of special analysis by Simon Hughes.
>
> Yes, when we edit the Sky live coverage, we can storyline it, because we already know the day's outcome. But there's less time, than in football, between end-of-play and our edited highlights. A lot of cricket coverage may look formulaic. But it's not easy to follow the ball as it comes off the bat. The director and/or the vision mixer must decide in a fraction of a second, where the ball is going.
>
> We, the production team, get closer to the cricket players than happens with football players. We follow them around the UK and on foreign tours we spend many days and weeks with them. Cricketers are not like footballers who live in a closed world and want to avoid the media, especially print journalists. Footballers are defended by PR people.

> Making sports TV is an incredible team thing. It's the next best thing to being a sportsman. We're all passionate about TV sport. When England defeated Australia for the Ashes at Edgbaston in 2005, the emotion was explosive. There were people in the OB truck just shouting and screaming with joy. You also feel close to the cricket viewers. E-mail was big. Now all the cricket fans do Twitter and Facebook.

During the Sky era of TV Sport, since 1990, certain negative aspects have grown – especially corruption and match fixing involving bribery-and-betting, plus doping with banned substances. Horse Racing negatives have included bans or prison for some of the most eminent jockeys. Cycling has produced perhaps the most spectacular single corrupt example in the form of Lance Armstrong who won the Tour de France seven times while using banned substances. Equally systemic corruption seems to exist in South Asian Cricket, where the betting often involves a single batsman, or bowler, or a single ball. Very senior Pakistan and South African cricketers have been guilty. Television may have helped to encourage this corruption and gambling; but television replays can also supply some of the best and strongest incriminating evidence.

There is fierce competition between sports to obtain the most lucrative TV contracts. UK Football has, ever since 1990, always had the best UK contracts. Inevitably some sports, which did well on British TV previous to 1990, have done less well since 1990. Two leading examples are the pub 'sports' of Snooker and Darts. A short version of Snooker, called *Pot Black* did well on BBC2 from 1969 to 1986; Snooker, with its different coloured balls on the green table, needed colour television which only BBC2 initially provided. Snooker was subsequently a big success in its long form version of lengthy knock out competitions based in Sheffield. Snooker could be televised cheaply because the small playing table could be well covered by as few as three cameras; and even the top players earned only comparatively modest pay.

The other successful televised pub sport was Darts, seemingly dominated by large middle-aged men. Darts also could be performed in a small space and was cheap to televise. Both top Snooker players and top Darts players appeared, while on camera, to consume ample quantities of alcohol. Both Snooker and Darts players can look back nostalgically to the large TV audiences their sports once attracted. Snooker and Darts retain a modest presence on the larger audience TV channels; both have a much bigger presence on daytime TV. Snooker and Darts together occupy many hundreds of hours each year on Sky's sports channels; they are accompanied there by other, once super-popular, sports such as Boxing, Wrestling and Speedway. These smaller sports, it seems, need to develop stronger narratives, bigger flawed-personality stars, and other familiar soap ingredients.

Sports stars and managers

Although the nineteenth century had its own sports stars (such as W.G. Grace in Cricket), modern sports stardom was largely created by television. Today many UK sports stars are paid at least £1 million per year and a small number are paid much more. But sports stardom typically lasts ten years or less. A stellar player may shine brightly at 22 or 23, but then lose form or suffer a crippling injury. In UK sport, Football has the most stars. But some of the biggest individual stars are the one or two UK leaders in sports such as Tennis, Golf and Formula One. Despite there being many horse racing jockeys, a small number of star flat racing jockeys achieve hundreds and thousands of racing wins.

Many young sports stars are inarticulate on TV; they also seem dull because their team managers and personal agents have advised them to say little. Nice quiet hardworking players get picked for the team and may later be picked to advertise snack food, watches or clothes. Television producers obviously prefer the good-bad boy. Many football players develop their own visual signature – the weird haircut or the exuberant victory dance. At the 2012 London Olympics, the sprinter Usain Bolt further developed his diagonal (advertising) pose, while the 5,000 and 10,000 metre champion Mo Farah, adopted his two-hands-on-head victory sign. Less advised by talent agents is the behaviour of some Rugby Union gentlemen who like to engage in drunken brawls with people smaller than themselves.

How did David Beckham become a Football superstar? Like many other talented footballers he was a very good looking and very inarticulate young man. But Beckham perfected the live action television clip – his trademark free kick, which, bend-it-like-Beckham, curved round the defensive wall and into the top corner of the goal. Beckham focused on becoming also a male model – one of the few Football stars to have played for Manchester United and England, and to have played in Madrid as well as in the fashion locations of Los Angeles and Paris. He became half of the Beckham brand which also included his pop music star, and fashion label, wife. Beckham was one of the fairly small number of sports stars who develop a second career as a national television talker. But there are many other more modest second careers available, for example as a local or regional ex-star who appears frequently on regional TV and local radio shows.

Another category of TV sports stars are the manager-coaches in general and the Football managers in particular. Compared with their players, the Football managers know more and are willing to say more. The leading managers tend to manage teams for twenty or even thirty years; but their careers typically have included many job moves. This is another highly paid and insecure job. Few managers have not been sacked at least two or three times. The Football manager often conforms to the common TV hero pattern of Alpha male with flawed and insecure personality. The most difficult management job is the England one. England managers themselves tend to be short stay; there are two familiar exit points – after the European Cup and after the World Cup. The England manager only has his team for a comparatively few international games each year. Meanwhile the England manager gives press conferences and TV interviews.[1]

Managers in the English Premiership have three major tasks. Firstly they assemble the team, which includes buying and selling players for

1 Niall Edworthy, *The Second Most Important Job In The Country* (London: Virgin, 1999). Barney Ronay, *The Manager: the absurd ascent of the most important man in Football* (London: Sphere, 2009). Simon Kuper and Stefan Szymanski, *Why England Lose* (London: HarperSport, 2010).

multi-million pound sums. Secondly the manager runs the team, and its support staff, on a daily, weekly and monthly basis. He decides which formation to adopt and what tactics and which players to use against the next opponents. Third the manager handles the media. Football managers typically prefer TV rather than popular national newspapers, whose journalists like negative and scandal stories. Football managers can appear on television immediately after a game and while still on the field of play. Managers can give press conferences, which however – as the name suggests – are often of most interest to the press. Managers can also perform on television while a televised game is in action. Managers know that what attracts TV producers and directors is drama, action, and the visual. Each manager, in fact, has an assigned stage, alongside the pitch, called his Technical Area. Here he can gesture, jump, gesticulate, and applaud (for the TV cameras).

When José Mourinho arrived at Chelsea in 2004 he was the most camera ready Football manager ever seen in England or the UK. He had already won the European Cup twice, and unlike many managers (British as well as European) he was exceptionally articulate, subtle and amusing in spoken English. He was spectacularly successful at Chelsea before being sacked. Mourinho's second coming (to Chelsea) in June 2013 was equally striking. Although he was now exactly fifty years of age he fitted perfectly with Chelsea's self-image as the centre of London's fashion industry.

In some other sports the manager-coaches are equally important, although usually less television-visible. A successful horse racing trainer, such as Sir Henry Cecil, who died in 2013, could appear on television many times in a season – typically just before the race and just after (if his horse won). Coaches in both codes of Rugby and in Cricket are powerful figures and appear frequently on television.

Perhaps the most powerful is the manager in professional long distance cycling. The cycling manager not only employs and deploys the racing team (and a larger back-up and support staff) but he also chooses which single cyclist will be the team leader – to be protected and helped by all the other team members. However, most cycling managers seem shy of television.

TV sports producers and talkers

Today's TV sports producers are handling much bigger quantities of sport and of money than was the case in 1990. Producers at Sky Sport have formatted the delivery of many hundreds of hours of live sport. Even the BBC – despite having lost the contracts for several major sports – produces more hours than it did in 1990; the BBC's *Match of the Day* (which began in 1964) now covers more weekend Football matches than it did in 1990.

In the 1980s only token fees were paid to rights holders. Sports executives at both the BBC and ITV traditionally saw themselves as doing the rights holders a favour by agreeing to put some of their sport onto national TV. There was not much negotiation about contracts. In 1990 most BBC and ITV sport was handled by in-house producers. Both BBC and ITV had their own fleet of OB trucks.

In the late 1980s there were several deadly incidents, not least the Hillsborough disaster. One BBC producer, John Philips, told me in 1990:

> It's happened to me on about five occasions now – not only football crowd disasters, but guys being killed falling off motorbikes, and car racing. This is the most difficult thing; it exercises the mind and also your common decency and humanity.

Today there are, thankfully, many fewer deaths on live sports television. But several aspects of the sports producer's work remain much the same. For example, a sports executive producer, such as Brian Barwick, was in charge of several big BBC sports series. In March 1990 Barwick described his job to me; he was in charge of all BBC Football output and Editor of its leading Football series namely *Match of the Day*, *The Road to Wembley*, *Grandstand* and *Sportsnight*. He was also in charge of all BBC Boxing output. Several series producers reported to Barwick.

As today, a senior sports producer like Brian Barwick in 1990 spent much of his time liaising with the relevant rights holder. He told me:

> I'm aged 35 and have only been in television ten years ... I'm in love with the game of Football ... About 200 people work for me at least some of the time ... I was Editor, with John Philips as series editor, at Hillsborough ... But it still seems sometimes

> that I'm living out a fairy tale. To be servicing the FA Cup and to be in charge of this summer's World Cup 1990 coverage for the nation is fantastic. I speak on a day-to-day basis to the Football Association. And I'm glad to say they don't try to influence what we do. There's relatively little friction. It's a 12 million pound contract for the BBC; it's a 30 million pound contract between the BBC and BSB and the FA. With the FA I just pick up the phone and have a conversation.

Senior sports producers in 1990, as today, had good job prospects. Brian Barwick himself became Head of BBC Sport Production (1995–7), Controller of ITV Sport (1998–2004) and then Chief Executive of the Football Association. In both the BBC and ITV hierarchies, sports producers were regarded as serious TV executives – and seen as probably more suitable than comedy or entertainment executives for high office. Bryan Cowgill who was head of BBC Sport (1963–74) was then Controller of BBC1 (1974–7). Roger Mosey held senior positions in BBC News before heading BBC Sport and then being put in charge of BBC 2012 Olympic Games output. Mosey told me that being a sports executive was quite similar to being a news executive.

Today the most demanding job for a senior sports executive is not televising the sport, but dealing with the sports contracts and the rights holders. The TV rights now cost more than the cost of production. Today there is elaborate preparation previous to each contract bidding process. Big contracts, such as those in Football, are now affected by competition-monopoly regulation and the blind bidding system is used. All of this requires much detailed planning and intelligence work.

TV sports producers today often find themselves at odds with print journalists. This TV versus newspaper tension goes back to the earliest days of television. Several national newspaper journalists, who had covered England's Football World Cup win of 1966, subsequently revealed to me their resentment at television's ability to show the game live. They told me of incidents they had seen which the TV cameras had ignored. Ever since 1966, the TV producers have adopted a more positive view of the sports with which they are contracted. Newspaper journalists, now as then, prefer to give more critical accounts of what happened in yesterday's game, and to predict which Football manager will be the next to be sacked.

Sports producers and directors have to manage several categories of sportstalkers. These talkers include commentators, discussants, and presenters. A few leading sports TV commentators have had remarkably long careers. John Motson did BBC Football commentary for 40 years.[2] Martin Tyler at BSkyB for many years did the commentary on some 60 live Football matches each year. Murray Walker did Formula One live commentary (BBC and ITV) until the age of 77. Bill McLaren did BBC radio and TV Rugby Union commentaries for 49 years (1953–2002) until the age of 79. Several Cricket, Boxing, Tennis, Golf, Darts and Rugby League commentators are similarly known for their very lengthy careers. Why do TV (and radio) producers – working in an insecure and competitive broadcasting industry – continue to employ the same commentators for decade after decade? One answer is that good commentators get better (and more knowledgeable) with experience.

Sports producers back in 1990 told me how important sports presenters were: 'The audience sees it as his show.' Often the presenter has to link together live interviews or discussion with recorded clips of recent sporting contests. Des Lynam recounts how, when aged 48 and a highly experienced BBC sports presenter, he had a brief experience of total panic – similar perhaps to a mature actor suddenly experiencing stage fright in a live theatre performance. Des Lynam was desperately anxious to retain his 'Relaxed and Smooth' presenter reputation.[3]

A third category of on-screen talent are the discussants – the experts who discuss the contest at half time and before and after the game. Different broadcasters favour different types of discussants; and channels, such as ITV, which take advertising, find that advertising swallows about half of the half-time minutes. Some sports provide yet a fourth on-screen role – this is the person who interviews the grand prix drivers or the jockeys, just before or just after the race. Clare Balding when interviewing jockeys-on-horses, and Martin Brundle when interviewing

2 John Motson, *Motty: forty years in the commentary box* (London: Virgin Books, 2009).

3 Lynam, *I Should Have Been At Work!*, 174–7.

grand prix drivers on-the-start-grid, showed rare and impressive skill over a lengthy period. Some of these leading sportstalkers, including Clare Balding, have become multi-sport and multi-platform performers – on sports programming, on other TV shows, on radio, in writing books and press columns, and doing paid speaking.

An earlier horse race talker was (Sir) Peter O'Sullevan, who did horse racing commentary on BBC TV and Radio over a 50 year period (1947–97). In an interview, he told me that he had only two complaints. Firstly it was, on a grey day, rather difficult to pick out jockey colours at distances of half a mile or more. Secondly, he disliked having to climb wobbly ladders to some of the BBC's more rickety, cold and windy, high commentary positions (although, like all commentators, he never complained on air).

Senior sports producers and executives need to take big decisions about firing and hiring their top talkers. A very small number of sports talkers are seen as stars (who can shift audience ratings) and are thus paid million pound salaries. But what to do if one or more of these stars misbehaves? An incident of this kind occurred in 2011 when two top Sky Sports Football talkers, Richard Keys and Andy Gray, were revealed as having made (off camera) some lewd and highly sexist remarks. The resulting press explosion led to Sky sacking its two millionaire talkers, who were soon re-employed at lowly Talksport radio. A sports talker who felt he had been unfairly fired at age 72, was John McCririck, who had been a horse racing talker for ITV and C4 across 31 years (1981–2012).

New top talkers can be selected somewhat more cautiously, but an agent may issue an ultimatum: if you don't promote my boy or girl, we'll accept the competition's offer. Some sports producers prefer ex-players as sports talkers, while other producers favour some journalists such as Adrian Chiles. Sky Cricket has relied especially heavily on former England Cricket captains to be its talkers. But in TV Cricket, and in all other TV sport, the producers are in charge; they employ and deploy the talking team.

UK television and the sports industrial complex

The emergence of a TV Sports Industrial Complex could already be seen in the early 1990s:

> Recent developments in TV sports contracts involve a gradual merging of the interests of television with the interests of professional sport ... Playing an increasingly central role within this cash framework are agents, who now represent a variety of separate financial interests. Sports agents work for, and negotiate for, Governing Bodies or Associations; they also represent on-screen presenters, reporters and expert analysts. The same agents represent leading players and sports personalities ... In yet other cases agents control the entire national and world rights to a particular sports event. Various branches of Mark McCormack's International Management Group (IMG) perform all of the above functions, and control the rights to Wimbledon and the British Open Golf Tournament.[4]

Mark McCormack built IMG on the basis of agency contracts with a very small number of very prominent American Golf and Tennis players. Although IMG was soon involved in obvious conflicts of interest – by working for both players and rights owners – Golf and Tennis are two, perhaps the only two, world sports which seem largely to have avoided major corruption and illegality.

Since the 1990s, big television advertising and big television coverage have driven the growth of big sport. The domestic TV audience is typically one hundred times, or more, larger than the audience at the event. Typically the audience at the televised sports event generates a third or less of the total revenue. The television money takes two forms: firstly the amount paid by the television broadcaster to the relevant rights holder; and secondly the amount paid by advertisers and sponsors to place their advertising at the venue, on the players' shirts, footwear or cars, and on the playing area.

Advertising agencies play a larger role in all this than is generally realised. American models of sports marketing, advertising and business have tended to be copied by the rest of the world. But, paradoxically, the

4 Tunstall, *Television Producers*, 70–1.

world has not copied American styles of sports governance which tend towards co-operative cartels (such as the American Football NFL) in contrast to the more aggressively capitalist models of Europe. Nevertheless American sports entrepreneurs continue to buy sports companies in the UK, Europe and elsewhere; and IMG is making a massive effort to largely own-and-operate (with local partners) entire western sports in India, China and elsewhere.

In commercial televised sport, as in much else, the UK acts as a link, or staging post, between the USA and Europe. The UK invented a number of the big sports. Much of this tradition is now long dead, but some UK restraints on commercialism still remain in, for instance, conservative UK arrangements for betting on Football and Horse Racing. The UK and British people, are perhaps strongest today in managing Formula One and in the English Premier Football League – although most of the relevant owners and players in both sports are not British. The majority of English Premier League owners are Americans, Arabs, Asians or Russians. The UK is strong in both flat racing and jump racing, but much of the big money now comes from the Arab world.

Another, more traditional, UK sporting oddity is that in some sports (including the Olympics) there is a single Great Britain team. But in other sports separate England, Wales, Scotland and Ireland/Northern Ireland teams are allowed. All of this helps to ensure that UK involvement in international sports governance can be especially chaotic and confused.

Most sports are in some kind of continuing turmoil at the international level; and this turmoil is often being caused by changes in sports television. UK sports turmoil has often been linked to BSkyB and its ineffectual UK competitors such as Virgin, Setanta and the American ESPN. Since 2010–11, British Telecom has caused the TV turmoil in both Football and Rugby Union. This competition has been supported – hesitantly – by the UK regulator, OFCOM.

Major TV changes impact all levels of a particular sport – the local, national and European (and other world regions) as well as at the world level. Each sport is also internally segmented into its Governing Association, its major Franchise Owners and Leagues, its own Bizarre Billionaires, its own star players and agents, and its major advertisers. UK sports Governing

Associations – like the Football Association (FA)[5] have, in recent decades, been somewhat ineffectual, with much of the power (including TV power) going to the wealthy Franchise Owners, such as the English Premier Football League. The FA has also been extremely ineffective when negotiating with FIFA (the international Football Governing Association). FIFA itself, based in tax haven Switzerland, has been a ramshackle body. Sepp Blatter, as boss of FIFA, has spread his influence across no less than forty-eight years; Blatter became FIFA President in 1974 and led the proceedings which awarded the 2022 World Football Cup to take place (initially) in the desert heat of the Qatar summer.

Sport in the TV era has its bizarre billionaires. One such has been the owner of the Chelsea Football Club franchise, Roman Abramovich, who had a habit of sacking expensive managers after about one year (of often very successful) service. Another bizarre billionaire was Bernie Ecclestone, who succeeded in outplaying the Formula One franchise holders (the team owners). Ecclestone established a working alliance with another Brit, Max Mosley, who became the long-serving President of the FIA, the Formula One Governing Association. Ecclestone acquired, for himself, the television rights. By controlling Formula One television he obtained financial and other control over Formula One.[6]

The inadequacy of most of the big sports Governing Associations, and of most of the Franchise holders, leaves most international sports vulnerable to corruption. Television has encouraged corruption in some sports, because TV has generated such large sums of money. Corruption takes two main forms – Doping and Match Fixing. But these sports are also rife with conflict of interest. In recent years new forms of gambling on sport have created new opportunities for corruption. Cycling in general, and Lance Armstrong (who won his seventh Tour de France in July 2005) in particular has been perhaps the most spectacular case of sports corruption.

5 David Davies, *FA Confidential: Sex, drugs, and penalties: the inside story of English Football* (London: Simon and Schuster, 2008).

6 Tom Bower, *No Angel: The secret life of Bernie Ecclestone* (London: Faber and Faber, 2011), 133–209.

Any mildly sceptical newspaper journalist or TV producer could have seen that there was indeed something unusual about a mediocre Texan cyclist who became the greatest long distance cyclist of all time. A few gallant journalists did denounce Armstrong as a drug-cheat, and the (Murdoch-controlled) London *Sunday Times* fought and lost a 2004 libel case against Armstrong. Perhaps TV executives across Europe did not want to believe that such a televisual event as the Tour de France had been corrupted by drug cheats for decades. Long distance cycling had a remarkably high rate of deaths caused by doping.[7]

Athletics, since the days of East German achievements has long experience of doping. Horse Racing has suffered from horse doping. Snooker has sometimes been fixed; and in 2010 it became apparent that Pakistani, as well as South African, top Cricketers were taking bribes to throw games. Nor has Football been exempt. Just as corruption in sport has been encouraged by new, undetectable, drugs, so also sport has been corrupted by new forms of online and mobile phone betting. Another change has been the switch to betting on such details as the precise winning score of a game and on predicting details like the number of free kicks and corners, or betting on a particular player or one six-ball over in Cricket. These tendencies have been exacerbated by the huge profusion of betting-on-sport in India and other Asian countries.[8]

Corruption is also fuelled by the increased focus on the top talent, the star international performers within each sport. Football, for example, has developed a current list of perhaps one hundred top players, who are recognised as stars by television audiences around the world. The leading Football franchises in Europe, and especially the twenty English Premier League clubs, seek to buy up these players. The Sports Associations and top franchise companies develop more and more competitions – both national and international. Top Football franchise teams also play off-season games

7 David Walsh, *Seven Deadly Sins: my pursuit of Lance Armstrong* (London: Simon and Schuster, 2012).

8 Mihir Bose, formerly the BBC's Sport Editor, has provided perhaps the best account of corruption across a wide range of sports and countries. See Mihir Bose, *The Spirit of the Game* (London: Constable, 2011), 349–571.

in Asia and elsewhere in order to spread their appeal and the star appeal of their top players. Each English Premier League manager sees a need for twenty or more top players so as always to have eleven fit top players on the pitch.

In Cricket the leading players tend to spend most of their playing days in international Cricket contests of various lengths, from five days to three hours. It is these numerous international Cricket games which interest the television producers. Lower order games (such as English County Cricket) get little TV attention.

The small internationally recognised elite within each sport are, of course, the players who are paid the high salaries. These players have Agents who not only negotiate their clients' salaries but also negotiate transfers and transfer fees. Agents have become more salient as television money has become more salient in professional sport.[9] Agents come in several sizes. In the UK alone up to 200 people claim to be Football agents. The lowest level of agents includes numerous recent ex-players, who may be working for their former team mates. Middle level agents may work for several top Football players, each himself currently earning several million pounds a year; such an agent himself (or herself) will have revenue of at least one or two million pounds per year. Then there is a third and top level of Football and Sports agent. These top agency companies work for top sports stars, which includes negotiating advertising and marketing deals. The top talent agencies tend to be American-connected. Major Hollywood talent agencies, such as CAA and WME (Creative Artists Agency and William Morris Endeavor) have sports clients. Meanwhile WME now owns IMG, the leading sports rights and sports talent 'independent producer'. William Morris/IMG has become a new kind of Hollywood star/sports rights/sports talent colossus.

One Anglo-Hollywood agent is Simon Fuller who created the Spice Girls pop group and moved on to represent brand Beckham (David and

9 Tom Bower, *Broken Dreams: vanity, greed and the souring of British Football* (London: Simon and Schuster/Pocket Books, 2003), 251–314. *I Am The Secret Footballer* (London: Guardian Books, 2012), 115–41.

Victoria), the tennis player Andy Murray, and the Formula One driver Lewis Hamilton. Top sports agents work for players, managers, sports franchises and Governing Associations. Leading agency companies probably have the best combined knowledge of sport, television and commercial marketing. Agents become both highly knowledgeable and highly skilled at navigating through the chaotic structure of most sports. Agency companies advise and control each sport's top talent – its TV stars. Agency (and management) companies offer to manage the star's sports career and to extend it into a new post retirement career (of advertising, TV expert sports talking, book-writing, participation in charity work, and in entertainment TV).

American agency companies and American sports entrepreneurs have been active in expanding not only into the UK, but into Europe, Asia and the world. Three main examples are as follows. Firstly, American sports companies have targeted the most internationally famous franchises in English Premier League Football. Manchester United, Liverpool and Arsenal are all American owned. (The fourth world famous UK Football brand, Chelsea, is owned by a Russian.) The three American owners had certain things in common. Each had had significant success as a sports franchise owner in the US; each was attracted by the worldwide marketing opportunities provided by owning a top English Premier League franchise; each of the three American ownerships was somewhat uncertain as to how they would move beyond the UK and Europe into Asia. In the meanwhile, the American owners aimed to attract advertising from big American companies. In 2012 Manchester United agreed a big advertising deal with General Motors. Reuters reported that GM wanted to tap Manchester United's estimated 659 million fans to promote GM's Chevrolet brand.[10]

Secondly, Rupert Murdoch's News Corporation had begun its advance into world sports with its 1992 BSkyB contract with the English Premier League. Murdoch's Star Sports then competed across Asia against Disney-owned ESPN, the leading US cable sports company. Subsequently Star (and News Corp) took full ownership of the merged ESS (ESPN Star Sports)

10 Reuters, 31 July 2012.

which now runs numerous Asian sports channels in Hindi, Mandarin, English and other languages.

Thirdly William Morris owned IMG demonstrated the importance of thinking big and thinking long-term. With the Indian Reliance company, IMG owns the major long-term commercial rights to both Football and Basketball in India. IMG has similar major sports deals in Brazil, Indonesia, the Philippines and Nigeria. One key attraction is English Premier League Football, supplied around the world from IMG's London operation.

More than in most other nations, sport in Britain has become deeply involved in the international sports-TV-advertising industrial complex. Television sports programming itself cannot be expected to focus investigative journalism on the hands that feed it. A few British TV investigations of sporting corruption and malpractice have been conducted, especially by the BBC's *Panorama*. But the main journalism critical of sports TV and the sports industry has appeared in newspapers. The *Sunday Times* pursued Lance Armstrong over a decade and eventually caught up with him. *The Guardian* has done well on Football industry exposés.

But many of the less glamorous aspects of televised sport receive little attention, even from either television or the newspapers. This includes what happens to the majority of professional sports people who never earn one million pounds a year – including the many former sports people who commit suicide, or take to drugs and alcohol. Not only do horses die at that TV spectacular, the Grand National; many jump jockeys sustain incapacitating injury.

And the future? The sports industrial complex trends seem likely to continue. British television sport seems likely to follow the pattern of Formula One, the English Football Premier League, and English Cricket. British TV viewers will be offered ever larger amounts of top sports television which will be more international, more American and Arab[11] financed, and less British.

11 David Conn, *Richer Than God: Manchester City, modern Football and growing up* (London: Quercus, 2012).

CHAPTER 12

TV Policy in Fragments, Genres in Jeopardy

Ever since 1914–18, British audio-visual policy has been fragmented. In recent years British television policy has been fragmented across a range of political players, organisations and agencies. Policy is led by the Prime Minister, other senior ministers and their Whitehall Departments, Parliament, OFCOM (the official Communications regulator) and by the Office of Fair Trading/Competition Commission regulators. Additional significant players, in setting audio-visual and television policy, are the Newspapers, the BBC, ITV, BSkyB, and other TV companies, including the 'Independent Producers'.

The UK has in practice developed three quite different Television Policy regimes. There is one Public Service Broadcasting regime; secondly a regime of very light (or very little) regulation for American companies; and thirdly a more mixed regime for the Murdoch family interests.

Firstly a *Public Service Broadcasting* regime applies to the BBC, ITV, C4 and C5.[1] Everyone agrees that PSB requires these channels to offer a multi-genre diet of programming.

There is a second regime for *American/Hollywood commercial companies* which allows these companies to ignore PSB requirements. Hollywood-in-London and Silicon-Valley-in-London companies are secretive about their UK finances and typically pay little or no tax (by pretending that their UK business is based in Ireland or some other tax haven). These American companies benefit from extreme scale economies at home, and even more extreme scale advantages in the UK. The companies have long established

1 Jeremy Tunstall, 'The BBC and UK Public Service Broadcasting', in Petros Iosifidis, eds, *Reinventing Public Service Communication: European Broadcasters And Beyond* (London: Palgrave Macmillan, 2010), 145–57.

commercial marketing pipelines. The Silicon Valley companies have also benefited from Wall Street finance and have used new technologies developed with Department of Defense funding. Several of these companies have also cooperated with Washington spy agencies, such as the NSA.

Thirdly the Murdoch family-controlled media had a unique UK history. News Corporation as an American/Hollywood company, was not required to do any Public Service Broadcasting. However, some modest limitations were placed upon News Corp. In the past, News Corp controlled the UK's largest newspaper group and also held a controlling interest in BSkyB, the satellite and pay TV monopolist. In 2013 most of the Murdoch family's American media were rearranged under the (Hollywood) Fox label; the British newspapers were rearranged under the News UK label.

Los Angeles is the main location of an integrated audio-visual entertainment industrial complex. But few London policy people use the term Hollywood to encompass Advertising, Animation and Children's, Cable, the Internet, Movie Studios, Music, Networks (TV and Cable), Talent Agencies, Television Production and Video Games.

Decisive factors: Prime Minister, press, finance, Hollywood

At least since Harold Macmillan (PM 1957–63), British Prime Ministers have tended to make key media and broadcasting decisions.[2] This often involves the PM shaping television and radio in order to please powerful press owners. Both Margaret Thatcher (1979–90) and Tony Blair (1997–2007) across their own decades shaped their television policy to please the press in general, and Rupert Murdoch in particular.

2 Jeremy Tunstall, 'Media Policy Dilemmas and Indecisions', *Parliamentary Affairs*, 37/3, Summer 1984: 310–26.

Financial arrangements are often decisive. Each of the UK's main TV broadcasters must follow the logic of its own form of finance. The BBC must offer a service acceptable to the politicians who ultimately determine its Licence Fee. ITV, C4 and C5 must respond to the requirements of the relevant advertisers. BSkyB, with its monthly subscribers, needs a huge flow of entertainment and a selection of premium sport and movies, which are required to reduce churn (de-subscribing).

British TV has always been heavily dependent on Hollywood output. Two of British television's most dramatic changes occurred in 1955 (the arrival of ITV) and around 1990–1 (the arrival of BSkyB). At both times there was a massive increase in the quantity of Hollywood output available on British screens. Today the UK-California connection involves not just Los Angeles but also Silicon Valley. There is today a strong tendency for Silicon Valley technology to combine with Hollywood product and then to emerge on a range of British screens and hand-held devices.

Policy in fragments: Committees, Parliament, departments

For over seven decades, following the BBC's 1922 birth, British broadcasting policy-making was amateurish in both conception and execution. Across the 1970s and 1980s several central government departments (Home Office, Treasury, Foreign Office, Industry, Trade, Education, Defence) were all involved in media responsibilities.[3] Parliament debated the media but few MPs were well informed. Meanwhile up to, and including, the 1990 Broadcasting Act, Big Committees (Beveridge, Pilkington, Annan, Peacock) played a leading role. These committees were remarkably amateur. So also were the people who presided over the BBC (as Governors) and over the commercial TV regulators (as Members). These committees of various kinds typically involved about one day's work per week.

3 Tunstall, *The Media In Britain*, 241–6.

Most BBC chairmen have had little previous broadcasting experience. Several have said, on arrival, that they don't watch much television, but they like radio. Even today the BBC's chairmanship is not a full time job.

The whole UK broadcasting policy apparatus has become much less amateur since 1991 and especially since 2000. In particular the Culture, Media and Sport Department is much more professional than were the relevant civil servants before 1990. The related Parliamentary Select Committees are now active and well informed. But while the BBC has nine decades of tradition and ITV has six decades, there is no strong tradition of integrated, coherent, well considered, broadcast policymaking. The Prime Minister, in consultation with the Press, will still be making the key decisions about the future of the BBC, ITV, BSkyB, and Virgin.

New channels and technologies: Genre and Hollywood consequences

Big Committees between the 1930s and 1980s led to new channels and new technologies. But these Committees largely ignored such issues as Genre-mixes and probable levels of imports from Hollywood. These Committees typically included one or two financial experts (Economics and Business) who focused on the finance, and one or two Technologists who focused on the Technology. Despite (or because of) their specialised expertise, both the Finance and Technology experts tended to make over-optimistic predictions about the likely popularity and commercial viability of their proposals. These Big Committees typically called for one new TV channel and some new technology. The Selsden (chaired) committee led to BBC television in 1936. The Beveridge committee led to ITV in 1955. Pilkington led to BBC2 in 1964. Annan led to Channel Four in 1982. The

Part Committee led to Direct Broadcasting by Satellite in 1989–90. The Peacock committee led to Channel Five in 1997.[4]

The majority membership of these Big Committees tended to leave Finance and Technology to a few expert colleagues. The main focus then became the maintenance of some vaguely defined Public Service in general and often upon the interests of Scotland, Wales and Northern Ireland in particular. A core, but very seldom stated, assumption was that British Public Service Broadcasting required predominantly good British programming and only a small quota of Hollywood's output. The Pilkington Committee, for example, said in 1962:

> television has created some forms of programming which particularly lend themselves to triviality, which lend themselves to the exploitation of artificial situations or of 'personalities' but have practically no subject matter or body of their own. Some quiz shows and panel games obviously come into this category … Programmes which exemplified emotional tawdriness and mental timidity helped to cheapen both emotional and intellectual values.[5]

It might have been more honest to say 'Much less Hollywood rubbish, please.'

From the 1950s onwards, both the BBC and ITV became, alongside the Press, significant television policy players which worked to protect their own interests. The BBC succeeded in persuading Pilkington in 1962 that the third UK television channel should be BBC2 and not another ITV-style channel. The BBC high command had focused almost entirely on stopping an ITV advance, and had given little thought to what programming genres should appear on BBC2. The original 1964 launch idea was that BBC2 would focus on a different genre for each of the seven nights of the week – to be known as 'Seven Faces of the Week'. Sunday evening was to be 'serious plays', serious music and the 'best continental films'. Monday

4 Anthony Smith, ed., *British Broadcasting* (Newton Abbot: David and Charles, 1974). Bob Franklin, ed., *British Television Policy: A Reader* (London: Routledge, 2001).

5 Pilkington (chairman) *Report of the Committee on Broadcasting, 1960*, 34, 47.

meant family entertainment and comedy. Tuesday was for education. This approach lasted for only three months.[6]

ITV was a major player in the lengthy debates which eventually led to Channel Four in 1982. ITV feared a strong advertising funded competitor. The eventual result was a compromise – a new Channel Four which was only a fairly modest commercial competitor. Few people (apart from Jeremy Isaacs) had realised that Channel Four's modest finances would inevitably involve big imports of (then) cheap Hollywood product. Since the legislation, as usual, had almost nothing specific to say about Genres, Jeremy Isaacs was free to make his own genre-mix of some very high UK culture, some very low UK culture, and a lot of Hollywood product.

Little consideration was, or is, given to the genre-mix required to match a Public Service goal or any other policy goal. A detailed examination of twenty-one Genres is seen as impracticable in the context of a large committee of busy people. Anyway most policymaking, and broadcast policymakers, focus primarily on news and other serious factual programming. Little attention is paid to British crime, soap or entertainment formats and even less attention goes to Hollywood output in these genres. Consequently British TV policymaking has tended to understate the costs of PSB and new technology and also to understate the UK appeal of Hollywood entertainment.

UK cultural policy in fragments

The UK's Department for Culture, Media and Sport came into existence only in 1997. Previous to 1997 responsibility for Culture, Media and Sport had been spread across a range of government Departments. DCMS was descended from the Department of National Heritage (1992–7).

6 Briggs, *Competition, 1955–74*, 402–16.

The UK has never had an equivalent to France's tradition of government support for the French language, for Agence France-Presse, and for the French film industry.[7] In 1984 France introduced a major TV subscription service, Canal Plus, to present French and American film as equals. But the UK in the last hundred years has had no English language policy and no realistic British film industry policy.

Until 1956 London cultural policymakers were mainly concerned with English language and British media policies across the shrinking British Empire. 1956, as the year of Suez failure and ITV success, might have been a suitable time for developing some UK Cultural Policy. But Harold Macmillan, a Prime Minister with a book publishing background, missed the opportunity. So did his successors.

Alongside its failures, British Cultural Policy can claim some successes. National Lottery Funding, the National Theatre, the National Trust and funding for Art, Opera, BBC Orchestras, Sport and Scotland, Wales and Northern Ireland – these and other Arts initiatives are well known. But there have also been numerous failures, including these four:

1. *UK Newspapers* have long been attractive items for wealthy and eccentric foreigners. *The Times* was 'rescued' by Jacob Astor (1922). During the Thatcher 1980s, *The Times* and *The Sun* were controlled by Murdoch and the *Daily Telegraph* was controlled by Conrad Black. Subsequently Murdoch was mired in the large scale illegality of phone hacking and Black served time in an American prison.
2. *The UK Film Industry* has, for nearly a century, been effectively an off-shore subsidiary of Hollywood.
3. *UK Book Publishing* has seen many of it larger companies acquired by American and German book publishers.
4. *Reuters News Agency* was for over one hundred years the world's leading single supplier of news. In the television era, and especially since 1975, Reuters was the leading supplier of fast foreign news film to virtually every TV network in the world. Reuters was sold in 2008 to

7 Palmer and Tunstall, *Liberating Communications: policy-making in France and Britain.*

> Thomson of Toronto and New York; Thomson's growth had depended on public franchises for Scottish Television and North Sea Oil. There was no public government reaction and very little political or press discussion of this sale, which ensured that both of the world's leading news agencies are now effectively New York owned and operated.

Even after the Department for Culture, Media and Sport came into existence in 1997, British cultural policy has seemed to retain much of its previous fragmentation. Meanwhile DCMS responsibilities include Advertising, The Arts and Arts Market, Alcohol and Entertainment Licensing, Architecture, the BBC, Broadcasting, Channel Four, Computer Games, Cultural Property and Heritage, Design, Disaster Humanitarian Support, Fashion, Film, and – later in the alphabet – Press, Publishing, Royal Parks, State Ceremonial Occasions and Royal Funerals, Telecommunications and Broadband. But the numerous G through to O items do not include any responsibility for Hollywood or News Agencies.

UK audio-visual policy: A century of unanticipated outcomes

From 1914–18 onwards, London governments began an endless misunderstanding of Hollywood in particular, and of American popular culture in general. British government attempts in 1927 and 1947 to limit the impact of Hollywood films lacked credibility and failed.

The 1954–5 arrival of commercial ITV also involved unanticipated consequences. Few people had predicted that ITV audiences would quickly outnumber BBC audiences by more than two to one.

The Comfortable Duopoly Era (1964–82), of two BBC channels versus one ITV channel, saw London again failing fully to grasp what Los Angeles was doing. The Comfortable Duopolists, BBC and ITV, agreed broadly not to compete against each other. Both BBC and ITV happily imported expensive Hollywood product at artificially low prices. This entertainment product was placed into both peak audience time slots and low audience time slots. Policymakers during 1964–82 did not fully grasp that the BBC/ITV duopoly was not only well funded – with a Licence-Fee-and-Advertising financial duopoly – but was also effectively being subsidised by Hollywood. Expensive Hollywood series were being acquired at negligible cost well into the 1980s.

Channel Four's early years, after 1982, were also subsidised by the 'thousands of films' which Jeremy Isaacs bought at low cost from Hollywood. Each of these Hollywood films (and series) was typically shown several times.

Thatcher's great satellite policy crash

Within a few weeks at the end of 1990, two contradictory events happened. The much debated, and amended, *Broadcasting Act 1990* passed into law. Then, within two weeks, the Murdoch-led merger of Sky and BSB bulldozed the brand new Broadcasting Act (and previous Thatcher TV and media policy) into irrelevance.

Official British/Thatcher policy had developed British Satellite Broadcasting (BSB) as a high technology innovation, using British developed technology. But BSB surrendered to Sky, and BSkyB continued to use its low technology, developed in Luxembourg with American support.

British/Thatcher policy required that BSB deliver high quality new British programming on a loosely BBC/ITV model. Murdoch's merged BSkyB avoided the BBC/ITV model and relied mainly on American programming, plus live Sport.

British/Thatcher policy in the 1990 Act involved shaking up the BBC/ITV duopoly, making Channel Four genuinely competitive and introducing a new Channel Five. The additional intention to loosen the grip of the broadcasting trade unions was largely successful. But this 1990 policy – with its auctioning of ITV franchises and other competitive detail – led, in fact, to a huge 1990s weakening of ITV, which in 1989 had still been a formidable commercial competitor. The arrival of BSkyB as satellite monopolist also permanently weakened the prospects for Channel Five, which might otherwise have become (along with ITV and C4) a third major commercial competitor, showing mainly British programming.

British/Thatcher policy of the 1990s also introduced a new era of 'lighter touch' regulation. The new Independent Television Commission (ITC) regulator was, from its January 1991 birth, completely ineffective in relation to the BSkyB satellite monopolist. The ITC deliberately slowed down the merger of ITV into a single company, and the ITC's Cable policy was almost non-existent. The ITC also allowed ITV largely to withdraw from some of its previous genre obligations – such as Current Affairs.

How could Thatcher's satellite policy in general and her Broadcasting Act of late 1990 been so comprehensively bulldozered by Rupert Murdoch at a time when he himself was in serious financial difficulty with his Hollywood and American television acquisitions?

Firstly, Margaret Thatcher herself is to blame. Throughout her eleven years (May 1979–November 1990) as Prime Minister, broadcasting was on Thatcher's policy agenda, but seldom at the top of that agenda. Nigel Lawson has amusingly described Thatcher's contradictory impulses.[8] Basically Thatcher wanted more Public Service 'good taste' and good British programming; but she also wanted much more aggressive commercial competition. Thatcher suffered from an especially strong strain of the BBC Love/Hate virus. When on her political deathbed in late 1990, she gave Rupert Murdoch the British Prime Ministerial nod of approval, using 'Presidential' PM powers which had little legal foundation.

The senior Conservative politicians who as Home Secretary during 1979–90, were responsible for Broadcasting were to blame. All four – Willie Whitelaw, Leon Brittan, Douglas Hurd and David Waddington – were conventional public school and Oxbridge Tories. The two longest serving of these Home Secretaries were Whitelaw (Winchester and Cambridge)

8 Nigel Lawson, *The View from No.11* (London: Bantam Press, 1992), 720–3.

and Hurd (Eton and Cambridge). All four wanted to maintain the BBC and PSB, while introducing some (but not too much) fresh competition. None of these Home Secretaries wanted, or even imagined, anything like BSkyB. David Waddington, who was Home Secretary during Thatcher's last 13 months in office, seems in his autobiography to have forgotten that he was in charge of broadcasting policy when Thatcher gave her nod of approval to Rupert Murdoch and his bulldozer. Waddington's sole comment on the 1989–90 policy crash is an 'amazing' anecdote about Margaret Thatcher, who still wanted to discuss how (contrary to her own 1990 Act) she could perhaps abolish the BBC licence fee.[9]

Relevant senior London civil servants who were kind enough to give me interviews – both before and after my 1983–4 year in Washington DC – seemed remarkably poorly informed. Some of the better informed civil servants left to join either the newly privatised British Telecom or Mercury. One civil servant involved with UK Satellite-and-Cable policy in 1987 had not even heard of Hollywood's MPAA trade association, whose output was inevitably going to fill many thousands of UK Satellite and Cable time slots. Some good research was being commissioned by the Home Office,[10] but neither the civil servants nor the Ministers seemed to be reading it.

Patrick Whitten, the head of CIT Research, told me (January 1989) 22 months before the official BSB (British Satellite Broadcasting) collapsed into Sky's arms:

> BSB is headed for a major disaster. When you go to talk to civil servants and ministers you still go into another world. They simply are not interested in data, background, figures. This whole thing is a tax loss business – and not only for the American cable and phone companies. BSB also performs a tax loss function for people like Bond and Granada.

Parliament and its Members are also to blame. There was, at the time, no effective backbench committee system. Most MPs in the winter of 1990–1

9 David Waddington, *Memoirs: Dispatches from Margaret Thatcher's Last Home Secretary* (London: Biteback, 2012), 181–95.

10 Booz, Allen and Hamilton, *Subscription Television, A Study For The Home Office: Final Report* (May 1987).

were obsessed with the exit of Thatcher, the arrival of John Major as Prime Minister, the impending (first) Iraq war, and with European issues. Most MPs were probably reluctant to confront the ever-more-powerful Rupert Murdoch.[11]

The Newspapers in general did not object very vigorously. Newspapers controlled by Rupert Murdoch were in 1990–1 selling about 34 million copies per week; these papers carried much Sky advertising and even more editorial boosting of BSkyB as an exciting new entertainment offering. Some other newspapers – not least the *Financial Times* group – were involved as major shareholders in the new BSkyB.

The commercial TV regulators – IBA in 1990 and ITC in 1991 – were guilty of falling asleep on sentry duty in the face of the enemy.[12]

Finally, the public Committees, which examined broadcasting/satellite/cable policy in the 1980s, exhibited all of the weaknesses – and none of the strengths – of this Committee tradition.

11 Colin Seymour-Ure, 'Mass Media', in Dennis Kavanagh and Anthony Seldon, eds, *The Major Effect* (London: Macmillan, 1994), 399–417.

12 Steven Barnett and Andrew Curry, *The Battle For The BBC* (London: Aurum Press, 1994). Richard Collins, *Television: Policy and Culture* (London: Unwin Hyman, 1990). Tim Congdon, Brian Sturgess, National Economic Research Associates, and others, *Paying For Broadcasting: The Handbook* (London: Routledge, 1992). David Elstein, *Lectures on Broadcasting Policy* (Eight Lectures, delivered at Oxford University, 1999–2000). Peter Goodwin, *Television Under The Tories: Broadcasting Policy, 1979–1997* (London: British Film Institute, 1998). Colin MacCabe and Olivia Stewart, eds, *The BBC and Public Service Broadcasting* (Manchester University Press, 1986). Tim Madge, *Beyond The BBC: broadcasters and the public in the 1980s* (London: Macmillan, 1989). Nod Miller and Cresta Norris, eds, *Life After The Broadcasting Bill* (University of Manchester School of Education) 1989. Tom O'Malley, *Closedown? The BBC and Government Broadcasting Policy 1979–92* (London: Pluto Press, 1994). Michael Tracey, *The Decline and Fall of Public Service Broadcasting* (Oxford University Press, 1998). Cento Veljanovski, ed., *Freedom in Broadcasting* (London: Institute of Economic Affairs, 1989).

1980s committees: Amateur, arrogant, ignorant

Margaret Thatcher set up several committees to look into broadcasting/satellite/cable issues. These were conceived as short-sharp-no-nonsense investigations which would focus on one specific issue and then report quickly. But, with little time, these committees were much more amateur, arrogant and ignorant than their slower-moving predecessors, such as Pilkington and Annan.

Three separate Committees reported in 1981 and 1982 on Satellite and Cable:

- *Direct Broadcasting by Satellite* (1981). This 100 page report came from the Home Office and enthused about DBS.
- Another *Direct Broadcasting By Satellite* (1982) report was chaired by Sir Anthony Part and focused only on technical standards. It supported the super-high technology MAC system, which was unwisely accepted as the official British DBS Technology. The Part committee lasted four months and produced a fifty-seven-page report.
- *Report of the Inquiry Into Cable Expansion and Broadcasting Policy* took six months in 1982 and ran to 46 pages. Chaired by Lord Hunt, it exuded enthusiasm for Cable television, but had very little to say about costs or genre mix.

These technology slim volumes had several weaknesses in common. Policy discussion was fragmented. Narrow expertise accompanied naive boosterism for cable, satellite and the other new technologies. These reports typically gave very brief consideration to other countries – perhaps just ten paragraphs to the USA, Japan, France and Germany combined. Both France and the US were producing much better policy documents at this time.[13]

In 1982 the BBC saw itself awarded the lead DBS programming role; the BBC agreed to run two satellite channels which would motivate the

13 Palmer and Tunstall, *Liberating Communications*, 162–85, 282–300.

great British public to become DBS consumers. The BBC soon recognised that it could not take on the large and risky investment. When the BBC withdrew, a new body was established, the Satellite Broadcasting Board, which was owned fifty per cent by the BBC, thirty per cent by the ITV companies and twenty per cent by five other companies. After one year of life, this SBB 'club of 21' collapsed in 1984, leaving the DBS project without any programming or cash supply. The Thatcher government's focus on technology and competition – and its reluctance to consider programming cost or genre-mix – had led by 1984 to an embarrassing failure. But worse was to follow in the form of the Peacock Committee. It was one of the most influential, amateur, arrogant and ignorant documents in the entire history of British broadcast policymaking. The new broadcasting committee was set up by Prime Minister Thatcher's government and was active for sixteen months under the chairmanship of a right-wing 'liberal' economist, Professor Alan Peacock. The Peacock committee was asked to look at the BBC and the likely impact of switching BBC financing from licence fee to subscription. But the Peacock Report largely dismissed BBC Advertising and favoured BBC subscriptions. It then switched its focus on to ITV.

It seems to have taken the Peacock committee some months to recognise the rather obvious point that an advertising-financed BBC would drastically reduce the advertising finance going to ITV. The committee then had less than twelve months to come up with its fresh proposals. But the committee only met fortnightly.[14]

Two decades later, Tom O'Malley convened a retrospective conference on the Peacock committee. His book neatly exhibits the reluctance of the committee members, even twenty years after the event, to admit how flawed and self-contradictory their conclusions had been. One example (out of many available) was provided in the O'Malley book by Samuel Brittan, who had, back in the 1980s, been – along with Alan Peacock – the intellectual leader of the committee. Brittan indicates his low opinion of quantified audience data, because: 'the ratings do not measure the intensity

14 Sir Alan Peacock (chairman) *Report of the Committee on Financing the BBC* (London: HMSO, Cmnd 9824, 1986).

of preferences – whether a viewer is keenly interested in a programme or barely conscious of what is in front of him.'[15]

But in fact by 1985 the BBC Audience Research Department had been studying television 'Audience Appreciation' for over three decades. Survey respondents had long been given five choices, varying from 'Like Very Much' to 'Strongly Dislike'.[16]

The Peacock members admit to having closely followed the advice of Peter Jay (who in 1985 was fresh from his disastrous management of TV am in 1983). The Peacock Committee members failed fully to appreciate what had already happened by 1985 in Italy, Germany, Luxembourg and the United States. In particular, perhaps, they also ignored what had already happened in France, not least the famous Nora Minc report.[17]

While discussing the future expansion of television, the Peacock committee members were remarkably uninterested in what Rupert Murdoch was already uplinking from the UK. But Peacock makes several references to Italian and German classical music in the committee's published report. The Peacock committee members cheerfully put their own high cultural capital on display and they demand special support for 'quality' programming.

Peacock proclaimed himself as not concerned with broadcast content and genres. The market must determine such issues. However Peacock then decided that – after all – market forces might not adequately provide for all the important genres. Without any discussion or data, the Peacock Report casually asserts that some 'minority, high quality or experimental work' might not be market delivered and would need special subsidy via a public service broadcasting council (PSBC). Public Service Broadcasting was thus quickly abolished and then resurrected with the very same name. But while

15 Sir Samuel Brittan, 'The fight for freedom in broadcasting,' in Tom O'Malley and Janet Jones, eds, *The Peacock Committee and UK Broadcasting Policy* (Basingstoke: Palgrave Macmillan, 2009), 101–20.

16 Robert Silvey, *Who's Listening? The story of BBC Audience Research* (London: Allen and Unwin, 1974), 153–73.

17 Simon Nora and Alain Minc, *The Computerization of Society* (Cambridge, MA: MIT Press, 1980).

retaining 'Public Service', the Peacock Committee failed to consider what kind of genre-mix would be required to deliver its version of PSB.

Nevertheless Peacock exerted significant influence – both intended and unintended. The Peacock committee's strong advocacy of more competition was reflected in the 1988 Thatcher Government White Paper, whose title put 'Competition' first – *Broadcasting in the 1990s: Competition, Choice and Quality*. The Peacock Committee (1985–6), the subsequent Thatcher-Lawson Cabinet sub-committees (1987), and the White Paper (1988) led to the Broadcasting Act (1990).

The final unintended consequence of the Peacock Committee –and its lack of interest in satellite-plus-cable – was to help Thatcher and Murdoch to dance around Thatcher's own Broadcasting Act and beyond, into the clear BSkyB Hollywood dawn.

OFCOM: Hesitant regulator

> It is a measure of Rupert Murdoch's enormous clout that it has taken Ofcom three years to declare the British pay-TV market to be less than wholly competitive. This, to set things in context, is a field in which one supplier, British Sky Broadcasting, has more than twice the number of subscribers of its three main rivals combined. The picture in terms of revenues is even starker, with Sky accounting for 76 per cent.
>
> The broadcasting regulator has prepared its ground with the care of a bomb disposal operative.
>
> — FINANCIAL TIMES, leading article, April 2010[18]

Since its birth in 2003, OFCOM (Office of Communications) has been a decisive regulator of telecommunications technology and a hesitant, or timid, regulator of media companies and media content. As the *Financial Times* commented, OFCOM behaved like a cautious bomb disposal

18 'Ofcom aims gentle first blow at Sky', *Financial Times*, 1 April 2010.

operative in relation to Rupert Murdoch and BSkyB. OFCOM had already attracted numerous explosive denunciations from BSkyB executives, from the Murdoch family and from the Murdoch controlled national newspapers. Meanwhile OFCOM cautiously devoted much energy and finance to developing a strong audience research and social research base.

OFCOM has had a difficult history; it was required to combine the functions of the previous commercial television, and the telecommunications, regulators.[19] Ofcom's main impact on broadcasting has come through a long list of decisions about technologies and channels. Ofcom has made decisions on many digital issues, on the reallocation of vacated spectrum, on Digital Terrestrial TV (DTT) and Freeview/Freesat, on Broadcast Transmission Services, on High Definition and on fast broadband.

OFCOM was modelled by the Blair Government on its Financial Services Authority. But the FSA was subsequently seen by all of the main UK political parties to have utterly failed to predict, or to handle, the financial crash of 2007–8. The FSA was subsequently abolished, but OFCOM soldiered on as a weak media regulator.

In 2009 the then Leader of the Opposition, David Cameron, announced that a new Conservative government would abolish OFCOM. In fact Cameron as Prime Minister kept OFCOM. He gave it some additional responsibilities but also cut its funds by 28 per cent during 2011–13.[20] The bulk of OFCOM's finance continued to be devoted to Spectrum and Networks and Service. Television spending was in third place, and was cut by nearly half in real value between 2008 and 2014.[21]

According to the Communications Act, 2003, OFCOM would give equal weight to the requirements of 'Citizens' and of 'Customers'. But,

19 The Independent Television Commission (ITC) and the Office of Telecommunications (OFTEL). Ofcom also encompassed three other previously separate agencies – the Broadcasting Standards Commission, The Radio Authority and the Radiocomunications agency. Subsequently in 2011, Ofcom took over the duties of the Postal Services Commission.

20 Ed Richards, 'The View From Riverside House', *Television*, October 2013: 41–3.

21 *The Office of Communications, Annual Report and Account, 2013–14*, 69, 83.

from the outset, OFCOM de-emphasised 'Citizens' and mainly used the more commercial term 'Customers' (or Consumers).[22]

Back in 2003–4, Ofcom's eager young professionals enthusiastically began a number of innovative investigations. But because of the big players on the playing field, Ofcom increasingly focused firstly on technology/channel decisions and secondly on Public Service Broadcasting. Ofcom was especially interested in how the BBC and Channel Four might strengthen their output in certain genres. Different Ofcom documents listed different genres. But a typical list specified: 'regional news, news from the nations, UK children's programming, current affairs, other programming in the devolved nations, UK drama, UK comedy and education.'[23]

In 2008 Ofcom's leaders were hoping to maintain Public Service Broadcasting across the large and small channels of the BBC, ITV and Channels Four and Five. Ofcom presented four different possible models of PSB. The least popular of these four options – with Ofcom and its respondents – was the BBC as the sole public service broadcaster. But the financial crisis years 2008 and 2009 were not good years for extending PSB and for protecting unprofitable TV genres. From 2008–9 onwards Ofcom's executives increasingly recognised that their chosen PSB genres would be found mainly on the BBC channels.

OFCOM was only a middle-weight player in media policy, politics and public relations. The Department of Culture, Media and Sport was getting stronger as were the related Select Committees in Parliament. Moreover OFCOM was dependent on publicity from the Press, from BSkyB and especially from the BBC's many outlets.

OFCOM had relatively few media powers. The UK had, and has, a separate apparatus for monopoly/competition regulation. OFCOM did not have the old regulatory power of allocating regional franchises within

22 Peter Lunt and Sonia Livingstone, *Media Regulation: Governance and the interests of citizens and consumers* (London: Sage Publications, 2012), 41–63.

23 *Ofcom's Second Public Service Broadcasting Review: Putting Viewers First* (London: Ofcom, 2009), paragraph 2.23.

the ITV system. OFCOM did not regulate the film industry and had only limited powers in relation to the Internet.

OFCOM has always lacked significant power over the three main sources of broadcast finance. OFCOM does not set the BBC Licence Fee; OFCOM does not regulate BSkyB and Cable subscriptions; and OFCOM does not regulate Advertising, the funding source of ITV, C4 and C5.

Nor does OFCOM have any effective oversight of American media in Britain. Neither the Hollywood, nor the Silicon Valley, companies are beholden to OFCOM. When Google-in-the UK attracted more advertising dollar billions than ITV and was rapidly catching up on the BBC's total revenue, OFCOM still lacked any relevant powers.

Selected Bibliography

Adey, Kate, *The Kindness of Strangers* (London: Headline, 2002).

Aitken, Robin, *Can We Still Trust the BBC?* (London: Bloomsbury, 2013).

Annan, Noel (chairman), *Report of the Committee on the future of Broadcasting* (London: HMSO, 1977).

Anonymous, *I Am the Secret Footballer* (London: Guardian Books, 2012).

Attenborough, David, *Life on Air: Memoirs of a Broadcaster* (London: BBC Books, 2002).

Baade, Christina L., *Victory Through Harmony: The BBC and Popular Music in World War II* (New York: Oxford University Press, 2012).

Baillieu, Bill and John Goodchild, *The British Film Business* (Chichester: John Wiley, 2002).

Baker, Michael, *The Rise of the Victorian Actor* (London: Croom Helm, 1978).

Baker, Richard, *Here is the News* (London: Leslie Frewin, 1966).

Baker, William, and John C. Ross, *Harold Pinter: A Bibliographical History* (London: The British Library and New Castle, DE: Oak Knoll Press, 2005).

Bakewell, Joan, and Nicholas Garnham, *The New Priesthood: British Television Today* (London: Allen Lane, Penguin Press, 1970).

Balio, Tino, ed., *The American Film Industry* (Madison: University of Wisconsin, 1976).

Barfe, Louis, *Turned Out Nice Again: The story of British Light Entertainment* (London: Atlantic Books, 2008).

Barnett, Steven, *The Rise and Fall of Television Journalism* (London: Bloomsbury, 2011).

Barnett, Steven, and Andrew Curry, *The Battle for the BBC* (London: Aurum Press, 1994).

Bates, Anthony, *Broadcasting in Education* (London: Constable, 1984).

BBC, *British Broadcasting: a Select Bibliography* (London: BBC, 1972).

Beadle, Jeremy, *Beadle's About: a behind the scenes look at LWT's hit series* (London: Sidgwick and Jackson, 1989).

Belfield, Richard, and Christopher Hird and Sharon Kelly, *Murdoch: the Decline of an Empire* (London: Macdonald, 1991).

Birt, John, *The Harder Path* (London: Time Warner, 2002).

Bolton, Roger, *Death on the Rock* (London: W.H. Allen/Optomen, 1990).

Booy, Miles, *Love and Monsters: The Doctor Who Experience* (London: I.B. Tauris, 2012).

Booz, Allen and Hamilton International Ltd, *Subscription Television: a Study for the Home Office, Final report, 1987*.
Born, Georgina, *Uncertain Vision* (London: Vintage, 2004).
Bose, Mihir, *Michael Grade: screening the image* (London: Virgin, 1992).
——, *The Spirit of the Game* (London: Constable, 2011).
Boulton, Adam, *Tony's Ten Years: Memories of the Blair Administration* (London: Simon and Schuster, 2008).
Bowen, Jeremy, *War Stories* (London: Simon and Schuster, 2006).
Bower, Tom, *Broken Dreams: Vanity, Greed and the Souring of British Football* (London: Simon and Schuster, 2003).
——, *No Angel: The secret life of Bernie Ecclestone* (London: Faber and Faber, 2011).
——, *Sweet Revenge: the intimate life of Simon Cowell* (London: Faber and Faber, 2012).
Boyd-Barrett, Oliver, *The International News Agencies* (London: Constable and Los Angeles: Sage, 1980).
Briggs, Asa, *The War of Words* (Oxford: Oxford University Press, 1970).
——, *Governing the BBC* (London: BBC, 1979).
——, *The Golden Age of Wireless* (Oxford: Oxford University Press, 1995).
Brown, Maggie, *A Licence To Be Different: The Story of Channel 4* (London: British Film Institute, 2007).
Brown, Ray, ed., *Children and Television* (London: Collier Macmillan, 1976).
Brunsdon, Charlotte, *The Feminist, the Housewife and the Soap Opera* (Oxford: Oxford University Press, 2000).
Brunsdon, Charlotte and David Morley, *Everyday Television: Nationwide* (London: British Film Institute, 1978).
Bryant, Marsha, *Auden and Documentary in the 1930s* (Charlottesville: University of Virginia Press, 1997).
Buckingham, David, *Public Secrets: EastEnders and Its Audience* (London: British Film Institute, 1987).
Buckingham, David, Hannah Davies, Ken Jones and Peter Kelley, *Children's Television in Britain* (London: British Film Institute, 1999).
Bunce, Charlie, *Great British Railway Journeys* (London: HarperCollins, 2011).
Burns, Tom, *The BBC: Public Institution and Private World* (London: Macmillan, 1977).
Butler, David, ed, *Time and Relative Dissertations in Space: Critical Perspectives on Doctor Who* (Manchester: Manchester University Press, 2007).
Cantor, Muriel, *The Hollywood TV Producer* (New York: Basic Books, 1971).
Cardwell, Sarah, *Andrew Davies* (Manchester: Manchester University Press, 2005).
Carpenter, Humphrey, *Dennis Potter: The authorized biography* (London: Faber, 1998).
Chalaby, Jean K., *Transnational Television in Europe* (London: I.B. Tauris, 2009).

Chester, Lewis, *Tooth and Claw: The Inside Story of Spitting Image* (London: Faber and Faber, 1986).

Clarke, Nick, *Alastair Cooke: a biography* (London: Weidenfeld and Nicolson, 1999).

Coates, Tim, *The Hutton Inquiry, 2003–4* (London: Tim Coates, 2004).

Cockerell, Michael, *Live From Number Ten: The inside story of Prime Ministers and Television* (London: Faber and Faber, 1988).

Collins, Richard, *Television: Policy and Culture* (London: Unwin Hyman, 1990).

Congdon, Tim, and Brian Sturgess, *Paying for Broadcasting: the handbook* (London: Routledge, 1992).

Conn, David, *Richer than God: Manchester City, modern Football and growing up* (London: Quercus, 2012).

Cook, William, *Morecambe and Wise Untold* (London: HarperCollins, 2007).

Cooke, Lez, *British Television Drama: A history* (London: British Film Institute, 2003).

Corner, John, ed., *Popular Television in Britain* (London: British Film Institute, 1991).

Cotton, Bill, *Double Bill* (London: Fourth Estate/HarperCollins, 2000).

Cowgill, Bryan, *Mr Action Replay* (Swadlincote: Sportsmasters International, 2006).

Creeber, Glen, ed., *The Television Genre Book* (London: Palgrave Macmillan, 2008).

Cunningham, Hugh, *Grace Darling: Victorian Heroine* (London: Hambledon Continuum, 2007).

Curran, Charles, *A Seamless Robe: Broadcasting – Philosophy and Practice* (London: Collins, 1979).

Curran, James, *Media and Power* (London: Routledge, 2002).

Darlow, Michael, *Independents Struggle: The programme makers who took on the TV* Establishment (London: Quartet, 2004).

Davies, Dan, *In Plain Sight: The life and lies of Jimmy Savile* (London: Quercus, 2014).

Davies, David, *FA Confidential: Sex, Drugs and Penalties, the inside story of English Football* (London: Simon and Schuster, 2008).

Davies, Hunter, *The Grades: The first family of British Entertainment* (London: Weidenfeld and Nicolson, 1981).

Davies, Russell T., and Benjamin Cook, *Doctor Who: The Writer's Tale, The Final Chapter* (London: BBC Books, 2010).

Day-Lewis, Sean, *Talk of Drama: Views of the television dramatist now and then* (Luton: University of Luton Press and John Libbey, 1998).

De Vany, Arthur, *Hollywood Economics* (London: Routledge, 2004).

De Vries, Leonard, *History as Hot News, the world of the early Victorians through the eyes of the Illustrated London News, 1842–1865* (London: John Murray, 1967).

Dimbleby, Jonathan, *Richard Dimbleby* (London: Hodder and Stoughton, 1975).

——, *Russia: A journey to the heart of a land and its people* (London: BBC Books, 2009).

Docherty, David, *Running The Show: 21 years of London Weekend Television* (London: Boxtree, 1990).
Docherty, David, and David E. Morrison and Michael Tracey, *Keeping Faith? Channel 4 and its audience* (London: John Libbey, 1988).
Donovan, Paul, *All Our Todays* (London: Jonathan Cape, 1997).
Doran, Susan, ed., *Man and Monarch. Henry VIII* (London: British Library, 2009).
Dougall, Robert, *In and Out of the Box: An Autobiography* (London: Collins and Harvill, 1973).
Downing, Taylor, *The World at War* (London: Palgrave Macmillan, 2012).
Duguid, Mark, *Cracker* (London: British Film Institute/Macmillan, 2009).
Eaton, Michael, *Our Friends in the North* (London: British Film Institute, 2005).
Edworthy, Niall, *The Second Most Important Job in the Country* (London: Virgin, 1999).
Elberse, Anita, *Blockbusters* (London: Faber and Faber, 2014).
Ellis, Clive, *Fabulous Fanny Cradock, TV's outrageous queen of cuisine* (Stroud: Sutton Publishing, 2007).
Ellis, John, *TV FAQ: uncommon answers to common questions about TV* (London: I.B. Tauris, 2007).
Elstein, David, Lectures on Broadcasting Policy, delivered at Oxford University, 1999–2000.
English, James, *The Economy of Prestige: Prizes, awards and the circulation of cultural value* (Cambridge, MA: Harvard University Press, 2005).
Etzioni, Amitai, and Eleanor Townsley, *Public Intellectuals: An endangered species?* (Lanham, MD: Roman and Littlefield, 2006).
Fabe, Maxene, *TV Game shows* (New York: Doubleday, 1979).
Ferris, Paul, *Sir Huge: the life of Huw Wheldon* (London: Michael Joseph, 1990).
Finch, John, ed., *Granada Television: The first generation* (Manchester University Press, 2003).
Fisher, John, *Tony Hancock* (London: HarperCollins, 2008).
Fitzwalter, Raymond, *The Dream That Died: The Rise and Fall of ITV* (London: Matador, 2008).
Flanders, Judith, *The Invention of Murder* (London: Harper, 2011).
Franklin, Bob, ed., *British Television Policy: A Reader* (London: Routledge, 2001).
Fraser, Nick, *Why Documentaries Matter* (Oxford: Reuters Institute for the study of journalism, 2012).
Freedman, Des, *The Politics of Media Policy* (Cambridge: Polity, 2008).
Frost, David with Bob Zelnick, *Frost/Nixon* (London: Macmillan, 2001).
Gilbert, W. Stephen, *Fight and Kick and Bite: The Life and Work of Dennis Potter* (London: Sceptre, 1995).
Glavin, John, ed., *Dickens on Screen* (Cambridge: Cambridge University Press, 2003).

Goddard, Peter, and John Corner and Kay Richardson, *Public Issue Television: World in Action, 1963–98* (Manchester: Manchester University Press, 2007).
Goldie, Grace Wyndham, *Facing The Nation: Television and Politics, 1936–76* (London: The Bodley Head, 1977).
Gomery, Douglas, *The Hollywood Studio System* (London: British Film Institute/ Macmillan, 1986).
Goodwin, Peter, *Television Under The Tories: Broadcasting Policy, 1979–1997* (London: British Film Institute, 1998)
Gove, Michael, *Michael Portillo* (London: Fourth Estate, 1995).
Gow, James, Richard Paterson and Alison Preston, eds, *Bosnia By Television* (London: British Film Institute, 1996).
Grade, Michael, *It Seemed Like A Good Idea At The Time* (London: Macmillan Pan, 1999–2000).
Gunter, Barrie, and Paul Winstone, *Television: the Public's View, 1992* (London: John Libbey, 1993).
Hall, Julian, *The Rough Guide to British Cult Comedy* (Edinburgh University Press, 2009).
Hallam, Julia, *Lynda La Plante* (Manchester: Manchester University Press, 2005).
Hampton, Benjamin B., *History of the American Film Industry from its beginning to 1931* (New York: Dover, 1970).
Hanna, Emma, *The Great War on the Small Screen* (Edinburgh: Edinburgh University Press, 2009).
Harris, Robert, *Good and Faithful Servant: The unauthorized biography of Bernard Ingham* (London: Faber and Faber, 1992).
Hayward, Anthony, *In the Name of Justice: The Television Reporting of John Pilger* (London: Bloomsbury, 2011).
Hill, Annette, *Reality TV: Audiences and Popular Factual Television* (London: Routledge, 2005).
Hills, Matt, *Triumph of a Time Lord* (London: I.B. Tauris, 2010).
Himmelweit, Hilde, A.N. Oppenheim and Pamela Vince, *Television and the Child* (Oxford: Oxford University Press, 1958).
Hobson, Dorothy, *Channel 4: The early years and the Jeremy Isaacs Legacy* (London: I.B. Tauris, 2008).
Hodgson, Patricia and others, *E-Britannia: The Communications Revolution* (Luton: University of Luton Press, 2000).
Holland, Patricia, The *Angry Buzz: This Week and Current Affairs Television* (London: I.B. Tauris, 1996).
Holmes, Richard, *The World at War* (London: Ebury Press, 2011).
Holmes, Su, *The Quiz Show* (Edinburgh: Edinburgh University Press, 2008).

Horrie, Chris, and Steve Clarke, *Fuzzy Monsters: Fear and Loathing at the BBC* (London: William Heinemann, 1994).
——, *Citizen Greg* (London: Simon and Schuster, 2000).
Horsman, Mathew, *Sky High: the inside story of BSkyB* (London: Orion, 1997).
Humphrys, John, *Lost For Words* (London: Hodder and Stoughton, 2004).
Hunt, Leon, *The League of Gentlemen* (London: British Film Institute/Palgrave Macmillan, 2008).
Hussey, Marmaduke, *Chance Governs All: A Memoir* (London: Macmillan, 2001).
Inglis, Fred, *A Short History of Celebrity* (Princeton, NJ: Princeton University Press, 2010).
Iosifidis, Petros, ed, *Reinventing Public Service Communication: European Broadcasters and Beyond* (London: Palgrave Macmillan, 2010).
Isaacs, Jeremy, *Storm Over 4: A Personal Account* (London: Weidenfeld and Nicolson, 1989).
——, *Look Me in The Eye: A Life in Television* (London: Little, Brown, 2006).
Jacobs, Ronald N., and Eleanor Townsley, *The Space of Opinion: Media intellectuals and the public sphere* (New York: Oxford University Press, 2011).
Jaffee, Larry, ed., *Walford State of Mind* (Weekawken, NJ: East End Company, 2010).
Jarvie, Ian, *Hollywood's Overseas Campaign: The North Atlantic Movie Trade, 1920–1950* (Cambridge: Cambridge University Press, 1992).
Johnson, Sophie, *Miranda Hart: the unauthorised biography* (London: John Blake, 2011).
Jowett, Garth, *Film: the Democratic Art* (Boston: Little, Brown, 1976).
Kavanagh, Dennis, and Anthony Seldon, eds, *The Major Effect* (London: Macmillan, 1994).
Kelner, Martin, *Sit Down and Cheer: a history of sport on* TV (London: Bloomsbury, 2013).
Kerr, Paul, *The Crimean War* (London: Boxtree, 1997).
Kershaw, H.V., *The Street Where I Live* (London: Granada, 1981).
Kirkland, Dennis, *The Strange and Saucy World of Benny Hill* (London: Blake Publishing, 2002).
Kompare, Derek, *Rerun Nation: How Repeats Invented American television* (New York: Routledge, 2005).
Kuper, Simon, and Stefan Szymanski, *Why England Lose* (London: HarperSport, 2014).
Kustow, Michael, *One in Four: A year in the life of a Channel Four commissioning editor* (London: Chatto and Windus, 1987).
Lacey, Stephen, *Tony Garnett* (Manchester: Manchester University Press, 2007).

Lambert, Richard, *Independent Review of BBC News 24* (London: Department of Culture, Media and Sport, 2002).
Lambert, Stephen, *Channel Four: Television with a difference?* (London: British Film Institute, 1982).
Lapping, Brian, *End of Empire* (London: Granada and Channel Four, 1985).
——, *Apartheid: A History* (London: Grafton Books, 1986).
Lawson, Nigel, *The View from No.11* (London: Bantam, 1992).
Leapman, Michael, *Barefaced Cheek: Rupert Murdoch* (London: Coronet, 1983).
Lee, Stewart, *How I escaped my Certain Fate: The life and Deaths of a Stand-up Comedian* (London: Faber and Faber, 2010).
Leiken, Robert S., *Europe's Angry Muslims: The Revolt of the Second Generation* (New York: Oxford University Press, 2012).
Leishman, Marista, *My Father: Reith of the BBC* (Edinburgh: Saint Andrew Press, 2006).
Leverette, Marc, Brian L. Ott and Carla Louise Buckley, *It's Not TV: Watching HBO in the post television era* (New York: Routledge, 2008).
Levy, Emmanuel, *And The Winner Is: The History and Politics of the Oscar awards* (New York: Continuum, 1990).
Lindley, Richard, *Panorama: Fifty Year of Pride and Paranoia* (London: Politico's, 2002).
——, *And Finally ...? The News from ITN* (London: Politico's, 2005).
Livingstone, Sonia, and Peter Lunt, *Talk on Television* (London: Routledge, 1994).
Lockyer, Sharon, ed., *Reading Little Britain* (London: I.B. Tauris, 2010).
Lunt, Peter, and Sonia Livingstone, *Media Regulation: Governance and the interests of citizens and consumers* (London: Sage Publications, 2012).
Lynam, Des, *I Should Have Been at Work* (London: HarperCollins, 2006).
Lynch, Gordon, *The Sacred in the Modern World* (Oxford: Oxford University Press, 2012).
MacCabe, Colin, and Olivia Stewart, eds, *The BBC and Public Service Broadcasting* (Manchester: Manchester University Press, 1986).
McCann, Graham, ed., *The Essential Dave Allen* (London: Hodder and Stoughton, 2005).
McCann, Graham, *Spike and Co: Inside the House of Fun with Milligan, Sykes, Galton and Simpson* (London: Hodder and Stoughton, 2006).
McIntosh, Andrew, ed., *Lifelong Learning: selected writings of Naomi* Sargant (Leicester: National Institute of Adult Continuing Education, 2009).
McQuail, Denis, *Analysis of Newspaper Content* (London: HMSO, 1977).
Madge, Tim, *Beyond the BBC: Broadcasters and the public in the 1980s* (London: Macmillan, 1989).

Mair, John, Richard Tait and Richard Keeble, eds, *Is the BBC In Crisis?* (Bury St Edmunds: Abramis/Arima Publishing, 2014).

Marr, Andrew, *My Trade: A short history of British journalism* (London: Macmillan Pan, 2005).

Martin, Brett, *Difficult Men: Behind the scenes of a creative revolution* (London: Faber and Faber, 2013).

Miller, Nod, and Cresta Norris, eds, *Life After The Broadcasting Bill* (Manchester: University of Manchester, School of Education, 1989).

Milne, Alasdair, *D.G: The Memoirs of a British Broadcaster* (London: Hodder and Stoughton, 1988).

Mjos, Ole J., *Media Globalization and the Discovery Channel Networks* (New York: Routledge, 2010).

Montgomery, Andrew, *ITN: 50 Years of News* (Long Hanborough: ESP Publishing, 2005).

Motson, John, *Motty: Forty years in the commentary box* (London: Virgin, 2009).

Newkey-Burden, Chas, *Simon Cowell: The Unauthorized Biography* (London: Michael O'Mara Books, 2009).

Newman, Kim, *Doctor Who* (London: British Film Institute, 2005).

Noble, Grant, *Children in Front of the Small Screen* (London: Constable, 1975).

Nora, Simon, and Alan Minc, *The Computerization of Society* (Cambridge, MA: MIT Press), 1980.

Norton, Graham, *So Me* (London: Hodder and Stoughton, 2004).

Oborne, Peter, *Alastair Campbell: New Labour and the rise of the media class* (London: Aurum Press, 1999).

O'Malley, Tom, *Closedown? The BBC and Government Broadcasting Policy, 1979–92* (London: Pluto Press, 1994).

O'Malley, Tom, and Janet Jones, eds, *The Peacock Committee and UK Broadcasting Policy* (London: Palgrave Macmillan, 2009), 101–20.

Palin, Michael, *Himalaya* (London: Weidenfeld and Nicolson, 2004).

Palmer, Michael, and Jeremy *Tunstall, Liberating Communications: Policymaking in France and Britain* (Oxford: Blackwell, 1990).

Palmer, Svetlana, and Sarah Wallis, *A War in Words* (London: Simon and Schuster, 2003).

Parkinson, Michael, *Parky: My Autobiography* (London: Hodder and Stoughton, 2008).

Partner, Peter, *Arab Voices: the BBC Arabic Service, 1939–1988* (London: BBC, 1988).

Paterson, Richard, ed., *Organising for Change* (London: British Film Institute, 1990).

Peacock, Alan (chairman), *Report of the Committee on Financing the BBC* (London: HMSO, 1986).

Peston, Robert, *Who Runs Britain?* (London: Hodder and Stoughton, 2008).

Peston, Robert, and Laurence Knight, *How Do We Fix This Mess?* (London: Hodder and Stoughton, 2012).

Philo, Greg, and Mike Berry, *More Bad News From Israel* (London: Pluto Press, 2011).

Pilkington, Harry (chairman), *Report of the Committee on Broadcasting, 1960* (London: HMSO, 1962).

Posner, Richard A., *Public Intellectuals: A study of decline* (Cambridge, MA: Harvard University Press, 2001).

Potter, Ian, *The Rise and Rise of the Independents: A Television History* (London: Guerrilla Books, 2008).

Pym, John, *Film on Four* (London: British Film Institute, 1992).

Ramsay, Gordon, *Humble Pie* (London: HarperCollins, 2006).

Read, Donald, *The Power of the News, the history of Reuters*, 1849–1989 (Oxford: Oxford University Press, 1992).

Rees, Laurence, *Auschwitz: The Nazis and the 'Final Solution'* (London: BBC Books, 2005).

Roache, William, *Soul on the Street: An Autobiography* (London: Hay House, 2007).

Roberts, J.F., *The True Story of Black Adder* (London: Preface, 2012).

Roedy, Bill, *What Makes Business Rock* (Hoboken, New Jersey: John Wiley, 2011).

Rogers, Everett M., and Judith K. Larsen, *Silicon Valley Fever: Growth of High Technology Culture* (New York: Basic Books, 1984).

Ronay, Barney, *The Manager: the Absurd Ascent of the most Important Man in Football* (London: Sphere, 2009).

Sambrook, Richard, *Are Foreign Correspondents Redundant?* (Oxford: Reuters Institute for the study of journalism, 2011).

Secombe, Harry, *An Entertaining Life* (London: Robson Books, 2004).

Seglow, Peter, *Trade Unionism in British Television* (Farnborough: Saxon House, 1978).

Sergeant, John, *Give Me Ten Seconds* (London: Macmillan, 2001).

Seymour-Ure, Colin, *Prime Ministers and the Media* (Oxford: Blackwell, 2003).

Shawcross, William, *Rupert Murdoch: Ringmaster of the Information Circus* (London: Chatto and Windus, 1992).

Silvey, Robert, *Who's Listening? The story of BBC Audience Research* (London: Allen and Unwin, 1974).

Simpson, John, *A Mad World, My Masters* (London: Macmillan, 2001).

Smith, Anthony, ed., *British Broadcasting* (Newton Abbot: David and Charles, 1974).

Snow, Jon, *Shooting History* (London: Harper Perennial, 2005).

Stanyer, James, *Intimate Politics: Publicity, privacy and the personal lives of politicians* (Cambridge: Polity, 2013).

Steemers, Jeanette, *Selling Television: British Television in the Global Marketplace* (London: British Film Institute, 2004).

——, *Creating Preschool Television: A Story of Commerce, Creativity and Curriculum* (London: Palgrave Macmillan, 2010).

Strachan, Hew, *The First World War* (London: Simon and Schuster, 2003).

Sutherland, John, *Inside Bleak House: A Guide for the Modern Dickensian* (London: Duckworth, 2005).

Sutton, Shaun, *The Largest Theatre in the world* (London: BBC, 1982).

Thompson, Ben, *Sunshine on Putty: The golden age of British Comedy from Vic Reeves to The Office* (London: Fourth Estate, 2004).

Thompson, John B., *Merchants of Culture: The publishing business in the twenty-first century* (Cambridge: Polity, 2010).

Tiffen, Rodney, *Rupert Murdoch: A Reassessment* (Sydney: University of New South Wales Press, 2014).

Toll, Robert C., *Blacking Up: The Minstrel Show in Nineteenth-century America* (New York: Oxford University Press, 1974).

Tracey, Michael, *In The Culture of the Eye: Ten Years of Weekend World* (London: Hutchinson, 1983).

——, *The Decline and Fall of Public Service Broadcasting* (Oxford: Oxford University Press, 1998).

Trethowan, Ian, *Split Screen* (London: Hamish Hamilton, 1984).

Tuccille, Jerome, *Rupert Murdoch* (New York: Donald E. Fine, 1989).

Tunstall, Jeremy, *The Westminster Lobby Correspondents* (London: Routledge, 1970).

——, ed., *Media Sociology* (London: Constable, 1970).

——, ed., *The Open University Opens* (London: Routledge, 1974).

——, *Journalists At Work* (London: Constable and Los Angeles, Sage, 1971).

——, *The Media are American* (London: Constable and New York: Columbia University Press, 1977).

——, *The Media in Britain* (London: Constable, 1983).

——, *Communications Deregulation: the Unleashing of America's Communications Industry* (Oxford: Blackwell, 1986).

——, *Television Producers* (London: Routledge, 1993).

——, *Newspaper Power* (Oxford: Oxford University Press, 1996).

——, *The Media Were American* (New York: Oxford University Press, 2008).

——, and David Machin, *The Anglo-American Media Connection* (Oxford: Oxford University Press, 1999).

——, and Michael Palmer, *Media Moguls* (London: Routledge, 1991).

——, and David Walker, *Media Made in California* (New York: Oxford University Press, 1987).

Veljanowski, Cento, ed, *Freedom in Broadcasting* (London: Institute of Economic Affairs, 1989).
Vine, Jeremy, *It's All News To Me* (London: Simon and Schuster, 2012).
Waddington, David, *Memoirs: Dispatches from Margaret Thatcher's Last Home Secretary* (London: Biteback, 2012).
Walsh, David, *Seven Deadly Sins: My Pursuit of Lance Armstrong* (London: Simon and Schuster, 2012).
Walters, Ben, *The Office* (London: British Film Institute, 2005).
Wasko, Janet, *Hollywood in the Information Age* (Cambridge: Polity, 1994).
Watson, Tom, and Martin Hickman, *Dial M For Murdoch: News Corporation and the Corruption of Britain* (London: Allen Lane, 2012).
Whicker, Alan, *Journey of a Lifetime* (London: HarperCollins, 2010).
Whitney, John, *The Whitney Memoirs: My Years at the IBA* (London: John Libbey, 2013).
Winnett, Robert, and Gordon Rayner, *No Expenses Spared* (London: Bantam, 2009).
Wolff, Michael, *The Man Who Owns The News* (London: Bodley Head, 2008).
Wood, Helen, and Beverley Skegg, eds, *Reality Television and class* (London: Palgrave Macmillan, 2011).
Wood, Michael, *In the Footsteps of Alexander the Great: a journey from Greece to India* (London: BBC Books, 1997 and 2004).
——, *The Story of India* (London: BBC Books, 2007).
Wood, Victoria, Fanny Blake and Frank Welsh, *Victoria's Empire* (London: Hodder and Stoughton, 2007).
Wyatt, Will, *The Fun Factory: a life in the BBC* (London: Aurum Press, 2003).
Yorke, John, *Into The Woods: a Five-Act Journey into Story* (London: Penguin, 2013).
Ziegler, Philip, *Mountbatten: The Official Biography* (London: Collins, 1985).

Index